MW00658725

MULTICULTURAL EDUCATION SERIES

James A. Banks, *Series Editor*

Just Schools: Building Equitable Collaborations with Families and Communities
Ann M. Ishimaru

Immigrant-Origin Students in Community College: Navigating Risk and Reward in Higher Education
Carola Suárez-Orozco and Olivia Osei-Twumasi, Eds.

"We Dare Say Love": Supporting Achievement in the Educational Life of Black Boys
Na'ilah Suad Nasir, Jarvis R. Givens, and Christopher P. Chatmon, Eds.

Teaching What *Really* Happened: How to Avoid the Tyranny of Textbooks and Get Students Excited About *Doing* History, 2nd Edition
James W. Loewen

Culturally Responsive Teaching: Theory, Research, and Practice, 3rd Edition
Geneva Gay

Music, Education, and Diversity: Bridging Cultures and Communities
Patricia Shehan Campbell

Reaching and Teaching Students in Poverty: Strategies for Erasing the Opportunity Gap, 2nd Edition
Paul C. Gorski

Deconstructing Race: Multicultural Education Beyond the Color-Bind
Jabari Mahiri

Is Everyone Really Equal? An Introduction to Key Concepts in Social Justice Education, 2nd Edition
Özlem Sensoy and Robin DiAngelo

Teaching for Equity in Complex Times: Negotiating Standards in a High-Performing Bilingual School
Jamy Stillman and Lauren Anderson

Transforming Educational Pathways for Chicana/o Students: A Critical Race Feminista Praxis
Dolores Delgado Bernal and Enrique Alemán, Jr.

Un-Standardizing Curriculum: Multicultural Teaching in the Standards-Based Classroom, 2nd Edition
Christine E. Sleeter and Judith Flores Carmona

Global Migration, Diversity, and Civic Education: Improving Policy and Practice
James A. Banks, Marcelo Suárez-Orozco, and Miriam Ben-Peretz, Eds.

Reclaiming the Multicultural Roots of U.S. Curriculum: Communities of Color and Official Knowledge in Education
Wayne Au, Anthony L. Brown, and Dolores Calderón

Human Rights and Schooling: An Ethical Framework for Teaching for Social Justice
Audrey Osler

We Can't Teach What We Don't Know: White Teachers, Multiracial Schools, 3rd Edition
Gary R. Howard

Teaching and Learning on the Verge: Democratic Education in Action
Shanti Elliott

Engaging the "Race Question": Accountability and Equity in U.S. Higher Education
Alicia C. Dowd and Estela Mara Bensimon

Diversity and Education: A Critical Multicultural Approach
Michael Vavrus

First Freire: Early Writings in Social Justice Education
Carlos Alberto Torres

Mathematics for Equity: A Framework for Successful Practice
Na'ilah Suad Nasir, Carlos Cabana, Barbara Shreve, Estelle Woodbury, and Nicole Louie, Eds.

Race, Empire, and English Language Teaching: Creating Responsible and Ethical Anti-Racist Practice
Suhanthie Motha

Black Male(d): Peril and Promise in the Education of African American Males
Tyrone C. Howard

LGBTQ Youth and Education: Policies and Practices
Cris Mayo

Race Frameworks: A Multidimensional Theory of Racism and Education
Zeus Leonardo

Class Rules: Exposing Inequality in American High Schools
Peter W. Cookson Jr.

Teachers Without Borders? The Hidden Consequences of International Teachers in U.S. Schools
Alyssa Hadley Dunn

Streetsmart Schoolsmart: Urban Poverty and the Education of Adolescent Boys
Gilberto Q. Conchas and James Diego Vigil

(continued)

Americans by Heart: Undocumented Latino Students and the Promise of Higher Education
William Pérez

Achieving Equity for Latino Students: Expanding the Pathway to Higher Education Through Public Policy
Frances Contreras

Literacy Achievement and Diversity: Keys to Success for Students, Teachers, and Schools
Kathryn H. Au

Understanding English Language Variation in U.S. Schools
Anne H. Charity Hudley and Christine Mallinson

Latino Children Learning English
Guadalupe Valdés, Sarah Capitelli, and Laura Alvarez

Asians in the Ivory Tower
Robert T. Teranishi

Our Worlds in Our Words: Exploring Race, Class, Gender, and Sexual Orientation in Multicultural Classrooms
Mary Dilg

Why Race and Culture Matter in Schools
Tyrone C. Howard

Diversity and Equity in Science Education
Okhee Lee and Cory A. Buxton

Forbidden Language
Patricia Gándara and Megan Hopkins, Eds.

The Light in Their Eyes,10th Anniversary Edition
Sonia Nieto

The Flat World and Education
Linda Darling-Hammond

Diversity and the New Teacher
Catherine Cornbleth

Frogs into Princes: Writings on School Reform
Larry Cuban

Educating Citizens in a Multicultural Society, 2nd Edition
James A. Banks

Culture, Literacy, and Learning
Carol D. Lee

Facing Accountability in Education
Christine E. Sleeter, Ed.

Talkin Black Talk
H. Samy Alim and John Baugh, Eds.

Improving Access to Mathematics
Na'ilah Suad Nasir and Paul Cobb, Eds.

"To Remain an Indian"
K. Tsianina Lomawaima and Teresa L. McCarty

Education Research in the Public Interest
Gloria Ladson-Billings and William F. Tate, Eds.

Multicultural Strategies for Education and Social Change
Arnetha F. Ball

Beyond the Big House
Gloria Ladson-Billings

Teaching and Learning in Two Languages
Eugene E. García

Improving Multicultural Education
Cherry A. McGee Banks

Education Programs for Improving Intergroup Relations
Walter G. Stephan and W. Paul Vogt, Eds.

City Schools and the American Dream
Pedro A. Noguera

Thriving in the Multicultural Classroom
Mary Dilg

Educating Teachers for Diversity
Jacqueline Jordan Irvine

Teaching Democracy
Walter C. Parker

The Making—and Remaking—of a Multiculturalist
Carlos E. Cortés

Transforming the Multicultural Education of Teachers
Michael Vavrus

Learning to Teach for Social Justice
Linda Darling-Hammond, Jennifer French, and Silvia Paloma Garcia-Lopez, Eds.

Culture, Difference, and Power, Revised Edition
Christine E. Sleeter

Learning and Not Learning English
Guadalupe Valdés

The Children Are Watching
Carlos E. Cortés

Multicultural Education, Transformative Knowledge, and Action
James A. Banks, Ed.

Just Schools

Building Equitable Collaborations with Families and Communities

Ann M. Ishimaru

Teachers College Press
Teachers College | Columbia University
New York and London

Published by Teachers College Press, 1234 Amsterdam Avenue, New York, NY 10027

Copyright © 2020 by Teachers College, Columbia University

Cover image by Ozgur Coskun / Shutterstock.

Chapter 2 is adapted with permission from "Rewriting the Rules of Engagement: Elaborating a Model of District-Community Collaboration." by A. M. Ishimaru, 2014, *Harvard Educational Review*, *84*(2), pp. 188–216, as well as "When New Relationships Meet Old Narratives: The Journey Towards Improving Parent-School Relations in a District-Community Organizing Collaboration," by A. M. Ishimaru, 2014, *Teachers College Record*, *116*(2), pp. 1–49.

Chapter 3 was drawn, in part, from "'Darles el Lugar': A Place for Nondominant Family Knowing in Educational Equity," by F. Barajas-López, F. and A. M. Ishimaru, 2016, *Urban Education*, *55*(1), pp. 38–65. Copyright © 2016 SAGE. Used with permission. doi.org/10.1177/0042085916652179

Chapters 4 and 6 draw from the following resources:

"From Family Engagement to Equitable Collaboration," by A. M. Ishimaru, 2017, *Educational Policy*, *33*(2), pp. 350–385. Copyright © 2017 SAGE. Used with permission. doi:10.1177/0895904817691841

"Disrupting Racialized Institutional Scripts: Towards Parent-Teacher Transformative Agency for Educational Justice," by A. M. Ishimaru and S. Takahashi, 2017, *Peabody Journal of Education*, *92*(3), pp. 343–362. doi.org/10.1080/0161956X.2017.1324660

"Reinforcing Deficit, Journeying Towards Equity: Cultural Brokering in Family Engagement Initiatives," by A. M. Ishimaru, K. Torres, J. Salvador, J. Lott, D. Williams, and C. Tran, 2016, *American Educational Research Journal*, *53*(4), pp. 850–882. Copyright © 2016 Sage. doi:10.3102/0002831216657178

"Families in the Driver's Seat: Catalyzing Parental Transformative Agency in Equitable Collaboration," by A. M. Ishimaru, J. Lott, K. O'Reilly-Diaz, and K. Torres, 2019, *Teachers College Record*, *121*(11). Retrievable from www.tcrecord.org/Content.asp?ContentId=22819

All rights reserved. No part of this publication may be reproduced or transmitted in any form or by any means, electronic or mechanical, including photocopy, or any information storage and retrieval system, without permission from the publisher. For reprint permission and other subsidiary rights requests, please contact Teachers College Press, Rights Dept.: tcpressrights@tc.columbia.edu

Library of Congress Cataloging-in-Publication Data is available at loc.gov

ISBN 978-0-8077-6319-3 (paper)
ISBN 978-0-8077-6320-9 (hardcover)
ISBN 978-0-8077-7815-9 (ebook)

Printed on acid-free paper
Manufactured in the United States of America

Contents

Series Foreword

This readable and informative book makes a compelling and research-based argument that empowering and engaging nondominant parents, families, and communities in schools can result in numerous positive learning outcomes for students, including increased academic achievement and affirmed cultural identities. When educators meaningfully engage with parents and families, they are more likely to recognize, respect, and incorporate elements from the homes and communities of students and to make schooling more culturally sustaining and joyous for students. Schools become more affirming and "identity safe" (Steele & Cohn-Vargas, 2013) places for students from diverse cultures and groups when they integrate the funds of knowledge and wisdom that exist in families and communities (Moll & González, 2004). Ishimaru describes how readers can reimagine, formulate, and implement creative ways for educators to collaborate with families and communities to create just, culturally affirming, and equitable schools.

Ishimaru describes why the potential positive outcomes that can result from engaging parents, families, and communities in schools are rarely realized, especially within nonmainstream communities with large populations of low-income minoritized and racialized groups such as African Americans, Latinxs, and Native Americans. The author details, with vivid and sometimes troubling examples, how low-income and minoritized parents are often viewed by teachers and school administrators from a cultural-deficit perspective. Low-income and minoritized parents are considered a problem when viewed from a deficit perspective rather than as a source of wisdom and knowledge that can be used to improve the education of their children. Ishimaru describes powerful examples and cases of how minoritized parents become frustrated by their marginalization when they try to explain to teachers and administrators the problems experienced by their children in school and recommend ways in which they might be solved. Ishimaru states that educators often "listen to respond" in order to fit the worries of parents into school-based assumptions rather than listening genuinely to comprehend the problems identified by parents and to take meaningful action to solve them.

This insightful and well-researched book will help school practitioners to conceptualize and implement promising strategies to engage parents and families in nonmainstream communities within the diverse racial, ethnic, and cultural groups that are now increasingly populating the nation's schools. American classrooms are experiencing the largest influx of immigrant students since the beginning of the 20th century. Approximately 12.6 million new immigrants—documented and undocumented—settled in the United States in the years from 2000 to 2016 (Zong, Batalova, & Hallock 2018). Less than 10% came from nations in Europe. Most came from Mexico, nations in South Asia, East Asia, Latin America, the Caribbean, and Central America. Although African immigrants make up a small part of the U.S. immigrant population (2.1 million were living in the Untied States in 2015), they increased by 41% from 2000 to 2013 (Anderson, 2017). The largest number of immigrants to the United States today come from India and China, not Mexico. The influence of an increasingly diverse population on U.S. schools, colleges, and universities is and will continue to be enormous.

Schools in the United States are more diverse today than they have been since the early 1900s, when a multitude of immigrants entered the United States from Southern, Central, and Eastern Europe (C. A. M. Banks, 2005). In 2017, the National Center for Education Statistics estimated that the percentage of students from ethnic minority groups made up more than 52% of the students in prekindergarten through 12th grade in U. S. public schools, an increase from 39.2% in 2001 (National Center for Education Statistics, 2017). Latinxs made up 25% of the children in the United States in 2017, African Americans were 15%, Asian and Pacific Island children were 6%, and American Indians were 1% (Annie E. Casey Foundation, 2019).

Language and religious diversity is also increasing in the U.S. student population. A Center for Migration Studies publication estimated that 21.6% of Americans aged 5 and above (65.5 million) spoke a language other than English at home in 2016 (Camarota & Ziegler, 2017). This percentage has doubled since 1990, and almost tripled since 1980. The significant number of immigrants from nations such as India and China has also greatly increased religious diversity in the United States. Harvard professor Diana L. Eck (2001) calls the United States the "most religiously diverse nation on earth" (p. 4). Islam is now the fastest-growing religion in the United States, as well as in several European nations such as France, the United Kingdom, and the Netherlands (Banks, 2009; O'Brien, 2016).

The major purpose of the Multicultural Education Series is to provide preservice educators, practicing educators, graduate students, scholars, and policymakers with an interrelated and comprehensive set of books that summarizes and analyzes important research, theory, and practice related to the education of ethnic, racial, cultural, and linguistic groups in the United States and the education of mainstream students about diversity. The dimensions of multicultural education, developed by Banks (2004) and described in the *Handbook of Research on Multicultural Education* and in the *Encyclopedia of Diversity in Education* (Banks, 2012), provide the conceptual framework for the development of the publications in the Series. The dimensions are content integration, the knowledge construction process, prejudice reduction, equity pedagogy, and an empowering institutional culture and social structure. The books in the Multicultural Education Series provide research, theoretical, and practical knowledge about the behaviors and learning characteristics of students of color (Conchas & Vigil, 2012; Lee, 2007), language minority students (Gándara & Hopkins, 2010; Valdés, 2001; Valdés, Capitelli, & Alvarez, 2011), low-income students (Cookson, 2013; Gorski, 2018), and other minoritized population groups, such as students who speak different varieties of English (Charity Hudley & Mallinson, 2011), and LGBTQ youth (Mayo, 2014).

This well-conceptualized and -written book describes transformative and culturally sustaining ways to engage low-income and minoritized parents, families, and communities in school collaborations. A transformative and culturally sustaining concept of building collaborations with schools requires that nonmainstream parents, families, and communities are viewed as having rich cultures and insights that can benefit schools and the education of their children, engaged as partners in decisionmaking rather than passive recipients of decisions made by teachers and school administrators, and valued for their rich cultural and insightful contributions. When parents, families, and communities are effectively involved in school decisionmaking, schools are better able to help students to acquire the knowledge and skills needed to become competent, thoughtful, and effective citizens in a racialized and polarized society. This book is a significant and rich contribution to the literature on ways to give voice to the myriad parents, families, and communities of color that have too long been ignored and silenced in schools.

—James A. Banks

REFERENCES

Anderson, M. (2017, February 14). African immigrant population in the U.S. steadily climbs. Pew Research Center. Retrieved from www.pewresearch.org/fact-tank/2017/02/14/african-immigrant-population-in-u-s-steadily-climbs/

Annie E. Casey Foundation. (2019). *2019 kids count data book: State trends in child well-being*. Baltimore, MD: Author.

Banks, C. A. M. (2005). *Improving multicultural education: Lessons from the intergroup education movement*. New York, NY: Teachers College Press.

Banks, J. A. (2004). Multicultural education: Historical development, dimensions, and practice. In J. A. Banks & C. A. M. Banks (Eds.), *Handbook of research on multicultural education* (2nd ed., pp. 3–29). San Francisco, CA: Jossey-Bass.

Banks, J. A. (Ed.). (2009). *The Routledge international companion to multicultural education*. New York, NY & London, England: Routledge.

Banks, J. A. (2012). Multicultural education: Dimensions of. In J. A. Banks (Ed.), *Encyclopedia of diversity in education* (vol. 3, pp. 1538–1547). Thousand Oaks, CA: Sage.

Camarota, S. A., & Ziegler, K. (2017, October). *65.5 million U.S. residents spoke a foreign language at home in 2016*. The Center for Immigration Studies. Retrieved from cis.org/Report/655-Million-US-Residents-Spoke-Foreign-Language-Home-2016

Charity Hudley, A. H., & Mallinson, C. (2011). *Understanding language variation in U. S. schools*. New York, NY: Teachers College Press.

Conchas, G. Q., & Vigil, J. D. (2012). *Streetsmart schoolsmart: Urban poverty and the education of adolescent boys*. New York, NY: Teachers College Press.

Cookson, P. W., Jr. (2013). *Class rules: Exposing inequality in American high schools*. New York, NY: Teachers College Press.

Eck, D. L. (2001). *A new religious America: How a "Christian country" has become the world's most religiously diverse nation*. New York, NY: HarperSanFrancisco.

Gándara, P., & Hopkins, M. (Eds.). (2010). *Forbidden language: English language learners and restrictive language policies*. New York, NY: Teachers College Press.

Gorski, P. C. (2018). *Reaching and teaching students in poverty: Strategies for erasing the opportunity* gap (2nd ed.). New York, NY: Teachers College Press.

Lee, C. D. (2007). *Culture, literacy, and learning: Taking bloom in the midst of the whirlwind*. New York, NY: Teachers College Press.

Mayo, C. (2014). *LGBTQ youth and education: Policies and practices*. New York, NY: Teachers College Press.

Moll, L. C., & González, N. (2004). Engaging life: A funds-of-knowledge approach to multicultural education. In J. A. Banks & C. A. M. Banks (Eds.), *Handbook of research on multicultural education* (2nd ed., pp. 699–715). San Francisco, CA: Jossey-Bass.

National Center for Education Statistics. (2017). *Enrollment and percentage distribution of enrollment in public elementary and secondary schools, by race/ethnicity and region: Selected years, fall 1995 through fall 2025*. Retrieved from nces.ed.gov/programs/digest/d15/tables/dt15_203.50.asp

O'Brien, P. (2016). *The Muslim question in Europe: Political controversies and public philosophies*. Philadelphia, PA: Temple University Press.

Steele, D. M., & Cohn-Vargas, B. (2013). *Identity safe classrooms: Places to belong and learn*. Thousand Oaks, CA: Corwin.

Valdés, G. (2001). *Learning and not learning English: Latino Students in American schools*. New York, NY: Teachers College Press.

Valdés, G., Capitelli, S., & Alvarez, L. (2011). *Latino children learning English: Steps in the journey*. New York, NY: Teachers College Press.

Zong, J., Batalova, J., & Hallock, J. (2018, February). *Frequently requested statistics on immigrants and immigration in the United States*. The Migration Policy Institute. Retrieved from www.migrationpolicy.org/article/frequently-requested-statistics-immigrants-and-immigration-united-states#Demographic

Acknowledgments

Although it is customary to end an acknowledgment with thanking one's own family and community in the writing of a book, to follow the guiding principles that shape this book, I begin with the family and communities who first taught me. They taught me what matters and showed me what it means to build from our histories and cultural resiliencies from immigration journeys to incarceration to reparations and solidarities beyond to educate and foster new possibilities for the next generations. I want to express my deep gratitude to my parents, Mikio and Vickie Ishimaru, and my Miyashita and Ishimaru grandparents—as well as their ancestors before them and the broader Japanese American community. I finished this book on the way to celebrating Bon Odori (the return of the ancestors) in Aoki village in Fukuoka, Japan, with my husband, children, and generous extended family. Doing so brought whole new layers to my appreciation of the legacies I have inherited and the giants upon whose shoulders I stand. *Okage sama de*—I am because of you.

This book would not exist without the families and communities whose knowledge, expertise, wisdom, and leadership illuminate and shape the pages of this book. Collectively, these youth, families, and communities represent formidable power, memory, and imagination in the quest to shape more-just schools and communities—at this current dim moment in our nation's history, they remain a reason for hope. I am deeply grateful to the many family and community leaders and organizers I have had the privilege of getting to know and learn *from* and *with* over the past decade and more. Educational practitioners have also been crucial partners in this work at every turn, from instructional assistants and classroom teachers to family engagement specialists, principals, and superintendents of small and large districts. If not for their humility, learning stances, and committed leadership practice, there would be no "collaboration" to write of in this book.

The work at the core of this book is the result of multiple partnerships (though any and all shortcomings are, of course, my own). An all-star team of coauthors, collaborators, educators, and graduate students have made all this work possible. Chapter 2 was adapted from a 2014 article in *Harvard Education Review* as well as an article in *Teachers College Record* from the same year (Ishimaru, 2014a, 2014b). Special thanks to the parent leaders of the Salem-Keizer Coalition for Equality, Eduardo Angulo, Sandy Husk,

John Lenssen, and the (now former) systems leaders of Salem-Keizer Public Schools for the foundational glimpses of equitable collaboration in that chapter. Chapter 3 adapts work collaboratively undertaken with Dr. Filiberto Barajas-López and published in *Urban Education* (Barajas-López & Ishimaru, 2016). Chapters 4 and 6 build from work done in partnership with Dr. Joe L. Lott, II, Dr. Melanie Quaempts, a number of districts and community organizations, and a team of terrific graduate students and emerging scholars who made up the Equitable Parent-School Collaboration (EPSC) Research Project (www.education.uw.edu/epsc/). Dr. Kathryn Torres played a crucial leadership role on that team, along with Dr. Ismael Fajardo, Karen O'Reilly-Diaz, Dr. Jessica Salvador, Christine Tran, Dawn Cameron Williams, Aditi Rajendran, Dalya Perez, Dr. Jondou Chase Chen, John Benner, Dr. Nathanie Lee, and Tram Dang. Those chapters draw from a solo-authored article in *Educational Policy* (Ishimaru, 2017), a coauthored article with Dr. Sola Takahashi in the *Peabody Journal of Education* (Ishimaru & Takahashi, 2017), a coauthored paper in the *American Educational Research Journal* (Ishimaru et al., 2016), and a coauthored article with Lott, Torres, and O'Reilly-Diaz in *Teachers College Record* (2019). Chapter 5 is coauthored with doctoral students Dawn Cameron Williams and Aditi Rajendran in partnership with three educational organizations. Finally, Chapter 7 is co-authored with three systems leaders, Dr. Kelly Aramaki, Dr. Justin Irish, and Dr. Keisha Scarlett, drawing from work done in the context of the University of Washington's Leadership for Learning Program (directed by Dr. Anthony Craig). That work also drew directly from the Family Leadership Design Collaborative (familydesigncollab.org/) in partnership with Dr. Megan Bang, Aditi Rajendran, and Charlene Montaño Nolan (as well as a host of other research assistants and a national network of collaborative members; see our website for a full list). Special thanks to Flint Community Schools superintendent Dr. Derrick Lamar Jones Lopez for his leadership in systems-based co-design.

Because the work in this book spans over a decade, many different organizations and fellowships have played an important role in funding the research. I would like to extend my appreciation to the Spencer Foundation, the State Farm Foundation, the Ruth Landes Memorial Research Fellowship, the Ronald R. Edmonds–Charles M. Cheng Memorial Fund, the Bill & Melinda Gates Foundation (special thanks to LiLi Liu), and the W.K. Kellogg Foundation (Valorie Johnson) for support of the research in this book. Thanks also to Dean Mia Tuan of the University of Washington College of Education for the sabbatical during which I was able to complete the writing of this book.

My academic mentors and s/heroes have also made this book possible. Many thanks to Dr. Jim Banks for his belief in this work and his consistent, persistent critical care in ensuring it came to fruition. Thank you to Dr. Mark Warren, my doctoral advisor, for his guidance and support long after the dissertation, along with the now far-flung but steadfast love of the extended"DRP," aka the beautiful humans of the Harvard Community Organizing for School Reform Project extended family. With Dr. Ron Glass (the master's advisor who first encouraged me to consider research so long ago) and many others, Mark showed me the way forward through his collaborative, engaged scholarship. My colleagues at the University of Washington's College of Education and the sister scholars of WIRED (Women Investigating Race, Ethnicity and Difference) have not only tolerated the kind of research I do but valued, supported, and enabled me to grow it—a rare dynamic in academia for which I count myself incredibly fortunate. Gratitude in particular to Megan Bang for helping to coax out the wolf within. And I have survived this journey only with the laughter, tears, and wicked sharp wits of the SMAHRTie lifeline: Liliana Garces, Cynthia Gordon da Cruz, Sola Takahashi, Amanda Taylor, and Mara Tieken. Thank you for pushing my scholarship and having my back. Special thank you to Jay Nalani for her final-hour editing help and to Teachers College Press editor Brian Ellerbeck for his patient support over the long haul.

My families have kept me grounded in all the big and small ways that families matter to well-being. Thank you to my siblings, Karen and David, and their families for Ishimaru traditions and cousin chaos. Love and cooking to the Solar Family, who first taught me families can be chosen as well as given. *Gassho* to the Seattle Betsuin community who remind me of my place (doing whatever the aunties say) and buoy our family with laughter and gratitude in the Dharma. And finally, to those who put up with my hair pulling, incessant keyboard-tapping, late-night theorizing, and absences away to research and write: Jani Semke and Darryl Robbins, you are the secret to our families' survival, and we are so fortunate to share the everyday with you; to my best friend, soulmate, and husband, Zack, thank you for being the one I want to share the highs and lows with at the end of each day; and to Mika, Kai, and Aki, my brilliant, quirky, laughing loves—you remind me why all of this matters—and anchor my faith in the future.

Introduction

> People, families, organizations in marginalized communities struggle everyday; it is a way of life that is necessary for survival, and when theorized and mobilized can become a powerful strategy for transformation.
>
> —Linda Tuhiwai Smith, *Decolonizing Methodologies: Research and Indigenous Peoples* (2012)

> One cannot expect positive results from an educational or political action program which fails to respect the particular view of the world held by the people. Such a program constitutes cultural invasion, good intentions notwithstanding.
>
> —Paulo Freire, *Pedagogy of the Oppressed* (1970)

We stand at a crossroads in the relationship between families and schools. At this moment in U.S. history, immigrant families are being separated and children imprisoned, explicitly racist sentiments have become commonplace in schools and in the media, Black lives continue to be imperiled, and federal policies and legal decisions have begun to undo decades of civil rights. A reimagining of the fundamental relationship between families, educators, and schools seems both elusive and, at the same time, never more crucial and relevant.

On one hand, it is a lot to ask public schools and families—especially those most marginalized by our systems—to engage each other differently when there's so much coming at them that threatens their very existence and survival. On the other hand, these broader sociopolitical dynamics both in and outside of schools throw into high relief how deeply the troubling assumptions and approaches to families of color are "baked into" our institutions and society—and the inner workings of schools.

Such an understanding also compels us to recognize the resilience, ingenuity, and agency that have existed *all along* among young people and their families from nondominant communities.[1] Indigenous scholars talk about this as "survivance"—not simply surviving, but finding ways to grow and thrive despite colonization, oppression, and marginalization (Vizenor, 2008). For certain, this means resistance to these forces, but this idea also calls us to remember forms of knowing, doing, and being that have existed and sustained communities of color all along—and that represent a formidable reservoir of possibilities for the future.

This book seeks to do the heavy lifting at this pivotal moment—not only of making these twin dynamics simultaneously visible, but of providing research, examples, and practices that can be undertaken at multiple levels to begin reconfiguring and redesigning the fundamental relations between families, communities, and schools. Based on over a decade of research across settings that ranged from complex, urban school systems to grassroots community-based educational spaces, the ambition of this book is to push us beyond the current paradigm and to fundamentally reimagine how families and communities might collaborate with educators at all levels to realize more just schools. If you are a teacher or other educator, parent, family member, student, community member, or an educational leader in a public school system, you already know that this is no small ambition. To anchor the studies and examinations that unfold in the following chapters, I rely on four principles that thread across the work: (1) begin with family and community priorities, interests, concerns, knowledge, and resources; (2) transform power; (3) build reciprocity and agency; and (4) undertake change as collective inquiry.

SITUATING "WHAT COUNTS" FOR FAMILIES IN EDUCATION

U.S. public schools recently opened their doors to a student population that is over half students of color, including an unprecedented and growing influx of immigrants and refugees (de Brey et al., 2019; Suárez-Orozco & Suárez-Orozco, 2001). Amid these sweeping demographic changes, troubling disparities in student outcomes and success by race and class persist (Darling-Hammond, 2015; Ladson-Billings, 2006). Faced with growing urgency to address these educational inequities, policymakers and educators have increasingly turned to parent and community engagement as a strategy to improve student success. Decades of research point to a positive association between a variety of parental roles in education and student achievement and success (Fan & Chen, 2001; Henderson & Mapp, 2002; Hill & Tyson, 2009; Jeynes, 2005, 2007, 2012, and many others). Some research even suggests that parent engagement has a greater impact on academic outcomes for marginalized students of color (Jeynes, 2015). Although debate rages on with regards to which behaviors help or hinder, the enthusiastic prescriptions and heated admonitions have one thing in common: They are mostly focused on an outmoded, deficit-based model of parent involvement. Rather than approaching parents and communities as contributors to the problem of racial and socioeconomic educational disparities, then, this book suggests that nondominant families can be—and are—vital collaborators and leaders in efforts to transform our schools and broader educational systems toward educational justice.

Given the realities of racism, historical trauma, poverty, unstable neighborhoods, and systemic inequities faced by nondominant students, families, and communities, it may come as little surprise that selling brownies at the school bake sale—a common enactment of traditional parent involvement models—has limited impact on educational improvement and student outcomes. For decades, scholars have called for a move "beyond the bake sale" from traditional *parent involvement* models to *family engagement* approaches that expand beyond biological parents to other family members, include the cultural practices and priorities of diverse communities, and position parents and families as critical actors in student academic success (Shirley, 1997; Warren, Mapp, & Community Organizing and School Reform Project, 2011).

However, even current "best practices" policy, practice, and research in family engagement often disregard the complex and contested dynamics of race, class, language, power, and privilege that pervade our schools and society. Despite an abundance of good intentions, both *involvement* and *engagement* approaches largely enact a theory of change focused on changing—or "fixing"—marginalized parents and families. In doing so, these efforts align with prevailing racialized narratives about low-income families and communities of color that implicitly blame them for their children's academic struggles. In most schools, family engagement continues to be operationalized as parent attendance at prescribed school events (such as open houses, parent–teacher conferences, and Parent–Teacher Association meetings) and "training" parents to ensure their children do their homework, attend school, behave in accordance with school expectations, and otherwise passively adhere to whatever policymakers and educational professionals say is best for their children.

An emerging body of research suggests that the asymmetrical, normative approaches that characterize many school-based efforts to engage families can actually foster *dis*engagement and resistance amongst families of color (Baquedano-López, Alexander, & Hernandez, 2013; Doucet, 2011; Dyrness, 2009; Lareau & Horvat, 1999; Olivos, 2006). Families can feel judged by educators and find their cultural practices, values, and priorities disregarded or even denigrated. Thus, efforts to involve and/or engage families not only fall short of closing so-called achievement gaps; a growing literature suggests that they can actually exacerbate racial and other inequities in education. "Best practice" efforts focused primarily on removing barriers to accessing the same individualistic, school-centric activities and events (e.g., translating fliers into different languages or providing childcare and food at school events) also fall short. They do little to shift the underlying assumptions and opportunities for engagement. They do little to disrupt the policies, institutional practices, and daily interactions that systematically structure marginalization and disengagement for nondominant students, their families, and their communities.

Moreover, this prescriptive, racialized lens about what "counts" as an appropriate role for families obscures vital knowledge and expertise possessed by nondominant families and communities. Such knowledge and expertise are a source of epistemic authority and a potent resource for transforming inequitable educational systems (Booker & Goldman, 2016). From Oprah to brain scientists and policymakers to iPhone apps (York, Loeb, & Doss, 2019), professional experts seem to be telling parents what to do to ensure their children's success. Yet rarely do parents and families—especially the ones with the most at stake in inequitable schools—have a place at the table to contribute *their* expertise in shaping the education agenda.

BEYOND CRITIQUE TO FOSTERING EQUITABLE COLLABORATIONS

Tapping the expertise of nondominant families and communities is not a simple task given the complexities of educational systems and the dynamics of race, culture, and power within and around them. Efforts to include marginalized parents in the conversation often take the form of window-dressing conventional activities to be more "inclusive" or tokenizing rituals that, contrary to intent, "reinforce the iron cage of [professional] authority" (Anderson, 1998). In other words, we cannot assign a lone parent to a committee and expect transformation; nor can we simply put a group of educators and families into a room and expect productive collaboration to emerge. Even brokering organizational partnerships between school districts and community-based organizations does not magically result in more responsive and equitable school systems, as the same hierarchical power dynamics often reassert themselves.

So how might we envision ways forward that recognize the historically rooted and ongoing processes of colonization and marginalization while reimagining and charting a different path for "engaging" families and communities in educational change? This book proposes building and enacting *equitable collaborations* as a process that seeks to move beyond the "good parent/bad parent" dichotomy to foster solidarities amid difference toward community-determined educational justice and well-being. Building from critical race, community organizing, and sociocultural learning theories, an equitable collaboration approach begins from the premise that nondominant families (which includes young people themselves, their caregivers, and extended relations) represent a largely untapped source of expertise and leadership for achieving educational equity and justice. This book aims to integrate insights from theory and research to offer principles and practices addressing complex systemic racial inequities in partnership with the families and communities most directly impacted by them. Rather than a prescriptive program or checklist of activities toward a predetermined end, though, equitable collaborations constitute a process, not an end in and of themselves. Rather than a linear journey predetermined by an all-knowing system, equitable collaborations lean into the inevitable complexities and tensions to move us beyond facile either/or propositions premised on a deficiency paradigm. The process itself allows us to reimagine and build the path toward systemic change with students, families, and communities themselves.

This book has five major goals: (1) to problematize well-meaning, but deficit-based approaches to marginalized parents and illuminate how even inclusive versions of the conventional model (which predominate in U.S. schools today) can still exacerbate existing educational inequities in education; (2) to highlight the expertise, knowledge, cultural practices, and organized power of nondominant families and communities that constitute critical resources in building more equitable educational systems; (3) to provide empirical data from programs, schools, and systemic initiatives that have made strides in leveraging the expertise of nondominant families and communities by building equitable collaborations with families; (4) to offer theoretical frameworks and methods that may be useful for researchers engaging in work related to family engagement; and (5) to provide guiding principles and recommendations to educators at multiple levels of educational systems about how to engage families in systemic transformation toward equity. To follow the first principle of starting with families and communities, though, means sharing my own positionality in this work.

SHOWING UP IN THE WORK

My own experiences and positionality are interwoven into this broader narrative in consequential ways. Because the move to play the "objective" researcher is tied up in a colonizing approach to research (Ladson-Billings, 1998; Smith, 2012), I also want to narrate my own learning and place in this work, as the chapters in this volume reflect an evolution of my own thinking, research, and practice across time. My family came to the United States as immigrants from Japan in the late 1800s and early 1900s, part of a wave of cheap labor to work on railroads in the West. They were eventually farmers—settlers on stolen Native lands—who worked land they could not legally own. My connection to many of the places and spaces I study across the country has been built through the communities and educators I have had the privilege to come to know, but those connections are often preceded—some would say haunted—by other memories. My family's efforts to establish new lives as Americans runs up and down the West Coast—from Seattle to Imperial Valley at the Mexican border—and they were incarcerated during World War II in Colorado, Arizona, and Arkansas. My father was born on the Colorado Indian Reservation, in one of the largest of the incarceration camps, in Poston, Arizona. Ultimately, my family's postwar "relocation" brought them to places like New York and Chicago, where I was born. My parents—of the Sansei (third) generation who led the fight for Japanese American reparations—made sure I knew my history from a young age, as well as my responsibility in ensuring injustice would not persist. *Kodomo no tame ni*—for the sake of the children.

So as a young teacher, my sense that families had a particular stake and expertise in education collided with my socialization into a predominantly white profession and my own feelings of insecurity as a new teacher. As an Asian American (and cisgender, heterosexual woman), I was privy to whiteness in a way the Model Minority myth uniquely provides—when the door to the faculty room closed, I heard white teachers deride a Black mother who had the temerity to suggest we integrate more history and content from other cultures into the curriculum. I thought the parent had a point, but as the lone teacher of color, I was scared to say so in that environment and scared to reach out to the mother.

When I became a parent, what had been theoretical became lived reality. I went to the first preschool open house, determined to be a "good, involved" parent. I sat in a tiny chair sipping apple juice from a Dixie paper cup and listened passively as the white woman director talked and talked at the handful of us who showed up (out of a preschool of over 100). She smiled and lectured in early-learning jargon to what she presumed to be low-income immigrant and refugee parents (I *was* low-income, but as a Harvard graduate student studying K–12 education with little familiarity with early learning!). The experience made me feel simultaneously infantilized, talked down to, and utterly confused about how to be a "good, involved" parent. As we filed out of the room my head was full of questions and conflict, and I vowed never to attend another parent night.

Around that same time, I asked a faculty member, a prominent, white male scholar, what the role of parents could be in school reform. He shrugged dismissively and said they could be involved by supporting individual student learning at home—and that had already been studied. These experiences all brought me to the conclusion that something was amiss. In short, my own family and community had taught me powerful lessons about historical injustice as well as community resistance, cultural practices, and ethical responsibilities that fundamentally shaped how I approached education, whether teaching, parenting, or researching. And in nearly every role I took up as an adult, schools seemed to dismiss, disregard, and even actively denigrate parents and families of color and the knowledge they brought to the education of their children. The system positioned outside others as knowing what's best for their children. Families of color didn't have all the answers, I reasoned, but surely the mostly white, middle-class educators who fill our public schools didn't have the *only* expertise that mattered for educating children. Ironically, the more I studied education reform and saw states and districts struggling to address racial disparities in student opportunities to learn and outcomes, the more I saw educators, educational leaders, policymakers, and funders hungrily casting about for knowledge, resources, and ideas about how they might become more culturally responsive and more equitable.

Only as a cultural and community organizer and eventually as a researcher studying education organizing did I begin to glimpse the potent agency of young people and families in shaping their own education as a force for liberation, sometimes in partnership with teachers, principals, and district leaders (though that seemed to be more the exception than the rule). As the director of an environmental justice organization and then co-lead of an Asian American cultural arts group, I learned challenging and powerful lessons about leadership in nondominant cultural contexts and about the complexities of power within communities. Since then, as a researcher, I have had the privilege of learning from and with many different community organizations as well as parent, family, community, *and* formal educational leaders, both in and out of school systems. Powerful activist scholars have also shaped my ability to see new possibilities and take up new theories and methodologies from fields and disciplines outside my own, not only to critique the system and to understand how inequities unfold and default back, but to remember the ancestral and cultural knowledges (Bernal, 2002; Khalifa, 2018; Yosso, 2005) that can help us begin to shape fundamentally different kinds of relations and aims. This book seeks to share some of the lessons these leaders and scholars have taught me—and that we have learned together—over the course of the last 15 years. Most of the studies in this book are published as peer-reviewed collaborative academic journal articles, but this book represents my effort to synthesize across that work and offer a more integrated narrative of journeys toward equitable collaboration across multiple contexts.

A FEW NOTES ON LANGUAGE

Parents, Families, and *Communities* have come to signal particular people and ways of thinking about these groups of people. The field of family engagement has largely come to recognize that the term "parents" carries with it a set of assumptions about two-parent heterosexual biologically related households that excludes the full range of familial and nonfamilial caregivers who are raising children. Thus, I use the term "family" to designate not only parents but older siblings, grandparents, cousins, foster parents, step-parents, and both the related and unrelated aunties, uncles, and other caregivers who collectively care for children. Although considerations of school-based family engagement often default to only adults, many communities approach children as *part* of families and foster *intergenerational* forms of engagement that recognize the powerful learning and interaction that has always unfolded between adults and children (Garcia, 2019). Although this book largely focuses on the adults around young people, a burgeoning literature has begun to explore youth voice as a form of educational leadership (Bertrand & Rodela, 2018; Lac & Mansfield, 2018; Mitra, 2006).

As for "community," a close colleague once puzzled that her intensive community work was perceived by others as somehow *not* related to families. Particularly in the context of conventional school-community partnership frameworks, "community" has become a code word solely for nonprofit organizations, social service agencies, businesses, churches, or libraries. I use the term "community" more expansively. Although my usage may include community-based organizations and community leaders without children in a particular school or educational organization, I mobilize the term to include groups of *people* who share a racial or cultural identity, a neighborhood, or a group of children. In that sense, then, families are inevitably *part* of larger communities. Just like individuals, they may or may not actively participate in those communities or engage particular practices in relation to those communities.

Nondominant families refers to those impacted by systemic oppression, such as marginalization based on race, class, language, or immigration status, and is a term that explicitly references relationships to dominant power. I have struggled mightily with this descriptor as it is flawed in its own ways, but I prefer this term to a number of others for specific reasons. For example, "diverse" or "multicultural" presume that some families are so-called diverse (code for non-white), whereas white families are racially neutral or the norm relative to whom others are defined as different from (Sensoy & DiAngelo, 2017). These terms obscure the recognition that *all* families are racialized (whether white, Black, Asian, Latinx, Indigenous, Pacific Islander or mixed) and, in doing so, veer toward "color evasion" in disregarding how powered hierarchies shape experiences and opportunities (Annamma, Jackson, & Morrison, 2017).[2] "Color evasion" here refers to the ideological assertion that race does not matter and that the way to end discrimination is to deny the experiences and legacy of racism and treat everyone the same (Bonilla-Silva, 2010). Stephanie Fryberg (2010) and many others have shown how this approach erases important aspects of people's identities and justifies the status quo.

Alternatively, "families of color" does not explicitly encompass the range of families who experience inequities in schools because there are multiple, intersecting dynamics of marginalization that this term does not include—that is, race is a central dimension, but it is not exclusive—dynamics of oppression also exist across class, gender, sexuality, ability, language, citizenship status, and religious identities. Other terms, such as "minoritized," problematize older terms such as "minority" and highlight the processes through which even those with numerical "majority" can be marginalized; however, this term often gets taken up by those unfamiliar with its particular intent as a typo for "minority," and the concept tends to still pivot around numbers and notions of representativeness. Families "placed at risk" is also too easily taken up as "at-risk," a pathologizing label that presumes a trajectory of problems and denies agency to individuals and communities. "Historically marginalized" accurately highlights the historically rooted nature of marginalization, but it doesn't encompass how these dynamics continue into the present, nor does it recognize that certain groups of people are newer to U.S.–based marginalization (for example, families from particular refugee communities) but are nevertheless subject to the powered hierarchies that structure educational inequities.

Although a growing body of scholarly work has taken up the term "nondominant," I often get pushback on this term from community members themselves and would greatly prefer a term that does not lump vastly different groups of people together and define us by what we are *not*. How might we better encompass what families *do* possess, along the lines of Tara Yosso's (2005) community cultural wealth framework? Dr. Yosso riffed off Bourdieu's (Bourdieu & Passeron, 1977) notion of social and cultural capital (relationships, knowledge, and abilities that provide access to material resources and opportunities), which are often framed as lacking in communities of color. She identified multiple forms of "capital" that serve as important resources for navigating unjust institutions. Could this reframing help us develop language, like "community-wealth families"? Resilient families? Survivance families? Knowledge-rich families? Unfortunately, terms such as these don't yet exist and don't speak to practitioners or families themselves. I am confident these terms will evolve over time, but until then I begin with "nondominant" as an imperfect descriptor and am excited to be part of evolving language that better encompasses both the strengths and challenges faced by our communities.

Race, racism, and *racial inequities*—entire books, and indeed, entire careers, focus on understanding racial categories, racialization processes, and the multilayered, dynamic structures and systems of racism and racial inequity. Those are beyond the scope of this modest book. In Chapter 2, I explain how different theories inform how the framework of equitable collaborations takes up race. In brief, though, I draw from many scholars and theorists to conceptualize race in three parts. Part 1: Race is a historical construction. So-called science was used to distinguish different "races" in order to rationalize conquest, genocide, slavery, and exploitation. Part 2: Race is a biological fiction. Studies of DNA have confirmed that there are far more differences within so-called races than there are between them. Part 3: Race is a social reality with very real consequences. Racism accounts for the present-day inequities in just about every facet of modern life, from employment to banking and home ownership, from the justice system to health care, and in every aspect of education. Eduardo Bonilla-Silva's (2010) work reminds us that these systems do not need individual "racists" to maintain them—historically rooted racism persists in the supposedly race-neutral policies and practices that shape our everyday lives.

We hear all the time about the so-called racial achievement gap. But a more precise understanding of racial categories and the historical context of racism helps us to understand why many (including myself) critique the language of "achievement gap" for misdirecting the focus on students—and their families and communities—as the source of the problem. Instead, we might ask how the system of education in this country has created inequitable opportunities, access, and learning environments. Linda Darling-Hammond (2015) points out that low-income students of color have less-well-qualified and less-experienced teachers, less access to high-quality curricula, less access to materials and equipment, to counselors, library, and learning supports; we might recall that race and class are intertwined. Gloria Ladson-Billings (2006) calls this an "educational debt" owed to those who have been denied access for generations. This debt is one of the very real consequences of the social construction of race.

Equity and *educational justice*—many in the field have made the distinction between equality ("sameness as fairness") and equity (providing whatever individuals need to produce equal outcomes) (Gutiérrez & Jaramillo, 2006). Equity has often been constructed as a finite "won and done" outcome achieved primarily through legal remedies, like *Brown v. Board of Education.* I use the term "racial equity" in a more expansive, ongoing sense, but I increasingly use the term educational justice to push our conversation and work beyond legally defined notions of remedies and a Rawlsian notion of "equality" (an ahistorical and individualistic assumption that everyone starts at the same place and is governed by the same set of both formal and informal rules and norms) (Ryan, 2006). Again, whole books have been and will continue to be written on philosophies and approaches to justice, but I use educational justice in this book to refer to a dynamic process toward community-determined aims and ends, not simply individualistic achievement and "escape" to a different class and neighborhood, as framed by a neoliberal market-based logic.

Educational systems—In this book, I recognize that both schools and districts constitute complex systems unto themselves, but I generally refer to "educational systems" and mean both formal schools and the institutions, organizations, and informal spaces that constitute learning environments for young people (and adults).

Leadership—In spite of the long history of studying leadership as the traits, characteristics, or behaviors of individuals in formal roles of authority (such as superintendents or principals), this book approaches leadership as the actions undertaken to make change in an organization, group or community—by necessity, this implicates multiple people. In this sense, I often conceptualize leading as a verb, not a noun. Although formal educational leaders are important actors, they are by no means the *only* individuals enacting leadership. The premise of this book is that nondominant families and communities are critical—but typically overlooked—actors in educational leadership for educational justice.

ORGANIZATION OF THE BOOK

This book elaborates how equitable collaboration entails ongoing processes of building relationships, inquiring into and designing new organizational routines, and building systemic and community collaborative capacity and transformation. Based on empirical research and inquiry-driven practice, such processes offer promising possibilities not only for improving student outcomes and success in schools, but for developing robust partnerships between families and educators that build from the resources, assets, culture, and contributions of nondominant students, families, and communities to enact educational justice, community well-being, and a society premised on care and dignity.

The chapters in this book chart the beginning of a journey toward equitable collaboration with families and communities toward educational justice. After situating the book in the problem space using the literature (Chapter 1) and offering a conceptual lens of equitable collaboration featuring four guiding principles (Chapter 2), this journey begins with nondominant family experiences and narratives of education and inequities. Through brief vignettes and exchanges, families unveil how educational inequities unfold at multiple scales, leading to the principle of *beginning with families and communities* (Chapter 3). To fully understand the import and implications of everyday individual interactions between educators and families/communities, we need first to comprehend how inequities have been historically and structurally shaped, and then how those dynamics are operationalized in organizational contexts that open or constrain possibilities for equitable collaboration.

Each subsequent chapter thus highlights practices of equitable collaboration with families and communities in education and guiding principles at three overlapping scales: the *systemic level* at the intersection of multiple institutions, the *organizational level* within schools, districts, and educational organizations, and the *individual level* as played out in moment-to-moment interactions. In reality, all three levels are implicated in any given interaction, decision, or family–school context, but I foreground each level in turn for clarity's sake and use each chapter to delve into one or more of the guiding principles of equitable collaboration (see Figure I.1 for a conceptual representation of these levels).

At the systems level (Chapter 4), I examine a cross-sector collaboration to illuminate how the policy context shaped cultural brokering within multiorganizational efforts to address educational inequities. Amid powered dynamics playing out across agencies, districts, and community organizations and a predominance of assimilative approaches to families, my team and I identified systemic brokering approaches across organizational boundaries, highlighting guiding principles of *building reciprocity and agency* and *transforming power*.

At an organizational level (Chapter 5), we illuminate how educational organizations use data inquiry processes with families to catalyze organizational improvement and transformation. With Dawn Cameron Williams and Aditi Rajendran, I examine inquiry processes in early childhood, K–12 district, and community-based educational organizations to share practices, tensions, and openings for enacting the guiding principle of undertaking change as *collective inquiry and capacity-building*.

Figure I.1. Inequities and Collaborations at Three Overlapping Scales: Systemic, Organizational, and Individual Levels.

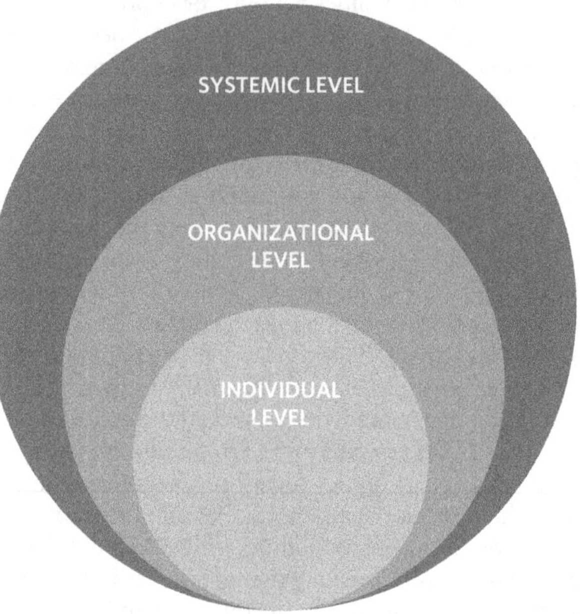

At the individual level (Chapter 6), I focus on how the moment-to-moment interactions between educators and families can foster collective learning for both families and educators and replace historically rooted power asymmetries with new relationships and ways of interacting to co-create change. Weaving together all four guiding principles of equitable collaboration, the chapter offers solidarity-driven co-design as an opportunity to foster new forms of activity and cultivate collective agency in the journey toward equitable collaboration between families, schools, and communities.

Finally, I conclude the book (Chapter 7) with a focus on systems-based co-design, drawing from research conducted with Dr. Kelly Aramaki, Dr. Justin Irish, Dr. Keisha Scarlett, Aditi Rajendran, and a host of other families, community partners, and systems leaders within a broader project with Dr. Megan Bang called the Family Leadership Design Collaborative (FLDC). Situated within the transformative research-practice agenda envisioned by the national FLDC network, this final chapter explores how district leaders shifted their leadership practices to undertake solidarity-driven co-design. Drawing on the four guiding principles simultaneously again, I illuminate how three leaders learned their way toward enacting "both/and" approaches as they negotiated key dilemmas in implementing co-design. Their practices suggest critical systemic leadership capacities for starting from family and community priorities, transforming power, building reciprocity and transformative agency, and undertaking change as collective inquiry. I conclude with a call to reimagine research and practice in collaboration *with* nondominant families and communities to build solidarities across difference and enact transformative change toward educational justice at multiple levels of education.

EQUITABLE COLLABORATIONS IN REACHING FOR TRANSFORMATION

This book builds from a critique of the old "remediation" paradigm of parent involvement to examine the challenges and possibilities for building more equitable forms of collaboration between nondominant families, communities, and schools. Centrally focused on the dynamics of race, class, power, and privilege across multiple levels of complex educational systems, the book seeks to generate new insights, contribute new knowledge, and illuminate useful theories and "next" practices (Hargreaves & Fullan, 2012) to help educators learn from and with nondominant families to disrupt racial inequities in educational systems and improve the schooling experiences, academic outcomes, and life chances of their children.

Transformative change in education is difficult to envision given the disturbing current sociopolitical context that draws sustenance from centuries of oppression and colonization. But as Leigh Patel (2017) argues, if we cannot imagine a different reality in which "all living beings, human and nonhuman, are afforded well-being, care, and dignity," how do we expect to work toward it? Nondominant families and communities are complex and tension filled, and they are not immune from the dynamics of power, racism, and hierarchies we must navigate in schools. And yet, they are also potential collaborators and leaders we have yet to take seriously in change efforts. *Equitable collaborations* between families and schools call us to move beyond our current paradigm, in which schools are the central actors (and holders of expertise) who reach out to "engage" families around *educators'* and *policymakers'* visions of what is best for children. Rather, a justice-based educational change agenda can only be *co-constructed* by both professional educators and those with the greatest expertise on their own children, their learning priorities and needs, their languages and cultural practices, their histories and nondominant ways of knowing—that is, the families and communities of children themselves. Only then can we reimagine what education might become. In this way, equitable collaborations ask us to step beyond the well-established bounds of thinking that educators should engage families and communities for *their* children's and *their* own benefit. By the time you are done reading this book, I hope you will begin to grasp the imperative of collectively taking up these new relationships, roles, and possibilities to reimagine what education might do to heal the past and cultivate thriving futures *kodomo no tame ni*—for the sake of *all our* children.

Fuzzy Families, Prickly Racism

Framing the Problem Space

> [Educators] can make imagined possibilities of equity a reality, but they can only do so with a different understanding of the power relationships between parents and schools. (Baquedano-López et al., 2013)

> The push for "parents as partners," empowerment, and parent education, then, may need to be calibrated to reflect the desires and goals of particular communities rather than politically laden assumptions made by outsiders about what parents need. (Doucet, 2011)

When my own children were preschoolers, they brought home the concepts of "warm fuzzies" and "cold pricklies" to describe how different words or interactions with their peers or teachers made them feel. Warm fuzzies are words, behaviors, or situations that make you feel happy, safe, good. Cold pricklies make you feel uncomfortable, alienated, or unhappy.[1] These may seem simplistic or childish but they are also unerringly good descriptions of what comes up for many adults when entering this problem space.

Despite the rhetoric and education jargon, competing feelings arise quickly in discussing the intersection of families, education, racism, and injustice in policy and practice. Even the jargon around families and education feels warm and fuzzy: Family engagement. Two-generation supports. Parent–teacher partnerships. Dual-capacity. We can all come together around feel-good efforts that bolster parents as children's "first teachers," support families in raising healthy, happy children, and help them to partner with teachers and school systems to ensure their children's academic success. But talk of racism, exclusion, marginalization, and colonization rains cold pricklies on those warm family fuzzies. Many educators would just as soon avoid talking about these dynamics, given our limited knowledge and training to engage around these issues, the political stakes for doing so inexpertly, and the discomfort we must face in reflecting on how our own default practices may be implicated. And though community-based leaders largely understand how the dynamics of racism play out in schools for the families they work with, they are beholden to funders and institutions that re-enact those very dynamics at organizational levels and hold them accountable to school-centered agendas and metrics. But the research—about both families and systems of oppression in education—suggests that if we are serious about fulfilling the potential of every child and about the well-being of our communities, we must lean into the complexities and discomfort of these twin dynamics. Only by doing so can we begin to learn our way toward policies and practices of educational justice.

In this chapter, I begin by drawing on the research literature to provide an overview of the positive association between family engagement and a wide range of student outcomes and share brief historical context for the shift from traditional models and research on *parent involvement* to *family engagement*. Despite the long history of research and an abundance of rhetoric about the importance of parents, my own and others' research suggest that the approaches and assumptions of family engagement still largely default to a deficiency paradigm on the ground. Thus, I propose moving beyond incremental efforts and "best practices" in family engagement to foster more *equitable collaborations* between families, communities, and educational systems. In the next chapter, I introduce a model and set of principles for how we might undertake "next practices" toward enacting equitable collaborations.

In this chapter, I take stock of the constrained, normative structures, routines, and expectations of nondominant parents and families in schools and where they came from historically. Why not jump directly to solutions? I sometimes encounter resistance in the form of impatience from educators or leaders who don't want to talk about the underpinnings of the problem—"We know there's a problem. Just tell us what to do now!" goes the refrain. To approach families and communities differently, though, we—as educators and researchers, as organizations and organizers, and even as fellow family members—must understand where, why, and how we often unwittingly reinforce the underlying dynamics of inequity when we envision and undertake solutions.

I close this chapter by overviewing a different branch of research, this time highlighting studies that illuminate the places and spaces that nondominant families and communities have been and continue to be powerful actors and changemakers in education. I highlight studies of community organizing and empowerment as well as participatory design of community learning as offering new lenses and directions forward for considering how to bridge divides of experience, education, culture, and understanding to enable educators and nondominant families to work together toward educational justice.

START WITH WARM FUZZIES: FAMILIES MATTER

Decades of research and policy efforts have focused on parents as key levers for improving children's educational success, and parent and family involvement is consistently associated with positive educational outcomes for children. For instance, research has found that when parents, teachers, and other adults in schools work together, students experience a broad range of positive outcomes, from better grades and test scores to more positive social-emotional outcomes and engagement in school, higher attendance at school, enrollment in more challenging coursework, and a greater likelihood of graduating and attending college (Epstein, 1995; Fan & Chen, 2001; Henderson & Mapp, 2002; Hill & Tyson, 2009; Jeynes, 2005, 2015).

More recently parent–school relations have become part of the broader school reform conversation, fueled by longitudinal analyses and a renewed focus on whole school reform. For instance, in Chicago, Tony Bryk (2010) and his colleagues examined the improvement of schools over an 11-year period and found that elementary schools with positive parent–school ties were 10 times more likely to improve in mathematics achievement and 4 times more likely to improve in reading achievement. Likewise, a recent evaluation of public elementary schools in Washington, DC, found that family engagement practices like home visits were associated with improved student attendance and grade-level reading proficiency (Sheldon & Jung, 2015). Although a critical read of these studies raises important questions about what behaviors and actions researchers do and do not "count" in their studies (see Chapter 5), for now let us note only a small handful of exceptions (whose methodologies and causal claims have been questioned by the field) to the largely positive associations between various forms of parental involvement or engagement and student achievement and other forms of academic success.

Thus, a robust body of research suggests that families are critical to educational success both in terms of their role in their own children's education in and out of schools and in terms of their advocacy and leadership in school change efforts. So if the research is that compelling, *why aren't we involving parents and realizing educational justice and success for all students?*

If you have ever tried to revisit or dispute a decision in schools as a parent or guardian, family member, community advocate, or student, your experience likely suggests it's not that simple. Especially when those interactions span differences of race, class, culture, language, and power, judgments about expertise, knowledge, and roles profoundly shape whose voices get heard, what changes, and who gets excluded, dismissed, or disregarded. Some families have far more influence on educators and the system than others.

What do we mean by "parents"? By "involvement"? By "educational success"? Who decides which behaviors and actions are legitimate and productive? Whose norms and expectations shape those assessments? What are the consequences of violating those norms and scripts? And how do interactions with families shape schooling practices and experiences? These questions are more than semantics or the strategic framing of policy wonks—or even the hand-wringing of ivory tower academics.

They have real consequences for children and families, both in everyday moment-to-moment interactions with schools and over the broad arc of communities' histories with U.S. schools. To dig into these complexities, we must first assess our conventional approaches to involving parents through a more critical historical lens.

ENTER THE COLD PRICKLIES: RACIAL INEQUITIES FROM PARENT INVOLVEMENT TO FAMILY ENGAGEMENT

The following fictitious case highlights some of the complexities of the power dynamics and assumptions that infuse the relationship between schools and nondominant families. Although this is only one specific example and an amalgam of many different stories I have heard through the years, the themes strike a chord across communities. The research may argue for the positive benefits of schools involving parents in education, but the "cold pricklies" enter when we begin to see how the structures, policies, and systems of schooling are experienced by young people of color and their families.

> After the first few days of kindergarten, Alejandro started crying and begging not to go to school. Maria, his mother, knew it was hard being away from home and having everything in English, but then Ale came home with a scraped knee. He said a boy "with yellow hair" had pushed him and said mean things. A week later, Maria got a call from the teacher, Ms. Laurie. Speaking too fast in English for Maria to catch everything, Ms. Laurie said Ale needed to learn to follow directions, to sit still, and get along with the other children. She asked Maria to use the same rules at home as they used at school. Embarrassed that perhaps her parenting was the source of Ale's struggles at school, Maria quickly agreed.
>
> Maria was worried. Ale was different from his big sister—he was a sweet energetic child who didn't do well if it was too noisy or things didn't happen the way he expected. Every day he came home with stories about Jordan, the boy who pushed Ale, made fun of his brown skin, or told him to go "back where he came from." Maria tried to talk about it with Ms. Laurie at drop-off, but the teacher said it was school policy not to talk about another student. Ale would be fine, the teacher reassured her, when he got better at keeping his hands to himself.
>
> After months of this, Maria found a crumpled flyer in Ale's backpack about the parent–teacher conferences and thought perhaps this was her chance to bring the issue up again, but the conferences were during the day when she had to work, so she couldn't go. Maria shared her worries with her neighbor Blanca, who had a 2nd-grader at

> the school. Blanca told her about a group of Mexican parents whose kids were being bullied. They were going to talk to the principal together. Relieved to realize she wasn't alone, Maria agreed to come to the meeting.
>
> At the meeting, when Blanca talked about their children being bullied, the principal, Ms. Shannon, explained that children were learning how to get along in their diverse school and not all behavior was bullying. She then told the parents not to worry because the school district had recently adopted a new social-emotional learning curriculum. When Blanca asked which parents were involved in choosing the curriculum, the principal said they would have to talk with district personnel about that. Ms. Shannon gave them all a fact sheet in English with the goals of the social-emotional academic development curriculum and the social-emotional learning standards a student must "know and be able to do" by the end of each grade level. Ms. Shannon encouraged them to talk with their teachers if they had any questions about how to support their children's social-emotional learning at home.
>
> Maria and the other parents left feeling frustrated and not sure how the curriculum was going to help their children right now. Blanca said maybe they should take their concerns to the district and the superintendent.

This case raises a multitude of tensions and questions—from the current enthusiasm about social-emotional learning to racialized bullying and interactions in our schools; from individual parent–teacher interactions to the relations between organized families and district decision-makers; and from federal privacy policies to everyday leadership practice. Across all of these issues, the dynamics of power are literally "baked in" to the conversations. At the most basic level, though, the case illustrates how limited our current paradigm of parent involvement is for enabling any of us—parents, families, teachers, principals, superintendents, organizers, and young people themselves—to navigate these complex, overlapping, and power-infused situations to best support our youth. The expectations and roles designated for parents in schools are bounded by a set of institutional norms and deeply entrenched racialized assumptions about what it means to be "involved."

Parent Involvement and the Logic of Deficiency

Parent involvement has come to signify a particular approach to the role of families as enacted across decades of racialized policy and practice in education. It is marked by a familiar litany of behaviors and activities, such as attendance at open houses, parent–teacher conferences, and PTA meetings, volunteering in the classroom or on fieldtrips, and fundraising for school needs. Scholar Veronica Terriquez (2011) calls these "plug-in" opportunities because they do not allow for any variability or meaningful interactions. Parents in this paradigm are expected to "plug-in" to a preset program of activities and interactions. Defined and controlled by school personnel, these activities and events for parents largely function to limit their participation and influence in the core work of the school (Cooper, 2009b; Hands, 2014). In Maria's case, these opportunities included the teacher calling her at home when a problem arose, and the parent–teacher conferences that conflicted with Maria's work schedule.

Along with these events come a set of unspoken dominant norms and expectations that assume parents' passive support of the school's agenda—organizational theorists call these "institutional scripts." Institutional scripts refer to the "taken-for-granted assumptions" that underlie educators' interactions with each other and with other stakeholders, such as families (Mawhinney & Smrekar, 1996, p. 494). These default organizational scripts constitute a set of unspoken norms and assumptions that shape the possibilities for what happens and how people interact in schools (Burch, 2007; Meyer & Rowan, 2006). I'll unpack these scripts in more detail in Chapter 6, but I want to introduce this concept here, not because it's a new way of thinking about the role of parents and families in schools but because it helps us to "see" the norms that shape our interactions in and around schools, regardless of which roles we inhabit.

In Maria's case, the teacher expected her to listen passively to her reports about Alejandro's behavior and to adhere to the school's expectations and rules for behavior and discipline at home. The teacher also dismissed Maria's attempt to discuss and try to understand Ale's interactions with another student at school—Ms. Laurie's response reinforced the gatekeeping nature of her professional role (referencing privacy concerns with regard to another student) and implied that Maria's role was to support the school's expectations for Alejandro's behavior at home, not discuss dynamics regarding children at the school. Blanca's meeting with the principal departed from the strictly controlled involvement activities in that a group of parents came together and requested the meeting to discuss a common issue. However, the principal asserted her power through almost exclusively one-way communications that presumed the parents didn't fully understand the nature of the dynamics unfolding between children at the school—her claim that "not all behavior" [constituted] "bullying" served to undermine and dismiss their concerns while (re)establishing her greater expertise and claim to "the truth" of what was happening at the school. Rather than listening and engaging with the experiences of students and parents, Ms. Shannon then reinforced her professional role by telling them their concerns were already being addressed by the new social-emotional learning curriculum. She reverted to educator jargon (via a flyer in English referencing "standards for what students should know and be able to do by each grade level"), reinforced the notion that parents' role was to support their children's learning of the curriculum at home, and referred the parents to unnamed district personnel for questions regarding decision-making (a move that absolved her of responsibility). Ms. Shannon then ended the meeting with the parents without attending to their continued concerns.

Nearly 2 decades ago, scholars critiqued these presumed roles and expectations of parents as "circumscribed and institutionalized" (Crowson & Boyd, 2001, p. 12). Parents from nondominant communities, in particular, are expected to defer to educators as the sole source of expertise in the education of their children (Auerbach, 2011). When they do *not* behave in accordance with these unspoken expectations, families and communities of color are often labeled "problem parents," which research has linked to teachers' diminished sense of responsibility for students' learning. In their research on teachers, John Diamond and his colleagues (2004) found that teachers who perceived that the "problem" of achievement resided in students or families themselves were less likely to persist in their efforts to teach students at high levels and to engage in the professional learning to improve their instruction. These expectations for parents' roles relative to schools have been codified by policy and practice—as well as research—over decades, to the extent that they often feel like "common sense" to educators, parents, and communities alike.

While all parents need support in raising healthy, happy young people and ensuring their academic success within complex schooling systems, our policy, discourse, and practices presume that *some* parents need this help far more than others. In particular, low-income parents of color are presumed to be deficient—and part of the *problem* of racial inequities. The logic goes like this: Some parents' inability (or unwillingness) to be involved in their children's education is the cause of persistent disparities in student educational outcomes, from preschool enrollment to college attainment. In other words, "they"—and their cultures and communities—are implicitly to blame. Many policy and decision-making processes consider low-income immigrant, refugee, and other parents of color to be needy beneficiaries whose best interests are known only by others. At worst, complaints about "uncaring" parents or cultures who "don't value" education reveal widespread racialized assumptions that nondominant families are to blame for so-called achievement gaps. The simple fact is that this "logic" actually flies in the face of empirical research; parents of color *do* care about their children's education (Lightfoot, 2004; Valencia & Black, 2002).

Even so, assumptions about "uncaring" parents of color continue to undergird an invisible logic about the solutions to educational inequities. If nondominant parents are part of the problem, goes the logic, then in order to eliminate racial disparities, our policies and practices must aim to "fix" these parents so that they may become more "involved" in the ways professional educators and policymakers believe they ought to be. Though it may sound benign, this theory of change constitutes a form of cultural racism—that is, it rests on the idea that racism will disappear if those impacted by it are the ones to change (Bonilla-Silva, 2010; Lewis & Diamond, 2015).

But these assumptions about the need to address parent deficiencies are so embedded in structures, policies, and practices that we do not think to question them. Therefore, efforts to "involve" parents in education are likely to re-entrench inequitable dynamics until we challenge the underlying logic of deficiency and blame that infuse our typical approaches to nondominant parents, families, and communities.

A Brief History of Parents of Color as "Deficient"

Current educational policy and practice thus implicitly frame nondominant parents, families, and communities in terms of inherent deficiencies. These deficit-based structures and assumptions about families of color in schools didn't materialize arbitrarily out of a vacuum. They are embedded in policies and practices that go back as far as the beginnings of formal schooling in this country. Although it's beyond the scope of this volume to detail the histories of inequities in U.S. public schooling, we must at least acknowledge the founding of the United States on stolen Native lands and the ways in which formal schooling has largely operated as a vehicle of colonization and assimilation throughout the history of this country. As many have pointed out, separating children from their parents and communities is not new; boarding schools for Indigenous children forcibly took them from their homes, punished them for speaking their native languages or engaging in cultural practices, and explicitly aimed to "kill the Indian, save the man" (Brayboy, 2006; Garcia, 2019; Mackey, 2015; Tuck & Yang, 2012). Segregated schools for African Americans and other separate-and-unequal schools for Mexican, Chinese, and other communities are also part of the history of structural inequities in a U.S. public education system designed to assimilate immigrant, native, and rural children into dominant American culture and into the industrial workforce (Ladson-Billings & Tate, 1995; Ladson-Billings, 2006; Tyack, 2000). In large part, education has been done *to* children and families (Jordan, 2010), and schools have been the vehicles of that oppression and colonization (Khalifa et al., 2018).

A historical lens on educational and social policy in the United States also reinforces this deficiency framing of families of color. After the Coleman Report (Coleman et al., 1966) found that students' educational attainment could largely be explained by students' family background, the "culture of poverty" emerged to describe the behaviors, attitudes, and traits of a monolithic deficient culture that created its own circumstance of poverty and low education, thus blaming low-income people for their own predicament. Though based on six families and discredited by study after study, the stereotype has persisted and has even been reinforced in widely accepted professional development programs delivered to thousands of educators (Gorski, 2008). Similarly, the contested Moynihan Report on Black families (Moynihan, 1965), written by an Assistant Secretary of Labor (not a researcher), reinforced racialized assumptions of deficiency by focusing on family structure—particularly the destruction of patriarchal Black families by white oppression—as a fundamental aspect of racial inequality.[2] Fordham and Ogbu (1986) later theorized that Black students underperformed academically because, as "involuntary minorities," Black youth associated high academic success with "acting white" and embraced an oppositional culture that rejected academic success. Although Fordham and Ogbu developed oppositional culture as a theory to distinguish non-white groups that succeed from those that do not, their theory essentialized racial group experiences and left little agency—beyond acceeptance of dominant norms or self-defeating resistance—for challenging oppression (Solórzano & Bernal, 2001). Despite an abundance of empirical research challenging the framing of racial inequities in terms of self-defeating Black (and other nondominant) cultures or behaviors (P. L. Carter, 2005; Lewis & Diamond, 2015; Nasir, 2011), these tropes live on. Policy discourses fueled by these deficiency assumptions remain remarkably enduring in popular media and decision-making rationales (Warikoo & Carter, 2009).

Thus, "blame the victim" logics implicating Black and other families of color build from deeply rooted racialized assumptions codified by social and educational policies and reinforced by popular media as well as current political rhetoric. However, a growing consensus in educational research conceptualizes the disparities we see today as the result of structural and systemic forms of racism. Gloria Ladson-Billings (2006) conceptualizes these disparities as an "education debt" of centuries of accumulated sociopolitical, historical, economic, and moral exclusion and oppression of people of color in the United States. Despite desegregation and decades of efforts to improve schools and academic outcomes, educational injustices live on in the current structures and processes of schooling. For instance, resource allocations to schools are often based on tax bases—which are linked to income and to real estate values, legacies of long histories of redlining and racial covenants that prevented people of color from living in particular areas or accessing loans to become homeowners. Indeed, Orfield and Frankenberg (2014) note that segregation is actually increasing. Decades ago, Jeannie Oakes's (1985) research called out how tracking within schools structures opportunities and advantages, especially to white, middle-class students, while limiting access for others, especially Black and Latinx students. Dynamics at the level of individual interactions reinforce these structural mechanisms for inequity. For example, Lewis and Diamond (2015) show how racialized assumptions and implicit bias of educators shape discipline and expectations across a school, including assessments of which students are "smart" and "capable" and which are "troublemakers" or "at risk" of failing. Study after study highlights how schools and educators privilege Western cultural norms, behaviors, and ways of knowing and being in ways that lead to traditional notions of academic achievement, while devaluing the nondominant cultural capital of students of color (Carter, 2005; Delpit, 1988; Lee, 2001;Valenzuela, 1999).

If these racialized assumptions and structural dynamics shape students' experiences in schools, it's not much of a stretch to recognize them in how schools interact with families and communities. Thus, it's not an accident that some parents—especially from African American, Latinx, Indigenous, and Pacific Islander communities—are considered "deficient" or "unable to support their children."

Asian Americans are often positioned within a stereotyped "Model Minority" status, even though they experience many similar barriers and systemic inequities, especially those from refugee and more recent immigrant communities (Kao, 1995; Takaki, 1989; Zhou & Bankston, 1999).[3] The myth that all Asian Americans are successful in school obscures dramatic variation within these communities, even among those with supposedly similar cultural backgrounds (Lee, 2006). For example, in my research I have encountered "Chinese immigrant families" from markedly different contexts. In one case, Toishanese families from a particular rural province in China mostly came from contexts of poverty and had limited formal education. Their children attended low-income, highly diverse urban U.S. schools. These parents spoke little English, struggled to navigate the complex American educational system, and expressed feeling disregarded and ignored in schools. In contrast, in a relatively wealthy suburban district, many immigrant Chinese parents had come to the United States on work visas to become professionals in the high-tech industry. They were mostly highly educated (a number held PhDs in technical fields), financially well-off, spoke English well, and regularly exercised their voices and privilege in the school system (for instance, running for and winning seats on the local school board). Thus, even within this group of supposedly similar Chinese immigrant families lies dramatic variation. We also know that particular Asian American students (such as Hmong, Laotian, Filipino, and Cambodian) face disparities in schooling outcomes that get overlooked when they are "lumped" into a monolithic racial category (Pang, Han, & Pang, 2011). Thus, viewing these families through a monolithic "Model Minority" lens further reinforces inequities experienced by some Asian families as well. Asian Americans are not unique in this variability, of course; look closely, and every simplistic racial category masks variation within it.

For certain, some parents are unable or unwilling to support their children. But the research does not bear out any systematic association between the *racial* group of parents and their ability to parent and support their children. We know that there is cultural variability in raising healthy children (Rogoff, 2003), and that parents of color socialize their children in particular ways to exist in a racist society (Wang & Huguley, 2012). The only associations that do seem to exist between race and parenting are those that make comparisons to white, middle-class childrearing practices and involvement expectations. In other words, just knowing someone's race tells us little about their ability to support their child's learning and healthy development; however, it does suggest something about their experiences with schools.

Barriers to Participation for Families of Color

Although the voices of families themselves best convey their own experiences and their complex lived theories of inequities (see Chapter 3), I want to briefly lay out what the research literature has learned about how the deficiency paradigm plays out in practice to foster exclusion and disengagement. First, the field has long acknowledged barriers of language, poverty, lack of childcare, bureaucratic school processes, and other issues faced by low-income immigrant parents and families of color (Carreón, Drake, & Barton, 2005; Turney & Kao, 2009). These are no small matter. In the opening case, for example, Maria must speak to the teacher in English on the phone even though she does not fully understand all the teacher is saying. She attempts to follow up with the teacher about her son's trouble with a classmate, but the teacher quotes school policy as preventing her from speaking of another student. Finally, Maria receives information about a parent–teacher conference from a crumpled flyer in her child's backpack but cannot attend due to her work schedule.

From a systems perspective, these represent realities of public school life—that is, limited or nonexistent supports for language translation and interpretation, privacy policies like the Family Education Rights and Privacy Act (FERPA) that constrain what can and cannot be discussed, lack of time and avenues for effective communication, and union contracts that dictate work obligations and schedules. From the perspective of families, though, these dynamics accumulate and intersect to form an inaccessible system. Anne Henderson, Karen Mapp, and their colleagues (2007) characterize the extreme cases of these barriers as "fortress" schools. But that characterization implies that such dynamics are exceptional. My work suggests that such barriers are embedded in the everyday workings of schools and the conventional practice of educators—rather than exceptions, such barriers have come to be seen as part of the "normal" functioning of schools. The barriers are real and consequential for the increasingly diverse families in our schools. But they represent only the surface issues.

Let's engage in a thought experiment that I learned from a scholar (as well as friend and mentor) whose work has profoundly reshaped conversations in the field. In his work with families, Dr. Gerardo López has asked: What if we removed all the barriers in the scenario? Everything was translated into Spanish; transportation and childcare were provided for Maria to attend PTA and other school meetings; the parent–teacher conference was scheduled to accommodate her work constraints. And school policies and procedures were clearly explained to Maria so she understood whom to talk with and what was and was not permissible to discuss in which contexts. Would Maria have been able to resolve the problem and ensure that Ale feels safe, has a sense of belonging, and is learning in a culturally responsive environment that recognizes not only his special needs but also his brilliance?

One study by Stallworth (1984 in Carreón et al., 2005) may shed some light on the answer. Many educators are surprised to learn what parents in that study said was missing *most* from their involvement in their child's education. Despite the existence of the multiple barriers I just elaborated, parents in the study overwhelmingly pointed to two things: inauthentic opportunities for participation and a lack of influence over important decisions, including a partnership "that [does] not center around fault-finding conversations." These responses hint at the deeper issues below the surface barriers. For parents like Maria, they are issues of power, culture, and racialized assumptions, not simply an issue of her limited English proficiency and knowledge of educational procedures. In the case above, the teacher's first interaction with Maria was a call home about Ale's behavior problems in class. The teacher did not ask questions to help her learn more about Ale from the person who knew him best or work to establish a relationship with Maria. Rather, Ms. Laurie presumed that the problem related to a lack of discipline at home—and requested that the parent change her parenting to be more consistent with the expectations of the school (e.g., parents as the target of change). Without inquiring further, the teacher situated the problem in Ale himself—and by extension, his home and perhaps culturally based childrearing practices related to behavior. As a Somali mother explained to me wryly in one of my research projects, "Just because we do not speak the language, we are not blind [*sic*]. We know when we are being judged."

When the group of parents in the fictitious scenario came together to share their concerns about racially based bullying, the principal dismissed their concerns (based on the presumption that they did not know what bullying was), and gave them a district fact sheet about a social-emotional curriculum couched in education jargon. She also closed further discussion by referring the parents to either a district staffer involved with the curriculum adoption or their teachers, to discuss the content of the lessons. Without having to say it explicitly, the principal conveyed to the parents that their concerns were misplaced or unimportant, a decision had already been made about a curriculum (without them), and their "place" was to be informed and support their children *at home* in learning the school's expectations. When I share this case with educators, they are often quick to criticize the teacher and principal. But if you talk to enough nondominant parents and families, they will tell you that these educators are not behaving exceptionally in any way—these dynamics are a "normal" feature of their experiences of school.

For many families and communities marginalized by educational and other systems, the default parent involvement paradigm—and the assumptions of deficiency that underlie it—can actually reinforce racialized dynamics and inequities in education. For instance, African American parents who advocate for their children often get labeled as "obstacles" or "problem parents" while white parents who advocate for their children are considered positively "involved" in ensuring their children's success (Lareau & Horvat, 1999; Freelon, 2018). These labels then result in moments of exclusion that have negative implications for the young people in these families. For some parents, these dynamics foster their disengagement—as a mother of four children in one of my studies explained,

> I went to the parent nights and events for the first year, then afterwards I just walked away. We were just getting talked at, and we were just there by ourselves. We couldn't talk to anybody else. I haven't gone too much after that because I had other activities.

Some parents are quite intentional and agentic in navigating boundaries between their families and the school—for example, Fabienne Doucet (2011) documented Haitian immigrant families' deliberate efforts to create distance between the worlds of home and school as a result of their ambivalence about dominant U.S. culture. Whether families persist, disengage, or resist, the irony is that many well-intentioned school efforts to involve parents may actually reinforce the notion that nondominant families have no place in education—and thus function to *worsen* racial inequities.

The Role of Research: From Reinforcing to Critiquing White Normativity

Although it's tempting to think of educational research as the "objective" arbitrator in separating fact from fiction, we must acknowledge that the research, too, has been implicated in this conundrum. Put simply, conventional research on parent involvement has largely elevated white, middle-class (heterosexual, patriarchal, Christian) parenting behaviors as the gold standard to which all other families should aspire. The activities and linked expectations of parent involvement reflect Epstein's (1995) well-known and oft-cited model of family involvement, which situates students within three spheres of influence—home, school, and community—and suggests that when there is greater overlap between the spheres, students receive more coordinated support. However, this framework does not acknowledge the existence of powered dynamics in how these realms converge; in practice, this has typically meant subsuming home and community to the institution of the school. The framework translates into a set of activities that conveniently adheres to educators' expectations for individualistic parental support of school agendas, especially through compliance behaviors at home (for instance, ensuring homework completion, home discipline that is consistent with school expectations, and timely school attendance). Although higher levels of participation such as decision-making do exist in the continuum—and a community engagement level was added in more recent years—these behaviors are still defined in relation to school-based involvement structures and expectations with no explicit recognition of their intersection with the dynamics of race, class, culture, power, and privilege.

In a historical context, the overlapping spheres model was groundbreaking for its time in its conceptualization of the potential synergies among home, community, and school and asserting the importance of parents in education (at that time, assumed to be only two biological heterosexual parents). Anne Henderson, one of the pioneers of family engagement research, shared that the policy conversations largely ignored parents in education early in her career (personal communication, February 2017). So we owe a debt of gratitude to this framework (and the work of other researchers and practitioners, to be sure) for the inclusion of parent involvement in much educational policy, educator standards, and education reforms.

However, the *use* of this model in practice has reinforced (and continues to emphasize) white *normativity* in family–school relations in ways that have very real, very troubling implications for children. That is, the model designates white, middle-class parenting and school involvement behaviors as "normal"—and, by definition, anything else as problematic or lacking. This seemingly innocent list of what "counts" as involvement implicitly positions families who do not conform to these expectations as deficient and to blame for racial and other group-based disparities in education. This contributes to what Mapp and Hong (2010) note as the "hard-to-reach" parent narrative—when parents (of color) don't attend a school-based event, and (predominantly white, middle-class) educators presume they don't care or don't value education. In this way, the Epstein framework has functioned to reinforce or rationalize educators' deficit-based assumptions about families of color. As we have seen, these assumptions can, in turn, serve to constrain the participation of nondominant communities in schooling and to rationalize the abnegation of educator responsibility for student learning.

A body of research has offered critiques of the white, middle-class normative school-based behaviors and activities that "count" as involvement. Studies that attend to the dynamics of race, class, power, and exclusion in family–school relations attest to the need to expand narrow conceptions of "involvement" normed in whiteness, particularly given the growing number of immigrant and other families of color, whose cultural practices supported their children's learning in other ways (Baquedano-López et al., 2013; Carreón et al., 2005; Lareau & Horvat, 1999). For example, many Mexican American parents pass on culturally embedded *consejos* (advice) to their children and emphasize the value of hard work as forms of engagement, but these practices are often disregarded by schools (Delgado-Gaitan, 1994; López, 2001).

What About the PTA?

At this point, some may object to the charge that there are few opportunities for parents to participate and influence schools. But what about participation in parent–teacher organizations? Let's talk about the PTA.[4] I have said relatively little yet about the white, advantaged parents who represent the normative "good," "involved" parents. Some of these parents and families have disproportionate influence in schools, and the PTA often serves as both a vehicle for that influence and a particular context of exclusion. Notwithstanding the distinct historical role of the PTA in segregated Black schools (see Siddle Walker, 1996), the PTA of today in most schools largely mirrors the structures, cultural norms, and racialized expectations of schools themselves. In practice, the PTA often functions to consolidate power and influence for a select few, typically more privileged white parents who speak English, are fluent in dominant cultural norms and behaviors, have access to financial and valued social resources, and know how to navigate American schools and interact with educators. In addition to using electronic listservs and other forms of electronic communication that can exclude and marginalize many parents (Freidus, 2016), PTAs in gentrifying communities can also inadvertently push parents of color to the margins. For instance, one study found this happen when newer, white parents worked to "professionalize" the PTA by emphasizing economic skills such as grantwriting and fundraising (Posey-Maddox, 2014). As Lareau and Horvat (1999) explain, "Whiteness represents a largely hidden cultural resource that facilitates white parents' compliance with the standard of deferential and positive parental involvement in school" (p. 49). This "resource" provides greater voice, influence, and credibility via the PTA as well, especially when white parents feel their contributions of skill and financial resources entitle them to influence.

Even typical PTA meeting procedures—like the use of Robert's Rules of Order, English as the only language, and fundraising as a primary expectation—can contribute to an alienating environment for working-class families and families of color. For instance, in her research with Mariana Souto-Manning and Tasha Tropp Laman, Sally Brown, a former PTA secretary and early childhood classroom teacher, described what she called a "PTA FundRACEer" event at her school, in which children were exhorted to sell candy in order to win prizes as "good" students. She explains,

> It was not until I began to look at everyday schooling practices more critically that I realized how racial, linguistic, and class lines can be drawn further through familiar events such as PTA fundraising campaigns. This PTA was very concerned with improving the education and resources available at the school. It was not the aim of the PTA to cause harm to children or their families, yet these practices negatively affected working-class children and children of color as well as their families." (Brown et al., 2010, p. 519)

To talk about the deficiency paradigm that underlies approaches to families of color in schools requires that we also name the *opportunity hoarding* that represents the flip side of these dynamics. Opportunity hoarding, a term coined by Charles Tilly (1998), refers to the monopolizing of "goods" (such as educational opportunities) by those with power. White, middle-class families are often positioned as saviors, without whom our public education system will fall apart, particularly in urban and gentrifying communities. Fear of white flight often plays a key role in district and school decision-making that constrains equity-focused change (Lewis & Diamond, 2015; Turner, 2015).

Thus, schools often disproportionately attend and respond to white parents' concerns and demands not only because parents are able to mobilize whiteness as a resource in their interactions with educators but because of the material and social resources that would be lost if white, middle-class families chose to leave the district. Although operating within a notion that "good parents" secure the best advantages for their own children, professional white parents often use their influence to "hoard" those opportunities to maintain their children's privilege at the expense of other children (Hagerman, 2018; Lewis-McCoy, 2014). When PTAs raise money to secure the best materials or learning opportunities for the children in their school, they can not only marginalize parents of color and low-income parents in their own schools, they can perpetuate and reinforce inequities between schools. Thus, PTAs can serve as a platform for opportunity hoarding. For certain there are exceptions to this dynamic. Although there are parents and organizers who have leveraged the PTA toward equity-based school change and who are working to foster more inclusive and equity-focused spaces for all parents,[5] the normative expectations and racialized scripts that shape parent involvement are "baked" (pun intended) into the structure and practices of the PTA.

Shifting to Family Engagement

The move to expand conventional conceptions of involvement and highlight community empowerment built the foundation for a burgeoning community-focused education reform literature and a call to move "beyond the bake sale" (Henderson, Mapp, Johnson, & Davies, 2007; Warren et al., 2008). Dennis Shirley (1997) first articulated the distinction between traditional parent *involvement* and parent or family *engagement* in his landmark study of community organizing in education:

> Parental *involvement*—as practiced in most schools and reflected in the research literature—avoids issues of power and assigns parents a passive role in the maintenance of school culture. Parental *engagement* designates parents as citizens in the fullest sense—change agents who can transform urban schools and neighborhoods. (p. 73)

This distinction launched a renewed conversation among scholars and practitioners about *engaging* families in their children's education and success. The shift from "parent involvement" to a discourse of "family engagement" has emerged in tandem with growing attention to the need to address race- and class-based educational disparities in the United States. The U.S. Department of Education's family engagement framework (Mapp & Kuttner, 2013) broadened the focus from parents (exclusive to the parent–child dyad) to families (including siblings and nontraditional family constellations such as foster care, blended families, and multigenerational caregivers). The framework also prioritized building the "dual capacity" of *both* families and educators to collaborate in supporting student learning. The framework contrasts with conventional parent involvement approaches in important ways, such as focusing on learning as a central aim, acknowledging the key role of educators in shaping opportunities for engagement, and attending to relational dynamics between educators and families. Yet most frameworks in the field do not center family engagement in the pursuit of systemic and institutional change for educational equity, nor do they explicitly address the power, race, class, language, citizenship status, and other dynamics that infuse educational institutions and shape opportunities for nondominant families to "partner" with schools in educational reform.

Some in the field argue that the involvement paradigm and its deficiency logic are a thing of the past, that our "best practices" have evolved. Now, they argue, we talk about listening, respecting, and building learning-focused relationships with families. We go to families in home visits to learn about students. We invest resources in family liaisons who can advocate for and support families. We foster welcoming school environments.

But if we look closely, many of the practices and implicit assumptions of parent involvement *still persist* in approaches reframed as "family engagement." For instance, my colleagues and I did research on the role of cultural brokers such as parent/family liaisons. As I describe in Chapter 4, we found a contradiction between the empowering language of "engagement" and "leadership" and the dominant approach of socializing nondominant families into school-centric norms, expectations, and agendas that had been set without them. And spend enough time listening to young people and their families talk about their under-resourced schools, and the racially oppressive treatment they often experience within them, and you will recognize soon enough that we have by no means "arrived" at a moment of equitable engagement.

As I discuss in Chapter 6, the racialized scripts and logics in our schools with regard to nondominant families are powerful and deeply embedded in our schools. "Tweaks" around the edges aimed to "include" more diverse families are likely to fall short of educational justice. Incremental changes in our definitions and approaches—like those embedded in the discourse shift from parent involvement to family engagement—often fail to question the underlying goals and assumptions about how schools and families intersect to cultivate and often exacerbate racial and other powered inequities. I have found Leigh Patel's (2017) notion of "incremental inclusion" helpful for understanding this distinction. She distinguishes token or incremental changes to include people into the existing status quo system from fundamental shifts to power or the system itself. That is, we might take steps to broaden our notion of "parents" to include other family members and to "reach out" to families of color by valuing nondominant forms of involvement and proactively building relationships with more "diverse" families. But at the end of the day, we must also ask the question: What are we trying to "include" these families in? If we are merely working to include *more* families in the conventional paradigm of schooling, we have tinkered around the edges but not reshaped the fundamental assumptions, structures, or powered practices that underlie the existing system.

In practice, then, efforts to enact more reciprocal engagement within highly politicized school contexts continue to place the onus of change on parents themselves without a primary focus on educational systems and *their* engagement. That is, rather than seeking to involve "hard-to-reach" parents, critical family engagement research and practice suggest the need for "hard-to-access" systems to fundamentally redesign their goals, values, routine practices, and interactions with parents and communities. If the new language of family engagement and its "best practices" have not gotten us to that place, then how might we need to begin to shift toward more meaningful and transformative change? A first step is to work toward getting a fuller picture of both the families themselves and the systems that reinforce the inequities we are seeking to transform.

Agency and Power Despite Schools

My educational leadership students sometimes complain at this point that ignorance was bliss, that they wish they had never become aware of how deeply entrenched these dynamics are in the everyday workings of the educational system. To that I offer only that nondominant students, families, and communities have lived these inequities for generations, yet they—we—persist in pursuing education as a form of liberation, as resistance, as cultural survivance, and as a means for realizing humanizing relations and community well-being. Thus, I close this chapter by offering a brief overview of two different branches of research that offer glimpses of the places and spaces where nondominant families and communities have been and continue to be powerful actors and changemakers in education. These are the bodies of work that have fueled the vision of what is possible (and this book).

First, studies of community and youth organizing and empowerment highlight parents and families as potent agents for school change benefitting entire school communities. This literature has provided studies of nondominant families and communities as central and powerful actors in equity-based school change. Concha Delgado-Gaitan (2001) was among the first to illuminate what she called a "parent-school empowerment process" in which a community of Latinx parents in California came together to learn from each other about schools, recognize their rights, and create change in their schools to better support their students. Likewise, community organizing seeks to actively engage "everyday" parents and community members in advocating *for themselves* to influence decision-makers in the institutions that affect their lives (Shirley, 1997; Warren, Mapp, & The Community Organizing for School Reform Project, 2011).

In this approach to school reform, community organizers build the capacity of nondominant youth, parents, and communities to exercise power and leadership in efforts to create more equitable schools (Mediratta, Shah, & McAlister, 2009; Warren, 2005). These organized reform efforts position students, families, and communities as resources, collaborators, and leaders in the hard work of improving educational systems. For instance, the Oakland Community Organizations (OCO) in Oakland, California, prompted the school district to open 40 new small schools to address overcrowding and school failure in the "flatlands" of the city (Mediratta et al., 2009). The Community Collaborative to Improve District 9 Schools in New York created the Lead Teacher Program, which put master teachers in schools to support the development of other teachers, a program that expanded to more than 100 schools (Fabricant, 2010). Logan Square Neighborhood Association (LSNA) in Chicago organized a Parent Mentor program to place parents in classrooms and develop their leadership for educational change (Hong, 2011).

Youth organizing has also come to the fore as a vehicle for fostering youth resilience and leadership to make change, particularly to address inequities in education (Warren, Mira, & Nikundiwe, 2008). For instance, the well-established Philadelphia Student Union has chapters in six schools in the city's most under-resourced neighborhoods and has mounted campaigns to limit the charterization of the school district, institute a fair state school-funding formula, and address violence in the city's schools (Rosen, 2019). These are only a few examples of the organizing happening in communities across the country; scholars estimate that there are at least 500 organizing groups focused particularly on education reform in the United States (Warren, 2014). This literature (including my own studies) offers a starting point for imagining new, more collective and critical approaches to working with families in educational changemaking.

A second body of research highlights the pivotal role and expertise of families and communities in education beyond schools. This work grows from the acknowledgment that children spend a very small proportion of their waking hours in formal school settings. Rather, families and communities comprise a primary source and context for learning. This body of research suggests that nondominant families and communities possess forms of expertise in their cultural and linguistic repertoires, lived experiences, social and economic "funds of knowledge," social and cultural resources, and community leadership (e.g., Bang et al., 2014; Barton et al., 2004; Gutiérrez & Rogoff, 2003; Heath, 1983; Ishimaru, Barajas-López, & Bang, 2015; Lareau, 2003; López, Scribner, & Mahitivanichcha, 2001; Moll, Amanti, Neff, & Gonzalez, 1992; Valdés, 1996; Wang & Huguley, 2012; Warren et al., 2009). For instance, Luis Moll and his colleagues (1992) studied how particular household and economic skills among Latinx immigrant families might become resources and opportunities for young people to learn traditional content. More specifically, though, *participatory* design of community learning contexts offers new lenses and directions forward for considering how to bridge divides of experience, education, culture, and understanding to enable educators and nondominant families to work together toward educational justice.

CONCLUSIONS: FROM INVOLVEMENT AND ENGAGEMENT TOWARD EQUITABLE COLLABORATION

In the end, the warm fuzzies and cold pricklies depend on who you are and how you perceive what's at stake in the interactions between families and schools. For nondominant families and communities, schools themselves have historically been, and often continue to be, places of "cold pricklies." The well-intended efforts of educators to involve and engage families can inadvertently reinforce racial inequities. Rather than clinging to the relatively static, often racialized notions about what families can and should do in schools, I argue that the bodies of research described above—as well as the ongoing practices of many nondominant communities—point to the need to undertake the work as a *process* shaped not by school-driven agendas but by families themselves. What happens if we shift from a dominant-culture, school-centric model of training or "fixing" students and parents to an approach to young people and their families and communities that recognizes their expertise and prioritizes their collective well-being, self-determination, and dignity? My work suggests that a change of perspective from seeing strengths instead of deficits is *not* sufficient alone. Asset- or strengths-based approaches are a start, but they do little to shift power or change the system and the consequential determinations about what matters and what counts—and who gets to decide.

Rather than operating from the premise that schools are the central actors with the agency to involve or engage families, a journey of *equitable collaboration* asks that we recognize schools as *part* of broader communities within which we foster new kinds of relationships between families and schools, premised on a different paradigm. I use the term "paradigm" deliberately here to evoke the kind of shift implied from a conception of the Earth as the center of the universe to one in which the Earth is revolving around the sun. We currently live in a school-centric universe of family engagement. What would it mean for us to move toward a community-centric universe, in which schools play a critically important role but are no longer the *sole* source of what Erickson (2001) calls the "social gravity"? How might our educational systems—schools and other educational institutions—operate differently if we were to build a "new relationship" in which the expertise of educators and policymakers were combined with the knowledge and brilliance of young people and their families and communities, especially those who have been marginalized by the conventional school-centric model?

This is no small ask! Many educators and schools instinctively react with fear that such a shift means they are no longer experts or leaders, that their agenda no longer matters. But when we realized that we were orbiting the sun (rather than the other way around), it didn't suddenly mean the Earth no longer mattered. The Earth still mattered deeply, but the shift to a heliocentric worldview did require a fundamental reconceptualizing and reordering of the world. Similarly, a community-centric approach to education *requires us to reconsider* some of the fundamental assumptions we hold tight—beliefs about the aims of our education, the roles played by various actors, and the processes through which we seek to make change. Although such a system does not yet exist, we do have glimpses of what it could begin to look like. Building forward from the bodies of research on community organizing and family- and community-based learning described above, the next chapter proposes a framework that grew out of my research for beginning the journey toward more equitable forms of collaboration and leadership.

CHAPTER 2

New Rules of Engagement

From Conventional Partnerships to Equitable Collaborations

> We want to change the paradigm. Parents are your partners. We are part of the solution, not a roadblock. —Parent organizer

> If we have been gagged and disempowered by theories, we can also be loosened and empowered by theories. (Anzaldúa, 1990, p. xxvi)

If the conventional practice of engaging families and communities in schools positions them as part of the problem in education, we first need to conceptualize how else nondominant families and communities *could* be a part of education in order to begin to imagine alternative approaches. In other words, a robust critique is important, but how do we move beyond critique? How can families and communities of color become integral to defining and realizing systemic solutions to the inequities in education? In this chapter, I draw from multidisciplinary theories and from more than a decade of empirical studies to argue that nondominant families and communities have crucial expertise and potential leadership that formal educators need in order to meaningfully address injustices in schools. I offer a framework of equitable collaborations that departs from dominant school-based approaches to nondominant families and communities along four key dimensions: roles, goals, strategies, and change processes. The underlying ideas of the framework are by no means new. They build from critical race and decolonizing theories to center community-based expertise and practices, while drawing upon concepts from community organizing and theories of race, culture, and learning. Together, the concepts in this framework offer a starting place for addressing the deeply embedded nature of racial and other inequities in our schools.

To highlight emergent distinctions between equitable collaborations and conventional partnership approaches, I draw from a mixed methods study of a district-organizing collaboration in a new immigrant destination. Though far from perfectly realized, the case study suggests a political and relational model of long-term, collective engagement characterized by

- *roles* for nondominant parents and communities as educational leaders (versus passive beneficiaries about whom professionals know best);
- *goals* of systemic transformation within a culture of shared responsibility (versus "fix the parent" aims within a culture of implicit blame);
- *strategies* of relationship and capacity-building for systemic change (versus special events or material resources to "fix" students and families); and
- an approach to *educational change* that addresses political and social issues in the broader community (versus isolated technical efforts within the four walls of schools).

These "new rules of engagement" constitute a departure from business-as-usual relations between schools, families, and communities.

The model offers an important snapshot of emergent equitable collaboration in a particular context. Once we have a lens to distinguish deficit-based approaches from more justice- or solidarity-based models of educational change, we must then ask: *How* might we begin to enact new approaches to work with families and communities in the journey to educational justice? One peril of the journey is that, in our haste in getting from status quo to more just systems, we can easily reinforce the very problematic dynamics we set out to change. For instance, we can presume that parents are leaders and "train" them to advocate for policies that others have determined to be "good" for them. I have often seen this unfold in practice with little regard as to whether those would be the forms of change (e.g., a particular policy) or action (e.g., testifying at a hearing or sitting on a taskforce) those families would prioritize for themselves, had they been shaping the agenda from the outset. At best, such arrangements accomplish short-term policy or resource wins that families helped to achieve (but which often fall short in implementation or sustainability). At worst, families can be positioned as pawns in a power play that treats them as instrumental means toward predetermined ends (J. Scott, 2013). In this sense, justice lives not just in the outcome or the product, but also in the process of getting there.

To support efforts to both pursue and enact educational justice simultaneously, then, each dimension of the equitable collaboration framework relates to a principle to guide practice. The principles thread through the subsequent chapters: (1) Start with family and community priorities, interests, concerns, knowledge, and resources; (2) transform power; (3) build reciprocity and transformative agency; and (4) undertake change as collective inquiry.

WHY EQUITABLE COLLABORATIONS? CRITICAL RACE THEORY, COMMUNITY ORGANIZING, AND SOCIOCULTURAL LEARNING

When I first encountered theory in graduate school, I found the jargon and concepts paralyzing and abstract—epistemologies, discourse, hegemony, interest convergence, post-this and post-that. I couldn't imagine how these could be of any practical use in the everyday world. But the more I learned, the more I began to understand that theories surround and undergird how we think about and move in the world, even if we are not aware of them. Scholar bell hooks suggests that our "lived theories" shape our sense-making and practice—from daily moment-to-moment actions and interactions to broader routines and approaches over time. As many have noted of young people and families of color, they already have knowledge from their lived experiences; they simply use different language to name these dynamics than those given value by the academy. And yet this naming can be a powerful act of self-transformation and agency. Thus, our discussion of equitable collaborations begins with grounding in theory—not only to acknowledge the intellectual "giants" whose shoulders provide the foundation for many of the concepts and practices that follow, but to challenge you to reflect on the implicit theories that shape your interactions and practice in education. Although the framework draws across multiple disciplines, the concepts overlap and intersect in powerful ways like a lattice to undergird the dimensions and principles of equitable collaboration.

CRT and Decolonizing Theories—Starting Premises for Justice Projects

Building from critical race theories (CRT), an equitable collaboration perspective recognizes race and racism as central features of U.S. schools that fundamentally shape how students, families, and communities engage with and experience schooling (Bell, 1995). An equity- or justice-focused approach to engaging families and communities acknowledges and reckons with both deep-seated histories and ongoing dynamics of racism and, in some cases, generational community trauma, in relation to formal U.S. schooling. In short, for some young people and their communities, schools reinforce trauma and injustice. Any effort to enlist nondominant families and communities in partnering for educational change must therefore contend with the historical and ongoing dynamics of racism, particularly in light of ongoing material inequities and a contemporary sociopolitical landscape that condones and even encourages explicit displays of racism and policies of family separation.

Critical race theories also illuminate the powered and racialized ways in which public schools control the narrative and assumptions about what counts as "good" parent and student behaviors, positive engagement, and academic success. According to these theories, "whiteness" refers not to an individual's racial identity but to a social construct premised on inequitable power and Black (and other people of color) domination. Cheryl Harris (1993) demonstrated through her legal scholarship that the notion of whiteness is embedded in our very laws and institutions. She points out that the meaning and substance of race has changed over time, but "what persists is the expectation of white-controlled institutions in the continued right to determine meaning—the reified privilege of power—that reconstitutes the property interest in whiteness in contemporary form" (p. 1,762). In other words, schools—as white-controlled institutions and agents of whiteness—have the right to define what counts, what doesn't, what matters, and what doesn't. Think about all the times you have heard certain students labeled as "disengaged," "disruptive," or "defiant." And certain parents labeled as "uninvolved," "uncaring," or perhaps even as "scary." Schools recognize, value, and reward particular behaviors and ignore, disregard, or erase others as a routine part of legitimizing and maintaining a set of privileges and exclusivity associated with whiteness. So, rather than assuming at face value that certain engagement practices are "good" and helpful—like deferent support of the school's agenda or reinforcement of school discipline expectations at home—this lens helps us to question how such expectations of nondominant families of color may function as subtle forms of assimilation and control that preserve privilege and a status quo of racial inequity.

Critical race theories also offer ways forward: the perspectives, counternarratives, and cultural practices of nondominant youth, families, and their communities provide a critical resource for understanding inequities, as well as a starting point for constructing alternative possibilities. Counternarratives—the voices and stories of those impacted by racism and intersecting oppressions—do help us to recognize that racism is a prevailing feature of U.S. schools, but alongside those dynamics are *also* histories of resistance, community agency, and cultural practices that have been sustained and that have evolved over time. For example, a broader notion of "family" beyond the nuclear unit of two parents and children has long been a feature of many so-called non-Western cultures, as have collective approaches to parenting. Many children growing up in Asian American and Pacific Islander communities, as well as Indigenous communities (Garcia, 2019), have aunties or uncles whose relationships are not defined by biology. Similarly, scholar Camille Cooper's (2009a) work has illuminated African American community traditions of "othermothering," and extended families living together is a commonplace practice in Indigenous and other communities of color. Despite being considered the "norm" in schools and institutions, the dominant white, middle-class, Christian heterosexual conceptions of biological nuclear families may well constitute the outlier. In fact, a study by Canadian scholar Joseph Henrich and his colleagues (2010) examined who was studied to make claims about a vast array of "human" psychological behaviors, perceptions, and attitudes. They concluded that the samples were overwhelmingly "WEIRD"—that is, 96% of the samples were of *W*estern, *e*ducated people from *i*ndustrialized, *r*ich *d*emocracies—a decidedly skewed sample to be making claims about human development and behavior!

Theories of settler colonialism and decolonizing theories also contribute key notions to what it might mean and look like for families of color to be centered in educational justice endeavors (Brayboy, 2006; Patel, 2016; Smith, 2012; Tuck & Gaztambide-Fernández, 2013; Tuck & Gorlewski, 2016). Through my research collaborations and learning with and from key colleagues and mentors, particularly Indigenous scholars, the principles of equitable collaborations have also come to be shaped by a recognition of the colonization of people and land as a fundamental dynamic underlying public institutions like schools. More specifically, the aim of settler colonialism is the forced removal and erasure of Indigenous peoples in order to take the land and resources for the use of settlers (Wolfe, 2006). This notion extends to the enslaved labor of Blacks as a form of white property. And while recognizing Latinx, Asian, and Pacific Islanders as settlers in this paradigm, we can also begin to see how cheap immigrant labor served to fuel and reinforce European settler colonialism in particular.

In my own family, the incarceration of Japanese Americans during World War II, though certainly fueled by racism and xenophobia, also implicated racialized economics of what many have characterized as a "land grab" by white farmers (40% of all the vegetables in California were grown by Japanese Americans despite the legal prohibition against their land ownership, and over 90% of particular produce). My father was born in an incarceration camp sited on the Colorado River Indian Reservation. Keeping mindful of Eve Tuck and K. Wayne Yang's (2012) reminder that decolonization is not a metaphor (everything these days seems to be a "decolonizing project"), this lens can help us to begin to see and understand how deeply rooted the dynamics and paradigm of settler colonialism are in our country—and by extension, our schools and formal educational systems.

Although John Dewey and others envisioned public schools as sites for democracy and opportunity, decolonizing theories help us to anchor our understanding of schools in relation to Indigenous, Black, and other nondominant communities, in particular. U.S. public schools were literally built on land seized from Indigenous peoples in the so-called Westward expansion—in fact, an 1872 painting of "Western progress" depicts a white woman floating across the plains, laying telegraph lines in her wake, holding a "School Book" in her arms, and driving out Indigenous people and buffalo and other animals (Dunbar-Ortiz, 2014). Rather than offer that image to you here,[1] I want to paint a different picture. In this picture of education, the U.S. government used Native boarding schools to separate children from their families, destroy Native languages and cultural practices, and forcibly assimilate children into whiteness. The logic of settler colonialism persists today in the erasure of Indigenous presence, in the dynamics of gentrification and school closures in many cities, and as Linda Tuhiwai Smith (2012) suggests, in the fundamental ways we think about education, research, and the possibilities for change. Although schooling has become less explicit and more subtle about these aims, many argue that the underlying logic persists in schools and can be seen in commonplace policies and practices, such as boundary assignments, tracking, and punitive discipline regimes that fuel the pipeline or nexus from school to prison.

Although recognition of our country's history of genocide may not sound like a hopeful way forward, I would argue that this lens helps us situate educational change within a much broader arc of history and efforts toward justice than simply what happens inside the four walls of a school building. This set of ideas also problematizes the notion of equitable collaborations with families as a "settled" end—that is, a set of activities or events we check off a list or a singular predetermined outcome achieved, which we then consider to be established and done. Rather, collaboration is a dynamic process that operates on multiple levels, from broader structures to everyday moments. In efforts to build equitable collaborations, these theories highlight how we can inadvertently play out the same powered dynamics and scripts that we thought we were disrupting.

Similar to the counternarratives of critical race theories, Indigenous scholarship and decolonizing lenses also help us to recognize ancestral knowledges and ways of being in the world as resources for change that have persisted and continued to evolve in spite of concerted efforts to destroy them. Fortunately, these sources of knowledge and possibilities are not buried in books or sequestered in ivory towers, but embodied in the collective histories, communities, and cultural practices of Indigenous and other minoritized peoples in the here and now. As Anishinaabe scholar Gerald Vizenor (2008) first explained, *survivance* isn't just about survival in the face of oppression—it's also about how to remember, evolve, re-imagine, and thrive. So, as a starting place, the frameworks that undergird the notions in this book look to education as a powerful force for broader justice projects and envision education beyond settler colonial aims of individual achievement, social mobility, and property ownership. Rather, drawing from the notion of "survivance" and the ancestral knowledges of families and communities of color, equitable collaborations aim for education that can help further the collective thriving of people and education justice as defined by those communities. This also means that the particular solutions and definitions can't and won't be the same for every context or community. That's the work and the necessity of equitable collaborations.

Community Organizing—Beyond an Individualistic Paradigm for the Roles of Youth, Parents, and Families

A second set of theories and ideas that inform the foundation for equitable collaborations are conceptions of community organizing. As highlighted in the previous chapter, community organizing illuminates how those closest to inequities—who typically have the least voice in decisions—can build relationships and collective power to advocate for themselves and change schools and other institutions. In particular, these approaches inform on-the-ground practices for engaging in collective action and leadership to change institutions and systems. Consistent with the prior theories, community organizing centrally focuses on disrupting systems of power; relationships are a means through which to grow people power. Transformative forms of organizing recognize the need to challenge powered hierarchies, sustain community leadership, and make systems change, not simply win short-term campaigns to pass policies, gain resources for programs, or hold institutions accountable to concessions.

Scholars of education organizing, in particular, have argued that policy wins in education are precarious—as my doctoral advisor and education organizing scholar Mark Warren (2011) explains, you can't force a teacher to teach well. Any education policy "win" lives in its implementation, which depends on the relationships, understandings, capacities, and practices of the teachers, administrators, families, and communities—in short, the adults—around young people in and around schools. This body of work has informed a turn toward more collective forms of engagement and leadership development in schools and a recognition of the need to attend to broader community challenges and well-being as inextricably linked to education.

Sociocultural Learning Theories—Remediating Family-School Activity

Finally, an equitable collaboration perspective draws from sociocultural learning theories to move beyond efforts to "remediate"—or fix—individual nondominant students, families, and communities toward "re-mediating" activity and the interactions between families and educators (Gutiérrez & Vossoughi, 2010). Sociocultural learning theories recognize learning as "mediated" by a variety of objects, tools, ideas, expectations, rules, and roles (Engeström, 2001; Vygotsky & Cole, 1981). Learning does not happen in a vacuum or in the abstract solely in our heads; rather, we learn through interacting with other people toward specific aims (or "objects") within particular contexts. Even though we often think of learning as the task of students in classrooms, these theories help us to see that adults are engaged in learning in schools as well, particularly when we interact across roles in educational change work. We can thus think of an educational system as multiple overlapping "activity systems." Similar to the organizing concepts described above, this means that even when we have a new structure or policy, we often default to our old forms of activity—so we need to undertake collective learning to create new practices and different ways of interacting toward shared aims. Such a complex process needs to unfold at multiple levels of educational systems to build the capacity of all the adults around children to improve the learning trajectories and well-being of nondominant students *with* their families and communities.

The framework I describe next relies most on critical race theories and community organizing concepts. The remaining chapters of this book will examine practices beyond our current "best practices" to enact more equitable collaborations. The principles that undergird these practices draw particularly from decolonizing and sociocultural learning theories to begin to suggest ways forward in the ongoing journey toward educational justice.

TOWARD EQUITABLE COLLABORATIONS: CASE STUDY OF A "NEW RELATIONSHIP"

To illustrate equitable collaborations as a model, I draw on research I conducted on a district–community organizing group collaboration in the small metropolitan town of Salem, Oregon. The collaboration I examined in my research was by no means perfect, nor does it offer a straightforward blueprint for change. However, the evolution of a "new relationship" and the inevitable tensions in the work are instructive for imagining what a different set of arrangements might look and sound like within a particular time and context. I use this case to draw out some key distinctions between more conventional partnership approaches and community-school relations that aspire toward more equitable forms of collaboration.

Across the country, many low-income Latinx parents experience their children's public schools as alienating and disempowering contexts, yet in the Salem-Keizer School District, parents and community leaders of the Salem-Keizer Coalition for Equality (the Coalition) built a collaboration with the Salem-Keizer district leadership that appeared to be shifting the practice and culture of schooling, particularly for the growing population of emerging bilingual students (in that context, referred to as English language learners [ELLs]). Four years of collaborative efforts between the Coalition and the Salem-Keizer district appeared to be positively impacting schooling for Latinx students learning English, including relationships between and among parents and schools. District leaders pointed to modest but consistent increases in overall and ELL student performance on state standardized tests (in reading and math) as a testament to their collaborative work with the Coalition. My quantitative analyses found more positive parent–school relations associated with focal schools, and Coalition parents expressed increased confidence in their ability to support their children's learning, stronger relationships with other Latinx parents, and a growing sense of leadership and influence in partnering with educators to make the system more responsive to their children's collective needs and interests. Thus, both quantitative and qualitative indicators seemed to point to systemic impacts. Additionally, both district and Coalition leaders talked about the dynamics in schools as a "microcosm" of the response to the demographic shifts in Salem; the collaboration between the district and the Coalition was a way to address the "demographic denial" in the broader community.

The case opens with community context to illuminate the deficit approaches that constituted the first response of the Salem district and community to changes in their student populations. I then describe the formation of the Coalition and the emergence, enactment, and evolution of the district–community collaboration as they relate to four key dimensions of *roles, goals, strategies,* and *change processes*. These findings regarding the promise and inevitable challenges of the Salem-Keizer collaboration offer insights about how educational and community leadership might work together to catalyze equitable change in schools.

A CHANGING COMMUNITY: TRADITIONAL APPROACHES, DEFICIT CONCEPTIONS

A blanket of lush green covers the famed fertile, volcanic Willamette Valley soil just outside the state capital of Salem, Oregon. Yet inside the city limits, to the northeast, long stretches of industrial warehouses are interrupted by a scattering of *taquerias*, money transfer shops, and the occasional beauty salon or bakery with advertising in Spanish. Laughing neighborhood children call out to one another in Spanish as they play in a park known for shootings, gang violence, and drug deals. Like a growing number of "second-tier" new immigrant destinations throughout the country, Salem was a relative newcomer to these dynamics, increasing by ten-fold the number of Latinx students classified as English language learners in a 20-year period. Although some Salemites saw this increasing diversity as a strength, a significant group of longtime white Salemites did not believe or want to accept that their community had changed, a reaction referred to as "demographic denial." For many Latinx community leaders, this denial maintained a status quo of inequity and enabled Salemites to shirk responsibility for providing resources and support for immigrant students and families.

By the late 1990s, the district's lack of academic supports for the growing population of Latinx students learning English converged with parents' experiences of alienation in their children's schools. Latinx students and parents routinely experienced mistreatment in schools, and many felt that the district's inability to address their needs and concerns was not benign neglect or ignorance, but rather outright racism. Children came home asking their parents what "wetback" meant and struggling in an unfamiliar cultural and linguistic environment. To illustrate a common story told by Salem-Keizer parents, Maritza Martinez, mother of three students in the district, drew a happy face on a piece of paper and explained how her young children started the year eager to go to school. She crumpled the paper into a ball and opened it again as she told how her children—and the children of the parents she was addressing—began crying and pleading not to go to school after a while: "This is the face of my kids. Your kids. They get so frustrated—and we say, 'Oh no, my child doesn't want to go to school!'"

Many parents tried to talk to teachers and principals, but were brushed off, ignored, or sometimes treated with hostility. A defining moment occurred at Holbrooke Elementary, a school with one of the highest Latinx student populations in the district, when a child on his way to school was hit and killed by the side-view mirror of a passing truck. The district assumed no responsibility, pointing out that it was the city's job to manage the roads, while the city argued that the district should never have built a school at that site. Amid the finger pointing, parents whose children attended the school were left out of the conversation. According to a parent, this incident left the Latinx community feeling that "Nobody—nobody, not even the school district, not the city of Salem, cares."

"WE HAD TO TAKE ACTION": NEW ROLES FOR PARENTS IN THE FORMATION OF THE COALITION

This sense of crisis about Latinx students' experiences in the schools catalyzed the formation of the Salem-Keizer Coalition for Equality, a coalition primarily of Latinx community-based organizations, dedicated to equity and social justice for children in the Salem-Keizer district and throughout the state. Eduardo Angulo was named chairman—and eventually executive director—of the Coalition, and the board of directors was made up of organizational representatives, a number of whom were grassroots leaders who had cut their teeth in the civil rights, farmworkers, and Chicano movements. Angulo, a dark-skinned Puerto Rican most recently from Los Angeles, had just finished his studies in political science at a local college and was an aide for the Oregon Commission on Hispanic Affairs. Though local school district leaders dismissively described him as a "radical" for his attempts to "expose the crisis" of Latinx youth in Salem, he had come to be known and respected as a fiery and charismatic activist among local community leaders of color.

In the early days of the Coalition, Angulo and his wife represented and advocated *for* immigrant Mexican and Central American parents, but community and union organizers on the board soon pushed for a more "bottom-up" approach. Inspired by Freirean approaches to popular education, the Coalition started to offer workshops in Spanish that actively validated the parents' own ways of knowing, engaged them in active learning from one another, and improved their capacity to advocate for themselves and their children. These trainings helped parents understand their rights and the public education system, strengthened their relationships with other parents, and promoted leadership in organizing other parents to participate in school decision-making. One outgrowth of these workshops was a series of gatherings, trainings, and district advocacy events called the Parent Organizing Project (POP). Through the POP, a growing group of parent leaders began to advocate at school board meetings, district hearings, and key decision-making meetings, particularly for supports and resources for English language learner students.

The Coalition's new combined "top-down, bottom-up" approach called for a kind of leadership that was shared more broadly across the organization with other parents. "I'm not the boss and you follow me," explained Angulo to a group of parents at a training, "We have to balance the dynamics of power." Coalition board member Ana Ceballos described: "In the Coalition, it's not dependent on one leader but it's more like the ducks flying south where people are always rotating the leadership." Although Angulo's charismatic personality meant he was often the first to speak in public events or the spokesperson framing an issue for the media, a core group of volunteer parent leaders, mostly mothers, emerged from the POP and took up new roles as facilitators of others' learning and leaders of Coalition advocacy. Among them were two Indigenous Mexican women with little formal education who had been timid and afraid to talk in the group prior to the trainings. After participating in the workshops and POP trainings over the course of several years, they began facilitating workshops for other parents, and several POP parents talked about them as being among the most confident facilitators in the group, particularly skilled at encouraging other parents to find their voices. Other POP parents noticed the core leadership team as well; POP parent Juan Jose referred to them as *"las directoras de la Coalition"* (the *female* directors of the Coalition). Although these changes created complex and sometimes challenging gender dynamics both within the group and within families, Angulo was no longer the singular voice or contact point for the majority of POP parents.

The Coalition's capacity-building approach also played a key role in addressing the power asymmetries that typically prevent parents from being at the table alongside school personnel with formal authority. For instance, Coalition parent leaders always met ahead of time as a group to plan their questions, priorities, and input before participating in district feedback events or meeting with members of the district leadership team. At the superintendent's annual School Summit Talk (at which Angulo was not present), a group of 10 Coalition parent leaders queried the superintendent and a board member with prepared questions. Their questions about ELL students dominated the discussion, comprising about half of the overall questions asked from the audience of roughly 200 attendees. Jorge Ruiz, a parent organizer, described the parents' questions as a form of collective advocacy that pushed the district to recognize and respond to their concerns:

> So when all these questions come [from parents], the principals and administrators have to move a bit more because the people are asking to let us into the school. The parents are not happy with what is happening in the school, they want more. So in a manner, they are advocating in the district.

The combination of leadership trainings and experiences such as these introduced Coalition parents to a sense of nascent political empowerment for transforming the broader educational institution.

A COLLABORATION EMERGES: SHARED RESPONSIBILITY FOR SYSTEMIC CHANGE GOALS

With an unprecedented turnout of about 800 Latinx parents, the Coalition launched the first No Child Left Behind (NCLB) Parent Conference in the district in 2005. The event strategically leveraged federal policy and built the Coalition's power by demonstrating its credibility and political capital as a contributor with strong ties in the community. Coalition parent leader Amparo Meza explained that "with the Coalition's presence and parent education, the teachers see the interest that we have as a community." Other educators also began to perceive a relationship with the Coalition as beneficial. The district's elementary director reflected that his relationship with the Coalition emerged from a need to learn about the community: "I didn't know virtually anything about ELLs, but I knew I could be a learner, and I needed to learn about the community's needs." District leaders saw in the Coalition an opportunity to partner, communicate with, and learn from members of the Latinx community.

The Coalition had seen the limits of their earlier "fire and brimstone" adversarial advocacy, and they undertook a more collaborative approach in their work with educators and district leaders. In a workshop, Coalition mother Maritza Martinez emphasized that parent engagement is "not about being against the schools—it's about being *with* them. Change isn't going to happen at the district with just the teachers." The Coalition's efforts to raise the issues of English learner student performance, build key relationships, and develop parent capacity positioned the Coalition to participate in selecting a new superintendent who would engage with the Latinx community.

Recognizing shared reform priorities, the Coalition supported new superintendent Sandy Husk as she assembled a leadership team that included more Latinx administrators and educators experienced working with emergent bilingual populations, crafted a strategic plan that explicitly highlighted English learner instructional improvement, and shifted resources to the department focused on support for English learners. The Coalition strategy shifted to holding the district accountable to its own strategic plan and providing political "cover" for the district's efforts to improve teaching for students learning English by speaking out about the need to invest limited funding in professional development. At the same time, the Coalition cultivated the engagement and advocacy of low-income Latinx parents, and the district provided resources, legitimacy, and support to these efforts. For example, the NCLB conference, once a Coalition event, became a product of the collaboration. Former state administrator David Jorgenson explained:

> That [Parent] conference is a good symbol of the collaboration. It started out with the Coalition doing it by themselves and then gradually the school district joined in a little bit, more and more. Now the conference is pretty much a total partnership that you see.

Likewise, district administrator Paul Reza pointed to shared goals as a key element of their collaboration: "We both believe in the same mission and the same vision and goals for our district."

The Coalition shifted from demanding accountability of the district to calls for "mutual accountability" of parents and community along with educators for the educational success of emergent bilinguals and other students. That is, both the district and the community were responsible and should be held accountable for the education of students learning English. Organizer Sonia Vasquez explained: "We're not going to just point fingers at the school district and pat ourselves on the back, we did everything that we needed to do. We hold parents accountable just as much as we hold the school district accountable. I would say that's part of our strategy and it's been a part of our strategy all along, to have that 50/50 partnership." Likewise, superintendent Sandy Husk worked to build a culture of shared responsibility for those goals by challenging the notion that Latinx children and other immigrant students learning English could be considered the responsibility of another sector, another school, or another educator. Husk emphasized that they are "all our children" and therefore a district-wide *and* community-wide responsibility. District administrator Ana Ceballos described:

> We're moving into the whole district. Before it used to be oh, that's the ELA [English Language Acquisition] department or those kids don't belong to us because they're bilingual kids. We weren't concerned if [Holbrooke] was failing. It was that principal's problem and that community's problem, and the [other] schools didn't care, but with this new superintendent, all English language learners have become a district-wide challenge that we all have to address. So right now in our district, we're responsible for all of the kids.

CAPACITY- AND RELATIONSHIP-BUILDING STRATEGIES FOR SYSTEMS CHANGE

The district and Coalition focused on three key coordinated initiatives to transform the system as a whole, and each stakeholder leveraged its own strengths and resources to enact capacity- and relationship-building strategies. First, district leaders prioritized *improving classroom instruction for students learning English system-wide*. The district provided professional development for differentiating instruction for those learning English and offered all teachers the opportunity to obtain their English as a Second Language (ESL) endorsement at the district's expense. The number of English language acquisition instructional coaches deployed in schools increased ("more than double, from 7 to 15, amidst a $26 million budget deficit," pointed out one senior administrator), and the district trained principals on English learner versions of classroom strategies and asked them to adapt them on their own for native English speakers. Thus, the district moved teacher and staff capacity-building for English language learner instruction and support to the center of the district's improvement work.

The second collaborative strategy consisted of the Coalition's *parent professional development activities* (a term used by both district and Coalition leadership). The workshops built the skills, knowledge, and confidence of low-income Latinx parents. Although these primarily emphasized traditional forms of parent involvement in the schools, the parent workshops became a *vehicle* for parent empowerment and more meaningful engagement through the POP and the parent lead organizing team. Parents who had been through the workshops often joined POP activities, such as advocacy at district events, cultural gatherings, parent conference planning and participation, and periodic trainings on district budget and English learner issues. A subset of 12 long-time POP parents from across the district eventually became a cadre of Coalition parent lead organizers (including two staff organizers, fellow immigrant parents). This core parent leader team revised and facilitated the workshops, built extensive networks of parents, cultivated relationships with school and district leaders, trained parents and educators in other districts, and developed their own initiatives.

Finally, in the third collaborative strategy, new and different relationships were forged through a jointly-led *civic engagement initiative* called the MACSS (Marshall Area Coalition for School Success). The MACSS sought to engage the primarily white civic, faith, business, and union leaders of the city in improving student achievement in high-poverty, high-English learner-population schools. Spearheaded by Angulo and influential used-car salesman Herb Waters, the MACSS aimed to bring resources, political clout, and volunteerism to support students in the Marshall feeder schools and to provide visible civic leadership to challenge the "demographic denial" in the broader Salem community. Waters, an outspoken white conservative with deep roots in Salem and influential connections with the "downtown" business community, saw the MACSS as part of his own and his fellow citizens' responsibility to the schools. The group acted as a conduit for strategic communications with the broader community about the changing demographics of the schools and the need for new educational approaches. Even more concretely, school board chair Simon Chambers attributed the passage (by 60% of the vote) of a $242 million school bond measure "when the recession was in full bore" to the key support of MACSS leadership team members. Thus, as a third collaborative strategy, the MACSS projected the notion of community accountability for student success onto an even larger stage, providing the district an opportunity to *proactively engage* with the broader community while addressing implications of changing demographics for the schools and for the future of Salem.

These capacity- and relationship-building strategies began to realize change in the system, including a shift in the power between Latinx parents and the district leadership. The collaboration entered new territory as the political process of educational reform led to tensions between the district and the Coalition.

"NAVIGATING INSECURE GROUND": CHANGE PROCESSES AT THE END OF THE HONEYMOON

After the economic downturn, the Coalition sought and received a district contract to subsidize the parent workshops. This meant the Coalition had to seek permission to make changes to the contract and report to the district on their workshops, something that had never been required before. This new dynamic, fueled by concern about impending staff changes on the district senior leadership team, drove the Coalition to call an end to the "honeymoon." They shifted to demanding an assessment of English language learner student progress (in the form of test scores) and fiscal accountability for resources allocated for students learning English. By 2010, tensions had grown between the Coalition and the district over differing expectations about the pace and magnitude of change. Many parents and board members of the Coalition felt there had been too little progress made in closing the academic performance disparities between English language learners and other students. At the same time, district leaders perceived the same standardized test results as promising evidence of movement in the right direction. Tensions became so high that the district leadership team and the Coalition board both agreed to mediation by a local lawyer who had been a strong supporter of the collaboration. As a result, both parties remained publicly cordial and collaborative, yet subsequent interactions between the district and the Coalition entailed cautious renegotiation of the relationship and roles.

This conflict exposed differing notions of the role of politics and tension in the collaboration. District leaders saw public tension as "delicate" and something to be avoided in a partnership, whereas—for the Coalition—conflict and political tension were instrumental to their larger strategy and foundation as an independent community voice. As Angulo described: "the key to the success of the whole thing is for us to stay at the table as watchdogs forcing the healthy tension concept at all times." While the Coalition felt that their assertion of independent power merely activated the "healthy tension" that propelled their work with the district, the district perceived the Coalition moving from "positive" "problem-solving" to an "adversarial" "political" approach.

CASE DISCUSSION: A "NEW RELATIONSHIP"

The collaboration between the district leadership and community organizing group in Salem-Keizer provides key insights into a "new relationship" and model for how families, community leaders, and educators might work together to create change. As summarized in Table 2.1, equitable collaborations contrast with conventional involvement and partnership approaches along four dimensions: *roles*, *goals*, *strategies*, and *processes*.

1. Roles: Parents and Communities as Educational Leaders

As in many schools and communities across the country, the origins of the Salem-Keizer case show how systems marginalize nondominant children and families. At best, these children and parents were considered needy clients "at risk" for failure without the intervention of predominantly white professionals and educators who knew what was "best" for them. At worst, as the child's death at Holbrooke Elementary highlights, the school system was complicit in exacerbating existing inequities. As many scholars of inequities have pointed out, no individual person or policy intended this tragedy or the collective abnegation of responsibility (Bonilla-Silva, 2010). However, the system's "default settings" functioned to compound intersecting structural inequities rooted in poverty, racism, and lack of political influence across multiple institutions. From business interests in housing and city ordinances about land zoning, commerce routes, and traffic safety to district resource allocations and busing policies, inequitable decisions and outcomes quickly compound. Ironically, those with the insights and experiences—and

Table 2.1. Contrasting Rules of Engagement Between Conventional Partnerships and Equitable Collaborations

Conventional PARTNERSHIPS	Equitable COLLABORATIONS
ROLES: Nondominant parents and families as clients and beneficiaries	ROLES: Nondominant parents and families as educational leaders who contribute and help shape the agenda
GOALS: Individual remediation aims within a culture of denial or implicit blame	GOALS: Equitable systemic change within a culture of shared responsibility
STRATEGIES: Technical changes with existing practices and system. Formal leaders buffer from outside "intrusion."	STRATEGIES: Build relationships and capacity for systems change. Formal leaders bridge.
CHANGE PROCESS: Apolitical approach focused on schools in isolation	CHANGE PROCESS: Change as a political process that addresses broader issues in community

lived theories—of how inequities unfold on the ground (e.g., nondominant students, families, and communities) are typically relegated to the margins or considered beneficiaries whose needs should be considered and supported only as those in power deem fitting.

As the Salem-Keizer case illustrates, though, new possibilities can emerge when parents and families are approached as educational leaders and collaborators with expertise and resources of their own to contribute to improving the educational system. Through advocacy and interactions with immigrant Latinx parent leaders, the district came to recognize the valuable resources—such as cultural knowledge, credibility and trust with the Latinx community, political and social capital with the state education agency and policymakers—that organized, low-income Latinx parents brought to the table as legitimate representatives of affected parents and families. Thus, a foundational principle related to this dimension of the framework is *begin with families and communities*. Only when we initiate educational change with nondominant families and communities—and center their priorities, concerns, expertise, knowledge, and resources (rather than that of the system, or of white, middle-class parents or educators)—can we begin to counter the status quo normative assumptions in the system about what and who matters. We begin to leverage all the expertise at our disposal, not just that of professional educators. And we begin the journey to educational justice with those most impacted by inequities as fellow agents of change.

Scholars of participatory design refer to this as "role remediation"—a fundamental shift in the underlying assumptions that govern who is expected to do what and how people interact, from parents deferring to teachers about knowledge of mathematics to principals presuming control over teachers. As we will unpack in the coming chapters, this principle may sound straightforward, but putting it into practice is no simple task. This principle challenges in profound ways the predominant emphasis in education on standardization, efficiency, and effectiveness. For now, however, let us also recognize that beginning with families and communities also opens the door to more expansive aims than we might otherwise have undertaken.

2. Goals: Shared Responsibility for Systemic Aims

The Salem-Keizer case highlighted a shared *systemic focus* embedded within intentional efforts to shift the *district culture* from blame or denial to collective responsibility and mutual accountability. Although the district had tried to address "the problem" of English language learners with discrete interventions for individual students and families early on, once the Coalition became a key actor (partly in response to those efforts), the collaboration evolved to a focus on improving the system's ability to better educate Latinx emergent bilingual students. Beyond the goals themselves, systemic education reform "must involve the spread of underlying beliefs, norms, and principles" (Coburn, 2003, p. 8), and the Coalition's mantra of "mutual accountability" merged with the new superintendent's reframing of district priorities to initiate a shift from a culture of denial and implicit blame to one of explicitly shared responsibility for the success of all students, particularly Latinx students learning English.

Collaborations characterized by shared responsibility for goals of systemic change suggest a second principle: *Transform power*. This means targeting the inequitable power that lives in schooling structures, routines, policies, and everyday relations, rather than trying to change individuals or groups of people to better conform to an existing oppressive system. Another deceptively simple principle, transforming power does not rest on an assumption of a zero-sum game, in which discrete amounts of power over people or decisions can accrue (or be taken) by different "sides." Rather, this principle challenges us to identify and reshape structures and policies that reinforce racial and other hierarchies (for instance, tracking based on parent or teacher recommendations), as well as decisions and processes that influence material resources and opportunities for young people. Our everyday interactions are also infused with power dynamics—as we'll explore in subsequent chapters—so simply flipping the power dynamics does little to transform the underlying paradigm. This principle challenges us to name and disrupt existing power asymmetries, and then to construct new ways of interacting and working collectively to target systems that anchor or enable those inequities.

This principle also relates to what Leigh Patel (2016) calls "answerability"; although she refers to researchers' responsibility to learning, knowledge, and context, transforming power in educational practice means that we—educators, leaders, and community organizations—must also answer to students, families, and communities as partners in the work of creating more just schools. The Salem-Keizer case highlighted this in the culture of collective responsibility that was established, not merely through the words of the superintendent or principal, but through the actions and interactions of the formal educators with students and their families.

3. Strategies: Building Relationships and Capacity for Systemic Change

The primary change strategies in the Salem-Keizer collaboration focused on building the relationships and capacity of the people throughout the system to address systemic change as an adaptive, rather than technical, challenge (Heifetz & Linsky, 2002). The district and organizing group worked to build and transform *relationships* within and across stakeholder groups. Relationships between nondominant parents and educational leaders were vital to ensuring that decisions did not result in unintended negative consequences for the very students and families they were designed to benefit. The strong relationships and collective action of the parent leaders helped to counterbalance the typical power asymmetries with district and school leaders.

In the Salem-Keizer case, the district and the Coalition both implemented complementary strategies to build the *capacity* of the adults in their organizations to foster the learning of emergent bilinguals as part of broader systemic change work. Though the case does not offer examples of building the collective capacity of teachers, principals, and parents to work *together* (the case highlights more parallel, coordinated efforts), years later the Coalition offered a summer bilingual professional development institute for teachers across the district. Through neighborhood tours and youth and parent panels, teachers developed new capacities for teaching Spanish-speaking English language learners, as well as relationships with Latinx parent leaders. The collaboration also required shifting existing relationships and people's understanding of their work. For example, the district shifted its approach to parents from positioning them as an external audience to an internal constituency. For example, the Salem-Keizer 2008–2009 strategic plan called for greater permeability across traditional boundaries by including parents as an "internal" constituency, along with staff.

These strategies suggest a third principle: *Build reciprocity and agency.* Although these are two different concepts, they are linked to each other. Reciprocal relationships entail both two-way communication and presumption of expertise and capacity on the part of all parties. The Salem-Keizer case and a growing number of other studies highlight the knowledge and capacity that nondominant families have that might contribute to teaching and learning and to transforming broader educational systems. Reciprocal relationships enable families and educators to perceive each other as *both* experts and learners. When we attend to this principle, educators begin to recognize families' oft-overlooked "funds of knowledge" (historically and culturally based skills and knowledge related to household functioning [Moll et al., 1992]), as well as cultural and intellectual resources that can contribute to new visions and possibilities for transforming schools. This principle also reminds us that such relationships can neither be abstract nor based on an extractive or instrumental dynamic of trying to get something from people. Rather, reciprocal relationships can foster—and develop *through*—collective or transformative agency, or the ability of a group of people to break from a given frame and take initiatives to transform their activity over time (Engeström, 2007; Virkkunen, 2006). Such agency moves beyond the predominantly individualistic focus of the conventional deficiency paradigm and recognizes systemic change as a necessary broader focus of collaborative effort.

4. Change Process: Education Reform as Political Process

Finally, the Salem-Keizer case highlights the inherently *political* process of engaging a broad range of stakeholders and organizations in educational change. Although many systems implement so-called objective or neutral technical reforms that aim to avoid considerations of race, language, power, community voice, and politics, both district and community leaders understood the project of transforming Salem-Keizer to be an exercise in political and civic engagement, addressing urgent issues in the broader community. From this perspective, the Salem-Keizer schools were stages on which the larger political dynamics in the community played out. The case highlights how both district and community actors worked proactively to address—rather than avoid—those dynamics. The Coalition leveraged key local, state, and national relationships to *create* the political climate and priorities that fostered the collaboration. The district leaned on the Coalition to provide political "backup" for their reforms, directed toward increased support for English language learners across the district.

However, equitable collaborations are never static; institutional norms differentially shaped how educators and community leaders made sense of and used inevitable tensions. Whereas educational leaders sought to *avoid* potentially contentious political encounters and interpreted relational tensions as personal betrayals, the Coalition sought to *use* reform tensions as a vehicle for addressing broader concerns beyond schools. A model of equitable collaboration recognizes that what happens inside of schools is inseparable from the broader political and social context outside the educational system—and that the generative power of district–community (or school–family) collaboration lies in *how* actors engage the inevitable tensions in these "new relationships."

Thus, the final principle relates to the need to undertake change processes as a journey of learning for the individuals and organizations who are a part of the work: *Undertake change as collective inquiry*. As scholars of cultural historical activity theory argue, because all learning happens socially and within particular contexts, it necessarily entails tensions and contradictions. Sometimes those are conceptual tensions—like differing ideas about what constitutes "meaningful" engagement or "inclusive" climates—but they can also be relational and political tensions. By engaging in collective and ongoing inquiry processes, we can leverage those tensions as a source of learning that can open up new ways forward that we otherwise might not have imagined. Undertaking change as collective inquiry also implicates expanding both how we engage with data and how we can broaden the conversation beyond the narrow confines of the school walls.

CONCLUSIONS

Drawing on the example of the Salem-Keizer collaboration has enabled us to conceptualize how equitable collaborations might differ in key ways from our more conventional approaches to engaging with families and communities. Though far from a simple roadmap, the framework offers four dimensions (roles, goals, strategies, and change processes) and a set of principles that emerges from them as a starting point on the journey to more just systems and relations. The principles are intended as guiding supports in the shift toward more equitable forms of collaboration that

1. Begin with families and communities;
2. Transform power;
3. Build reciprocity and agency; and
4. Undertake change as collective inquiry.

Given the complexity and likelihood of multiple trajectories for evolving collaborative efforts, the journey must begin with a frank assessment of the nature of existing relationships between families/communities and systems that serve them (see Appendix A for a tool to begin this assessment).

As I hope you are beginning to see, the field of "family engagement" has evolved an important critique of conventional parent involvement, but as a number of scholars have noted, our research has gotten rather stuck at critique. In practice, much of the work to improve family engagement constitutes somewhat incremental changes to build relationships or foster more welcoming climates without any fundamental change from the assumptions underlying the conventional deficiency paradigm of "fixing" young people and their families. To shift toward greater equity in the role of nondominant families and communities in education, we must address inequities at different layers of the system. We also need guidance for constructing and enacting a different paradigm for the role, expertise, and leadership of families and communities. After a more in-depth examination of how inequities play out in schools through the perspectives and voices of families themselves, the subsequent chapters draw on research-based examples and studies to apply the four principles of equitable collaborations in efforts to reshape institutional policies, organizational processes and routines, and interactions among schools, students, families, and communities. Although these examples—all "works in progress"—look different in different contexts, they offer insights into how the four principles can serve as a kind of social "DNA" for justice-centered collaborations.

Nondominant Families on Their Own Terms

Lived Theories of Educational Injustice

> Those who have been most systematically excluded, oppressed, or denied carry specifically revealing wisdom about the history, structure, consequences, and the fracture points in unjust social arrangements. (Fine, 2008, p. 215)

> Despite long-standing claims by elites that Blacks, women, Latinos, and other similarly derogated groups in the United States remain incapable of producing the type of interpretive, analytical thought that is labeled theory in the West, powerful knowledges of resistance that toppled former structures of social inequality repudiate this view. Members of these groups do in fact theorize, and our critical social theory has been central to our political empowerment and search for justice. (Collins, 1998, p. xvi)

INTRODUCTION

Following the first principle of beginning with families and communities, this chapter centers the voices and experiences of nondominant parents and families in narrating their experiences and insights about systemic inequities in schools. Although African American, African immigrant, Latinx, Indigenous, Asian American, and Pacific Islander families and communities have unique histories of racism, exclusion, and colonization, they also have overlapping insights and experiences of schools and educational injustice. As Michele Fine points out in the opening quote, this "specifically revealing wisdom" constitutes an overlooked source of knowledge about the mechanisms and impacts of educational injustices. Each community also possesses unique community-based ways of knowing and cultural practices that constitute resources for imagining new ways forward for educational justice.

In this chapter, I draw from design-based research studies to examine how nondominant families narrate their lived experiences, and I highlight key convergences with recent scholarship on systemic racial inequities in education. Using three episodes, parents from different racial/ethnic communities narrate their own and their children's experiences of inequity in schooling across intersections of language, race, culture, class, and power. For each episode, I begin with families' insights to highlight their reflections on their lived experiences as complex understandings of inequity in education and the forces that shape learning in and out of schools. I then contextualize these conceptions in the research, not merely to legitimize them from the point of academic scholarship but to point out emerging convergences in the literature that echo their insights. To be clear, I am not proposing that nondominant parents have comprehensive insights or expertise, only that their lived theories of inequities constitute often-overlooked but vital knowledge. Recognizing and tapping this knowledge requires scholars and professional educators to move beyond our tendencies to simplify family-based understandings of inequity and privilege dominant institutional norms and language.

NONDOMINANT FAMILY INSIGHTS AS LIVED THEORIES OF INJUSTICE

As discussed in the prior chapters, conventional approaches to engaging nondominant parents in education are rooted in conceptions of parents and families as deficient, sometimes lacking knowledge, skills, capital, and capacities, and, at other times, as lacking more fundamentally in caring or will (Baquedano-López et al., 2013; Valencia & Black, 2002). Given those assumptions, the voices, insights, and contributions of nondominant families are rarely central to educational theory, policy, and practice. In a study conducted with my colleague Dr. Filiberto Barajas-López as well as Dr. Joe Lott, Dr. Melanie Quaempts, and a team of graduate students and emerging scholars of color, we partnered with African American and immigrant Latinx and Asian families, white teachers, white principals, and district leaders of color. Drawing on the parents' insights, we suggest a different narrative about nondominant families and communities—a narrative not only of strength and resilience but of untapped insights, understandings, and opportunities for fundamentally reshaping how schools and school systems educate children. While much of the research has moved beyond deficit-based perspectives on families, the expertise of families has not figured prominently in conversations about racial equity in education. Neither academic theories of inequity nor typical practices are grounded in the "lived theory" (hooks, 1994) of nondominant families. And despite instances of local influence and partnering, the expertise of nondominant families has yet to become central to broader educational reform movements. Rather, policymakers and formal educational leaders continue to position nondominant families as clients and beneficiaries—or in the case of "choice" initiatives such as charter schools and vouchers, as instrumental levers of power in the form of individual consumers in a marketplace of constrained choices (Baquedano-López et al., 2013; J. Scott, 2013). Yet the lived experiences and insights of nondominant parents and families can open possibilities for change within the complex dynamics of race, culture, community, learning, and, ultimately, educational justice. These lived theories also help us to reimagine the role of nondominant families beyond the simplistic dichotomies of "engagement" versus "disengagement" or "good parents" versus "bad parents."

The following episodes address families and schools at three overlapping scales: the systemic level across institutions, the organizational level within schools and districts, and the individual level played out in moment-to-moment interactions. Although some frameworks and approaches focus only on one level—for example, focusing on engagement policies, structures, and personnel or aiming to improve individual parent–teacher relationships, decades of my own and others' research suggest that singular approaches are likely to fall short of realizing sustained change. For instance, even with powerful family-centered policies, implementation often falls back into marginalizing practices and assumptions. On the other hand, we might construct reciprocal, learning-focused parent–teacher relationships in one classroom, but once that teacher moves on, deficit-based policies and structures may continue to constrain those possibilities in classrooms, schools, and districts. Systems are dynamic and complex because people and relationships are dynamic and complex; technical tweaks and singular level changes nearly always result in adjustments elsewhere to maintain the status quo. When we keep our eyes on the relationships and interactions, we can begin to see how policies, structures, norms, assumptions, and decisions play out at multiple levels to either reinforce or disrupt inequities.

We know from research that inequities in education play out at multiple levels (Lewis & Diamond, 2015; Sullivan & Artiles, 2011)—and like racism in the broader society, those mechanisms often adapt to change in dynamic ways over time. Thus, our understanding of inequities and attempts to address them must operate at multiple levels simultaneously and continuously. Drawing on the "specifically revealing wisdom" of nondominant families from empirical studies, the following sections highlight how racial inequities unfold in education beginning at the systemic level and working our way down to the individual level.

"THEY JUST WANT TO PASS THE KIDS": SYSTEMIC DYNAMICS OF ACCOUNTABILITY POLICY AND EQUITABLE LEARNING

This first episode arose in a parent discussion about how race matters in student academics and schools at a systems level. In this instance, nondominant parents' insights illuminate how accountability-driven educational reform often results in differential learning opportunities for students determined by race, class, and neighborhood. Initiated by one Latina mother (Natalia) and then built upon by another (Lourdes, the interpreter, is also a Latina mother in the district), their brief exchange points to how the implementation of policies—designed to produce equitable outcomes—can exacerbate existing disparities between white, middle-class, English-only schools and lower-income schools serving predominantly linguistically and racially diverse students.

Natalia: Yo he visto que en la escuela cuando hay un niño Americano se enfocan mucho en los estudios, incluso les tiene que pagar clases extra a los niños. En cambio donde hay muchas culturas, como en la escuela de nosotros, lo que ellos les interesa es que pasen el examen de . . .

Lourdes: What she has seen is that in other schools that commonly [are] Caucasian they will pay for extra help and do different things to better their education. Where in the school that she [is] at, like in our school, there's so much other cultures and different races, that she's noticed that they're more concerned about—it's just making sure the kids pass, it's just pass, just pass, but they don't actually put anything else into it.

Researcher: So there's more discrimination towards schools that have more races, that they don't encourage . . .?

Lourdes: They don't encourage they just want to pass the kids, it's just more, let's get them to pass instead of teaching them.

Natalia first distinguishes the school her own child attends (characterized by many cultures and races) from a school in the same district that serves predominantly white, middle-class students. She points out that these more privileged schools have a different set of assumptions and standards when it comes to both their investments in and conceptions of student learning. For instance, white parents and schools pay for extra help and provide additional learning opportunities for students.

Here Natalia highlights the inequitable distribution of parental and school financial resources to support students in and out of schools, explicitly linking these dynamics to the intersections of race and class. We know from the literature that predominantly white schools tend to have access to greater resources, both among families in the neighborhood and within the community itself. Historically rooted policies restricted educational and work opportunities as well as housing options for many communities of color. Today, ongoing mechanisms—such as the use of tax bases to allocate funds to districts—perpetuate these structural inequities across institutions. Even the seemingly innocuous Parent–Teacher Association often represents a hidden sources of inequity; fundraising by wealthier parents to support their local schools can "essentially buy better education" for their own children (Nisbet, 2018, p. 5; Posey-Maddox, 2014). For example, within a single district, the funds raised by school PTAs ranged from zero to the half a million dollars a year netted by one school (Raftery, 2018). As discussed in Chapter 1, in addition to these financial disparities, middle-class white parents also tend to exert greater influence in school matters (Freidus, 2006).

Natalia's insight about the differences in support across school communities is also substantiated by a body of research from the economics of education that has examined the money that parents of different socioeconomic classes and education levels invest in their children's child care and educational enrichment. Enrichment includes learning materials like books, computers, and toys, as well as out-of-school learning opportunities, such as art and music classes, tutoring, summer camps, and other extended learning or extracurricular programs. Over the past 30 years, all families have increased their investments in enrichment, but the highest-income U.S. families have increased their investments *three times more* than families with the lowest incomes (Duncan & Murnane, 2011). In addition, middle-class children's participation in out-of-school activities enables their parents to develop more extensive social networks. Erin Horvat and colleagues (2003) found that these networks enabled parents to intervene collectively to obtain more desirable results in addressing school-based problems. These differences in parental resources may also contribute to disparate opportunities to learn for students living in poverty. Although not all of these studies explicitly attend to racial disparities, we know that race and class intersect; in the episode above, the mother, Natalia, recognizes that these dynamics center on schools like her own, that are both racially diverse and low-income.

In the exchange above, the Latina mothers also highlight a systemic dynamic in their own context related to the negative effect of accountability policies supposedly intended to close "achievement gaps." That is, Natalia emphasizes that these more-privileged schools are more focused on studying and learning. In contrast, Lourdes, interpreting for Natalia, emphasizes how in "our schools" (with greater racial diversity), the primary focus is on their students passing high-stakes tests—"just pass, just pass"—rather than "teaching them" and "bettering their education." Natalia and Lourdes are homing in on a widespread dynamic that converges with scholarly findings about a pattern across public schools in the wake of accountability policies. A common educator response to accountability policy in schools struggling under sanctions for their performance has been to engage in practices "that improve accountability status but not necessarily student learning" (Diamond, 2012, p. 152). Although high-quality instruction has become a commonly espoused focus of educational equity efforts, Diamond (2012) found a predominance of didactic (in contrast to interactive) instruction and unequal resource distribution between low- and high-performing schools. Studies have documented such schools engaging in practices such as focused test preparation for "bubble" students—those who are just below the standardized assessment proficiency cut-off score. In some cases, schools even undertook strategies for referring students with the lowest scores to special education or encouraging them to miss school on testing days (Booher-Jennings, 2005).

A robust body of research now attests to the limitations of standardized assessments as the sole measure of student learning and teacher and school effectiveness (Koretz, 2008). Nevertheless, educational policy continues to assess schools based on test scores; many schools ranked on the "bottom" (based on scores) focus on getting students to pass standardized tests at the expense of fostering more robust learning. In short, the mothers highlight how schools' organizational responses to accountability policies have functioned to *counter* educational equity in their children's schools and to reinforce inequities across systems.

"ARE YOU SPEAKING FOR YOURSELF OR FOR ALL THE PARENTS?": POWER AND ENGAGEMENT AT THE SCHOOL LEVEL

The second episode highlights how families experience racial inequities at the school level within the context of interactions between nondominant parents and principals. Historically rooted structural inequities across institutions and policies shape the dynamics of inequity in education *systemically*. In addition to these influences, principals play a critical role in mediating the relationship between families and educators at the *school* level. The next episode features an exchange between a parent and a principal at a meeting that was part of a year-long process in which families and educators developed a parent education curriculum for their schools. This particular meeting included seven parents, three teachers, two principals, two district leaders, and researchers. Erikah (an African American mother) first introduced the activity by stating that parents were going to share the topics that they had identified *together* (prior to the educators joining) as their top priorities for the parent curriculum. Thus, the activity was presented as an opportunity for parents to share their collective work with the principals and teachers. Immediately after Erikah's introduction, a brief exchange between the principal, Barbara—a white woman with a long history in her elementary school—and one of the parents, Binh—a Vietnamese immigrant father—constituted a subtle but key moment of tension over control of school matters.

In the excerpt below, Binh shares out to a group of teachers and principals the parents' top picks for the parent programming topics:

> *Binh:* We picked up this topic which is bullying, you know . . . [inaudible] myself didn't have [any] positive feedback. What we would like to hear is some kind of announcement from the school or the teachers when people are reporting a violation. For me it was

up in the air. I don't know what's going on but the thing seemed to be resolved by itself without me knowing and what I'd like to have is some kind of collaboration response regarding the issue, but that was my hope.

Barbara: Can I just clarify, Binh, are you speaking for you specifically or are you speaking for all the parents right now?

Binh: For myself and also from hearing from other . . . parents as well.

Barbara: So it's a recap of the conversation you guys had . . .?

Binh: Right. (Meeting, March 22, 2014)

Researcher fieldnotes noted the tense silence that ensued following this exchange. One of the district leaders who was co-facilitating the session immediately sensed the tension in the exchange between Binh and Barbara, and she interrupted the discussion. She expressed that people were "personalizing" and redirected the activity to establishing norms before continuing with the presentation of the rest of the parent priorities, followed by a group prioritization activity to decide the final topics.

The joint meeting among parents, teachers, and principals highlighted a contradiction between the ideal of "partnership" and the enacted dynamics of power and tension. Parents and principals ascribed quite different meanings to the principal's question. Prior to the joint meeting, the two principals had met separately with the district leader and researchers. Barbara expressed some trepidation with regard to the process of inviting parents to co-design their own education curriculum, "because other people and things are kind of controlling this process because it's a different way of doing things, but ultimately I'm the person responsible for it, so you do feel like you want to kind of make sure you do have some control over it." On the surface, the principal framed her question simply as an attempt to get clarification. The other principal who was present claimed the entire meeting was a good example of collaboration with parents.

However, the parents interpreted the question as an exercise of power that questioned the legitimacy and validity of their insights about the importance of bullying in their schools. The context and historical tensions surrounding what might seem like a benign request for clarification shaped how parents interpreted her comment. For instance, when prompted to reflect on the meeting later, the parents on the design team seemed to have already developed a shared critique of the power dynamics in their interactions with educators. For example, Mary (a Vietnamese mother) referred to the interaction between Binh and Barbara (whom she referred to as Mrs. Wells) surrounding bullying. She reported picking up on the principal's body language as "defensive" and argued that "they [educators] have to hear from the parents' truth, be open minded and then we can have the whole picture." Mary perceived an unwillingness to listen during Binh's interaction with the principal:

> . . . on the bullying subject. Binh was presenting it and Mrs. Wells got defensive and she's like "Are you talking for yourself or the group?" In my mind, things [we are] talking [about] are for so many other parents who have silent voices that had the same experience, you know. Listen, have an open mind, not get defensive at this point in time. Just listen! (Meeting, April 22, 2014)

In this reference, Mary interpreted the interaction as a direct challenge to Binh, in order to possibly diminish the power of his statement. Mary pointed out that they, as parents, were representing not only themselves but "silent voices that had the same experience[s]"; that while they were speaking from personal experience, they were *also* voicing issues they had heard from other parents from their community. She saw this as an example of how parents' "lay[ing] out their truth" can often be uncomfortable for educators. Finally, Mary switched to hypothetically addressing Mrs. Wells (who was not present at the moment) by asking her to "listen, [and] have an open mind" to what they have to say about parent community concerns and "not get defensive." Mary later shared an experience of her child being bullied, in which she felt the teachers did not intervene because of their assumptions that it was "normal" for children of color to behave negatively toward one another. Despite her perception of racially discriminatory responses, Mary expressed feeling at a loss as to "where to even begin that conversation," as the principal's "defensive" behavior in the meeting was indicative of what she could expect to encounter in raising an issue of racial discrimination at the school.

Other parents' reactions also highlight how this momentary exchange between a parent and principal acted as a microcosm of historically infused inequities in schools. La'Kisha, an African American mother, explained:

> I just knew that it always going to be head to head because they're [the principals] here. What we're talking about. Especially with the bullying I just knew that was going to be an issue, because they try to sugarcoat that all the time. With us bringing that to the forefront, I can't sugarcoat it because we're dissecting it. I knew that it was going to bring some tension.

As described above, the sharing of priorities had been introduced as an opportunity for educators to hear about the collective work parents had done together. Yet, in framing the question in either/or terms (i.e., speaking for yourself *versus* speaking for all parents), the principal ensured that either response could be subjected to further scrutiny. On one hand, asking if Binh was speaking only for himself framed his experience as an isolated incident, a means of minimizing or dismissing the experience. When principals and other educators individualize an issue with a parent, they maximize the power differential and frame the problem as unrelated to broader issues in the school. This move minimizes both the extent of the issue and the scope of their responsibility in responding to it. That is, if one child is experiencing bullying, the solution involves intervening in interactions between two children. However, if multiple children are bullying and being bullied, this suggests a broader dynamic within the school that implicates the culture of the school, the role of teachers and other educators, and—perhaps most threatening—multiple parents and families with shared concerns.

On the other hand, inquiring if he was speaking for *all* parents cast other doubts about the validity of this chosen topic. Thus, a father (a member of a traditionally marginalized community whose voice and perspective had been historically excluded from the discussion of important issues in school) brought forward an issue that mattered to him personally *and* also to the rest of the parents in the group. Echoing well-documented inequitable parent–principal dynamics (Anderson, 1998; Auerbach, 2009), the parent's voice and legitimacy were both challenged by an authority figure accustomed to deciding policies on important issues in school (such as bullying).

This episode illuminates key dynamics of inequity at the *school* level. Second only to teachers in their influence on student learning (Leithwood, Louis, Anderson, & Wahlstrom, 2004), formal school leaders play a pivotal role in shaping the culture of a school and the possibilities for equitable collaboration with families and communities (Auerbach, 2011; Khalifa, 2018). As recognized in the national Professional Standards for Educational Leaders,[1] leadership for family and community collaboration can impact student achievement and school improvement through the school culture and expectations for teachers, as well as direct relationships with parents that facilitate their participation and contributions to teaching and learning.

However, like the principal in this episode, many school leaders perceive increased parental influence as a threat to their own power and control (Auerbach, 2007; Crow, 1998). Even among educational leaders known for their commitment to parent engagement, most engage in largely symbolic behaviors (such as "open-door policies") and traditional management tasks (e.g., delegation and budgeting) that take "a wishful view of parents as supporters of the school agenda" (Auerbach, 2007, p. 724). This approach dovetails with the conventional expectations of leadership, which favor arrangements that "seek to *control* community organizations, parents, and others outside schools" (Honig, 2004, p. 67). Leading in this way also presumes that the school—and principal—alone know what's best for children, particularly low-income children of color. However, the unintentional message that parents have nothing to contribute can actually deter marginalized parents from engaging with the school. Even efforts in which schools ask for parent "input" or "feedback" often impose an agenda that limits the powerful experiences, ideas, and solutions that parents and families can bring to the table. When parents bring priorities or concerns to the table that differ from the school's agenda—especially in contexts in which race and culture are salient—powered interactions often ensue.

These patterns are not the exception to the rule—rather, nondominant families recognize and regularly encounter such tensions as they undertake change. Asked to reflect on a transcript of an excerpt of the meeting, La'Kisha expressed her perception that the educators at the meeting were attempting to shut down the conversation about parent priorities:

> I mean, I see a lot of blowing off—"I think it's best how we're doing it. Just don't come to the principal just with your problems. Go find somebody else." Sending you to—they'll say, "Go to the Handbook." No, it don't talk back. That's why I have the outside source come in for my child so I'm out of it because now, me and you, we can talk and be cordial because it's my child—so it can go, really, somewhere else. When it comes to my child, let me get somebody on the outside come in with the professional—so they can see what's really going on—[picks up transcript and waves it] because this is what's going on! [others laugh, she does not] This is not acceptable! Serious! This is not!

La'Kisha was very explicit about how she felt the educators were "blowing off" their input, by verbalizing her interpretations of their statements that emphasized not wanting to change their practices or hear feedback from parents. "Go to the Handbook" referred to educators sending parents to written materials as a way to communicate their school policies without having parents "talk back" to them about their concerns and feedback. She referred to a personal experience she had shared earlier with other parents, referencing her sense of having been "blown off" by the administration, and her move to bring in an outside psychologist to evaluate her son so that someone from the outside would "see what's really going on." That is, parents' knowledge and information on their child's learning needs must be legitimized by an outside professional in order to validate the parents' concerns to the school surrounding necessary learning supports. When La'Kisha then picked up the meeting transcript and waved it around saying, "This is what's going on!" she highlighted her own experiences and the interactions between parents and educators at the prior meeting as instantiations of the fundamentally inequitable power dynamics between parents and educators in schools. In concluding that "This is not acceptable. Serious! This is not!" La'Kisha refused the dominant dynamic embodied by the meeting interactions as the terms of engagement with her children's school. Throughout La'Kisha's speaking, other parents were nodding and making sounds in the affirmative as though they agreed with her. After a series of energetic exchanges among parents debating how to change these dynamics in the design team, La'Kisha again picked up the meeting transcript and proclaimed, "This shows that we're not a team!"

Lest principals or educational leaders be simplistically cast as "villains," it is important to note that not only principals but teachers, counselors, parent liaisons, community-based organizational partners, researchers, and *even other parents themselves* can enact and reinforce traditional scripts with regard to roles and power asymmetries, even as they are seeking to change them. Though significant and often pivotal, principal leadership is only one aspect of institutional inequity experienced by nondominant families in schools. A number of structures (like tracking and special academic programs), policies (such as student discipline policies), and especially decision-making processes at the school level (such as referrals for special education or English language learner designation) function to exacerbate racial disparities in schools. Across these structural and policy dynamics, parents and families are often routinely excluded from decision-making processes or isolated and "managed" through individualistic interventions targeting their children. Even simple organizational routines designed for efficiency and order—such as preventing parents from walking their children to class in the morning, daytime decision-making meetings, reliance on elected PTA officers for parent "input," and bureaucratic procedures for registering concerns and filing complaints—often serve to keep families outside the core work of teaching and learning.

As nondominant parents' lived theories illuminate, schools are never neutral spaces. Even in processes designed to balance power between families and educators (such as the co-design process in this episode), powered differentials between families and schools often reassert themselves. School leaders play a pivotal role, but all the adults in and around schools are implicated in these organizational dynamics. As La'Kisha and Mary suggest (in tandem with Martin [2011] and Ray [2019]), schools are racialized institutional spaces that reflect the broader dynamics in society. Race and racism take shape in school and in society through power and practice. Although nondominant parents may be uniquely positioned to perceive and address problems experienced by their children in schools, the racialized dynamics and power asymmetries "baked" into routines and leadership practices at the school level often work to isolate and dismiss families' concerns and insights.

LISTENING TO RESPOND: INEQUITIES IN THE MOMENT AT THE INDIVIDUAL LEVEL

The final episode in this chapter highlights how families experience racial inequities through individual moment-to-moment interactions with educators and other systems-based actors. As we've seen in the prior two episodes, families readily narrate how historically rooted structural inequities across institutions and policies shape the *systemic* dynamics of inequity. And families' experiences at the *school* level illuminate how school leaders and organizational routines mediate the relationship between families and schools. At both these levels, the dynamics of inequity are often compounded at the individual level when systems-based actors interact with families in everyday conversations.

The final brief episode, also from a design team meeting in this study, illuminates what often happens when the complex lived understandings of nondominant parents and families come into contact with educator conceptions and assumptions about parent capacity. Like the prior episode, this brief exchange occurred within a broader set of conversations over time. In the initial set of conversations, parents had elaborated their ambitions for their children's education in ways that envisioned far more than good grades, higher test scores, and graduation as forms of success. The following episode revisited those discussions as two parents express their wish for their children not only to perform academically, but to develop social skills to confront issues that might arise in school. In this discussion between two mothers about the complex dimensions of students' education, a teacher interjected her interpretation of the parents' discussion.

> *Violeta* [Latina parent]: I think it's because when you talk about academic [learning], there's a lot of parts that play into that, right? We have discussed health, so they're healthy. They're being fed. They're being nourished. All these parts do play into that so if we only focus on the academic achievement—it is a big part of our goal, but it is also . . . for them to be good socially . . . and all these different parts . . .
>
> *Mary* [Vietnamese parent]: I've just been thinking we teach our kids how to be successful academically, but we don't teach them how to cope in the process, to resolve their own issues and understand what's happening in school. They don't feel like, "Oh, who do I ask? Or should I ask? I'm scared to ask my mom because I don't want to burden her." For someone to go up to them and teach them how to cope with all the process of each . . . problem, anything that they're dealing with.
>
> *Sandra* [teacher]: It sounds like they're talking about the social-emotional fulfillment of school, the PBIS culture, Second Step, those kinds of things that fall in very well with our counseling home as well as leadership. (Meeting, March 22, 2014)

The parents begin by articulating a conception of learning that moves far beyond conventional school discourses focused on performance on standardized assessments and core content mastery. They highlight a vision of their children's learning that speaks to broader well-being—from physical health to social skills, from problem solving to an ability to navigate complex issues of relational and ethical responsibility. Insights such as these are not unique to the studies my colleagues and I have conducted with nondominant families.

When families discuss their dreams, priorities, and values with regard to the education of their children, they rarely (if ever) emphasize the kinds of measures referenced by reformers and policymakers as indicators of "good" schools. Notably, their focus is not on test scores or grades as measures of academic achievement or even proxies like attendance at school.

Nor do groups of families, when given time and space to reflect together, generally hope for a few isolated individuals to "escape" their community, never to return. Meritocratic notions of individualistic social mobility are certainly alive and well, but time and again, when families who have been marginalized by our systems came together to engage in what researchers call "social dreaming" (Espinoza, 2008), they began to imagine how they might change schools, other institutions, broader systems, or their own communities to foster the collective well-being of all of their children and families. For example, families speak of broader well-being for their children and their communities as a more expansive aim for their education. They envision their children's success in school not simply as good grades but as becoming good people, as learning to work with others who are different from themselves, and as holding onto—and flourishing with—their home language, cultures, and knowledge, and for the opportunity to determine their own futures.

These insights converge with a body of research alluded to briefly in Chapter 1. This literature has identified culturally rooted conceptions of education and socialization among nondominant families and communities that expand beyond narrow, normative measures of school "success." For example, the notion of *educación* in many Latinx families denotes a broader aim of cultivating the moral and character development of young people as members of a community (Auerbach, 2011; López, Scribner, & Mahitivanichcha, 2001; Valdés, 1996). Likewise, studies of Native youth and families highlight the importance of learning the expectations and responsibilities of being a part of a broader interdependent network of relations in communities (Garcia, 2019; Kulago, 2016). African American caretaking practices of "critical care" emphasize cultural affirmation, concern, advocacy and activism toward seeking justice and community uplift for those disempowered or marginalized in a context of inequity (Cooper, 2009a; Siddle Walker, 1996). And yet another body of work highlights the critically important racial and cultural socialization that African American, Latinx, Native American, and Asian American families provide their children to instill a sense of pride and knowledge as well as prepare them to encounter racism in society (Wang & Huguley, 2012).

In this sense, then, Violeta and Mary's brief interchange highlights holistic conceptions of child development and educational aspiration that are well documented already in the research literature, but it is the teacher Sandra's interjection in this episode that particularly illuminates an everyday dynamic of inequity in family–school relations. In this case, a white teacher attempts to make sense of what the two mothers have shared by reinterpreting their comments through educator jargon and school intervention programs (for instance, simply saying "PBIS" without explaining that it stands for Positive Behavioral Interventions and Supports or explaining what that means). In this attempt, the teacher reduces the mothers' concerns about their children's learning, broadly construing the problem to be about social-emotional learning and how the range of programs (e.g., PBIS and the Second Step social-emotional learning curriculum) offered at the school addresses such concerns. Focused on trying to "fit" what the parents have said into existing school programs and administrative units (such as "counseling" or "leadership"), the teacher misses the connection that the mothers suggest about what it means to be able to be academically successful—the intimate connection between academic success, social development, familial and community relationships, and broader well-being. In this way, the teacher's seemingly well-intended attempt to respond to Violeta and Mary inadvertently functioned to erase the parents' complex insights and reduce them to concerns to be addressed by packaged curricula or programs.

Given the many challenges of teaching in the current era of U.S. education, expecting educators to be up on the latest research on the cultural practices of nondominant families seems a tall order. Why, then, don't we take up the insights of parents in their own schools to expand our understanding of the problem and explore new possible solutions?

Educators like to think of themselves as good listeners. Too often, though, especially given the deep de-professionalization of teaching, their desire to demonstrate their expertise (coupled with implicit assumptions of families' lack of expertise) can get in the way of their ability to notice and learn from the lived experiences and knowledge of nondominant families. When families and caregivers approach educators with concerns or issues about their children's learning or well-being at school, those insights are often rooted in a more holistic conception of children's growth and development than schools typically address and, thus, the interactions can be opportunities for deep listening and learning for educators. However, especially when those concerns are raised by caregivers of color in ways that depart from white normative expectations for parents, educators can engage in what I call "listening to respond." That is, they are listening primarily for how to fit caregivers' concerns into school-based assumptions, programs, or organizational units so that they might be ready with a response. Though likely intended to affirm the competency of educators and assure families that the school has a plan in place to remedy the situation, the "listening to respond" dynamic can actually make families feel they are not truly being heard. And what's more, such interactions constitute missed opportunities for teachers, educators, policymakers, and researchers to move beyond dominant institutional knowledge and systems (what Dr. Muhammad Khalifa [2018] calls school-based epistemologies) to begin to learn about nondominant families' knowledge and ways of being (what he calls community-based epistemologies).

Such everyday interactions represent missed opportunities for teachers to engage parents in meaningful dialogue about the long-term positive development of their children within a complex society. In this example, the teacher missed an opportunity to explore what parents hope children will learn with regard to advocating for themselves in schools and resolving issues across home and school contexts amid complex relational, ethical, and cultural dynamics. This "opening" occurs when the immigrant Vietnamese mother narrates her child's awareness of not wanting to burden a parent with a problem they know they may not be able to resolve. Although this teacher likely intended to be helpful to parents and to reassure them that the school was already working to address the issues they were raising, her "listening to respond" behavior inadvertently resulted in reasserting the dominance of her power, knowledge, and expertise, thus reinforcing rigid teacher–parent roles and constraining possibilities for change.

When educators intersect with parents, families, and communities and their more expansive conceptions of learning, teachers and principals often reframe parents' language and meanings into educational jargon in ways that change or narrow the meaning or focus. Accustomed to "managing" parent concerns or issues, teachers and other educators often operate from white normative assumptions that nondominant families lack sufficient knowledge about schools to be able to name what they believe is missing from their child's education. This particular exchange highlights these dynamics at play at an everyday interactional level even in the relative absence of the intense emotional charge often present in racialized parent–teacher interactions that arise as a result of student "problems" at school, whether behavioral or academic (Lawrence-Lightfoot, 2004). For instance, we know that discipline is a pivotal context for the reproduction of racial discrimination in schools (Skiba, Michael, Nardo, & Peterson, 2002). Maisie Chin, the director of a parent organizing group called CADRE, has been working with Black and Latinx parents in Los Angeles to disrupt the school-to-prison pipeline for nearly 2 decades. She calls discipline the "holy grail" of racial equity in education because of its connection to the school-to-prison pipeline. Scholars have shown how student behaviors are often interpreted through the racialized lenses of mostly white female educators in ways that are presumed to be problematic. Black (and to some extent Latino, Native, and Pacific Islander) students who behave in particular ways are more likely to be noticed and selected by educators for disciplinary referral, and those students are also subsequently assigned harsher punishments and consequences for problem behaviors (Gregory, Skiba, & Noguera, 2010; Lewis & Diamond, 2015; Skiba et al., 2002). Now add to those dynamics the racialized assumptions about those students' families, and the moment-to-moment powered interactions between nondominant families and educators at the individual level can compound systemic and organizational dynamics of inequity across other levels.

CONCLUSIONS

This chapter sought to draw on the "specific revealing wisdom" (Fine, 1993) of nondominant families to glean insights about the complexities and compounding dynamics of racial inequities at multiple scales in educational systems. The lived experiences of families illuminated *systemic* dynamics embedded in federal policies, resource allocation, and implementation across multiple institutions; *school-level* structures, routines, and processes shaped by principals; and *individual-level* interactions in everyday powered exchanges between families and educators. Their insights converge with research about the mechanisms of inequity while also suggesting possibilities for how we might begin to construct a new model for the role of family-based experiences, epistemologies, and solutions to inequity. When we enact the principle of *beginning from family and community priorities and knowledge,* it becomes clear that nondominant parents may have insights, knowledge, and expertise that can be a source of professional learning for educators in creating more inclusive and holistic learning environments.

To begin to shift these dynamics, principals (and other systems-based actors and leaders) may need to confront their default stance of control and recognize how efficiency-oriented decisions can constrain parental agency and the potential for collaborating for systemic change (Khalifa et al., 2013). Formal educational leaders must begin to recognize the ways in which their engagement practices can default to "symbolic gestures" that merely reinforce their control and power, such as open-door policies, visibility at drop-off and pick-up, and allowing community access to the school (Auerbach, 2011). Starting from families and communities means leading by first *learning* and participating to support community priorities and contexts (Green, 2017; Khalifa, 2018).

The experiences of parents voiced in this chapter also begin to suggest how nondominant family expertise might contribute to re-mediating issues that arise in schools that depart from the dominant repertoire, norms, or assumptions in schools. For example, early on in the design process, parents identified helping their children to develop a positive racial and cultural identity as a high priority and an essential part of their children's learning that would enable them to be successful productive adults. This converges with the literature highlighting high-performing students' positive racial identities (Carter, 2008) as well as research regarding how parents of color—especially African American parents—socialize their children to prepare them for a racialized society (Wang & Huguley, 2012). Although the (white) teachers in the design process recognized they lacked the training and experience to support students' positive racial identity development alone, they eventually realized they could turn to the expertise of their students' parents to help them build more culturally sustaining learning environments for their children.

Finally, these episodes illuminate schools as racialized spaces infused with power asymmetries at multiple levels, in which there are few, if any, spaces to name, question, or raise issues of racism, particularly for students, parents, and families. As the demographics of U.S. public schools have shifted, scholars have urged educators to move beyond "color muteness" (Pollock, 2009) to recognize and acknowledge the ways in which racial dynamics and implicit bias shape interactions with students. Heeding this scholarship, schools and districts have increasingly focused on educator cultural competency and equity initiatives built on frank conversations about race. However, nondominant families and communities have been notably absent from many of these efforts. Along with students themselves, nondominant families are uniquely situated among educational stakeholders to perceive, understand, and narrate how racism unfolds in school settings. Although educators often constrain or silence the voices of nondominant parent and family voices, the findings in this chapter suggest that providing nondominant parents with opportunities to narrate daily school life and tensions can augment existing efforts to bring about equity by centering the experiences of the students and communities that schools purport to serve.

As these families' insights suggest, racial inequities play out in often complex and subtle ways across multiple levels of the educational system. There is no book or static body of knowledge that can reveal how those dynamics operate because they are often shifting and always specific to context. However, the expertise of nondominant families closest to inequities can offer key insights; trust and reciprocity are required to open the conversation, along with skills to recognize openings to explore, but as we begin to understand how inequities play out in schools, our journey beyond critique and into possibility can begin.

CHAPTER 4

Systemic Collaborations

Multiorganizational Educational Equity Initiatives

> Education reform, then, cannot be considered mainly in technical or organizational terms but rather should be addressed as a profoundly political problem. The failures of public education reflect the lack of power held by low-income communities of color, in resources, accountability, and performance. (Warren, 2014)

When we begin with the experiences, priorities, and stories of families and communities marginalized by educational systems, we see that racial injustices in education are historically rooted and tied to structural inequities that implicate far more than schools alone. Given these broader inequities, it is not surprising that families of color and others marginalized by the system often experience on-the-ground implementation of educational policies as exacerbating—rather than ameliorating—inequities in schools. My research suggests we follow families' insights and begin exploring solutions to the problem of racial inequities in education from their historical and broader systemic roots. This chapter examines efforts to transform *complex educational systems across multiple institutions.* We will explore how districts, schools, community organizations, funders, and other public and private agencies can work together—in theory, *with* families and communities—to address racial disparities in education. District–community partnerships and broader cross-sector collaborations for education represent a recent wave of policy "solutions" that seeks to address the intersecting challenges within broader community contexts experienced by students in low-income, marginalized communities (Henig, Riehl, Rebell, & Wolff, 2015; Horsford & Vasquez Heilig, 2014; Lawson, 2013; Park et al., 2013).

I begin this chapter with a brief overview of the appeal and potential of cross-sector collaborations as a policy solution to the problem of educational disparities, then situate such efforts in a broader historical context. We will dig into one such partnership to highlight the need to attend to practice and implementation beyond the policy, as "new" structural arrangements can inadvertently be operationalized in ways that can actually replicate power inequities between organizations. I then examine the hiring of "cultural brokers" as a common reform intended to help "bridge" between institutions, communities, and families. Despite a predominance of strategies and practices that fostered adherence to the conventional deficit-based parent involvement paradigm, my research team identified cultural brokering practices focused on *systems* change that leveraged key actors' work at organizational boundaries toward more equitable collaboration. The chapter closes by revisiting two of the guiding principles and offering recommendations for how initiatives and leaders might *transform power* and *build reciprocity and agengy* in district–community and cross-sector organizational relationships.

CROSS-SECTOR COLLABORATIONS: NEW POLICY CONTEXTS FOR ENGAGEMENT

Policymakers have long seen parents and families as key levers for improving student outcomes and success (Marsh, Strunk, Bush-Mecenas, & Huguet, 2015; Nakagawa, 2000). But recently, a wave of cross-sector collaboration efforts has emerged as a new policy context for work to "engage" diverse parents and families in education. Cross-sector collaborations are strategic partnerships between schools, community-based organizations (CBOs), advocates, businesses, governmental agencies, philanthropies, and the public-at-large around a shared vision and indicators of improved educational outcomes for students from "cradle-to-career," especially within a particular neighborhood, city, or region (Henig et al., 2015; Horsford & Vasquez Heilig, 2014; LeChasseur, 2016). Such partnerships have recently spurred a great deal of enthusiasm from policymakers, funders, and agencies—and have launched a new set of high-profile initiatives (Kania & Kramer, 2013). Well-known versions of these collaborative efforts include the federal Promise Neighborhoods Initiative, the Harlem Children's Zone, and the Strive Network.

At first glance, these efforts across multiple institutions and organizations seem highly promising and, indeed, necessary for broader systems change, given the intertwined nature of educational inequities. That is, poverty and racism also shape inequities in health care, housing, and work opportunities that directly impact young people's ability to succeed in school. Limited job opportunities for families can mean unstable income and housing, which, in turn, can increase students' mobility and stress, thus negatively impacting young people's ability to engage or attend school (as well as their well-being). Likewise, inequitable access to high-quality health care—from dental care to mental health—can negatively affect students' academic success. Particularly when we recognize that these interlocking dynamics are not simply related to poverty but are also a legacy of racism, colonization, and assimilative governmental policies carried over generations, the notion that schools alone can "solve" inequities seems increasingly far-fetched.

And yet, given the overlapping institutional dynamics, what better place to focus and intervene across systems than education?

Thus, in theory, cross-sector collaborations have important potential for better aligning efforts and making sustained change within *and* beyond schools themselves. Such initiatives have helped to focus disparate efforts, consolidate and target resources, and build common understandings, approaches, and goals (Henig et al., 2015). They have also increasingly positioned nondominant parents, families, and communities as key stakeholders in educational equity efforts (Pekel et al., 2015). Although an emerging literature has begun to examine the impact and complexities of cross-sector collaboratives, this chapter focuses on the implications of this context for efforts to build more equitable relations between nondominant families, schools, and communities. Research—my own and that of others—suggests that efforts to bring families and communities into the conversation as equal stakeholders can often fall short of the rhetoric and aspirations. Efforts to align and coordinate different social and support services around education across institutions and fields are hardly new. A look back historically can be instructive for contextualizing the role of families and communities in earlier such efforts.

NEW CONTEXT, FAMILIAR TERRITORY: CONTEXTUALIZING EDUCATION BEYOND THE SCHOOL WALLS

Outside of formal state-run or sanctioned institutions, many communities of color and Indigenous communities have long recognized and attended to education as linked to their families' and communities' broader well-being. Education, after all, has never solely been the domain of formal institutions; families and communities comprise the first learning contexts for children prior to any interactions with schools. "Since time immemorial,"[1] Indigenous communities have shared stories as a form of community knowledge and taught young people cultural practices that link their own well-being to that of their families, communities, non-human relations, and the land (Brayboy, 2006; San Pedro et al., 2017; Smith, 2012). Scholar Muhammad Khalifa (2017) highlights the "Ancestral knowledges" of Indigenous and other minoritized peoples as the knowledge systems and ways of being embedded in written, oral, and spiritual traditions. From the perspective of Ancestral knowledges, "there are not barriers between spirituality, education, family, and other aspects of life." Although these knowledge systems have been impacted by colonization, slavery, and other forms of oppression, they have also persisted and evolved over time.

Historically, African American schools in the segregated South—as well as some present-day community-based schools—tended to the priorities and needs of their students and communities beyond the four walls of the school in tandem with their academic growth (Siddle Walker, 1996). And many community organizing groups engage in multi-issue organizing, recognizing how education intertwines with other issues, such as immigration, voting rights, affordable housing, environmental injustices, or health inequities. From this perspective, then, strengthening education by attending to other supports and systems beyond schools is not new; within this context, it's actually "new" to think of education as somehow distinct from other aspects of well-being for whole children and families.

Within the context of formal state institutions in the United States, though, the notion of integrating social services with education goes back to the late 1800s and the days of Jane Addams and the settlement houses. At that time, education reformers began to recognize poverty, violence, housing insecurity, lack of health care, and other economic and societal challenges as major barriers to education (Henig et al., 2015). Recent decades have seen a renewal of interest in addressing the linked fates of urban schools and communities (Anyon, 2009; Horsford & Vasquez Heilig, 2014; Noguera, 2003; Warren, 2005). Prior to the most recent wave of cross-sector collaborative efforts, the comprehensive services movement of the 1990s targeted public schools as a hub for providing health, employment, recreation, and other services for students and families (Mawhinney & Smrekar, 1996). These "comprehensive community initiatives" in major urban centers sought to mobilize broad, multisector civic capacity in support of community-wide causes such as community revitalization, economic development, and education (Henig et al., 2015; Stone et al., 2001).

Research on the comprehensive community initiatives of the 1990s found that the strategies employed in those efforts largely reinforced the conventional "parent involvement" dynamics we discussed in the prior chapters. That is, parents were treated as clients or beneficiaries whose best interests were known by professionals outside of those communities (Crowson & Boyd, 2001; Fine, 1993; Mawhinney & Smrekar, 1996). For instance, principals and agency directors generally decided which services to provide and how to link them to the school. Likewise, low-income families had little or no say in decision-making, neither in setting school priorities, nor in shaping the broader initiatives. Rather, the well-intentioned service coordination models often reinforced power inequities between families and schools and consolidated dominant institutional agendas. Around this time, Clarence Stone and his colleagues studied 11 U.S. cities that had undertaken broader civic initiatives around education reform to examine the *civic capacity* of those efforts, what they defined as the mobilization of "core stakeholders" around a community-wide cause. They found that most initiatives ended up "rounding up the usual suspects" of elites (p. 341), which was largely insufficient for moving and sustaining transformative change. None of the initiatives engaged affected parents or families except as intended beneficiaries of services, and Stone and his colleagues concluded dimly, "parents, as the most directly affected constituency group for public schools, are a weak counterweight to professional autonomy" (Stone et al., 2001, p. 85).

So what lessons might we bring forward from these prior efforts to collaborate with families and communities across organizations and institutions to transform education? First, we might begin any effort to improve schools by enlisting the knowledge and practices that nondominant families and communities often bring with them; these insights can help systems-based actors not only to better understand inequities but to rethink our dominant assumptions and models. Second, we would be wise to temper our enthusiasm and excitement about the latest fad in education with the recognition that even our best designs and intentions can—and often do—default to structural arrangements that reassert conventional power asymmetries. To realize the promise of equitable collaboration in cross-sector educational change initiatives, we must learn from the mistakes of prior efforts and push beyond good intentions and rhetoric to recognize and intervene when the deficiency paradigm reasserts itself.

CROSS-SECTOR "COLLABETITION": REINFORCING INTERORGANIZATIONAL INEQUITIES

As I have established, in theory, a cross-sector collaborative initiative is an ideal context within which to embed efforts to build more authentic forms of parent and community participation, as it draws on a broader segment of the community than typical engagement approaches have sought to do. These initiatives also explicitly seek to build public understanding and political will for sustained educational change. Such a context could also provide opportunities for mutual and collective learning to push beyond our current "best practices" for engaging families and communities in education.

As part of a broader project, my research team examined efforts to more authentically engage families and communities within the context of one such cross-sector collaboration, what I will refer to as the Pathways Project. Albeit in its early phases, this effort emulated a national "collective impact" model in which a single "backbone" organization serves as the common anchor for the many different organizations and efforts. The theory of change underlying such efforts relates to coordinating disparate efforts and uniting around a set of common metrics. I will share some of our findings from within these specific efforts in the second half of this chapter, but I want to begin with the policy assumptions and structural arrangements that comprise that context, as they profoundly shaped the work and interactions within the initiative in fundamental ways.

This cross-sector collaborative effort embodied a particular paradox at the ground level. One of the community partners in the initiative dubbed this dynamic "*collabetition.*" That is, the districts, agencies, community organizations, and institutions involved in the Pathways Project were ostensibly collaborating around a common vision and set of indicators, but in practice, the structures and processes in the initiative created a sense of constant competition for financial and human resources, media attention, priorities, and opportunities for many of the project partners. This competition reinforced old hierarchies and powered dimensions between organizations. From the top on down, those hierarchies looked something like this, with power decreasing vertically:

POWER ↓

- Foundations and white-led policy organizations
- School districts
- Large social-service and white-led agencies
- Community-based organizations
- Community of color–led grassroots groups and coalitions
- Working-class students, families, and communities of color

In other words, policy elites and executives had the greatest power and ability to set the agenda, whereas those most directly affected by the systemic injustices the initiative sought to address—young people, families, and communities—had little voice or influence.

In the case we studied, this strategy was pursued with little disruption to the default assumption that only the "usual suspects" of elites would determine those metrics, shape the agenda to which efforts should align, and consolidate resources and opportunities around the organizations "onboard" with the initiative. When Maria (a staff member of a community-based agency) first named this "collabetition" dynamic in a room full of community organizations in the collective impact initiative, there was an audible exhale of recognition around the table. To be clear, this is a dynamic we identified in a single cross-sector collaboration, but other scholars have identified similar dynamics in other initiatives (Horsford & Sampson, 2014; Geller et al., 2014; LeChasseur, 2016), and I have been surprised at how much the concept has resonated with scholars and practitioners across very different contexts.

The concept of *collabetition* became a useful lens for making sense of the normative power dynamics between organizations within the initiative. First, collabetition favored larger, predominantly white organizations, which set the tone for the entire initiative in terms of the role of families. For instance, the districts within the project jointly applied for and won a major grant, but the districts had to compete with each other for the bulk of funds through a grant award process. Within the school–community partnerships portion of the grant, only districts could select community partners and apply for the funds. This stipulation reinforced power inequities between districts and communities and structured competition between community organizations, favoring larger, predominantly white-led organizations with preexisting district contracts or relationships. Likewise, the Pathways Project's award for collective impact efforts required district or CBO applicants to demonstrate their ability to work extensively with data and write about their accomplishments, a requirement that community leaders argued further pitted organizations against one another and disadvantaged smaller, grassroots organizations with less capacity. Notably, nondominant parents and families had no direct voice or influence in shaping the agenda or affecting change in either competitive process.

If grassroots organizations led by people of color had been chosen to lead, we could imagine that parents and families might have had influence in shaping the agenda and been positioned as true partners and not merely service recipients. For example, the project strongly promoted an intervention aimed at changing parenting behaviors, in the form of an electronic app that would send parents messages about things to do to stimulate their children's brains and engage them in learning activities at home. In spite of the novel technological delivery, the strategy of professionals informing parents about what they should do differently defaulted to conventional involvement approaches and put the onus of change solely on parents. Notably, there was no app to provide information *from* parents *to* educators or schools about what *they* should do differently.

Likewise, nondominant parents had little voice or influence in the Pathways Project itself. "Unaffiliated" parents (who did not work as staff for a participating organization) and families did not sit on committees or participate in project meetings, and a survey of organizational partners conducted for the formative evaluation of the project indicated that 77% of the respondents "did not know how parents were represented in the Project." Although some argued that "real parents" should have a role and voice in project decision-making, others questioned whether parents would be interested in or capable of participating meaningfully in such meetings. Rather, some district and CBO staff claimed that their frequent interactions with parents and families enabled them to "know what parents need," and suggested it would not be a good use of parents' time to have them participate in such meetings.

Second, collabetition hindered the ability of districts to use data and research to improve their family engagement. A collective impact initiative should, in theory, be an ideal context within which to cultivate parent leadership and improve engagement practices. However, district and community leaders in our study also voiced concerns that the data and research on their efforts to engage parents and families created comparisons between them that were politically challenging to navigate, both inside and outside districts. On one hand, if our research highlighted areas of growth in fostering equitable engagement, administrators feared that their image-conscious superintendents would perceive it as a critique of the work that might undermine future commitments to staffing and resourcing family and community engagement. On the other hand, organized parents focused on equity concerns can operate at odds with public relations efforts to highlight district successes and garner public support (Mediratta et al., 2009). *Collabetition* may well have contributed to district leaders' reluctance to foster collective parent voice and influence that could disrupt the public narrative of district commitment and success in eliminating opportunity gaps.

Despite the intentions of Pathways Project staff and funders, sharing our research with the sites and the broader initiative also did little to catalyze collective learning. Rather, the *collabetition* dynamic in the broader context of these initiatives seemed to limit the extent to which district-, school-, and community-based organizational leaders were willing to be transparent about their practice and to engage with one another in improvement-focused professional learning. For instance, when our team facilitated a discussion across sites focused on sharing of problems of practice, organizational leaders shared vague generalizations about principals' and teachers' low priority on family engagement and the limited time and resources for the work. Some of these leaders later confided in private that they felt nervous or constrained in discussing potential limitations of their work in the presence of the others, including the funder from whom they hoped to secure additional future support for their work. Thus, rather than providing an ideal context for realizing collective learning and engaging broader participation beyond the "usual suspects" of education reform (Stone et al., 2001), the norms and powered mechanisms in the cross-sector collaborative context actually seemed to limit the extent to which organizations within it could learn from, align, or connect with each others' strategies and approaches.

How does *collabetition* inform our understanding of broad-scale interorganizational education reform and what do we *do* with this recognition? In some ways, cross-sector collaborations may represent the proverbial new label for old wine, on a larger scale. In his book *So Much Reform, So Little Change*, scholar Charles Payne (2008) called out the dysfunctions of urban educational reforms, with their focus on short-term solutions and lack of accountability to the very communities they are supposed to help. What's more, these dynamics are racialized both within organizations and between them, often through processes that appear neutral (Ray, 2019). Referencing as an example the post-Reconstruction debate about Black education (between industrial education and full inclusion), Ray points out, "Non-White organizations often depended on the largess of White institutional (state-level) benefactors. This dependency constrained collective action for political and social equality" (p. 39). Despite their innovative sheen, then, cross-sector collaborations can mimic the default logic of accountability policies and meritocratic market-based reforms (Trujillo, 2014) and reinforce racialized inequities between school systems, agencies, and CBOs at interorganizational levels.

Like broader accountability policies, cross-sector collaboratives often rely on a technical-rational logic—the idea that "by shining a light on students' performance, examining differences across groups, and maintaining high expectations for all, schools can provide more equitable outcomes for students" (Garner, Thorne, & Horn, 2017, p. 408). We have learned a great deal about how accountability policies operate within contexts of historical and ongoing inequities: Rewards (such as funding and public recognition) and sanctions (public scrutiny and competitive comparisons) produce limited change to racial disparities in student outcomes. More than that, though, as parents Natalia and Lourdes in Chapter 3 perceived, and scholars have found in other contexts (Oakes & Rogers, 2006), the implementation of accountability policies according to a technical-rational logic can actually *reinforce* business-as-usual in ways that further racial inequities.

Consolidating resources, attention, and decision-making in a single "hub" controlled by a small group of policy elites can also consolidate hierarchical power and undercut the agency, funding, and decision-making by smaller CBOs and grassroots organizations and networks, especially those who work closest with families themselves. Rather than ameliorating racial inequities, then, cross-sector collaborations that privilege technical solutions can affirm existing racialized power structures and institutions in ways that inadvertently exacerbate the overlapping dynamics of racism, poverty, and, ultimately, of inequitable political power. As scholar Mark Warren (2014) argued in the quote that opened this chapter:

> Education reform, then, cannot be considered mainly in technical or organizational terms, but rather should be addressed as a profoundly political problem. The failures of public education reflect the lack of power held by low-income communities of color, in resources, accountability, and performance.

To the credit of the cross-sector initiative we studied, these dynamics sparked a conversation about the role of parents and families of color that catalyzed a renewed effort to engage them in the leadership of the initiative (albeit without challenging the conventional organizational hierarchies described above). Conversations about racial equity have also begun to infuse the cross-sector collaborative field more broadly, as can be seen in a plethora of conference presentations, reports, webinars, and other guidance.[2] Even some funders have undertaken work to explore how to become more racially equitable and, thanks to Villanueva's (2018) influential book, have begun conversations about how to "decolonize" their wealth. These are promising conversations and efforts—arguably, efforts that have begun asking questions and exploring possibilities that most policy elites and systems-based actors have not before considered.

And yet, collectively, what we know thus far suggests that this is not easy or straightforward work—our "new" initiatives often default to "old" powered narratives, structures, and assumptions. Cross-sector collaborations must constantly work to transform power and build reciprocity at interorganizational levels, lest they default to the historically based structural arrangements that produce and fuel inequities. We must attend to—and work to reshape—the broader contexts within which reforms and efforts to engage families and communities are taking place. The underlying logics within those contexts can make certain approaches feel like "common sense," when in fact they are merely adhering to the dominant scripts about the "proper role" of students and families as recipients and sideline players whose interests are best known by others. Given this broader understanding of how interorganizational relations shape the approaches and assumptions about nondominant families and communities, we can now turn to the strategies within these initiatives that seek to bridge across organizations to families and communities themselves.

CULTURAL BROKERING AS BRIDGING

Cultural brokers have been taken up as a common policy solution intended to "bridge" between nondominant families, communities, and institutions. Community-based organizations themselves can act as cultural brokers, and many districts and schools currently hire family liaisons or parent leaders to facilitate coordination and communication between communities and schools. In theory, cultural brokers have a foot in two worlds: the world of the school and other formal institutions and the world of a specific cultural community (Jezewski, 1990). These individuals—many of whom share the cultural and linguistic background of the families they seek to engage—translate between those worlds and help families from nondominant cultural communities to understand and access information, resources, and opportunities from dominant institutions.

When undertaken with an aim of fostering equitable collaboration, cultural brokering by organizations or individuals offers the potential of building greater reciprocity by shifting the default ways of doing business and brokering knowledge, resources, and practices across efforts and organizations. Research related to the role of community-based organizations in education (including my own early work) suggests that organizations can act as cultural brokers to build the networks and access of families and communities, enabling them to access and influence schools and other systems (Geller et al., 2015; Small, 2006). Such work may involve helping families to decode, translate, and rehearse how to navigate the dominant culture of schools; providing access to institutional knowledge or networks; and affirming the cultural values and resources of parents, families, and communities to foster more inclusive environments (Howland et al., 2006; Lopez & Stack, 2001; Martinez-Cosio & Iannacone, 2007).

However, my rosy view of cultural brokering has shifted over the course of examining how institutions tend to undertake this strategy within the current policy context. When I examined the work of cultural brokers for instances of transforming power and building reciprocity, I found that the "brokering" more often than not was unidirectional—from higher-status individuals within schools or systems (family liaisons, parent leaders, or allies) toward lower-status individuals (in this case, nondominant parents) in ways that maintained those powered roles. I began to question whose "culture" was being brokered—and toward what ends.

In the next section, I'll share what that actually looked like on the ground, but before you get too disheartened about the possibilities for cultural brokers, I want to share a quick "spoiler" about my own evolving thinking. Although my research identified a predominance of assimilative strategies undertaken by those designated as cultural brokers (across disparate contexts and multiple studies), my research team also found promising approaches that sought to shift power and institute greater reciprocity between families and schools. More importantly, though, I came to realize that seeing "cultural brokers" as embodied in individuals or organizations was limiting and could actually set them up in problematic ways as tokenized representatives who speak *for* parents or on behalf of essentialized cultures and communities. Instead, like leadership, cultural brokering offers more transformative ways forward when we use it as a verb. No longer attached to particular individuals by virtue of their formal role or cultural identity, cultural brokering can be undertaken by a variety of actors, including systems-based roles like teachers, principals, counselors, nonprofit staff, and district administrators. Importantly, when focused on actions and interactions rather than roles or institutions, cultural brokering can reckon with power inequities to foster reciprocity and agency between families, schools, and other organizations.

I first came to these understandings through research that my team and I conducted on "cultural brokers" in three initiatives within the Pathways Project that were seeking to better engage parents with schools: two school districts and one neighborhood-based community organization. Each initiative operationalized the roles of cultural brokers quite differently: The Fairview district hired full-time school-based family liaisons; the Kellogg district stipended parent leaders to faciliate a 9-week evening parent academy; and the Westfield Center community organization hired "family allies" to support specific families who had been identified for their caseload. Despite their varied approaches, each site shared the local policy context of the cross-sector collaboration and its underlying logic; not surprisingly, then, the strategies that predominated within each of these sites also aligned with traditional parent involvement approaches.

The cultural brokers mostly socialized families into dominant institutions and norms to support the agenda of schools and, within that, the broader cross-sector collaborative (and its logics, as described above). These strategies included informing parents about school expectations and the importance of home support activities (like nightly reading and homework completion), encouraging parents to attend conventional school activities (such as open houses and parent–teacher conferences), and connecting families with resources to meet basic needs for food, housing, and health care. They also addressed school-related needs for language translation and information about whom to talk with about additional student learning or behavioral supports.

In Fairview, the liaisons offered workshops that informed parents about why they should be involved in their children's education and shared a list of 25 behaviors to promote their child's success, such as attending open houses, talking with their child about school, and getting them to school on time. The Kellogg parent facilitators used a scripted curriculum that emphasized how schools worked, as well as the need to foster a more "school-like" home learning environment. Finally, the Westfield Center cultural brokers referred parents to culturally and linguistically appropriate therapists and assisted parents with paperwork for health and social supports or after-school care.

To be clear, I am not arguing that these activities are unnecessary or that families with basic needs should not be supported in accessing them. However, when those are the *sole* activities and opportunities made available to families, we can reinforce asymmetric power between families and schools and imply that parents *alone* must change their behaviors and attitudes to improve student learning and outcomes. If reciprocity and agency were at the core of cultural broker work, we might ask: Where are the opportunities for educators to learn about the Ancestral knowledges and what Tara Yosso (2005) calls the "community cultural wealth"[3] of students and their families? How do cultural brokers enable families and communities to leverage their expertise about their own children to redesign systems and agendas to become more responsive and equitable? How do brokers build families' capacity not only to support and advocate for their own child individually but *also* to collectively influence broader policy and reform? And what cultural brokering might reshape the organizational policies and practices that relegate families to the margins of teaching and learning?

By now you may be recognizing a pattern with regard to proposed solutions to addressing the role of nondominant families in cultivating more racially equitable educational systems. The latest "silver bullet" often gives us new language and focus for reforms (and often new funding as well), but such interventions often disregard a starting point of historically rooted racial injustices and colonization. In doing so, we can replicate the very dynamics we set out to disrupt. In short, many districts across the country and even many community organizations recognize the power of cultural brokering and have created and funded new positions for individuals to take on this function. This move can feel like a big win for a system that has struggled to recognize families and communities as important players in their children's education. But they are not silver bullets. As in cross-sector collaborative initiatives, hiring cultural brokers within a policy context that mirrors the assumptions of the deficiency paradigm can position them as institutional gatekeepers whose sole job is to assimilate families into dominant cultural norms and school agendas. These individuals may even become agents of the institution whose job is to "train" parents to act as compliance officers to ensure their children behave as schools and educators desire (e.g., doing their homework, attending school regularly, following rules, etc.). And hiring individuals into cultural broker roles can function as a self-congratulatory "check" in the invisible "family engagement" box for systems leaders or policy elites—one that leaves largely intact the broader systems of inequity.

Yet, as promised above, my research—and that of others—also offers a glimpse into potential ways forward. Looking beyond individual actors in particular roles toward the act of cultural *brokering* highlighted practices and approaches that people in different roles across systems were undertaking—in ways that often took advantage of being at the borders of organizations.

EMERGING APPROACHES TO EQUITABLE CULTURAL BROKERING

Despite the predominance of conventional parent involvement strategies in the Pathways Project and the three initiatives within it, all the sites were working to improve their work and enact more equitable interactions with parents and families to support their children's education and success. Because other books and articles have so thoroughly documented the problematic nature of deficit-based practices, I deliberately focus here on the cultural brokering strategies that were more collective, reciprocal, and/or relational in nature and, as such, suggest possibilities for equitable collaboration between families and schools:

1. Fostering relational cultures and politicized trust
2. Scaffolding family leadership and influence
3. Redesigning the system

1. Fostering Relational Cultures and Politicized Trust with Educators

Nondominant families often experience schools as hostile or alienating environments. Through both subtle and explicit messages, schools and educators can signal that parents do not belong in the school and have no "place" in the education of their children. For example, Latinx parents in my research routinely share experiences of school secretaries who do not acknowledge their presence, and teachers who avoid them or talk down to them because they do not speak English well. Likewise, Black parents share being aggressively questioned when they show up unannounced at their children's school, while white parents at the same school are welcomed with smiles and allowances for flexibility. Multiple studies highlight how low-income parents and parents of color feel teachers treat them with paternalistic condescension or outright hostility (Olivos & Mendoza, 2009; Yull et al., 2014). Seemingly benign school policies and oganizational routines can exacerbate such racialized exclusion. Several elementary schools I have studied established rules to prevent parents from walking their children to their classrooms in the name of maintaining order during the morning drop-off. And many typical involvement opportunities at schools take an individualistic approach that functions to isolate families. This isolation precludes families from talking to each other and perceiving patterns in their treatment that may implicate educators and schools more broadly. In our work, many such families are surprised to realize they are not alone in their experiences of alienation.

In the study of Pathways Project family engagement initiatives, one set of cultural brokering practices focused on building relationships between parents and educators as well as between families through a relational, "home-like" climate in schools. For example, bilingual (Spanish/English) Fairview family liaisons called families to attend school events, greeted parents with hugs, encouraged parents to talk with them any time, and visited homes to help address issues when needed. Two Latina mothers contrasted their experiences at different times and in different schools, alluding to a perception of racial discrimination related to the lack of welcome:

> Flor: *Antes nos hacían a un lado . . .*
> Victoria: *Aja, cuando yo venía aquí yo no me sentía como que era bienvenida en ninguna escuela yo me sentía que era bienvenida, he visitado las escuelas de mis hijos mayores y yo no como siempre ha habido esa discriminación hacia los hispanos"*
> Flor: Before they pushed us aside/ignored us . . .
> Victoria: Yeah, when I used to come here I did not feel that I was welcomed, I did not feel that I was welcome in any school, I have visited the schools of my older children and like always there has been discrimination toward Hispanics. (Parent focus group, Fairview District, June 5, 2013)

In these instances, the focused attention and welcoming approach helped to build positive relationships between parents and the school. Likewise, a Somali father experienced a new sense of connection with and trust in Kellogg School District staff as a result of becoming a facilitator in the parent academy:

> For me, now I can just walk into the school district, and see all the faces I know. . . . So I know that I can come to them if I need some help. That's the difference. Before, they were like outside. You were looking at displays. . . . But now, if you have a wrong question, you can still come and tell them, so they will tell you if it's wrong to ask. Because you know that you can actually trust them, because you're already involved with them. . . . They are there for you.

In a number of schools, the designation of a physical space specifically for families in the schools provided a location for families to gather, share resources, ask questions, and connect about common concerns or issues.

Though not sufficient on its own for fostering a relational culture, the decision to allocate such a space signaled that families had a "place" in the education of their children. For instance, a Westfield Center Family Ally referenced such a room in one of the neighborhood schools:

> That's a space where parents know they can come in any time to connect with each other, but at the same time, in that room we will have different family bilingual staff who will speak whatever language the families need. And they can come in there and they will be able to get whatever support they need for their families. There can be training happening . . . based on what the families need, whether it's understanding the school system, what the assessments are, how to navigate [resources], or different things like that. But it really starts with having a place where they can go to get that support.

Likewise, one of the shifts at a Fairview elementary school that parents referenced repeatedly was the designation of a room. Located at the front of the building in what used to be the principal's office, the new family room was where the family liaison was based and where regular parent coffees and meetings were held.

To varying degrees, cultural brokering in the initatives we studied also created opportunities for families to meet and develop relationships with one another, particularly with those who shared their home language and culture. Kellogg's teaching of the parent academy curriculum in English, Spanish, Russian, Somali, Vietnamese, Punjabi, Kurdish, Burmese, and Arabic was perhaps the clearest example of this strategy. Although they were working from a common set of procedures and curricula, the parent facilitators adapted their recruitment and instruction to their cultural context. For instance, Somali parent leaders went door to door in their community; phone calls and in-person reminders connected Latinx families; and a Burmese cultural broker picked her students up in her car and brought them to the school together. Kellogg parents pointed to the relationships that developed between parents in the workshops as a critical aspect of the program's success, echoing a sentiment expressed broadly across participating parents:

> The key strengths of the program was, I believe, what I saw, was seeing the parents be engaged with each other. And though each one come[s] from different avenues, they have the same concerns. And addressing those concerns and finding out what are different areas. Even with me, I'm a parent, but also [a] facilitator/recruiter, and for me, hearing other parents' strategies on how to perhaps get one child to do something, then another one, I took a lot of stuff home for me and utilized at home. And then what I've used, other parents are like, really? And so to get that was nice. (Parent facilitator, Kellogg School District, May 6, 2013)

Parent participants and facilitators alike highly valued the opportunity to build relationships with other parents. Often formally designated by language, these alternative spaces enabled nondominant parents to interact in culturally specific ways, share experiences, identify common concerns, and offer support, ideas, and resources—in short, to engage collectively with each other. A Fairview cultural broker saw opportunities for immigrant parents to develop relationships with one another as a foundation for building a schoolwide sense of belonging:

> We know those parents will feel—wow, that's what I used to do in my country—[we] used to get together with the same group, we used to speak the same language and we can connect, and we develop friendship and relationships and we feel welcome in the whole community.

A limitation of language-specific spaces, though, was the unintended exclusion of English-speaking parents of color, particularly African American families, but also Pacific Islander and Native American families, who were largely absent from these initiatives. Similarly, district leaders in both Fairview and Hartland (Westfield Center's district) had heard concerns from African American families that they were not provided the same opportunities as those who spoke languages other than English. When asked why the district did not designate race-specific spaces, the Kellogg district administrator was adamant that it would be far too politically volatile to even talk about designating groups by race. Thus, although language was a proxy that enabled spaces tailored to the cultural practices of many groups, some African American and other nondominant families felt overlooked by these practices.

Despite these limitations, the research suggests that relational climates may provide a foundation for more robust forms of engagement and educational improvement (see Ishimaru et al., 2016, for an in-depth treatment of cultural brokering practices in this context). Bryk and Schneider (2004) highlight relational trust as a critical "social lubricant" in the hard work of school improvement, and the social capital literature suggests that such relationships between nondominant parents and educators can provide access to institutional knowledge, opportunities, or resources that can aid students' academic success (Stanton-Salazar, 2010).

Beyond welcoming gestures and warm relationships, though, cultural-brokering strategies might begin to build what Vakil and colleagues (2016) call *politicized trust*. As discussed earlier, the interactions and relations between families and educators are shaped by historically rooted and racialized power dynamics. Building politicized trust requires that we attend not simply to whether families believe in the integrity of educators or feel they can rely on teachers or principals to follow through on what they say they will do, but that we also recognize how trust is shaped by race and power and must be constantly renegotiated and cultivated in everyday interactions and over time. These types of relationships move beyond purely technical fixes to more explictly addressing the political dimensions of change in schools (Geller et al., 2015).

In our study, we saw politicized trust develop in one Fairview school when Latinx mothers became increasingly frustrated with the principal's lack of response to their concerns that a single combined classroom did not meet the needs of students in special education or those learning English. Although the family liaison initially supported the families in sharing their concerns with the principal, the mothers helped the liaison to recognize the principal's racialized power moves to disregard parental concerns and further marginalize students in the name of efficiency. The cultural brokering in this case eventually shifted to facilitating parent communication with the principal supervisor at the district (an institutional agent), which ultimately led to the principal being counseled out of the position. In this case, families built politicized trust with the family liaison and a district leader over time and across roles and racial differences to address the marginalization of students with special needs and those learning English.

Overall, cultural brokering strategies focused on building relationships between educators and families, as well as between families, seemed to foster more reciprocal and collective interactions at schools. However, for all the warmth and cultural specificity, these strategies were still primarily school-centric and largely maintained the unilateral power dynamics between schools and communities (Crowson & Boyd, 2001). That is, they focused on bringing parents and families *into* schools and, through relationships with each other, returning to school, to get information, access programs, or interact with educators in ways that mostly reinforced educator-set agendas and power asymmetries. The relationships themselves appeared to have little impact on the core of teaching and learning in classrooms or schools, beyond minor adjustments to better serve individual students, and did little to balance power or reshape schooling. Relationships and a sense of shared experiences and concerns nurtured new conversations and understandings but they were not sufficient, in and of themselves, to catalyze systems change toward more just education. Rather than interpreting this simplistically as "relationships don't cut it," though, I want to emphasize that they are foundational for developing politicized trust and transforming power in ways that can reshape schooling.

2. Scaffolding Parent Leadership and Influence

All the initiatives in the study sought to develop parents as "leaders" of their own children and sometimes of other parents, and a handful of parents had the opportunity to be hired into formal cultural broker roles or to take on formal leadership roles (like school board membership). Beyond the school level, Fairview's district-level parent leadership council met quarterly to review the district's family engagement work, coordinate with other stakeholders about district strategy, and set priorities for family and community engagement. However, Kellogg's program stood out for providing scaffolded leadership development opportunities in the form of multiple roles at multiple levels for parents/family members to engage other parents and contribute to the success not only of their own children but of children across their school, community, or district.

Kellogg's model provided supports and opportunities for parent and community leaders to take on new "stretch" assignments with increasing responsibility and influence in the system and in their communities. Stretch assignments are tasks or roles that require knowledge or skills beyond individuals' current capacity to enable them to grow in their leadership (Hill, 2003). Kellogg parents and community leaders became recruiters, interpreters, workshop facilitators, trainers, curriculum developers, and even (formal) teachers within their communities. For example, Yates, a Somali father whose youth had been spent in a refugee camp, started as a recruiter for the program, making phone calls and home visits to encourage his friends and neighbors to attend the academy. With his cousin, he facilitated the workshops, and he continued to facilitate conversations with Somali families at his home after the program ended. With one district leader's support, Yates subsequently created and taught a Somali parent–child native language class at his subsidized housing unit. Although not all the facilitators took up this range of leadership, most expressed a sense of new agency and identity as leaders in their communities. A parent participant explained:

> I think what made the facilitator so special is that it wasn't the principal teaching it and it wasn't a teacher teaching it, it was just moms and grandmas and aunties teaching it. And they know how to teach because that's who's in the class. I thought that was what made it really special. (Parent focus group, May 16, 2013).

Because these facilitators were themselves parents, family and community members similar to participants, they were able to leverage their expertise and become seen by other families as leaders.

These leadership opportunities fostered more reciprocal dynamics with the system and enabled parent/family leaders to contribute their expertise on their children and communities. For example, a principal talked about what they had learned from parent leaders about communicating with the different cultural communities in the school:

> And so, we're learning that we have to really make face-to-face contact with [Somali families] . . . We've also learned from some of our groups that having our print materials translated is sometimes helpful and sometimes not, because the parents aren't necessarily literate in their first language. And so for some of them it doesn't

> matter what language the print materials come home in, there's going to be a challenge to interpret and read. . . . So now we're asking ourselves a lot of questions.

The Westfield Center family allies took a more community-based approach to building family leadership. Parents themselves could be hired as family allies or other staff members of Westfield Center, and all the family allies were mothers of color who had originally participated in WC's programming as parents seeking to navigate schools or identify resources to support their families. More recently, the organization initiated a Family Education Council (FEC), an effort to build and support the leadership of families themselves across cultural communities in Westfield to impact change in schools. The FEC echoes a growing recognition within the Pathways Project of the need to leverage parent leadership, and the region has seen a proliferation of efforts to cultivate parent and family leadership in more recent years (including at the level of the collective impact initiative).

However, as other studies have found (Geller, 2016; Quezada, 2016), parent, family, and community leadership in schools goes only so far without parallel openings, shifts, and capacity on the part of educators and school systems. Rather, equitable collaborations that transform power and build reciprocity must not only address families but must also cultivate change on the part of educators and systems.

3. Redesigning Systems

Though far less common than the other strategies we found, we did identify cultural brokering strategies to change the structures, systems, and practices in educational systems that systematically exclude or marginalize families and their influence. These approaches were not fully realized in the study we conducted in the Pathways Project context, but they do suggest opportunities for building more equitable and reciprocal collaboration between families and educational systems. This systems-focused cultural brokering seemed to be enabled by individuals' positioning on the borders of organizations. That is, systems actors whose daily work entails interacting with individuals who do not work directly for the district (e.g., families, government agency staff, community-based organizations, researchers, etc.) often have access to multiple sources of knowledge and information that are less available to others in the district. This positioning on the "border" of the district combined with a degree of ambiguity and autonomy with how they accomplished their goals (associated with those higher up in the organizational hierarchy) seemed to create conducive conditions for systemic brokering.

Both district initiatives in our study built new infrastructure, systems, and capacity to support family engagement, but cultural brokering in the Kellogg district initiative to scaffold leadership represented a more fundamental level of systems redesign. As Kellogg administrator Monica Summers explained, this entailed significant "behind the scenes" work across departments, in particular those often not considered directly involved in either the work of family engagement or equity, such as the department of human resources, communications, finance, and operations. Monica emphasized the importance of ensuring "executive understanding and investment" in the district's efforts to foster more robust engagement with families. Systemic shifts implicated many areas of the district and could easily be stymied by administrators insistent on maintaining control or adhering to status quo procedures. This systemic investment, which began with the superintendent's vision and support, deepened through ongoing and strategic communications at executive leadership meetings, in which Monica and her supervisor narrated the work and celebrated accomplishments made possible by internal district partners.

For example, Kellogg created new systems and policies to hire nondominant parents and family members, some of whom had limited formal education, in order to leverage their particular expertise. Monica explained that previously, individuals could not be hired by the district without high school completion and/or advanced education certification, which prevented a number of parents from immigrant and refugee backgrounds from being hired to support outreach or facilitation in the program:

> It required a lot of executive work . . . to get the people in Finance and HR to value things like cultural expertise, language expertise at a level of acknowledgement as formal college training. You can't get a college certificate for having lived in a refugee camp and intimately knowing how to community organize.

The district also negotiated contracts with culturally specific community-based organizations and developed a system of training and ongoing coaching to support parent facilitators in leading the parent academy.

Another cultural brokering strategy focused on redesigning systems involved building the capacity of educators to engage and partner differently with families. Like a number of districts across the country, Fairview district had undertaken a home visit pilot program. Loosely modeled on the Parent–Teacher Home Visit Project[4]—in which teachers approach home visits as learners—this effort represented a potentially promising strategy that aimed to build teachers' understanding and ability to engage with their families and students to improve classroom instruction. However, this pilot engaged a small number of teachers, and there appeared to be little follow-through to support changes in teaching practice as a result of the home visits. In addition, research from other contexts suggests that efforts to bring teachers into community spaces can confirm or exacerbate deficit-based perspectives of students as much as they can remediate those views (Rubel, 2017). Perhaps in part to address this danger, the Fairview district also partnered with a national technical assistance agency to provide a series of equity-focused workshops to integrate classroom teachers and counselors into family engagement efforts alongside family liaisons and parents. Due to challenges in getting release time and other issues, few classroom teachers participated in the trainings, and after the external grant funding ran out, the learning was not sustained. However, the effort led the district department to explore new efforts to build educator capacity in working with families.

In my more recent work, I supported systems-based administrators in taking co-design approaches to their leadership practice. Like the Kellogg administrators who changed human resource policies to hire parent leaders with less formal U.S. education, the district leaders who undertook co-design were working to shift how the system engaged with families and communities—what I might now reframe as *systemic* brokering. Notably, the focus in these efforts was not on changing families and communities in order to "engage" them in schools but rather on changing how schools and districts engaged with families in consequential interactions and decision-making processes. Although I examine co-design as a leadership practice in Chapter 7, I will highlight here three key leadership practices that I argue constitute systemic brokering strategies for transforming power and building reciprocity and agency.

First, systems leaders let go of the notion that only those whose formal roles explicitly reference families should be "engaging" them. Rather, reshaping systems toward educational justice meant that key decisions that impact students and families needed to be made *with* them, not *for* them, regardless of the formal role or charge of the educational leader. For these leaders, this meant examining their own contexts for opportunities to reshape consequential policies or decision-making processes—such as the development of a family engagement policy, a principal hiring process, addressing student absenteeism, or the selection process for a district-level parent advisory council. In these cases, the district administrators moved from enacting leadership as a *role* that embodied sole decision-making authority to approaching leadership as an *action* that included facilitating collaboration with students, families, or communities. This seemingly simple shift represents a profound transformation of hierarchical and institutionally based power.

Second, district administrators also partnered with other individuals—both in and out of the system—to help build politicized trust in contexts of historical oppression and institutional mistrust. For example, one district administrator partnered with culturally specific community-based leaders to build relationships and foster more reciprocal exchanges with Latinx families. Not only did these moves enable more fluid facilitation and open trust-building opportunities, such partnering spread leadership across actors (and in some cases, organizations) and built greater investment by other district actors in reshaping decision-making processes to cultivate collaboration with families.

Finally, leaders also undertook systemic brokering to build reciprocity in the process of decision-making itself. Rather than defaulting to a unidirectional exercise of seeking stakeholder "input" and "voice" and then making the final decision behind closed doors, these leaders created processes that shared responsibility and power with families. To be clear, this did not mean abnegating their own voice and participation, but neither did it mean reverting to individualistic power moves to get to the end they alone deemed best. This was perhaps the most challenging aspect to navigate for those accustomed to holding formal power and authority. This practice asked them to acknowledge the institutional power they held as representatives of the district; use it to hold space for new voices, conversations, and solutions; and also bring their own multiple identities—not only as a district leader but as a community leader, neighborhood resident, and mother of Black children in the system, for example—into their participation. This systemic brokering thus reshaped spaces and power in which families and systems-based actors interacted, resulting in fundamentally different relationships, decisions, and solutions (see Chapter 7 for more on systems leadership and co-design).

CONCLUSIONS

By examining both the context of cross-sector collaborations and the cultural brokering strategies undertaken within it, this chapter revisits two of the guiding principles of the book to suggest how initiative leaders might *transform power* and *build reciprocity and agency* in district–community and cross-sector educational equity initiatives. Across empirical studies, *structural constraints* (shaped by collabetition) and *cultural brokering strategies* offer insights for either reinforcing status-quo institutional dynamics or building equitable collaborations across organizational boundaries. First, despite ambitious equity-focused aims, cross-sector collaborative endeavors—and the funding mechanisms that sustain them—can inadvertently reinforce inequitable relations and constrain family and community roles in decision-making. This context, in turn, shaped the largely assimilative practices of cultural brokers within the cross-sector initiative. Cross-sector collaborations will not realize their potential for addressing racial inequities if they replicate or exacerbate meritocratic competition, deficit-based assumptions about students and families, and technical-rational logics that disregard histories and structures of racism, colonization, and power.

However, systems-focused cultural brokering practices, especially by those at organizational boundaries close to students, families, and communities, offer potential ways forward for transforming systems' default way of approaching nondominant students, families, and communities from within those organizations or efforts. Top-down, policy-driven approaches can be reconfigured or even subverted by family-centered and practice-driven efforts to change systems. Shifting our focus from individuals in cultural broker *roles* to cultural brokering *strategies or practices* can be a start in reorienting to more collective, relational, or reciprocal actions to foster systemic capacity and transformation. To be clear, then, cultural brokering is not about simply hiring individuals with particular cultural identities into prescribed roles—in fact, the ability of the typical school- or district-based family liaison to make systems change is severely limited by the hierarchy of schools and the fact that they often share some aspect of the marginalized status of the families they are intended to reach. In this way, we might begin to understand leadership—both systems-based and community-based—as a form of *systemic brokering* to transform power and build reciprocity between organizations and individuals.

In sum, systemic brokering represents a "next" practice strategy for fostering equitable collaborations across institutions and organizations. Moving from the systems level to the organizational level of education opens new avenues for change. The next chapter explores how data inquiry with nondominant families and communities might be leveraged as a vehicle for organizational transformation.

Collaborating in Organizational Improvement

Data Inquiry with Families, Communities, and Educators

with Dawn Cameron Williams and Aditi Rajendran

> For apart from inquiry, apart from the praxis, individuals cannot be truly human. Knowledge emerges only through invention and re-invention, through the restless, impatient, continuing, hopeful inquiry human beings pursue in the world, with the world, and with each other.
>
> —Paulo Freire, *Pedagogy of the Oppressed* (1970)

Data and families are rarely discussed together in education. They occupy almost entirely different spaces, literatures, and frameworks in the scholarly world. Families and data also rarely intersect in the everyday realities of practice in schools and districts. Not incidentally, data has been imbued with significant power in educational decision-making; families and communities are rarely situated in this way. This chapter is about how we might reconfigure the relationships between families, power, and data via collective inquiry to foster more just schools and educational organizations.

In the current standards and accountability era, data has become central to conversations about organizational decision-making, improvement, and compliance, particularly with state and federal policies (Sandall, Schwartz, & Lacroix, 2004). The prolific research on data use in education suggests that collaborative analysis and use of data can build leadership, shift practice, and fuel continuous improvement in teaching and learning (Bertrand & Marsh, 2015; Coburn & Turner, 2011; Garner & Horn, 2016; Knapp, Copland, & Swinnerton, 2007; Leithwood & Riehl, 2003; Marsh & Farrell, 2015; Wayman & Stringfield, 2006). In fact, data has come to have so much power in education that it's not uncommon to hear scholars and practitioners alike referencing the need for "data driven" decision-making

(Derrick-Mills, 2015; Gullo, 2013; Ikemoto & Marsh, 2007; Mandinach, 2012; Park & Datnow, 2009).

On the other hand, families—especially those marginalized in our systems—are often completely absent from the research and practice of organizational decision-making and improvement. To the extent that families are visible in these processes, school and district leaders often consider them barriers to overcome or peripheral actors to inform. Nondominant families are hardly ever ascribed the power to "drive" decision-making; in fact, district leaders often use data to counter the priorities and demands of organized families and communities (for example, in school closure decisions [Khalifa et al., 2014; Kirshner & Jefferson, 2015]). School and district administrators can see nondominant families as a threat to the status quo.

With so much faith in the power of data to "drive" us to better schools, we might wonder: "Where does equity come in?" Brette Garner, Jennifer Thorne, and Ilana Horn (2017) asked precisely that question as they observed teachers interpreting data to inform their instructional practice. Within a high-stake accountability policy context, they found that educators tended to interpret achievement data about students in ways that positioned individuals as deficient. By extension, this positioning implicitly blames nondominant families and communities for so-called racial achievement "gaps" (Ladson-Billings, 2006; Milner, 2013). Only certain kinds of data get on the table, and a technical-rational policy context obscures historically rooted inequitable structures, systems, and racial ideologies. Efforts to use data in schools thus often reinforce inequity far more than they disrupt it (Diamond & Cooper, 2007). Garner and colleagues explain:

> As a consequence, students' academic trajectories are reduced to a series of test scores, enabling teachers, administrators, and the public to reinstate deficit narratives about marginalized subpopulations as they are measured against the White, middle-class norm. This functions to reify the racism, colonialist values, and White supremacy and privilege that are ingrained in the fabric of US society. (Garner et al., 2017)

Back to the paradigm of deficiency! Not surprisingly, many families and communities of color have experienced data as "weaponized" against them—sometimes to racialize and implicitly criticize their parenting and other times to rationalize ongoing or renewed injustices in their schools and communities.

Given these dynamics and an educational measurement history rooted in racist ideologies,[1] some wonder if throwing data out the door entirely would be the most equity-focused move we could collectively make. However, current U.S. federal and state education funding mechanisms generally preclude that as a viable short-term strategy, and nondominant families and communities are not hapless victims in relation to data. The accountability logic of current educational policy has also been used by youth, parent, and community organizing groups to make inequities visible and demand overdue educational change. This strategic use of data, from a *community* accountability stance, offers important insights into how data might be reclaimed to transform power and demand systemic action (Oakes & Rogers, 2006).

While such uses of conventional data will likely remain in community-based toolkits for educational change, Eve Tuck (2009) cautions that efforts to illuminate the problem can unintentionally reinforce simplistic notions about nondominant students, families, and communities. That is, the strategy underlying efforts to make inequities visible is based on the legal presumption that a remedy will be provided if communities can demonstrate sufficient damage to those with formal power and authority. However, data and research *solely* about conventional achievement and academic success disparities can unintentionally magnify the deficiency paradigm. Ironically, this exclusive focus on narrow metrics and racialized comparisons can paint particular nondominant communities as unidimensional victims without agency or resources. What's more, conventional forms of data and data use can also obscure the resiliency, adaptivity, and creativity of young people and their families and communities. In this sense, achievement scores don't just tell us how well students can answer particular kinds of questions, they also indicate what our educational system (and dominant society) currently values—and does *not*.

Given the power imbued in educational data, what if we could reclaim and expand data as a *tool* for fostering equitable collaborations and schools? How could we expand and shift our narrow, school-centric, colonizing conceptions of data and data use toward cultivating justice in education? This chapter draws from 5 years of work across early childhood, formal K–12, and community-based settings to explore this unlikely prospect. We shift to an organizational level in this chapter and focus on the *role of nondominant families and communities in organizational improvement efforts* using data inquiry as a form of joint work[2] to foster families' and educators' collective capacity for change. Our work suggests the need to shift from a focus on data itself toward using data to help catalyze broader organizational change processes in partnership with nondominant families and communities. Synthesizing learning and findings across contexts and time, we offer a model of collective inquiry with nondominant families that aims to build new capacities, stronger relationships, and deeper understanding of equity-based problems of practice. Operating from neither a deficiency paradigm nor an accountability logic, this model fosters transformative agency for equitable change across educators, families, and communities.

In what follows, we start by situating the data inquiry work within a continuum of relationships between families and data; we think of this as orienting to the "what." We then highlight promising practices we observed (and supported) across three phases of the collective inquiry cycle; these constitute the "how." We also discuss both challenges and "next level" opportunities for realizing transformative organizational change. The chapter closes by returning to the guiding principle of undertaking change as *collective inquiry* and capacity building for fostering more just schools and educational organizations.

CONCEPTUALIZING RELATIONSHIPS BETWEEN FAMILIES AND DATA

To help make sense of the interactions between families and data, we adapted a typology developed by Dana Mitra (2006), originally focused on student voice, to conceptualize different types of relationships between families (including their children and young people) and educational data uses (see Figure 5.1). We merged Mitra's triangle with ideas from Michael Fielding's (2001) spectrum of student involvement in school-based research to indicate both the prevalence of the practices closer to the bottom as well as the greater agency and power ascribed to families as the practices proceed upward. The most common and basic practice of schools and systems at the bottom of the pyramid is the use of data *about* students and families. The next group of practices recognizes families as holding insights and perspectives

Figure 5.1. Relationships Between Families and Data in Educational Changemaking

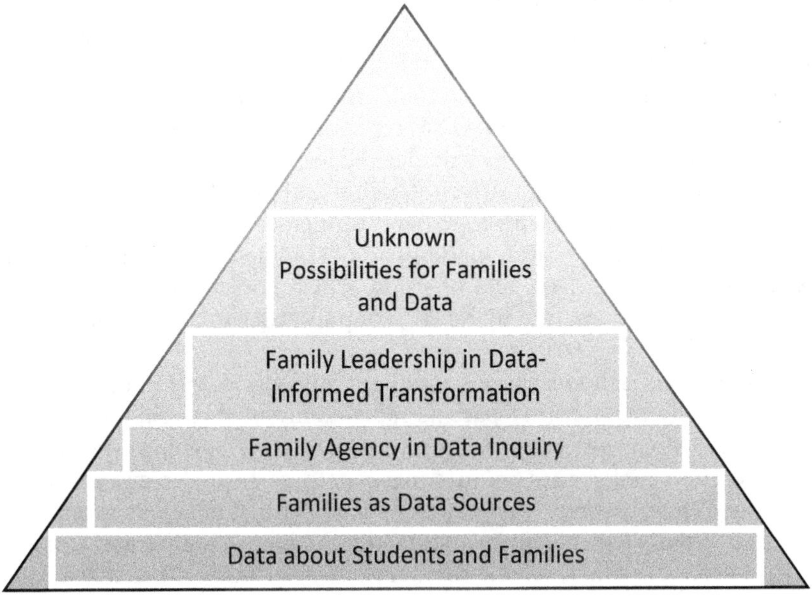

for informing organizational assessments; such practices draw on students and families as *sources* of data. At the next level, we place practices in which families take up *agency* in using data in inquiries to inform or advocate for organizational change. Closer to the top and more infrequently found are practices in which families play *leadership* roles alongside educators and positional educational leaders in organizational decision-making and transformation work that is informed—but *not driven*—by community-owned and -defined forms of data. Finally, drawing from work by Mansfield, Welton, and Halx (2012), we recognized that exceedingly little has been studied on this topic; we added a final set of practices at the top to represent the yet-unknown possibilities for how families might mobilize data in educational changemaking.

In our research across multiple organizations and contexts, we noted nearly all types of practices represented in this pyramid, sometimes in sequence, other times occurring simultaneously in different parts of an organization. This chapter focuses primarily on these organizations' efforts to "move up" the pyramid toward practices that use data inquiry to transform power and foster reciprocity and agency. For our research partners, this most typically indicated focused work on fostering family *agency* and *leadership* in data inquiry processes (the two higher tiers). However, the bottom of the pyramid represents the majority of practices in the field, so we discuss those practices first in order to place the practices described later in the chapter within a broader continuum.

Data about Students and Families

The most common relationship at the bottom of the pyramid is that of schools generating and using *data about students and families* for policy-driven accountability purposes. This represents most of the conventional data about student achievement derived from grades or standardized tests referenced in the "data-driven decision-making" literature. In recent years, student data has begun to expand to include other indicators, such as attendance, discipline rates, kindergarten "readiness," and enrollment in specialized programs or courses of study, which equity-focused educators may disaggregate to analyze by racial group in order to surface disparities (Johnson & La Salle, 2010).

To the extent schools share data about students with families, the intent is generally to "inform" parents individually of their child's progress or struggles, often via online school information systems but also during parent–teacher conferences or meetings set to resolve perceived student problems. When teachers share student data with families in group settings, it is often with the aim of motivating or increasing parent support. For instance, "academic parent–teacher teams" bring families together in group settings with their children's teachers to discuss academic achievement data (Paredes, 2011). In this paradigm, teachers might share state or local achievement data with parents in an effort to motivate them to change their home learning support behaviors in order to improve individual and class performance.

We observed this type of approach early on at one of the organizations we studied. Two young, white teachers presented their program's Peabody Picture Vocabulary Test (PPVT) early literacy data to parents. We witnessed a small group of mothers of color, some with strollers or rocking young children, listening quietly as the teachers reviewed percentages and comparisons for different tasks on the assessment from a set of charts on the wall. Following lengthy explanations of the statistical reports, the teachers asked if there were any questions. The handful of parents still in the room by the end (many left during the presentation) remained silent. They thanked the teachers, then smiled as they said their goodbyes. We wondered how these parents felt about their "engagement" with teachers and data; particularly across cultural contexts, silence and smiles can be interpreted in multiple ways—not only as signs of acquiescence and appreciation.

When data are only *about* students and families, they have little or no agency and power; indeed, they become objectified as numbers, and efforts to "share" this data generally position educators as experts or information providers to passive recipients: families (Starkie, 2012; Weiss & Lopez, 2011). Although many educators and leaders recognize the limitations of these forms of data, these practices still comprise the dominant mode of data use in both early childhood and K–12 education. Federal, state, and even private funding policies typically require such achievement data use to ensure accountability for their programming or schooling (Sandall, Schwartz, & Lacroix, 2004). Data *about families* often includes attendance rates at parent–teacher conferences and school events or teacher perceptions of parent involvement or support (reported in staff surveys).

As some of our work and that of others has examined (Au, 2009, 2017; Ishimaru et al., 2014), such metrics represent narrow conceptions of learning and family engagement that boil down to the ability to take standardized tests and behave in accordance with white normative school-centered expectations. In the field of early childhood education, scholars like Mariana Souto-Manning highlight how the very definition of "kindergarten readiness" is normed on a set of white, middle-class behaviors and expectations (Pérez & Saavedra, 2017; Souto-Manning & Rabadi-Raol, 2018). Similarly, Christine McWayne and her colleagues (2013) identified an entirely new dimension of family engagement in their study of Latino Head Start parents, leading them to conclude:

> With the behaviors of White, middle-class families and children naively used as the standard for developing measures' content and norms, our field is ill-informed to determine what is most culturally relevant for diverse groups of children and families. (p. 604)

Not only are "one-size-fits-all" approaches bound to fall short, then; the use of measures normed in these ways can further alienate families who perceive the brilliance of their children being disregarded or even reframed as problematic in school settings.

While the white-normativity of accountability data use may be somewhat invisible to many educators and has only recently been articulated in the research, this dynamic is often not lost on nondominant families. In the parking lot after hearing about early literacy data, a Somali mother said to me, "The teachers show us the data and compare our children to white children who [only] speak English. My child speaks two languages and is learning English [as a third language]. How do they say he is behind?" She went on to talk about how teachers had construed her son's behaviors (many of which were related to cultural differences) as problematic. She concluded our discussion with the comment from a prior chapter: "Just because we do not speak the language, we are not blind. We know when we are being judged." Rather than passively acquiescing to external accountability demands or interpreting parents' silence as an indicator of a low priority on education, the organizations in our studies all sought ways to move beyond conventional data practices and resist the racialized, deficit-based framings that arise from such approaches.

Students and Families as Sources of Data

At the next level of practice, students and families may become *sources* of perceptual data. Such practices recognize that students and families' perspectives and experiences hold important insights that can be used to assess services or supports, triangulate educator perspectives about school climate, or inform engagement strategies. For instance, the community-based early childhood center we studied conducted a survey of parents in their home-visiting program to determine which books and toys they preferred, and their Early Head Start program asked families about preferences for times and days of the week to hold family events. In another program, a family engagement coordinator conducted a family focus group about past parent nights and what topics and activities were of most interest to families (Community Place fieldnotes, 2014). All of these inquiries led to data that influenced program planning to better tailor engagement with families.

Many school districts conduct annual student surveys to examine school climate (for instance, students' sense of belonging at school, their perceptions of their teachers' expectations, or their sense of how other students treat them). Student perceptions can provide important means of triangulating other sources of data, and a growing body of research has substantiated correlations between student perceptions of teaching and other achievement measures (Wallace, Kelcey, & Ruzek, 2016). However, educators typically interpret such data and decide what to do about it in the absence of students and families themselves.

Districts also conduct family surveys to gauge satisfaction with things such as communication from the school, student supports, and their perceptions of a welcoming environment in their child's school. Oftentimes, data from these family surveys seem to indicate high satisfaction of families with their schools, but a closer look reveals that those who responded to the (generally online) survey are predominantly white, English-speaking middle-class parents. Although response rates are often difficult to locate, many school and district surveys of families appear to have overall response rates ranging from 5% to 30%, and they often over-represent white, English-speaking, higher-income and more professional parents. As you might imagine, data from only a *subset* of privileged parents can easily bias the results when they are interpreted as a representation of *all* families. Thus, in addition to telling an incomplete story, practices that query families as sources of data can inadvertently reinforce the existing dynamics of giving voice to a select few, privileged parents while invisibilizing others.

Listening sessions have also become increasingly common mechanisms of engagement in schools and systems (I will address these more specifically in Chapter 7). Like surveys, listening sessions run the risk of becoming new forums for furthering privileged voices. Even when conducted with attention to balancing voices, at the end of the listening session, the "listeners" (typically school or district administrators) decide what they will attend to and address. In this scenario, then, power remains solely in the hands of those with formal authority. Systems-based leaders who challenge dominant institutional practices in responding to family and community voices also risk negative consequences from those above them in the organizational hierarchy.

Thus, data practices that situate students and families as data *sources* align with the shift from involvement to engagement discussed earlier in this book. They mark an important shift away from deficit-based constructions and acknowledge students and families as holders of important experiences and insights. However, such data and practices are still largely driven by school-centric, normative white agendas. Likewise, formal leaders and educators decide in isolation whether and how such data will be used. Educators often make sense of the data *without* students and families in the conversation; families often end up as recipients of glossy school reports that tell them what their own data means and how it will be used. Although the education organizations we studied engaged in these practices to a lesser or greater extent, they also sought to evolve these approaches to foster agency and leadership among families.

Family Agency in Data Inquiry

At this third level on the pyramid, families might still be sources of data but they are also active participants and agents in collecting the data, making sense of it and sometimes using it to motivate change. In community organizing, students, families, and community members frequently select and use data strategically in campaigns to call out inequities and compel action. Sometimes this means using conventional data in new ways, such as mobilizing community concern and support for change. For instance, the faith-based organizing group PACT (People Acting in Coalition Together) in San Jose, California, used the low proficiency levels on state standardized assessment data to call out neighborhood schools' failure to provide high-quality education and to advocate for parent-driven charter schools (Warren et al., 2011). However, as mentioned earlier, this accountability-driven use of conventional achievement data can also reinforce a set of dominant assumptions about what counts as data, how it gets collected, and who ultimately gets to decide what to do with it.

Other times, organized parents and communities may collect and strategically use conventional and new data in tandem with each other. For example, the parent organizing group CADRE (Community Asset Development Re-defining Education) in Los Angeles issued a "shadow report" about the implementation of discipline policies in the district designed to stem the school-to-prison pipeline.[3] Parents conducted surveys and focus groups of other parents in addition to partnering with another organization to examine data on school discipline and intervention program implementation. They used this data to press the district to follow through on its commitments and to provide specific recommendations toward realizing a "culture of dignity" in South Los Angeles schools (CADRE, 2017). Youth Participatory Action Research (YPAR) also engages young people in identifying issues of concern, collecting data about them, and using the data to advocate for change (Cammarota & Fine, 2008; Fox et al., 2010; Mirra, Filipiak, & Garcia, 2015). These practices leverage data to transform power; in these efforts, families exercise their agency to collect and use data toward aims that *they* determine. As described in the second part of the chapter, the community-based organization in our study generated new data by refining an existing survey, collecting data in community-responsive ways, and advocating with school and district leaders for better communication. In these cases, families and community groups are reclaiming data to compel schools or systems to become more responsive to their priorities and needs.

Another example of these types of practices in educational organizations is the use of data to reflect on and improve the organization itself. When families are engaged in a data inquiry process, the focus shifts from individual students and parents to the children for whom they share collective responsibility. Though sparse, the existing research suggests that engaging parents and community members in organizational decision-making can build a sense of legitimacy around identified problems and solutions, strengthen problem-solving capacity, enhance broader civic engagement, and improve student outcomes (Ishimaru, 2018; Rogers, Freelon, & Terriquez, 2012). In such approaches, families are no longer passive recipients of data but active participants and interpreters of data—they participate as knowers and doers. Such practices foster student and family agency and a sense of ownership over their own data, as they determine what data to collect and how to make sense of it. This process can also broaden or expand what "counts" as data. Some districts have even begun to hire "parent evaluators" to identify areas of concern, reach out to specific nondominant families to collect data, then analyze and present their research to the district (Superville, 2019). We'll examine how the organizations in our study each approached these efforts and explore tensions and opportunities to evolve such efforts to family leadership in educational change work.

Family Leadership in Data-Informed Transformation

Found infrequently, *family leadership in data-informed transformation* entails families acting as leaders and decision-makers when using data to make consequential decisions about organizational transformation. In such practices, families not only influence determinations about what data to collect and participate in data interpretation; they play an integral part in decision-making and co-creating solutions for organizational change based on the data. This level requires ongoing collaboration between families and systems-based educators and actors. In the examples above, community organizing groups would not only hold up data about a lack of implementation or communication, they would have the influence and partnerships with school leaders to be *part* of implementing strategies to address the problem. Likewise, within schools and other educational organizations, inquiry processes would move from episodic engagements with families and data toward ongoing and continuous *joint* work to reflect, collect data, and transform how the organization operates, especially the everyday activities of teaching, learning, and schooling. Although such examples are few and hard to come by, family leadership practices *can* be cultivated between districts, students, families, and community organizers and organizations. Over time, as described in the second half of this chapter, two of the organizations in this chapter (notably, both community-based organizations) have worked to evolve practices toward family leadership in decision-making and organizational transformation work.

Unknown Possibilities for Families and Data

Finally, echoing Mansfield, Welton, and Halx's (2012) adaptation of the student voice pyramid, we added a final category at the top of the pyramid to suggest that we have much yet to learn about the potential for how families might interact with or use data toward transformative ends. There is exceedingly little research about how nondominant families, young people, educators, researchers, and other actors might mobilize and use "metrics that matter"[4] to dismantle oppression and work toward liberation in and out of schools. For instance, as our colleagues note, family and community partnerships tend to be adult-centric. Two-generation intervention models target low-income adults and children in the same family; they provide education, job training, parenting supports, or other health and social services to adults and early childhood education and sometimes counseling or health care for children (Chase-Lansdale & Brooks-Gunn, 2014). Such efforts emphasize addressing the basic needs of individuals within a family in order to get a "multiplier" effect; fostering agency or leadership for changing systems is generally not part of such models. A step into unknown possibilities for families and data might move toward truly intergenerational collaborations, in which young people and their caregivers shared cultural practices, knowledge, *and data* to create solutions together through their interactions and joint work. Efforts to realize cross-racial and cross-geography solidarities might also move into the arena of the possible. The possible dimensions of what lies beyond family leadership in transformation is speculative at best, but given the relative nascency of this area of work, we strongly suspect there are possibilities yet unrecognized that go beyond our current inquiries and conceptualizations.

A MODEL OF DATA INQUIRY FOR EQUITABLE COLLABORATION

Although the levels of the pyramid may appear to be neatly delineated categories, the messiness of on-the-ground work is such that one might identify—even within a single organization over time—everything from deficit-based conventional data practices to those fostering family leadership in organizational change. Thus, even though they were all working toward equitable collaborations with families and communities, each of the three research partnerships our team worked with emphasized a different aspect of their inquiry process.

The model we elaborate below (see Figure 5.2) was based initially on Community Place's "data carousel" process (Holcomb, 2004). It highlights six key phases or stages of a data inquiry process (see the Equitable Parent-School Collaboration website [www.education.uw.edu/epsc/] for additional resources and information). For the purposes of this chapter, we highlight three of these phases—Questioning, Engaging, and Making Sense—to demonstrate how *undertaking change as collective inquiry* can build joint capacity and foster more just schools and educational organizations.

To illustrate particular practices in these three phases, we highlight work we did in partnership with three educational organizations:[5] Community Place (CP), an early childhood program run by a community-based agency; the Riverview School District, a diversifying suburban K–12 school district in the Pacific Northwest; and SESEC (Southeast Seattle Education Coalition), a neighborhood-based education coalition to examine and evolve a model for using data inquiry to leverage parent and family expertise and decision-making in educational improvement

Figure 5.2. Illustrating Practices from Three Phases of Collective Inquiry

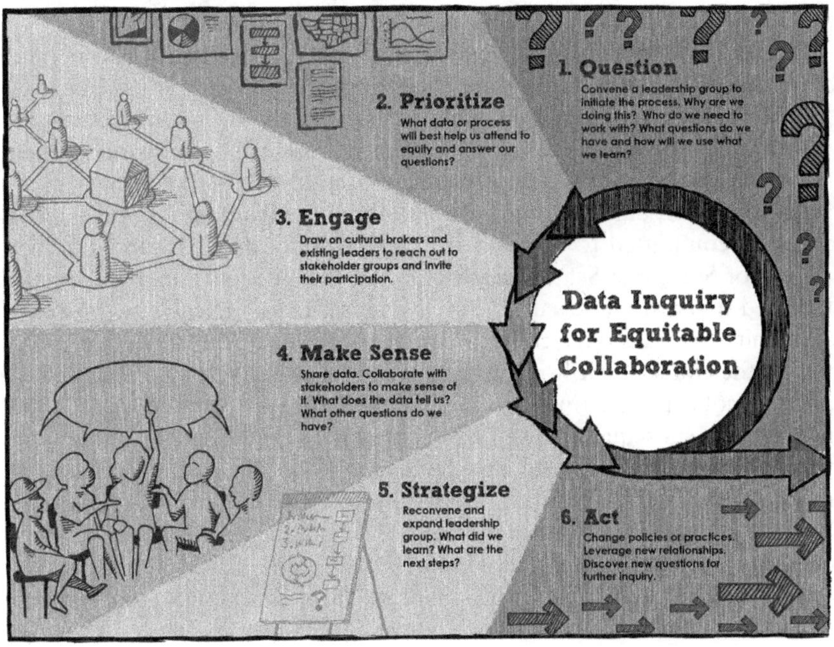

Figure by Paul Kuttner. © Copyright 2015 University of Washington.

efforts.[6] Community Place served as the starting place for our explorations, as they sought to use "data carousel" events to engage multiple stakeholders around an issue or problem of practice to improve their programming, services, and outcomes. The data carousel was a structured annual event at which staff, parents, and community partners collectively examined and interrogated existing program data together. Participants considered questions such as "What do these data seem to tell us? What do they not tell us? What else would we need to know?" (Holcomb, 2004, p. 114). We learned from and with Community Place as they developed their data carousel over the course of 4 years. Because their process served as the foundation for evolving the model and constituted our most intensive research, we foreground data from their implementations.

In 2014–2015, our team drew on the model of data inquiry for equitable collaborations as well as a previously designed family engagement survey in our partnership with district leaders and two focal elementary schools in the Riverview School District. Riverview is a diverse, high-poverty suburban school district outside a major urban center in the Pacific Northwest. The district had sought out and secured a federal grant to do focused work around family engagement in two Title 1 schools as part of a broader regional effort to bolster family and community engagement. The schools partnered with community-based organizations, the district, and our team to leverage the survey as a means of identifying and developing parent leaders, as well as surfacing priorities for school improvement.

Finally, we shared what we learned from Community Place and Riverview School District with SESEC to inform their inquiry process to redesign and use the family engagement survey to identify community priorities, a process which they have also built from and evolved over 4 years and counting. SESEC is a neighborhood-based coalition of community-based organizations, educators, community leaders, families, and caregivers committed to empowering families of color and improving education for Southeast Seattle students. Their first collective inquiry process mobilized a racially and culturally diverse set of organizations toward a community-engaged data collection process that cultivated new relationships in the community. It resulted in a dataset of immigrant, refugee, and parent-of-color perspectives on schools that had never before existed in the district. They subsequently used a subset of the survey data to partner with the Chinese Information and Service Center (CISC) in conversations with immigrant Toishanese families (a rural ethnic community from southeast China outside of Hong Kong and Canton). Those design sessions grew into an event at which families shared stories and spoke directly to school officials and district administrators to share their experiences and demand specific changes in their children's schools.

In the next part of the chapter, we describe each focal stage within the context of the entire cycle and illuminate practices across the three settings that shed light on fostering the *agency* and *leadership* of families and educators around expansive forms of data in the journey toward more just educational organizations.

QUESTIONING PHASE

Before jumping to the data itself, our partners realized that an initial stage of questioning was vital for ensuring a generative process. We encapsulate this phase in two primary questions: Why are we doing this? How should we set the table? Across our case study sites, the organizations endeavored to *begin with families and communities* to shift from compliance or accountability modes to reclaiming data as a tool for educational change and equity-focused improvement.

Why Are We Doing This? From External Validation to Ownership

Across differences in the settings and intentions of our partner sites, all three took up practices that moved from a compliance mindset in working with data about students and families (the bottom of the pyramid) to reclaiming data for their own purposes, understandings, and organizational improvement (Family Agency in Data Inquiry). The organizations all began with the intent of using data to gain validation or to satisfy an external powered audience. In the Riverview School District, a large federal grant spurred district interest and new resources to promote family engagement in two elementary schools, so their process began as a strategy to comply with grant expectations. Community Place had a similar obligation through their annual federally mandated self-assessment process to examine data to "drive" program improvement in Head Start and Early Head Start:

> With self-assessment, it's a requirement. Really what you're doing is at some point in the year you're reflecting back and saying 'How did our systems and services function?' There's an opportunity to do a lot of interviews and an opportunity to really build data . . . It [the data] is sitting there maybe to do more . . . I'd heard from staff all about self-assessment. It was a compliance tracking tool. That's all it was. I was like, this is a complete utter waste of time. (Allison and Victor interview, February 6, 2014)

Although SESEC was not beholden to a federal funding agency, the members initially approached the data collection as means of challenging the district's presumption that the low participation rates in prior surveys among families of color and immigrant families meant meaningful data could not be gathered from nondominant families in Southeast Seattle (they also sought to challenge the implicit assumption, by extension, that these families did not prioritize education). Members of SESEC's coalition may have also anticipated using the data to hold the district accountable for equitable engagement opportunities.

Many data processes start and end with these compliance and accountability goals, but these organizations each recognized data as an opportunity to move beyond externally driven agendas. For instance, the Community Place leadership saw the potential for using self-assessment data to foster learning, especially among their staff:

> I think what we're trying to do is create a learning community. That's our goal. The habits within that are really, they fit with this because, again, the notion, stopping what you're doing . . . and reflecting and asking some questions and deciding, "Are we good? If we are, great. There's things we want to do differently but what are those?" That's the conversation we wanted everybody in. (Allison and Victor interview, February 6, 2014)

In their first year, CP directors offered little direction and sought to give "ownership" of the process to their staff, which resulted in confusion, frustration, and even some tears about the purpose of the data carousel as organizational staff attempted to comply with what they imagined the directors wanted. A stressed-out and harried staff member was told to "calm down" by the director when she was visibly anxious about the event and later told us that she would be "happy when this [data carousel] was over" (Community Place fieldnotes, 2014).

With support from our research partnership over subsequent years and iterations, CP directors and staff redesigned their approach from an isolated, one-time event to a multifaceted, ongoing process to "develop a more reflective learning culture" with the help of families, caregivers, and community partners. Early on, they moved away from questions about what the data are "telling" us toward reorienting the conversations around families and their participation, feedback, and insights. Candice, a department director explained, "we started with talking about which questions we wanted to answer. . . . It turned out we didn't always have data that would answer that question."

CP created design teams of staff from across programs to take the lead on data, outreach, and logistics. The data team generated meaningful questions that cut across programs and identified data that could foster reflection about those questions. For instance, one question related to family outreach for student recruitment and enrollment, and the data team gathered enrollment data from each program and records of family communications by home visitors and family support workers. The design teams adopted the theme of "Tinker, Play, Collaborate, and Reflect" as a guiding vision for the work and sought out facilitation training (with the presumption that learning to better facilitate conversations with families and other educators was a form of capacity building that would serve the organization beyond the data carousel event itself). By leaning into the questions of purpose and organizing around a shared vision, organizational staff began to take ownership of the data carousel, not so much as a single event but as a *process* to improve their own organization and learn together with families and community partners. This shift in purpose also changed how staff understood the role of families in the process, from passive recipients of compliance reports to fellow sense-makers and central organizational stakeholders invested in improving Community Place. As they continued to evolve their inquiry, CP design teams began to consider how families might be part of deciding what questions to ask and how to share the data that would be collected.

How Should We Set the Table?

Building from the insights of an inquiry process led initially only by program staff at Community Place, both Riverview District and SESEC *began* their processes with family and community expertise at the table alongside key organizational leaders and staff. In the case of Riverview, the inquiry process began not only with school and district leaders (including teacher leaders) but with the existing community partners (in this case, the two school PTAs, the YMCA after-school program, and the county library) as well as smaller organizations focused on supporting specific communities (for instance, a grassroots group that worked with Latinx families and a nonprofit organization focused on supporting families whose children have special needs).

Similarly, SESEC drew on its existing network of community-based organizations and intentionally worked to ensure that the diverse racial and cultural communities in their neighborhood were part of the process from the beginning. As racial equity had long been a focus for SESEC, the coalition routinely used a set of norms that centered communities of color in their meetings and work. However, they recognized that simply bringing a diverse group of organizations together and using racial equity–focused norms was not sufficient, given the likely negative histories and experiences of their communities with data.

Part of "setting the table" in SESEC's case included explicitly naming the dynamic of weaponized data in communities of color. The first gathering of the design team began with Dr. Jondou Chen facilitating a conversation asking how each of the members and their communities had experienced data in the past. Starting the conversation with the experiences of communities of color with data (and with researchers) opened space to share how data has both supported and negatively impacted community efforts, particularly in terms of reinforcing views of communities of color as "deficient." Importantly, the conversation led the design team to expand the purpose of the survey project. As Erin Okuno, the executive director, explained:

> This conversation led us to decide the project had to build trust. Anything we did in the project had to build trust with each other, the community, etc. At decision points we asked, 'what would build trust?' and that led us to the answer.

While it was still essential to engage low-income, immigrant, refugee, communities of color labeled by schools as "hard to reach" or "uninterested," the survey process itself became about collecting, analyzing, and reclaiming data to build and rebuild trust between the partnering organizations, the University of Washington, and the community.

ENGAGING PHASE

Although "Prioritizing" is the second phase of the process we evolved from the CP data carousel, we highlight the "Engaging" phase here next, since the practices we saw our partner organizations take up in this phase illuminate particular efforts to transform power and foster reciprocity and agency. This phase entails enlisting families and other stakeholders in collecting data, particularly with the help of cultural brokers (as described in Chapter 4). Because CP relied primarily on more conventional approaches to invite families to their culminating data carousel event (e.g., teacher invitations, flyers, and emails), we focus primarily on how Riverview and SESEC used this phase of the process to cultivate family and community leadership, foster reciprocity across expanded relational networks, and build collective agency and capacity around data.

Identifying Latinx Parent Leaders in Riverview

At Riverview, district leaders and community partners used data collection for a previously developed family engagement survey[7] to identify nondominant parents—particularly Latinx in that context—who might act as cultural brokers and leaders in the school. The year started with a community cultural event at the park across from the school that explicitly centered the Latinx community, entitled "Celebrate our Heritage and the Education of Our Children." The event included a table staffed by Sofia and Marta, two Spanish-speaking community partners, whose roles were solely to listen to concerns and issues from parents about their schools and the district, and to foster relationships with parents. To the surprise of many on the planning team, the table had a long line all evening. Sofia and Marta collected over 100 names, with contact information. They later followed up with 24 Latinx parents via personal phone calls to explore their interest in helping to lead engagement work in the schools. In retrospect, this approach might be understood as an adaptation of "one-on-ones," a staple organizer practice to initiate relationships, gain insights into people's concerns and motivations, and identify potential leaders (Warren et al., 2011). Of those parents, eight Latina mothers later came together with Sofia and Marta as a group to debrief the community event, strategize about further outreach, discuss the survey and its purpose, and walk through each item in the Spanish-language version of the survey to better understand the concepts. In tandem with community partner efforts and conventional school-based outreach (e.g., flyers and surveys sent home with students, electronic links and notes in the newsletter, etc.), these Latina parent leaders supported other parents in completing surveys at drop-off and pick-up and at school events (like the PTA movie night).

Overall, these efforts boosted the proportion of families who responded to the survey, resulting in a 45% and 40% response rate in each school, respectively, a marked increase for these schools, particularly among families who did not speak English at home.[8] The Riverview case provides useful insights about more culturally responsive approaches to collecting data from nondominant families, but at the end of the day their strategies were not simply to boost response rates on their survey. Rather, the process identified and activated cultural brokers to expand the family-based relational networks at their schools and take up other aspects of the work. For example, a subset of the parent leaders later became facilitators for the schools' family engagement academies.

Cultivating Community Leadership and Capacity at SESEC

In line with their priority of cultivating trust in the community while collecting a robust, inclusive dataset, SESEC invested most of its energies in the "engage" phase. The partnering organizational leaders strategized about the needs of their communities and the types of supports necessary to authentically engage families in the data collection process. SESEC intentionally sought to design an inquiry process that would be culturally specific and responsive to each of the cultural communities, even if that pushed against "scientific best practices" in data collection. They expanded the survey translation and administered the survey in 10 languages[9] and took a multifaceted approach using multiple modes, determined by members of the cultural communities themselves. For example, Graham Hill Elementary asked for the survey to be online so they could route families to the computer lab after parent–teacher conferences. Wanting more data from Spanish-speaking families, Graham Hill included the survey in their Latino Family night with community volunteers to assist families and build relationships. The effort resulted in a 100% response rate for the evening. Powerful Voices YMCA, an after-school enrichment program, handed out paper copies in prestamped envelopes for students to take home and mail back. The Chinese Information Service Center (CISC) supported their families through focus group–like meetings to talk through and complete the survey. Idil, a multilingual Somali parent, went door-to-door in the New Holly neighborhood, a subsidized housing community, to directly engage with East African families. As she told Erin Okuno, the director of SESEC:

> This is really hard to knock on doors. My people don't know what to say. I talked to a lady from Ethiopia who refused to do the survey. Instead of taking the survey she asked if she could tell me what she prays to God. She told me she tells Jesus her problems her children have in school. I told her the survey will help and it is a powerful way to tell schools what we want. I completed the survey by listening to what she prayed for. (Okuno & Chen, 2016)

Erin explained that this interaction literally represented "a leap of faith for both women." One parent was Muslim and the other Christian, so "for this to take place meant setting aside religious differences in the name of . . . education." As a result of SESEC's efforts to support their members in culturally specific and community-driven data collection, they surveyed 639 families, of whom 82.8% were people of color, 61.8%

were members of immigrant families, and 64.8% qualified for free and reduced-price lunch. Collectively, they spoke 25 different primary home languages other than English.

MAKING SENSE PHASE

No matter how many different ways we crunch the numbers or make fancy charts, data never speaks for itself. People have to "make sense" of the data to make it meaningful and relevant to their local contexts. Teachers typically examine statistics and charts only with other teachers, on designated Data Days or during after-school meetings, but this conventional sense-making can often reinforce deficit narratives (Bertrand & Marsh, 2015; Irby, 2018). Instead, the "Making Sense" phase of data inquiry for equitable collaboration brings families, educators, community members, and other organizational stakeholders into conversation *with each other* about data in order to improve the work of the organization, while also building substantive relationships.

This phase differed significantly across the three settings; perhaps it represents a critical juncture for reverting to dominant dynamics or evolving toward more robust relationships and joint work. Community Place used this phase as their culminating event and a primary means to build relationships and deepen insights about the organization with families and community partners. Meanwhile, in Riverview, this phase never came to fruition. Dominant routines of schools prevailed, and principals' actions functioned to gate-keep the data from families and community partners and enable business-as-usual to proceed. Principals claimed "workload issues" and utilized their positional power with their supervisors in the district to stop efforts. Finally, SESEC hosted a community summit (as well as additional school-specific and organizational events) to foster collective sense-making of the data and identify strategic priorities for the organization's work in the coming year. Because such distinct dynamics played out in each setting, we narrate this phase for each organization separately.

Evolving Engagement at Community Place

Community Place's first data carousels consisted of "stations" featuring mostly poster boards of compliance data designed to showcase program accomplishments. Staff narrated the data and obtained feedback from families and community partners, who rotated periodically between stations (the early literacy vignette from the Head Start classroom came from this first year). In subsequent years, CP shaped the data carousel as family engagement events that provided opportunities to build relationships, foster deep listening, and cultivate reciprocity between staff, families, and community partners. For example, staff of color opened the Early Head Start (EHS) carousel with cultural practices to create a welcoming environment and foster the comfort and trust needed to build reciprocity. The cultural opening invited everyone to participate in a traditional Ethiopian coffee ceremony, hear Vietnamese songs and poems, and eat fresh homemade Mexican tortillas prior to any talk of data or program improvement. Lorraine, an EHS program manager explained the purpose of the cultural opening:

> The cultural piece, made it more exciting and fun. It really showed who we are as EHS. It was reflective of our families and of our staff. I liked that it was staff that wouldn't normally step forward and they put themselves out there, so it was a chance for professional growth. They volunteered. It's not necessarily about the coffee or tea but it was showing how we value that.

Because EHS staff themselves shared these practices as part of their broader identities, they opened a relational space with the families (who were predominantly families of color) in their program. This move emphasized their shared cultural communities and practices, de-centered the data, and challenged conventional power dynamics between teachers, administrators, and families.

Building from this experience, Community Place designed their subsequent data carousel to be more family-centered, participatory, and conducive to deeper conversations. On the day of the event that year, we walked into a large gathering room with about 25 round tables with seating for 8–10 people at each. We got our name tags, and the airy room was already alive with sounds of laughter, chatter in different languages, and children's voices; the aroma of warm food and coffee wafted from the corner; and bright, colorful balloons floated from each table, showcasing numbers so we could find our way easily to our assigned tables. Since when did data seem so fun? So many families and community partners came to participate that the main room was not large enough to hold everyone, so staff added three overflow rooms. Each table had a mix of staff, community partners, and families. Several language-specific tables hosted conversations in Somali or Spanish, but others had interpreters and the discussion proceeded in multiple languages. A facilitator sat at each table to ensure each person would have the opportunity to share his or her perspectives on sets of simple data displays, and a designated note-taker kept track of the conversation for later sharing. After a brief introduction by the directors, the groups dug into conversation.

For 2 hours the table groups appeared in deep, sometimes animated discussions. As Victor, an early learning director, explained:

> We changed how we structured the event so that instead of going around the room we are going to stay together in the table groups. That way people can have deeper conversations. We are looking at

> the data together to find out did we do what we said we were going to do. We can't sit in our offices alone and make good decisions, we need help from the community.

CP also focused on key questions that the program wanted to investigate for organizational improvement, drawing data from across programs as evidence to examine. For example, one question focused participants on staff diversity data and asked participants to talk about the extent to which they felt it was important for program staff to share the language and culture of families in their program. At one table, this led to rich and challenging questions about race and leadership. Participants noticed that the more significant the role and responsibility became in the organizational hierarchy of CP, the less frequently those positions were occupied by individuals whose race, culture, or language matched those of CP families. This observation aligns with the tendency of organizations to segregate internally in racially-structured hierarchies (Ray, 2019). A parent of color at the table then shared experiences in which she perceived white directors had not been responsive to issues she had raised. In reflecting on the event, Allison, a program director noted,

> We have a lot more feedback than we have in the past. In the past, we struggled to get beyond looking at the data. It was harder to get into the richer conversations where more questions are asked and more wonderings. We got tons of really good feedback.

Thus, the combination of family, community, research, and educator perspectives on new or different forms of data (collected to address meaningful questions) enabled a deeper examination of organizational-level challenges.

Defaulting to Dominant Routines at Riverview School District

When our team shared the Riverview data with the original planning team, the principals shared their intent to organize opportunities for families and educators to engage with the data together. However, with the end of the school year imminent and district personnel changes underway, the dominant paradigm of compliance and accountability reasserted itself. Despite questions from both district and community partners, no further action was instigated by school personnel. Both principals seemed to use their positional authority to stymie further engagement with the data. Although one principal facilitated a discussion of the data with her building leadership team, a year later, one of the Latina parent leaders asked our research team, "What ever happened with that data we collected?"

This example represents how processes with good intention can begin in powerful ways and then actually reinforce dominant, inequitable dynamics in family–school relations. We did not have an opportunity to follow up, so we do not know why the principals did not follow through. Perhaps they felt too busy with other demands (a rationale we often hear) or felt threatened by the data within a high-stakes accountability policy context. The departure of the district leader who had played a crucial coaching role probably compounded pre-existing power imbalances between community partners, parent leaders, and school leaders. Without a counterweight at the district level, the default organizational response kept the data in the hands of those with power. Thus, the ability of the principals to control and constrain further action in relation to the data served to reinforce the status quo. However, years later, the district still touts the success of the family engagement initiatives at those two schools, so it also raises the possibility that the parent leadership and cultural brokering practices initiated through the inquiry process remain as resources in those communities, even if the data inquiry itself never fully realized its aims. This experience also partly fueled our team's interest in exploring how the model might play out differently if community-based organizations were at the helm, and schools and educators were invited to participate on the organizations' terms rather than on their own.

Setting Organizational Priorities at SESEC

At SESEC, the design team prepared the data for a community summit that included over 60 community members and organizational partners.[10] For SESEC leaders, the summit represented an important event to demonstrate accountability to the community and to provide space for members to feel ownership over "*their* data." After a brief high-level presentation about key findings and survey processes and a review of racial equity norms, summit participants broke into racial affinity groups for those identifying as white, multiracial, and people of color. Each table examined the survey data disaggregated by specific racial and cultural communities, including white, people of color, biracial, East Asian, African American, African immigrant, Latinx, Southeast Asian, Native/Indigenous, and Pacific Islander. Facilitators at each affinity group table guided community members through a protocol to discuss the data from the heart ("seeing this data makes me feel . . ."), the head ("moving ahead I'm thinking or want us to know . . ."), and the hands ("moving ahead I want to or I want us to . . .").

While some tension arose—for instance, some in the white affinity group felt uncomfortable being separated from conversations with people of color—SESEC intentionally prioritized the communities of color present so they had time and space to share how the data resonated with their own experiences. The SESEC director clarified that the affinity group conversations were not meant to enable people to jump into "action" but to allow each group to sit with and "own" their own data. Following these discussions, participants split into role-based groups of families of color, community allies, educators, and education administrators to strategize and plan next steps.

TENSIONS AND OPPORTUNITIES IN STRATEGIZING AND MOVING TO ACTION

The final two phases of the inquiry process, Strategize and Act, raised specific tensions and opportunities across the three organizations. The Strategize phase involves reconvening and reflecting about the data inquiry process to consider what was learned and what next steps might be in distilling conversations and proposing change. The Act phase involves taking action on what was learned for organizational improvement. Both CP and SESEC struggled to move their rich discussions and interactions with families into specific organizational change, though the contexts and focus for their inquiries differed.

In Community Place's case, the post-carousel staff debrief meetings included ample reflection, but there was little synthesis about how feedback and insights could lead to concrete plans for organization-wide change. Although there was a broad sense that the conversations with families and community partners impacted organizational planning, the CP debriefs and planning tended to focus on how to improve the data inquiry process and carousel events themselves, rather than how insights from the sense-making conversations might contribute toward broader organizational changes.

In the case of SESEC, the data summit did result in a set of priorities for the coalition, but because the focus of the inquiry was on area schools and the district rather than on SESEC itself, the coalition was limited in its ability to make organizational changes directly. Rather, as described above, they partnered with (CISC), a Chinese social service organization, to support Toishanese parents in continuing their conversations and advocating with school and district leaders for improved communication. As a result of their advocacy, one elementary school added an additional parent–teacher conference to their typical schedule. Erin also felt that individual teachers recognized the importance of more positive, proactive communication with families, and changes in the district's robocalls may also have been related to the CISC advocacy. Lacking an on-the-ground daily partnership with the schools, though, SESEC and CISC were limited in their ability to be part of implementing additional changes. However, their conversations laid the groundwork for a broader process with a larger group of SESEC's partners. SESEC's subsequent design sessions with 15 organizations sought to build facilitative capacity among their partner organizations and foster inclusive intergenerational spaces and cross-racial solidarities. Thus, the dynamic of making sense of data to inform local schools' improvement rather than their own organization related to the group's vision of itself as a convener and broker in a broader coalition. Like CP, SESEC has continued their inquiry process as an iterative practice to grow toward realizing family leadership in data-informed improvement.

CONCLUSIONS

The strategies and practices we highlighted in the three phases of data inquiry for equitable collaboration illuminate ways forward for moving from data *about* students and families or families as a *source* of data to family *agency* and *leadership* in joint inquiry for improving and transforming organizations. While aspects of these educational organizations' approaches are yet works in progress, Community Place's and SESEC's adoption of collective inquiry with families as an ongoing organizational routine suggests a source of organizational learning identified by scholars as essential for addressing educational disparities and inequities (Bensimon, 2005). Their efforts help us to visualize how to move beyond the sole use of deficiency or accountability-driven metrics of individualistic academic success normed on white, middle-class behaviors and outcomes. Although the sites took up different kinds of data in their inquiries, all three struggled with accessing data to address the pressing issues they wanted to know more about, as there was little or no overlap between existing accountability metrics and measures about the outcomes of concern for families and communities. Rather, all three recognized the need to develop and collect new measures that would attend to the dynamics, relationships, experiences, and priorities of families and communities—when a similar dynamic arose in a subsequent project, we came to call these "measures that matter." Nonetheless, by approaching data inquiry as a *vehicle* for repairing and building politicized trust and fostering transformative agency, these approaches open the door to exploring, defining, and pursuing more ambitious aims of holistic human flourishing, community-determined well-being, and educational justice.

Another way forward toward evolving family leadership practices in educational change involves participatory design research—what we and our colleagues in the Family Leadership Design Collaborative have come to call solidarity-driven co-design. The use of the term "solidarity-driven" is quite intentional. Recall the talk of data "driving" decision-making from the opening of this chapter? How many of us get in our car and expect it to drive us somewhere important on its own? Data doesn't drive. People do. And we "drive" toward destinations that matter for ourselves and our work, families, or communities—for particular reasons and aims. The final two chapters of this book begin to explore what it might look like to "drive" toward solidarities in fostering educational justice and community well-being.

Rewriting Moment-to-Moment Interactions

Families as Co-Designers

> Everyone believes that parents and teachers should be allies and partners. After all, they are both engaged in the important and precious work of raising, guiding and teaching our children. But more often than not, parents and teachers feel estranged from and suspicious of each other. Their relationship tends to be competitive and adversarial rather than collaborative and empathetic. Their encounters feel embattled rather than peaceful and productive. (Lawrence-Lightfoot, 2004, xxi)

This chapter focuses on the granular-level daily practices and strategies that can catalyze (or constrain) familial agency and collaboration with educators in everyday interactions *within* schools. These moments may seem insignificant given the scale of complex educational systems. But whether within a cross-sector collaborative context or a single complex organization, the daily interactions between families and educators constitute everyday moments that are also microcosms of their broader systems. Recall the brief episodes featured in Chapter 3, in which parents narrated how racial inequities play out in schools. These interactions are pivot points at which we can either reinforce or transform power and systemic practices. Rather than considering these moments as incidental interactions, I see them as layered moments that reflect histories, structures, underlying assumptions, and prior activity, as well as future possibilities. For instance, when we notice an uneven power dynamic between a parent of color and a white teacher, we are also observing longstanding histories of oppression between schools and nondominant communities playing out in the discourse, cultural norms, and expectations, and outcomes of those interactions (Hands & Hubbard, 2011; Ippolito, 2015; Lawrence-Lightfoot, 2004; Schutz, 2006).

This doesn't mean that we are all automatons merely carrying out pre-scripted instructions; however, we often don't recognize the extent to which our daily practice is shaped by the dynamics at organizational and systemic scales. Thus, this chapter illustrates how the different scales operate *simultaneously*. I first offer a more detailed explanation of racialized institutional scripts as a concept to make those dynamics visible and explain how and why they are so durable across time and contexts. To keep the discussion grounded at the everyday individual level, I focus specifically on how racialized institutional scripts shape the interactions between nondominant families and teachers.

Second, this chapter offers theory and practices for change. Theories of sociocultural learning, race, and culture offer a powerful foundational idea for family–school relations and educational change work: Not just children, but *all* of us are in an ongoing process of learning as we go about our daily lives in and out of schools. Learning is not bounded by formal classrooms or structured formats—or even our conscious awareness. As adults, we are constantly making sense of the world around us, including how we understand an issue or topic under discussion, how we act out particular roles (like those of "parent" or "principal" in a given context), how we interpret the expectations of us from other people, how we decide how to behave and what to say (and don't say), and how we negotiate decisions about next steps. This means that even though histories, structures, and institutional assumptions powerfully shape how we "show up" and what we do in schools, our constant state of learning means we can also *change* our relationships, interactions, processes, and outcomes through everyday activity. It's through such collective learning for both families and educators that the study in this chapter aimed to replace historically rooted power asymmetries with new relationships and ways of interacting to co-create change.

Specifically, I elaborate practices from a collaborative research project with families, teachers, principals, and district leaders to illuminate how the four guiding principles in this book converged as part of a single iterative process to intervene in moment-to-moment interactions and reshape family–school relations. Angela Booker and Shelley Goldman (2016) refer to the spaces and opportunities for families to reclaim their agency as knowers and doers (in their case, of mathematics) as a kind of "systemic repair." Such efforts move us into the domain of participatory design research (PDR), which takes as a starting point two key notions: first, that research can be a vehicle not just for observing what already exists but also for designing and realizing change aligned with social justice; second, that formally trained scholars should not be the only ones to produce knowledge—that educators, families, and community members are also critical decision-makers and co-constructors of knowledge in research that builds toward educational justice (Bang & Vossoughi, 2016).

RACIALIZED INSTITUTIONAL SCRIPTS IN FAMILY–TEACHER RELATIONS

Despite the complex and often contested dynamics that shape family–school relations at systemic and school levels, nondominant families and teachers share expertise on the daily realities of students and are both invested in student success, as noted in the opening Lawrence-Lightfoot quote.

Collaboration at this micro level can directly impact students and their learning experiences on a momentary and daily scale. Indeed, the majority of the conventional parent involvement literature focuses on this level of interaction. In theory, coordination and reciprocal exchange of information and practices between the adults who spend the most time with young people can improve both parenting and teaching practices in ways that foster holistic learning and well-being for children. And yet, particularly amid intersections of race, culture, and class, we know this aspiration is rarely realized due to the histories, structures, and power embedded in schools. I turn now to unpacking the concept of racialized institutional scripts alluded to earlier to help explain the constraints on equitable parent–teacher collaboration in schools, particularly across lines of race and class.

The concept of institutional scripts derives from institutional theory, which largely focuses on how social structures shape organizational activities through rules and regulations, values and norms, and interpretations of the world shaped by cultural context (Powell & DiMaggio, 1991; Meyer & Rowan, 2006; W.R. Scott, 2013). In particular, institutional theory emphasizes the taken-for-granted school norms and routines that define individual identities, shape the actions that are associated with these identities, and even constrain the possible alternative identities and actions that might be imagined (Powell & DiMaggio, 1991; Jepperson, 1991; Meyer & Rowan, 2006). Institutional scripts are a blueprint for identities and actions for different roles within an educational organization. These scripts are "taken for granted" in the sense that they are accepted as reasonable and normal, in conscious or unconscious ways (Jepperson, 1991, p. 147). As I have illustrated in other chapters, the institutional scripts in U.S. schools assume families' passive support of the school's agenda. Especially parents from nondominant communities are expected to defer to educators as the sole source of expertise in educating their children (Ishimaru, 2014b). The dominant institutional scripts about parents in school favor involvement activities that conform to educators' expectations for individualistic parental support, especially through compliance behaviors (for instance, ensuring homework completion, discipline at home that is consistent with school discipline, and timely school attendance; Cooper, 2009b).

Like schools themselves, these institutional scripts are not neutral and do not come out of a vacuum. Race and culture infuse the institutional scripts enacted by parents and teachers in contexts of systemic inequity. These scripts and identities in schools are fundamentally shaped by broader racial narratives and stereotypes in society. They are also rooted in the history of a U.S. public education system designed to colonize or assimilate immigrant, native, and rural children into dominant American culture and into the industrial workforce (Tyack, 2000). Such historically rooted institutional scripts implicitly preclude more reciprocal engagement and collaborative leadership with teachers and other educators to improve teaching and learning in the school (Ishimaru, 2014b; Schutz, 2006; Shirley, 1997;

Warren, Hong, Rubin, & Uy, 2009). According to the U.S. Department of Education, over 80% of the public education teacher workforce is white, whereas more than half of the U.S. school-age student population (and their families) are now from communities of color (U.S. Department of Education, 2016). Given this context as well as the history of U.S. schools as vehicles for colonization and assimilation (Smith, 2012; Wolfe, 2006) then, racialization processes are woven into schooling practices, and racial and cultural differences are a daily reality of schooling for many teachers, students, and parents.

Scholars like Na'ilah Nasir (Nasir & Hand, 2006) have investigated how race, culture, and learning intersect for youth in and out of schools. In particular, she examined the relationship between the racial storylines about African American males in society, the racialized identities available to African American boys in different learning environments, and the engagement and learning of those youth (2009). Nasir and her colleagues (2012) highlighted how the predominant racial storylines about Black males portray them as "unintelligent, lazy, inclined towards criminality, and as constituting an endangered species" (p. 290). Such negative storylines also play out in the everyday interactions between students, teachers, and other school actors and become racialized institutional scripts that can preclude or constrain the development of agentic learning identities and engagement. In her 2011 study, Nasir demonstrated how African American boys developed positive and agentic mathematical identities outside of classrooms in the context of playing dominoes and basketball. In these out-of-school learning contexts, the boys saw themselves as knowers and doers, which led to their deep engagement in the learning. Likewise, Megan Bang and her research partners (2013, 2014) found that when they put Indigenous cultural practices, knowledge, and ways of being at the center of informal learning for Indigenous students, they nurtured agentic science learner identities that ran counter to the more typical dynamic of Indigenous erasure in schools. A critical takeaway across these and other studies (see Gutiérrez & Vossoughi, 2010; Lee, 2001) is that the racialized institutional scripts in a given environment have profound implications for individuals' engagement and learning.

If this is the case for students, it isn't much of a stretch to imagine that similar influences might shape how families engage in schools. The scripts in schools make available few racialized identities for nondominant parents. Likewise, these constrained identities and opportunities have implications for families' engagement and actions in schools, as well as teachers' engagement with and actions toward them. In practice, the "good parent" supports students where, when, and how educators deem appropriate (e.g., participating in fundraisers, classroom preparation, monitoring homework, talking to their child about going to college). They attend school parent nights and ask questions that further their understanding of the school's expectations and agenda, but do not call into question the school's agenda for their children or the professional judgment or authority of educators. These behaviors align with normative expectations and assumptions associated with white parents and families, as discussed in Chapter 1.

The *racialized* institutional scripts thus shape the possibilities for collective learning and agency between parents and teachers across divides of race, culture, and class—and become consequential for students as a result. Although the racialized scripts for nondominant parents share a largely negative connotation, they reflect the broader racial storylines in society and, thus, manifest in specific forms for families from different racial and cultural communities. The "problem parent" is often associated with African American (and sometimes African immigrant) parents who challenge educators in what are often perceived by (white) educators as "destructive" ways that interfere with or derail their child's achievement and undermine the professional authority and expertise of educators (Lareau & Horvat, 1999, p. 43; Wilson, 2019). For instance, Lareau and Horvat (1999) found that teachers in their study delegitimized working-class African American families' advocacy for their children and claims about patterns of racial injustice at the school, defining their interest and concerns as "singularly unhelpful" (p. 44). Despite the history of racial inequity in the school and broader community that shaped these contexts and provided warrant for the concerns, the teachers' reactions to parent demands and mistrust of the school led to what Lareau and Horvat (1999) referred to as "moments of exclusion" in which the school disadvantaged the child in her or his life trajectory.

However, social class appeared to mediate the relationship between Black parents and schools; although middle-class African American families shared concerns about racial discrimination toward their children, they often intervened in ways that adhered to educators' expectations of deference and support. Similarly, Diamond and Gomez (2004) also found that middle-class African American parents more often selected their children's schools and adopted supportive orientations to them, whereas working-class African American families were often assigned to schools in which they adopted a "reform-based orientation." Across socioeconomic class, though, African American families' higher mistrust of schools is hardly unwarranted, as evidenced by the racially disproportionate assignment to special education and to disciplinary referrals. The racialized scripts in schools disregard this legacy while dovetailing with broader societal stereotypes of angry Black women or men (Lewis & Diamond, 2015; Wilson, 2019).

The institutional script about the "hard to reach" parent (sometimes "lazy" parent) tends to be code for Latinx, other immigrant or refugee families, and sometimes Native American families who are presumed not to care about their children or their education, as evidenced by their absence from school events or lack of response to communications from the school (Delgado-Gaitan, 2001; Jimenez-Castellanos & Gonzalez, 2012; Olivos, 2006). This script frames Latinx parents as "uninvolved" or "uncaring"

(Valencia & Black, 2002). This script is misleading because cultural practices of many migrant Latino families constitute forms of parent involvement that are not recognized by schools (López, 2001); their absence from more conventional forms of parent involvement tend to be interpreted by white teachers and principals as evidence of a cultural disinterest in education (Valencia & Black, 2002). Similarly, Native families are often made invisible, assumed to be dysfunctional, or presumed to devalue education (Bang et al., 2018; Faircloth & Tippeconnic, 2013).

It's hardly a coincidence that the "problem" and "hard to reach" parents tend to be parents of color whose forms of participation often do not conform to predominantly white educators' expectations for parent involvement. These racialized institutional scripts are never absolute and vary by context. They may also exist alongside negative racialized scripts for white parents, and there may be seemingly positive identities available to nondominant parents as well. For instance, a racialized script of a "good" parent may also be envisioned as an immigrant Latino parent who defers to educators and places unquestioned faith in their authority (Carreón et al., 2005) or Asian parents who are seen as "model minorities" who work hard and passively do what is expected of them (Kao, 2004). Nonetheless, the unspoken rules of schools for families of color include normative scripts that are critical of parent engagement that extends beyond compliance to school agendas and expectations.

CHANGING RACIALIZED INSTITUTIONAL SCRIPTS

If racialized institutional scripts help us to understand why equitable parent–teacher collaboration is so constrained and rare in schools, how might they change? Although promising practices and models of equitable family–school collaboration do exist, we have a dearth of theories and practices about how to enact more equitable parent–teacher relations in schools. I next look to theories of learning to envision how collective agency might be developed not only across roles (parent/teacher) but across historically rooted boundaries of race, class, professional status, and perceived expertise in ways that might reallocate power and influence, rather than reinforce dominant interests.

To examine the micro-level, day-to-day social dynamics that can lead to change and transformation within organizations, I turn to sociocultural learning and third-generation cultural-historical activity theory (CHAT), in particular (see Engeström, 2001, for a more extensive overview of the origins and generations of CHAT). From this perspective, all learning is social and cultural in nature (involving both subjects and different communities) and is mediated by a variety of tools, norms, assumptions, labor division, and rules toward some object or goal (see Figure 6.1 for a representation of an activity system of parent–teacher relations with the elements referenced above). All of these objects, subjects, tools, and other aspects of an activity system are rooted historically and in broader sociocultural contexts.

Applying this theory to the context of family engagement, we might broaden our view to understand interactions between parents and teachers as part of an *activity system* of adult learning in which roles and identities are constantly being reinforced and negotiated toward the aim of supporting students in school. The normative actions associated with certain roles (e.g., "teacher," "parent") here manifest as rules that bound actions and as a division of labor that defines which actions are legitimate for whom; these are linked to broader sociohistorical contexts. The interactions between subjects (parents), community (educators), and tools (ranging from discourses and policies to newsletters and meeting agendas) are shaped by the rules and divisions of labor in collective, object-oriented activity. These adult interactions have implications not only for individual students but for the broader school and educational system within which parents and teachers operate.

Drawing on this lens enables us to make a key distinction. Conventional school-based models for parent involvement seek to "remediate" *individual* nondominant parents, implicitly framing them as a source of the problem. The racialized institutional scripts make such interactions seem normal in schools. However, this lens highlights how efforts to improve parent–teacher relations and, by extension, schooling more broadly, necessitate addressing the *entire activity system*—or set of interacting individuals, tools,

Figure 6.1. Family-School Activity System (adapted from Engeström, 2001)

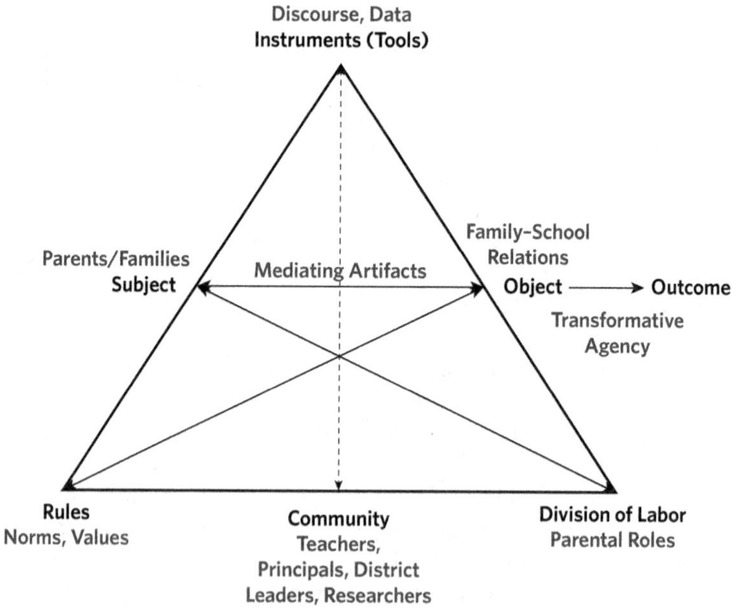

roles, assumptions, and goals and the broader sociocultural and historical contexts—within which parents and teachers interact. A focus on parent–teacher activity opens possibilities for "re-mediating" parent–teacher interactions and rewriting the rules and divisions of labor in the form of alternative scripts, or "counterscripts," that frame educational systems—not parents, families, or communities—as a source of inequities (Gutiérrez, 2008; Gutiérrez & Jurow, 2016; Gutiérrez & Vossoughi, 2010). This lens helps us orient toward fostering the collective agency of parents and teachers.

In particular, I want to highlight the concept of transformative agency (Engeström & Sannino, 2010; Haapasaari, Engeström, & Kerosuo, 2016). Transformative agency refers to the collective will and ability of individuals to break from a given frame and take initiatives to transform their activity over time (Engeström, 2007; Virkkunen, 2006). In this case, we are interested in how parents from marginalized communities might come together with teachers in racially inequitable educational institutions to collectively work through tensions, conflicts, and contradictions to "explicate and envision new possibilities" (Haapasaari et al., 2016, p. 2). In theory, then, focusing more broadly on the activity of family–school relations toward the end of transformative agency enables us to both acknowledge the power of racialized institutional scripts and structures in schooling contexts, and allow for the emergence of solidarities and collective action to change them.

PUTTING PRINCIPLES INTO PRACTICE IN PARTICIPATORY DESIGN-BASED RESEARCH

To illustrate these concepts in practice, I turn now to examples of how co-design concepts and practices might disrupt and shift the racialized institutional scripts about nondominant parents to build transformative agency between them and teachers. Drawing on participatory design research (PDR) methodology as a form of collective inquiry for transformative change, I highlight practices that: (a) begin with families and communities; (b) transform power; and (c) build reciprocity and transformative agency. Because the primary purpose of these examples is to illustrate co-design practices, I provide only a brief introduction to the context of the project (full accounting of the contexts, data, and analyses can be found in other articles—see Ishimaru, Lott, Torres, & O'Reilly-Diaz, 2019). I then describe PDR as a form of collective inquiry for change and overview the Kellogg co-design process prior to highlighting the specific practices that embodied the three remaining principles.

Kellogg School District Parent Education Curriculum Design

For 9 months in 2014, my research team (myself with Dr. Joe Lott, Dr. Melanie Quaempts [Strey], and a team of doctoral students including Dr.

Kathryn Torres, Dr. Ismael Fajardo, Dr. Jessica Salvador, Karen O'Reilly-Diaz, and Aditi Rajendran) partnered with Kellogg School District parents, teachers, principals, and district leaders in two high-poverty elementary schools to develop a new parent-education curriculum to help parents learn how to better support student learning. The curriculum was intended to replace the proprietary curriculum used in the district's existing 9-week parent academy, a train-the-trainer model using parent facilitators to teach mostly nondominant parents to navigate the school system and support their child's learning at home (i.e., a conventional parent involvement curriculum). Over the course of 13 design meetings held in one elementary school with two district leaders (multiracial Asian/Pacific American and African American), nine parents (four Latina, two African American, two Vietnamese, and one white parent), three teachers (white), two principals (white), and three to five researchers (African American, Asian American, and Latinx), the team identified priorities, developed lesson activities and design principles, piloted lessons, and refined them. Although both product (final curriculum) and process aimed to develop more productive relationships between families and schools to support student learning and success, the *process* of co-design comprised the primary focus of the study.

Co-design as Collective Inquiry Toward Transformative Change

Albeit different from the collective inquiry of data-informed organizational improvement described in Chapter 5, co-design represents another way of pursuing change as collective inquiry and joint work between families and educators. Our methodological approach in this project was central to the development of the co-design practices I illuminate below, so I want to take a moment to situate the methodologies in the broader field.

Participatory design research (PDR) is informed by and builds upon cultural historical activity theory and the change laboratories that have emerged from it (Cole, 1998; Engeström, 2001) as well as design research (Bell, 2004; Design Based Research Collaborative, 2003). As described earlier, design methods rooted in the learning sciences deliberately pose "how can" questions in order to generate knowledge and solutions toward new possibilities. In contrast to "how do" questions (understandings of the ways things currently are), "how can" questions aim research toward the future and the way things could be.

PDR is also shaped by critical, participatory, and community-engaged scholarship such as decolonizing methodologies (Patel, 2016; Smith, 2012), critical race theories (Brayboy, 2006; Ladson-Billings & Tate, 1995), participatory action research (Cammarota & Fine, 2008; Erickson, 1994); social design experiments (Gutiérrez, 2008; Gutiérrez & Jurow, 2016), community-based design experiments (Bang, Medin, Washinawatok, & Chapman, 2010); and community organizing and social movements (Anyon, 2009; Warren et al., 2011). Drawing from these approaches, PDR positions not only researchers and practitioners, but nondominant youth, families, and communities as co-designers of novel learning environments. Co-design processes within PDR attend to how the past shapes the present and constrains or opens possible futures, what scholars refer to as *critical historicity*. This understanding of historicity includes researchers' social locations and histories that, if unexamined, may "conceal racialized, classed, gendered, colonizing power dynamics, often under the guise of neutrality" (Bang & Vossoughi, 2016, p. 177).

Scholars of PDR have increasingly taken up issues of race, power, and the need to attend to critical historicity and relational dynamics in efforts to foster more equitable research partnerships (Vakil et al, 2016). The process of collaboration, particularly with historically marginalized communities, allows for the possibilities of authentic relationship formation, reciprocity, and accountability to one another and to the outcome. This project drew from PDR to explore how parents and educators might collaborate to design a parent engagement curriculum in ways that promote collective transformative agency. Drawing on these approaches, we can move beyond merely *documenting* deficit-based processes and historically rooted power asymmetries in family engagement toward beginning to *enact* equitable and justice-focused processes and solutions.

Through our work in the Family Leadership Design Collaborative (which I will discuss more in the final chapter), Dr. Megan Bang and I have come to define "solidarity-driven co-design" as a process of bringing diverse stakeholders together to collaborate in identifying issues, collectively imagining future possibilities, and iteratively designing novel solutions for change (see Ishimaru et al., 2018). Rather than centering data or centering the "object" of co-design (e.g., a particular learning outcome, tool, or environment), this approach to co-design aims to address both relationships and outcomes simultaneously. We seek to reconfigure the relationships and "rules of engagement" between families and educators through joint work generating new solutions. Solidarity-driven co-design aims to foster solidarities through collective inquiry by explicitly addressing and working to reconstruct how historically rooted power plays out in the process of co-constructing new knowledge and implementing change. Although the process I share below constituted in-depth, systematic empirical research, solidarity-driven co-design also offers insights for practitioner-based collective inquiry for educational transformation.

Overview of the Kellogg Curriculum Co-Design Process

In partnership with district leaders, we convened a design team of KSD parents, teachers, and principals to work with us (as researchers) and the district directors of student services and family engagement from two highly diverse, predominantly low-income elementary schools. The first sessions prioritized relationship-building among parents and helped them to identify common issues and priorities based on their experiences and concerns. Teachers, principals, and district leaders then joined the process to workshop priorities and develop lesson topics and plans. It was during the initial joint parent–educator session that racialized and powered tensions emerged between parents and educators. After examining transcript data from the prior meeting and reflecting on those dynamics, parents met on their own, then collected data from other parents to inform the bullying lesson and invited the teachers (but not principals) to rejoin the design process. Using jointly developed principles, brainstormed activities, and transcript data from the meetings, researchers drafted an initial lesson, and design team parents and teachers provided feedback for a next iteration. Design team members then rehearsed the refined lesson to test it, and parents on the team subsequently piloted the lesson in their native languages with a new set of parents. The parents reflected on the pilot and refined the lesson again, at which point principals rejoined the team. Finally, teachers from the design team used data from the sessions to draft the additional lessons, and the team reconvened a final time to reflect on the co-design process and observe lessons facilitated by others in a different school and district. All told, the team developed seven lessons that comprise the final curriculum: communication with teachers and schools (two parts), ensuring academic success, addressing bullying, fostering positive racial and cultural identities (two parts), and parent advocacy and leadership (see Appendix B for the final lesson topics and design principles).

1. Beginning with Families and Communities. First, we drew on co-design to disrupt the institutional scripts that position parents at the margins of schools by inviting them to become co-designers rather than research subjects or informants (Ishimaru, 2014b). Positioning parents as key decision-makers in the development of a parent education curriculum both acknowledged and challenged historical schooling practices that relegate parents to paper-cutting, chaperoning, and attendance at school events. Simply put, we began from the premise that parents were the experts on their own children and their own learning priorities and processes; the design team thus prioritized the expertise of families alongside that of professional educators, systems leaders, and researchers. However, simply inviting parents to the table would likely have defaulted to typical tokenizing dynamics had we not intentionally shaped *which* parents would be part of the process, *how the agenda* would be determined, and *how familial expertise* would be leveraged toward the dual aims of the project: creating a new parent curriculum and fostering solidarities between parents and educators.

To address which parents would be part of the co-design effort, we explicitly asked principals to invite parents who reflected the diverse racial and ethnic backgrounds of the student population in their schools. In particular, we asked the principals to invite parents of color who may not be involved in the way the school expected, such as by attending PTA meetings or by actively participating in other school events. In this way, we sought to diversify the typical actors in the broader ecology of family–school activity so that they might bring their distinct positions, histories, and experiences to the table. By intentionally reframing the role of low-income parents of color as experts, this design specification challenged educator assumptions about parents of color as barriers to student success by positioning them as "part of the solution" (Ishimaru, 2014a).

Beginning with families and communities also meant starting co-design by providing parents a dedicated space *without* educators present, thus enabling parents to build relationships, share their experiences, and determine priorities collaboratively in the relative absence of role-based power asymmetries. This move ensured that, rather than beginning from the aims of schools and setting parental expectations based on those outcomes, we were fostering parent relationships at the front end and infusing "critical historicity" (Bang, Faber, Gurneau, Marin, & Soto, 2015) in shaping the agenda. This also built a sense of solidarity and a foundation for collective power among parents (Warren et al., 2011).

Finally, consistent with critical race theories, the experiences and counternarratives of nondominant parents provided alternatives to dominant discourses and institutional scripts (Howard & Navarro, 2016; Ladson-Billings & Tate, 1995). Through the course of the study, we privileged families' stories and lived experiences as tools to draw out the distinctions between the performative aspects of school organizational routines and policies (what actually happens) and the ostensive (or idealized) notion often perceived by educational leaders and policymakers (Lewis & Diamond, 2015). Families' "lived theory" became a form of experiential expertise that shaped understandings and subsequent action in the co-design process (Barajas-López & Ishimaru, 2016).

2. Transforming Power. Second, the co-design process surfaced the dominant power asymmetries between parents and educators and worked to transform them by prompting design team members to reflect on their interactions in joint meetings and decision-making. After the parents shared their experiences and identified collective priorities for the lesson topics in the curriculum, the educators rejoined the team and parents shared the initial priorities they had developed together. At this point, the educators interacted with the parents in ways that aligned with the racialized institutional scripts to which they were accustomed. That is, the educators engaged in "listening to respond" and acted in ways that appeared to intimidate parents. For instance, they talked more than parents did and reframed parents' ideas in educator jargon, such as referencing "PBIS" (Positive Behavioral Intervention Supports) and emphasizing parents' need to learn to "navigate the schoolhouse." The principals, in particular, questioned parents' priorities on addressing bullying and racial identity in their schools and implied that the parents' purview was not about improving the school, but how they supported their own children at home. That is, principals' dominant assumptions about the division of labor and roles limited parental influence to matters that related strictly to their own children, particularly at home. The principals also framed the parents' desire to create a parent network to "resolve issues at the school" together as "so negative," and suggested that parents should come to the office for positive reasons more, such as introducing new babies or celebrating birthdays.

As the facilitators of this collaborative effort, our team was dismayed by these all-too-familiar dynamics. Our efforts to create the conditions for new, more equitable relations had quickly reverted to powered and racialized interactions. However, this tension served as a crucial catalyst in the process of fostering parent–teacher collective agency.

At the next meeting, we organized the meeting by role (i.e., parents, teachers, and principals/district leaders) to reflect on the interactions at the previous meeting and read a common excerpt of the meeting transcript as data. We used the data as "mirror material" (Engeström & Sannino, 2010) to make the interactions visible to the team. In reflecting on the meeting, parents heatedly pointed out their perceptions of educators getting "defensive," not listening, and dismissing their ideas. They discussed how the interactions in the meeting were typical of their broader interactions and histories with teachers and principals. One parent picked up the transcript and insisted, "This is what's going on!" as other parents nodded and made affirming sounds. She interpreted the design session interactions as an instantiation of the broader power dynamics between families and educators in schools.

As their discussion evolved, parents began to distinguish teachers from principals, noticing that some of the teachers were "really listening." Meanwhile, the principals, who met separately from the parents and teachers, read the *same* transcript excerpts the parents had read and expressed their perception that the dialogue reflected a positive collaboration between themselves and parents. The teachers, meanwhile, read the same transcript and noticed that parents' ideas were left behind when principals became active in the conversation. When asked how they thought the group should proceed as a team, the teachers expressed their interest in supporting parents in the process in whatever way the parents determined. These dramatically different interpretations of the very same meeting and data created an opening between parents and teachers, specifically in relation to their perceptions of power in the design team relational dynamics.

The co-design effort explicitly attended to issues of power and equity not only by putting this contradiction on the table, but by working to transform power asymmetries through adjustments in the process. Rather than researchers or district leaders deciding how to manage the situation or seeking to balance the perspectives equally, the parents collectively decided how to move forward (a key decision point in co-design). When, during the debate about how to proceed, one of the Latina mothers, Violeta, turned to me as "the professional" to make the decision, La'Kisha jumped in, reminding the group firmly, "It's our decision" (to which I readily agreed). Mary, a Vietnamese mother, proposed to invite the teachers back to the design team meetings, but not the principals, noting both teachers' knowledge and understanding of everyday interactions with their children, as well as the power dynamics with principals that might constrain teacher participation. Berenice, a Latina mother, agreed, explaining, "For surely, not the principals, because I think with the principals here, we're not able to get everything out." In this move, the parents transformed power by engaging teachers but positioning principals to the periphery in the design process for the time being. The parents also decided to collect data from other parents about bullying in schools to substantiate their claim about parent concerns to the principals and to get information about bullying from other parents as they prepared to create their bullying lesson.

Although the principals were eventually invited back into the process, they attended only a single meeting, at which the group used a protocol (a mediating tool) introduced by a district leader that structured feedback on a lesson draft that gave parents twice the opportunity to speak relative to that of educators. This strategy did allocate talk time more equitably, but the principals were not involved in the development or refining of the curriculum from that time forward (always citing their desire to remain involved but explaining that their hectic schedules limited their ability to attend).

3. Building Reciprocity and Transformative Agency. Finally, the co-design process built reciprocity and collective transformative agency between parents and teachers, in particular, through the process of developing, piloting, and refining the lessons in the parent curriculum. Starting from families and communities and transforming power cannot happen in the abstract or toward the sole end of building warm relationships. Because learning happens not only through the social and cultural dynamics between people but is also object-focused, efforts to shift family–educator relations must have some shared objective through which to build reciprocity and agency. In this case, the design principles underlying the curriculum served this objective, both for the lessons themselves and for the process of designing them. After the teachers rejoined the process, we supported the parent–teacher design team in jointly and iteratively developing a set of principles that would anchor each of the lessons they were designing. For example, the team felt it was important for activities to provide meaningful opportunities for family members to meet, make connections with one another, and share their hopes and dreams as well as common concerns or struggles in raising and educating their children. They also agreed that lessons should provide opportunities for parents to learn from each other (not simply receive information), to foster student success beyond school-centric definitions of academic achievement, and to develop their capacity to make change—both for their own children and for their schools.

For the design of each lesson, then, the team identified information they needed to develop the objectives and activities, which leveraged expertise from both parents and teachers and fostered reciprocity in building shared knowledge. For the bullying lesson, for example, parents on the team sought out other parents to determine issues to prioritize in addressing bullying. Teachers shared aspects of the new social-emotional curriculum adopted by the district to help ensure connections to what children were learning at school. Both parents and teachers sought out additional resources and information about bullying policies, responses, and initiatives. For the two lessons focused on fostering children's positive racial and cultural identities, parents shared their stories and experiences of how and when race matters, which led to profound learning for the white teachers. One of the white teachers reflected afterward that prior to hearing from the parents in the process, she had never before considered that children's racial and cultural identities were as important in their learning as any of the other content she taught.

Finally, the experience of piloting the bullying lesson with three groups of new parents (in English, Spanish, and Vietnamese) enabled design team parents to build new relationships with other parents but also deepened a sense of emerging agency among all the design team members to enact collective change. Particularly as they reflected on their learning in the process, both parents and teachers talked about possibilities for reshaping schools in spite of the top-down policies that seemed to constrain change. Mary, a design team parent, explained:

> This has been an empowering experience. I had the opportunity to go out into the community and started a conversation with other parents, to get feedback on issues and concerns that parents faced, it allowed me to see how important it was for parents to have a platform to network with other parents, to build relationships, offer support and resources.

Similarly, Lucy, a design team teacher, shared that her understanding of the expertise needed for education had shifted:

> My respect and understanding of families were greatly enhanced by my participation in the design process. I think that the greatest learning for me was that educators are great at thinking about what we want parents to know and do, but parents also have ideas about what they would like the school to be doing. If we only have the educators and legislators' voices, then we can't fully meet the needs of all students.

Schools typically focus on developing the individual agency of parents to advocate for their own children. In contrast, this process helped parents take hold of collective agency, which was focused on ensuring the success of *all* children (not just their own children) at school. Parents and teachers began to co-design new ways of interacting that disrupted the institutional scripts and transformed their joint activity over time to allow their roles and responsibilities to be more equitable. More than the curriculum itself, then, this emergent transformative agency became a key outcome of the co-design process (Engeström & Sannino, 2010; Haapasaari et al., 2016).

CO-DESIGN PRACTICES AS REWRITING RACIALIZED INSTITUTIONAL SCRIPTS

Though far from perfect, the co-design process described in this chapter offers examples of how we might begin to rewrite racialized institutional scripts in order to expand and foster collective parent–teacher agency within inequitable educational institutions. Through co-design practices centered on fostering equitable collaboration, we intentionally worked to build the conditions and opportunities for identities *beyond* the dominant racialized institutional scripts to be available to nondominant parents and families. Such identities entailed a form of agency and "self-authoring" (Nasir et al., 2012) that went beyond simply doing what they were told or resisting the school's authority—and beyond the false racialized binaries of "good/bad," involved/uninvolved parents. The parents in this case began to (re)claim their primacy over their children's learning and development. They framed themselves as essential team players—with teachers (and principals, in an ideal case)—who bring particular skills and knowledge to the "game" of school improvement, which they understood as a political process of organizational change. The parents also began to explicitly talk about power and their collective responsibility for schools to change. In this way, they began to renegotiate the terms of engagement with schools and reclaim their "epistemic authority" (Booker & Goldman, 2016). This process of reclaiming families' expertise about their own children's education and development represented a critical opportunity for systemic repair.

The case also suggests possibilities for making available new identities for teachers. We know that collective efficacy is vital for teachers of low-income students of color (Takahashi, 2011); participatory design theory and interventions offer potential for expanding this collective efficacy to include parents and address the intersectional dynamics of race, class, language, and professional status. For example, the teachers—all of whom were white women (like the vast majority of U.S. teachers)—began to see themselves as systems-based, white allies who could learn from parents' expertise about their children and their racialized experiences in schools to improve their own teaching and enact leadership with other teachers. Lucy, the white teacher, admitted that the process gave her a new appreciation for the importance of racial and cultural identities among her students, and later taught other teachers about racial microaggressions in a regional math education conference. She credited the co-design process as a space that enabled her to learn from parents about the complex dynamics of racial inequities.

REPOSITIONING RACIAL AND CULTURAL DIFFERENCES

Concerns about workforce diversity in education have recently come to the fore, particularly given a persistent "mismatch" between the racial and cultural makeup of the teaching profession and that of the student population. These longstanding issues have been heightened by newer research findings that the race of a teacher makes a difference for student learning and outcomes. For instance, Black students with Black teachers are associated with higher achievement scores and a higher likelihood of graduating from high school and college (Dee, 2004; Gershenson et al., 2018). The presumption that often underlies calls for greater teacher diversity is that differences in the racial identities and cultural practices between primarily white teachers and the students and families of color they serve are at the root of the problem of racial disparities in education. While we should certainly support efforts to diversify the teaching workforce, such efforts alone are unlikely to fundamentally change inequitable dynamics in schooling or in family–school relations, as teachers of color also struggle with racialized dynamics and marginalization in schools (Achinstein & Ogawa, 2011; Kohli, 2018). What if, instead of positioning racial and cultural differences as a barrier to change and educational justice, we were to instead intentionally *leverage* them as opportunities to expand possibilities for learning in and around schools, both for young people *and* for the adults around them?

To be clear, surface-level celebrations of diversity through a "holidays and heroes" approach can be a way to enact business-as-usual with the veneer of change, and, as such, further tokenize, alienate, and marginalize nondominant youth, families, and communities (Au, 2017). Instead, PDR and other social change design approaches suggest that explicit attention to historically rooted, power-infused racial and cultural differences in moment-to-moment interactions can shift decision-making and catalyze learning and transformative agency. Experts on racial disparities in education have long called for educators and leaders to undertake explicit conversations about race and power, particularly in reflecting on student data and school climate (Carter, Skiba, Arredondo, & Pollock, 2017; Irby, 2018). Solidarity-driven co-design takes this a step farther by putting the everyday lived interactions between people in schools on the table for scrutiny and discussion. Such explicit conversations become even more challenging when our own assumptions and interactions are directly implicated. In the case of this study, the "object" of the joint activity was to create a set of lessons for parents to learn about supporting student success in schools, but the broader outcome had to do with a new kind of relationship and collective learning and action between parents and educators. Co-design practices suggest how racial, cultural, and role differences might become sources of mutual and collective learning for parents and teachers, rather than barriers to authentic partnerships. This leads to critically important "how can" questions about solidarity, which I address in the final chapter of the book.

CONCLUSIONS

This chapter illustrates one iterative process in which all four guiding principles of equitable collaborations converged to foster generative adult learning for designing and realizing more just schools. As we have discussed, racial and other inequities in schools are embedded in complex systems that operate on multiple levels (Garces & Gordon da Cruz, 2017; Lewis & Diamond, 2015; Sullivan, Artiles, & Hernandez-Saca, 2015). Changing those systems will require significant adult learning on the part of both families and educators. Referring to educators and instructional improvement more narrowly, Harvard education reform scholar Richard Elmore often quipped, "If they knew how to do it, they would already be doing it!"

Although I echo his call for capacity-building (not simply accountability), my research suggests the importance of building the *collective* capacity—and leadership—of families and educators in fostering educational change. Broad-scale policy and institutional structures remain levers of systemic change, but the concepts and practices of co-design can begin to address the moment-to-moment interactions that are shaped by—and also have untapped ability to transform—the broader institutional structures that reinforce oppression in schools and school systems. The theory and practices in this chapter offer insights into how we might facilitate collective adult learning spaces that build transformative agency across boundaries of role, race, class, language, and educational background.

I also want to warn that co-design processes, though promising, are *not* a panacea to the complexities of systemic inequities in education. In this specific case, the design team parents did not continue to meet and act collectively beyond the design space, but each of the parents went on to enact leadership in other ways and cultivate the agency of other parents. For instance, after the process, Mary became an instructional assistant in one of the schools where she partnered with the principal to connect with parents in the school, and Natalia organized a committee for stay-at-home Latina mothers at her school. Likewise, one of the teachers subsequently taught other teachers about racial microaggressions in the classroom. And one of the district leaders went on to implement the curriculum in another district and support other systems leaders in co-designing a strategic plan with students and families. Scholars have increasingly pointed to the "ripples" of influence and changed activity that emerge from PDR work, often in unexpected ways or in entirely new spaces (Bang & Vossoughi, 2016). In addition, the design principles developed by the team have become an anchor for co-designing with families in other districts in the region and beyond. The diffusion and adaptation of design principles can also be considered a form of innovation spread (Sannino & Nocon, 2008).

That said, the emergent parent–teacher collaboration from this design process did not sustain or become institutionalized across the district. Family–school relations in the Kellogg district largely persisted in their conventional, individualistic, hierarchical dynamics. The next level of this work concerns the need to address mechanisms, organizational structures and routines, and systemic capacity for sustaining and spreading these new forms of activity across schools and systems. Deeply entrenched norms and assumptions embedded in systems are unlikely to change on their own. Thus, so-called "external" partners—such as university researchers, district staff, or community-based organizations—may also be critical in supporting efforts to reshape family–school activity in everyday life throughout a system.

More specifically, although the parents' decision to proceed in the design process without the principals for a while transformed power in that space, it may also have limited the extent to which these new forms of activity translated to other overlapping activity systems in schools. My other body of research focused on leadership for equity (for instance, Ishimaru & Galloway, 2014) recognizes principals as pivotal players in family–school relations. For instance, I was first introduced to the power of design teams with educators and families in a study of the role of principals in the creation of new schools catalyzed by education organizing. In that case (see Ishimaru, 2013), the principals who were part of school design teams experienced the process as a profound learning opportunity in developing their leadership, one that complemented their formal principal preparation. The trajectory of such learning can extend long after the process itself. Months after the co-design described in this chapter ended, one of the principals reflected that her initial defensive reaction to the process reflected the denial she felt in being confronted with her own practice in relation to parents. She subsequently shared her experiences with a group of leaders, calling it a profound learning experience "not for the faint of heart." The final chapter of this book explores how we might cultivate the learning and growth of professional educational leaders to undertake co-design approaches and practices.

Despite the challenges and complexities of co-design, I hope the concepts and practices in this chapter offer concrete examples and starting places for catalyzing shifts in power and new learning in your setting. Because of the way schools are structured, the historical relations between schools and communities, and the powered, racialized institutional scripts that shape interactions between parents and teachers in schools, equitable collaboration between nondominant families and educators is unlikely to ensue with incremental or technical improvements to existing individualistic school-based approaches. Many of the existing frameworks for family engagement provide broad policy commitments or prescriptions that fail to address the complexities of how race, power, gender, language, class, and other social markers shape family–school relations. Change undertaken as collective inquiry to foster equitable, learning-focused relationships between families and educators requires not only time and investment but also robust theory to inform the work and strategies at both macro and micro levels for attending to power and privilege in relational dynamics. Solidarity-driven co-design opens possibilities for tapping nondominant expertise and building collective capacity in the journey toward educational justice among families, schools, and communities.

CHAPTER 7

Co-Designing Justice and Well-Being with/in Systems and Conclusions

with Kelly Aramaki, Justin Irish, and Keisha Scarlett

> Whenever we love justice and stand on the side of justice we refuse simplistic binaries. We refuse to allow either/or thinking to cloud our judgment. We embrace the logic of both/and. We acknowledge the limits of what we know. (bell hooks, *Teaching Community: A Pedagogy of Hope,* 2003, p. 10)

Recasting families and communities in educational change is ultimately about leadership. Equitable collaborations ask us—both formal leaders and families and communities—to lead change and realize more just schools in ways that fundamentally depart from the ways we are accustomed to interacting. We can no longer easily check off a tidy box marked "family engagement" or compartmentalize it as someone else's responsibility. Nor do we simply demand to be heard and then wait to see if the powers that be will deliver on the change we wanted. I find the notion of "both/and" to be helpful for talking about what equitable collaborations ask of us all.

Scholar Kimberlé Crenshaw (1990), bell hooks (quoted above), Patricia Hill Collins (1998), and others proposed that we too often default to either/or approaches and ideas in the work of dismantling inequity. For example, social movements have been framed as being about *either* race *or* gender. But as a Black woman, Dr. Crenshaw was clear that it made no sense for her to have to choose one or the other—she was both Black *and* a woman—and the intersectionality of race and gender relates to very particular forms of oppression, experiences, and resiliencies. In the spirit of both/and, then, the journey to equitable collaborations is *both* about the leadership of nondominant youth, families, and communities *and* about the formal leaders and educators within educational systems. Our educational systems contain *both* historically rooted dynamics of oppression *and* possibilities for just futures and collective well-being. Change requires *both* disrupting what's already in motion *and* figuring out which practices, policies, and systems should replace the status quo. *Both* families *and* educators have expertise we need in order to "fix" our systems—*and both* need to build capacity to work toward systemic change.

That said, I would argue that we know a reasonable amount about how to foster the leadership of nondominant parents and families, thanks to decades of on-the-ground organizing and action research as well as decades and even centuries of culturally based community leadership (for example, in Indigenous communities). However, I have found through my research (and you may have begun to notice in these chapters) that equitable collaborations often stumble when it comes to the systems-based capacity to lead in fundamentally different ways. Thus, some of my most recent work seeks to bridge across strands of my research to chip away at a recurring puzzle: How can systems-based leaders learn to shift their practices and collaborate with family and community leaders in transforming education to become more just?

This final chapter again weaves the four principles of equitable collaborations together, but this time through an examination of systems-based co-design as a form of justice-focused leadership practice. Through the practices and tensions encountered by three district leaders, we will explore the possibilities for solidarity-driven theories of change in pursuit of educational justice (Ishimaru & Bang, 2017; Tuck & Yang, 2018). After providing a brief context of the broader project and the distinct co-design efforts within it, I will describe common dilemmas that the district leaders encountered in their efforts to transform the role of nondominant families and communities in educational change. Within the logic of conventional educational systems—and colonized minds, as Linda Tuhiwai Smith (2012) might say—these dilemmas often took the form of opposing binaries that seemed to present forced either/or choices. These educators' efforts to move through those seemingly forced choices reflect complex, nuanced *both/and* learning and approaches to collaborating with families and communities in their contexts. Though inevitably "works-in-progress," the lessons from these learning leaders point ways forward in the journey and call us to imagine and realize transformative possibilities for our educational systems and communities.

A CALL TO REIMAGINE FAMILY AND COMMUNITY ENGAGEMENT

When invited to share my research and thinking at the 2014 White House Convening on Transformative Family Engagement, I began to talk with other leading scholars, family leaders, and practitioners about what it would take to shift the field of education with regard to the marginalized roles and activities designated for families of color. What would it take to move beyond our current mode of school-centric, white, middle-class expectations? How might we shift away from prioritizing school events and checking boxes to "fix" parents, all the while inadvertently alienating families of color under the banner of "family engagement"? What would it look like to truly center racial equity in that work and tend to the flourishing of the young people in our collective care who have been and continue to be poorly served by our systems? And who would be crazy enough to take up that kind of charge?

With generous support from the W.K. Kellogg Foundation[1] and no small amount of trepidation, my colleague (as well as dear friend, co-design mentor, and Indigenous sister scholar-mother-organizer) Dr. Megan Bang and I took up the challenge. We reached out to a broad range of scholars, educators, and family and community leaders across the field of education to create the Family Leadership Design Collaborative (FLDC).[2] Today, the FLDC is a national, transdisciplinary network that works to reimagine how families and communities can lead collaborative efforts to create equitable educational spaces, schools, and systems. We seek to cultivate, enact, and sustain community well-being and educational justice through co-design with communities, families, and educational systems. Since 2015, we have been partnering with family–community collaboratives across the United States to develop practices, tools, and knowledge as well as cross-geography solidarities toward community well-being and educational justice.

Collectively, the FLDC developed an ambitious research-practice agenda (Ishimaru & Bang, 2016; 2017) and a series of design principles related to those that undergird this book.[3] In our first phase, we drew on solidarity-driven co-design in 10 local sites across the United States with geographically, linguistically, and racially diverse families and communities to imagine transformative aims for education and theories of change for getting to them. As discussed in the prior chapter, solidarity-driven co-design aims to foster solidarities through collective inquiry by explicitly addressing and working to reconstruct how historically rooted power plays out in the process of co-constructing new knowledge and implementing change. Building from Indigenous methodologies (Kovach, 2019; Smith, 2012) and community-based design research (Bang et al., 2010), we supported the 10 collaboratives in facilitating design circles—or in-depth reciprocal working groups—as a practice of solidarity-driven co-design (see Ishimaru et al., 2018 for a detailed methodology).

Our second phase undertook deeper dives with four of the original collaboratives to walk with them in co-designing context-specific practices, products, and measures with their communities and schools in Chicago, South Los Angeles, Southeast Seattle, and West Salt Lake City. For example, in Chicago, members of multiple urban Indigenous communities came together to build solidarities to foster global indigeneities. In South Los Angeles, the community organizing group CADRE partnered with UCLA to co-design role plays as a practice for developing new scripts to humanize parent–teacher interactions and build Black and Brown parent solidarities in the Los Angeles Unified School District. Members of SESEC, a coalition of primarily community of color–led organizations focused on educational equity, co-designed inclusive and intergenerational facilitative practices and space. Finally, University Neighborhood Partners, Community Advocates, and the University of Utah partnered with the Salt Lake School District to co-design a more meaningful and authentic role for nondominant parents in budget decision-making via the School Community Councils.

This chapter's inquiry into cultivating systems-based leadership for co-design grew out of the broader FLDC project, particularly the initial design circles facilitated by the then interim superintendent of Southfield Public Schools (in Michigan). The Southfield co-design sought to break down traditional hierarchical barriers between families and principals and served as an important "sister space" (educational context separated by space or history that embodies parallel values, Vossoughi in Melendez et al., 2018) for the district leaders in this study as they undertook co-design in their own contexts.[4]

DISTRICT LEADERS AND CO-DESIGN

All three of the district leaders in this study were in their final year of the 3-year Leadership for Learning (L4L) EdD program at the University of Washington. The program for preparing systems-focused practitioner leaders emphasizes equity and excellence as twin aims through a tightly integrated curriculum focused on Equity and Excellence, Inquiry, Leadership for Equitable Systems, Instructional Leadership, and Professional Growth. As a core faculty member in the program, I taught a yearlong Special Interest Group (SIG) for a subset of the cohort, with the invaluable support of PhD student Aditi Rajendran. The three district leaders in this chapter all collaborated extensively with others in their contexts to undertake their co-design projects, and this chapter builds not only from their work and consultations as part of the class, but also from presentations on their co-design projects at professional conferences that we have co-constructed together. Through this work, they have become partners and no longer students, and I acknowledge them as coauthors because it is both their work I am sharing and their learning that contributed to my own (though any shortcomings in the study are, of course, my own). I describe each leader and his or her co-design project and partners briefly below. In all three cases, their original notions of their co-design projects evolved through the process to become something entirely different than they had originally envisioned.

Kelly, an Asian American man, was an executive director (principal supervisor) in his large urban district. A former principal and teacher, he strongly identified as an equity-focused leader and oversaw 20 high-poverty schools in the region of the city with the most diverse student body in the district. His co-design work shifted from supporting an embattled principal in repairing family–school relations to teaching principals how to begin co-design and, ultimately, to partnering with a school community and the district director of racial equity in a process to hire a new principal at one school.

Justin, a gay white man, was the assistant superintendent of elementary instruction and equity in a suburban district with a growing (mostly immigrant) student of color population. He began with the ambition of "leading up" to co-design the district's strategic plan implementation and improvement process, then shifted to developing a family engagement policy to better leverage his existing relationships and points of leverage in his system. He eventually focused on an existing district community advisory group that had become somewhat entrenched and disgruntled. With several key district staff members and families, they co-designed a new selection process, charge, and operating norms to reshape the role and focus of the district community advisory group in relation to the core equity work of the district.

Keisha, an African American woman, was executive director of organizational development and equity in a diverse urban district. A former principal with deep ties in the community, she partnered with the local housing authority and with African American and East African families, initially to address chronic absenteeism among students in one housing authority development. Early on, the leadership team shifted to co-designing a program to address family priorities to improve the educational experiences of their youth. The project also attempted to address intraracial tensions between these two communities. The team drew on an existing $15,000 grant to ultimately co-design a youth mentoring program with a family engagement component.

MY TEACHING CHALLENGE: PROLEPTIC POLITIC AS PEDAGOGY

In lieu of a traditional methods section, I elect to narrate my own teaching pedagogy in the construction and facilitation of the Codesign Special Interest Group (SIG), as it is an integral part of these administrators' shared learning as well as the context within which they undertook co-design. From the beginning of the FLDC, we sought to cultivate a "proleptic politic" (Cole, 1998; Gutiérrez, 2008; Vossoughi, 2018) in which we tried to live or *enact* the here-and-now kinds of relations we envisioned for the future (Bang & Vossoughi, 2016). CADRE executive director Maisie Chin calls this "creating the future in the present." This notion relies on the understanding that, too often, in our efforts to realize equity and justice we reinforce the very dynamics we are trying to disrupt. We can undermine our own aims by reinforcing powered roles, deficit-based narratives, and unjust relations in the process. Thus, in considering how to approach teaching co-design as a professor in a university-based preparation program, I could not default to the same powered roles, normative expectations, and schooling routines that co-design seeks to disrupt. Rather, I had to figure out how to teach others to do co-design in ways that recognized them not only as district leaders, but also as members of families and communities as well as individuals with unique contexts and expertise; in ways that sought to transform conventional teacher–student power dynamics; that worked to foster reciprocity and agency; and that undertook the work as collective inquiry and capacity-building. Kelly, one of the district leaders in the class, later reflected on his own efforts to teach co-design to the principals in his district in their monthly principal professional learning sessions:

> Can you teach something like codesign—that's so inclusive, so equity-focused—in a way that's very not inclusive, in a non-codesign way? The delivery model is pretty much status quo, and we're trying to get at something that's very much not status quo.

In short, I had participated in or supported enough co-design in other contexts to realize that I had to teach students by changing our "rules of engagement" and modeling the work by co-designing the course *with* students.

Nothing in my training or professional socialization as a professor prepared me to undertake teaching in this way. Particularly as a woman of color, in a predominantly white (and historically male) field of educational leadership, in a predominantly white research institution, establishing my authority and expertise in the classroom has always been a complex undertaking (Martinez, Chang &, Welton, 2017; Motha & Varghese, 2018; Turner, 2002). The vulnerability and risk students discuss below for leaders of color is also very real in the university classroom—will it look like I don't know what I'm doing? Because I had been with these students for 2 years already, I was afforded some grace, and to its credit, the program sought to model continuous improvement in our delivery. At least in theory, then, co-designing with students as an approach to teaching was aligned with the program vision.

In practice, though, my teaching looked dramatically different from my usual approach of using a Powerpoint and facilitating classroom-based activities and conversations based on the readings. Although I had a broad agenda and the objective of supporting students in taking up co-design projects in their own contexts, I did not predetermine our destination or even know the course of the journey in any detail ahead of time. The course content and activities evolved entirely in partnership with students in their contexts—based on the needs, priorities, and interests of students as they took up their own co-design. We met for a full day once a month for 7 months, with pairs of students hosting us in their own (or their partner's) districts. Each daylong visit was the result of extensive planning with instructors, often preceded by a site visit to strategize with the local co-design team about how to ensure our visit would be useful or helpful to local efforts, not simply another extractive dynamic of a university coming to take advantage of local work. Over the course of the year, we developed and refined a set of principles for systems-based co-design:

- Recognize how positionality impacts power dynamics and trust
- Build politicized trust and solidarities
- Lean into tensions and disrupt hierarchical "business as usual"
- Sustain and advance the conversation over time through iterative feedback loops

The class sessions included meetings, data collection and sense-making, and even co-designing with members of the students' co-design teams, as well as conversations with the local superintendent, in most cases.

Finally, consistent with the formative interventionist approaches of design-based research in expansive learning (Engeström & Sannino, 2010), Aditi (PhD student teaching assistant) and I acted not only as teachers and researchers but also as collaborators and facilitators of the co-design process. I worked to bring my full identity as teacher, scholar, parent, and member of multiple communities (as a Japanese American and Buddhist, in particular) into the co-design, something I had never done as a professor before. It was at once the most intensive class preparation and teaching I have ever done and the most generative, research-based, and data-informed learning process I have ever facilitated. Keisha, a district leader in this study, once quipped that co-design required "strenuous use of qualitative data" in ways that are fundamentally different from the way we typically undertake learning or improvement work in formal educational systems (whether K–12 or higher education).

Beyond co-designing the course curriculum, we also collected multiple sources of data in the study. We collected student work, class session agendas, and detailed fieldnotes from the seven daylong sessions (approximately 42 hours), transcribed audio recordings of focal discussions during sessions, and took notes from one-on-one coaching conversations, pre-session site visits, and planning meetings. I also drew on the aforementioned conference presentations we have co-constructed since their graduation. As I analyzed data across these cases, I began to notice repeating patterns in the conceptual and relational tensions students grappled with in their co-design work.

DILEMMAS AS SYSTEMIC TENSIONS

According to cultural-historical activity theory (CHAT), tensions and contradictions are inherent in activity systems and can be a source of change and learning (Engeström & Sannino, 2010). Given the historically based power asymmetries and subordinate roles for families in schools, asking district leaders to center racial equity and nondominant families in their practice inevitably brought contradictions to the foreground. Whereas conventional approaches to engaging families often seek to avoid tensions, we collectively sought to interrogate them in order to generate new possibilities for how systems-based leaders and families and communities of color might collaborate in pursuing change in schools.

Below I conceptualize these contradictions as four key dilemmas that the district leaders encountered in their efforts to enact systemic co-design in their leadership. Although originally posited as opposing binaries by these leaders, I illuminate how they sought to take up "both/and" approaches to their leadership and navigate their way through these dilemmas to co-design more just educational systems.

Situating Co-Design in Formal Systems: Product or Process?

Co-design presents a particular challenge for most educational systems precisely because it is so at odds with the typical institutional structures and their underlying efficiency logics focused on standardized outcomes (Trujillo, 2014). District leaders are often selected for their ability to manage complexity and chart straightforward paths from inputs to predetermined products or outcomes, through a primarily technical, rational, and apolitical process. As Tina Trujillo (2014) explains, this factory-like efficiency model came originally from a mechanical engineer named Frederick Winslow Taylor, based on work he did for a steel company in 1899, and it quickly influenced industry and moved into education:

> Taylor's approach, later dubbed "scientific management," was characterized largely by methods for distilling work into discrete, quantifiable tasks; measuring observable outputs; exercising heavy managerial control over workers; and minimizing costs by appealing to workers' economic self-interests, as well as by engaging in systematically derived best practices and planning. (p. 2)

Despite decades of calls to abandon a "factory model" of schooling, these assumptions persist in the expectations of leadership (and teaching) in most systems in the country.

Scholars of participatory co-design, meanwhile, argue for foregrounding subject-subject relations, or the relationships, power dynamics, moment-to-moment interactions and overall process, in any collective learning activity (Bang & Vossoughi, 2016). Thus, when the district leaders first encountered co-design, they understood it as the opposing binary to the outcomes-focused standardization regime common in school districts. They understood co-design, instead, to be about prioritizing relationships above all else. For example, Kelly explained that in supporting one of his principals, he took up co-design with her not because he planned to but because the contentious parent–school dynamics "shoved" them into it and presented "an opportunity to embrace relationship building . . . to center the group on common values and relationships."

Likewise, early on, Keisha and her partners with the local housing authority abandoned their initial plan to co-design solutions to chronic absenteeism, as they realized that was a systems-centered, predetermined end decidedly not reflective of families' priorities. Her subsequent co-design and Justin's co-design with the district's parent advisory council both heavily emphasized relationship building and the sharing of stories and experiences. After several co-design sessions, though, the East African and African American families on Keisha's co-design team resisted the ongoing emphasis on getting to know each other. They expressed feeling that they had already invested a great deal of time in sharing their stories and did not have time to continue investing in those relationships if the immediate result was not change for their children.

This common dilemma reflects the limitations of approaching co-design as *only the opposite* of outcome-focused, efficiency-driven interactions. In CHAT terms, we might say that the foregrounding of subject-subject relations does not mean the elimination of any object at all in the learning activity. Thus, the district leaders began to understand co-design as a practice of *both* process *and* product, *both* relationships *and* outcome (although process and outcome in PDR dramatically depart from a Taylorian efficiency logic and instead are undergirded by solidarity aims, which we will return to later in this chapter).

This dilemma can often be observed in listening sessions. Listening sessions constitute an increasingly common approach to relationship building in districts, often used by school or district leaders to "engage" with families and communities or diffuse a volatile situation. They are considered a way to "give voice" to families who typically have few avenues for expressing their concerns in schools. However, they often result in what Megan Bang calls "trauma on display." In other words, these forums encourage youth, families, or communities to share their stories of harm or trauma inflicted by the system for the purpose of informing power-holders of problems they need to address, but they do little to shift power, roles, or assumptions about how issues will be resolved or decisions will be made. Listening sessions constitute an incremental practice that reinforces the status quo—and often exacerbates frustration—when systems leaders are unable to "deliver" on solutions that families desired. As we discussed in one of our planning sessions, listening sessions constitute "moves made by the system as concessions" under the guise of inclusion and democratic process, but, in practice, they solidify power in the system and its designees.

Through consultations with other district leader classmates and through collective examination of their scripted meeting data, both Kelly and Keisha realized the need to pivot from focusing solely on relationships to tending and fostering those relations *through* joint work toward a shared object or goal. Kelly narrated the shift in his practice from a focus solely on listening and building relationships to a more action-focused (object-oriented) conversation:

> A shift we did yesterday. How do you shift from trauma on display, how do you shift out of that? I think one of the ways you do that is to stop the listening session. Every time can't be a listening session. So we tried to do that yesterday. We said, next time, we're shifting to doing. And then the one who's always on display goes, yes, let's do something! It's kind of a shift. Maybe it might stop the every time, saying the same thing over and over and over. Because basically it's a shifting of control to that person—like, go ahead, let's design it. Let's figure it out.

Similarly, Justin described the shift in his understanding and approach in his closing reflections:

> I used to think co-design was about designing a final product. I now think co-design is making visible the multiple spaces, narratives, power structures and ways of being which promote positive relationships/partnerships that create equitable outcomes.

In other words, attending to fostering more just relations and process opens the door to different, more just solutions. Even as they discussed the challenge of making the "pivot" to action beyond abstract relationship building, the district leaders shifted toward practices that fostered *both* equitable, relational process *and* co-designed products.

Power and Positionality: "The Man" or "a Victim"?

Early on, all three district leaders grappled with multiple realities: their formal roles as designated representatives of the school district; the expertise and insight they sought to tap among families they were co-designing with; and the inherent power asymmetries between themselves and families. They also recognized that their historically rooted racial, gender, class, sexual orientation, and other identities shaped the way that others saw and interpreted their actions and intents. Keisha understood this tension in relation to the notion of critical historicity in co-design:

> Critical historicities [mean we] acknowledge the histories and stories of our experiences with education systems—the families and students. This includes the historical inequities and strengths we all bring. For me, I was feeling self-conscious about being associated, as being "the district" in that room. I felt like "The Man."

Very aware of the dynamic in which well-intended leaders take over meetings and wrest control of the agenda, Keisha initially sought to diffuse the power of her district role by doing little other than listening and taking notes in co-design meetings. Likewise, Kelly recognized early on that his district role and his positionality as an Asian American male in relation to many African American families, especially mothers, was a barrier to the trust he sought to build:

> The positionality of the person leading the co-design session matters. If our goal is to push the power toward families believing that families' funds of knowledge are the key to more equitable decisions and ways of doing school, then, we have to acknowledge that the positionality (intersection of identity—race, gender, religion, position, socioeconomic status) of the one leading the designing must be taken into account. If your positionality impedes trust, then you have to be willing to neutralize that factor.

Similarly, as a white man, Justin sought to be explicit about his role in upholding spaces of whiteness, especially in relation to the families and community members of color on the district advisory council. He worked hard to build trusting relationships with families, hosting them for meals at his home, working to enact a kind of servant leadership, and staying late into the night holding space for families to voice their frustrations with their schools in contentious meetings. However, he was at a loss when families of color became angry at him for not making the change they sought.

Thus, all three leaders recognized the power inherent in their formal authority and initially sought to diffuse it by playing passive roles or trying to act as "empty vessels" in relation to families. They initially understood their roles in co-design to be that of *either* representing The Man and taking over the co-design *or* getting out of the way and sometimes serving as "a punching bag" for families' frustrations. One principal on a site visit referred to herself as "feeling like a victim" whenever she opened the door to listening to families. However, by reflecting on their roles and collaboratively reflecting on data from a co-design session we participated in in another context, the district leaders began to perceive ways to *both* own the power and authority vested in them by their district roles *and* contribute in meaningful (and vital) ways to the process. Indeed, we discussed how their former well-intended silence and efforts to just "step aside" or passively absorb the hits could be construed as a form of withholding that unintentionally consolidated their power.

In Kelly's case, his both/and recognition meant bringing in another district administrator to partner with him, a Latina woman who had been a principal in a neighboring school and who had recently become the director of racial equity initiatives in the district. He noted:

> What this doesn't mean is that you give up your decision-making power completely. Co-design includes you as a decision maker. But what it does mean is that you have to share power, which may mean stepping aside for part of the process. In this case of the hiring of the principal, there wouldn't be trust in the process if I was the one leading it. It was hard for me. I felt hurt. But it was necessary. [Families] suggested that the process at the very least be co-led by a director in our equity department. That person led the subsequent co-design meetings with families.

Kelly likened his role in co-designing a new principal-hiring process at the school to the non-winning ice skaters on Olympic relay teams. The aim of those individual skaters was not to win for themselves but to make sure their team crossed the finish line first to claim the win.

In Keisha's case, leading from a both/and stance meant recognizing her multiple identities, *both* as a district administrator *and* as an African American longtime resident who was herself a student and was now a parent in those same neighborhood schools. She found that explicitly naming the power dynamics as well as her other identities opened new ways for her to participate:

> Bringing our whole selves can help us navigate through these histories. I had to re-enter this work thinking of the assets and strengths that I bring as part of my identities—as an African American, as a lifelong member of this community and a parent whose children attend the same schools their children attend.

In particular, Keisha was able to use her positionality to explicitly name tensions between African American and East African communities in their context, to begin to help families to work toward shared aims in light of their differences. She unpacked those complexities:

> The perception of many African American families in this community is that most of the resources are geared toward supporting East African families and not African American families. Due to gentrification and the relocation/suburbanization of low income African American families in this community, there is less of a cohesive social network amongst families, which has hampered their ability to organize, build solidarity and community leadership in the ways the East African families have been able to do in this same [neighborhood].

Keisha thus drew on both her district role and her personal experiences as a mother and member of the local African American community to acknowledge tensions and foster solidarities. Similarly, Justin "leaned into" the tensions of his positionality by partnering with other district staff to build their capacity and by putting whiteness on the table in district decision-making processes (I will focus on Justin's practice in the next dilemma). Though each leader did so in a different way, all worked to *both* own their power *and* use it in responsible and responsive ways.

Finally, the "messiness" of co-design processes raises particular tensions for how others perceive leadership. According to the literature and common wisdom, the very definition of a leader involves setting direction and getting others to move together toward shared aims. Under the header "What is Leadership?" a field-defining report concludes:

> In sum, school leaders are those persons, occupying various roles in the school, who provide direction and exert influence in order to achieve the school's goals. Formal leaders—those persons in formal positions of authority—are genuine leaders only to the extent that they fulfill these functions. (Leithwood & Riehl, 2003, p. 3)

However, as Kelly began to do professional learning sessions with principals to implement co-design across the district, he quickly realized that positionality also shaped how others perceived leaders' moves to share power and collaborate in an iterative "messy" process that deliberately refused predetermined outcomes. "Power for leaders of color is already tenuous. People don't always look at you as the leader. You're having to fight for that leadership," Kelly said, reflecting on a transcript from his last professional development session with principals about the "performance of power" with positional authority. The group discussed how easily the expertise of leaders of color can come into question; how a deliberate departure from the conventional straight-line "input, throughput, output" approach to leadership can be interpreted by the system and those with power as incompetence. "*You* [can be] messy and can get away with it," said a Latina principal to a white male district administrator in our discussion, "and *I* can get fired." Kelly agreed that there were both race and gender dynamics in the mix: "There's more grace towards people who have more privilege."

Finally, Keisha related the complexity of "performing power" as a Black woman leader to her own experience navigating and constantly recalibrating her role in the co-design space:

> The whole idea that—I may blow up my spot doing some of these things, and I just want to say that even as I'm working with [the housing authority] on the co-design project, and we're probably all experiencing some of the same things, I'm not an expert . . . and there's something about this that's a little bit immobilizing because you don't know how to show up. You're so afraid of who should be in the room, what should you say? What should you ask? Will it make

> all the parents run away? You know what I mean? Or who's not in the room, and so I'm finding it nerve wracking, to be honest [she and group laugh].

In other words, Keisha constantly balanced the fine line between being perceived as having expertise in order to maintain her position in the district as a Black woman leader, while also acknowledging her own learning and developing expertise in this new practice of co-design. She recognized that the fundamental shifts in her leadership approach—and the ongoing calibration of her practice—were consequential, in terms of how *both* families *and* the system perceived her leadership.

Thus, leading the "messiness" of co-design entails real risk and vulnerability, especially for leaders of color and those who experience intersecting lines of oppression (Kelly identified as a person of color, Keisha as a woman of color, and Justin as gay). They may face consequences for choosing to refuse the role of the decisive, "take charge" leader and instead pursuing joint work with families and communities so often framed as deficient or problematic by the system. That said, their identities also offered them insights and experiences from their own lived experiences to draw upon as resources in their co-design processes. For Keisha, Justin and Kelly, then, leading through the both/and of power and positionality also demanded a "strenuous" ability to navigate both community-centered contexts and system-centered interpretations of their leadership.

Leaning into Tension: Circle the Drain or Chart a New Path?

One of the core precepts of solidarity-driven co-design and our collectively designed principles of systems-based co-design relates to the use of tension to disrupt normative hierarchical dynamics or narratives. While this may sound simple, naming and addressing tensions in co-design means that they are never permanently resolved such that we then sail smoothly forward to our predetermined destination. Each tension we "lean into" opens a new one, as we evolve our practices and forms of activity. For example, early on, all three of the district leaders approached co-design as a something to take up "for" the benefit of families from marginalized communities. Underneath this assumption was the systems-centric logic that families need to be "educated" to understand the language and structures of the system in order to better support their children and advocate for what they need. Moving to the both/and of power and positionality enabled the district leaders to recognize the binary of *either* presuming families had to change *or* educators and systems needed to shift their engagement practices. Rather, they began to conceptualize co-design as a process that cultivates the collective learning of *both* families *and* educators. But even with that presumption, normative power dynamics inevitably re-emerged, oftentimes between families themselves.

I focus in this section primarily on Justin's co-design, as his efforts to "reset" a district family advisory council called EAACH (Equity Alliance for Achievement) hold particular insights for how he led through the tensions between *either* circling the drain of old conversations, interactions, and dynamics *or* charting an entirely new path. EAACH had existed for a number of years, and the youth and families (predominantly of color) and few white staff members who made up the committee both expressed deep dissatisfaction with it. Families expressed wanting more district staff to attend meetings, but when more staff came, families complained that they dominated the agenda. Students and families also felt their voices were not heard, perceiving another "strategic direction" council—made up primarily of staff and a few white families—as having greater influence on the district. The few staff in EAACH, on the other hand, felt "attacked" when they came to meetings and felt meetings were "too unstructured" and allowed students, families, and communities to "admire the problem" because they "don't understand the whole picture."

First, Justin brought together an EAACH leadership team comprised of both "strategic direction" and other key district administrators; specialists who worked with nondominant families as part of their formal roles; and a racially and culturally diverse (but smaller) group of families. They elected to co-design a revised structure and roles for general membership meetings and a new process for recruiting and selecting new students and families to join. Second, through examining transcripts of meetings that Justin brought to the team, they began to surface and talk about how the racialized institutional scripts in the district shaped a dominant culture "white space" in EAACH. Justin described how he "leaned into" the tension that subsequently played out as the team debated what kind of process to design for new potential EAACH members:

> This was the biggest controversy for the team and took the most time during meetings to discuss. Should there be a formal process (standard application with two short essay questions and a formal presentation to EAACH general membership) if you want to be an EAACH leader?

Justin highlighted the following scripted dialogue excerpt from a leadership team meeting to demonstrate how these conceptual *and* relational tensions were playing out between parents of color (two mothers in this case):

Callie: We need to be somewhat willing to play by the game in order to change it.
Frita: Noooo. You got to . . . (speaks under her breath . . . inaudible)
Callie (looking at Frita): This is my opinion.
Frita: You got to break the game (laughter from several people)

Callie: I think that you need to . . . Need to be able to be taken seriously—

Frita (interrupting Callie): So you think that just because someone plays the game by the rules, you're not being taken seriously?

Callie: I think that if someone is really unwilling to explain their skillset and how some of these skills . . . they wouldn't be an effective leader in our EAACH . . .

Frita: Says who?

Callie: This is me. This is my opinion.

In addition to the complex relational tensions playing out, Justin explained how this excerpt highlights parents debating competing theories of change. He distilled the argument for a formal application as: "If we want to change the white institution to become more culturally responsive, one must understand how the white institution works and change it from within." A formal "rigorous" application process, reasoned some, would screen for students, parents, and community members who can navigate the white system more like "professionals" alongside district and school staff while, at the same time, still representing the community. On the other hand, Justin narrated the argument for a more informal process as: "A formal process is doing what we have always done: using a white process in a white space." From this perspective, a formal process was intimidating, particularly for those who do not speak English fluently. As Justin encapsulated the debate, the formal process also discouraged the types of leaders "who understand the community and who will consistently advocate for culturally responsive practices."

This dialogue is evidence of a shift in Justin's leadership practice from primarily listening to actively shaping the conversation by putting whiteness and data on the table, enabling team members to notice and explicitly name dominant culture-normative assumptions, and play out competing theories of change. This excerpt illuminates a decision-making process in and of itself—it is a deliberation about the criteria to prioritize and the theories of change that matter in shaping another decision, the EAACH member selection process. Justin could have let the process default to the district's usual application procedure. Or he had the power to simply make the decision and move the group along on his preset agenda—following the script of the efficient, "decisive" leader. Instead, he intentionally held space for this "meta" decision-making process. The group ultimately agreed on a modified speed-dating process that would still screen people but in a less intimidating and more relational way. More importantly, though, the process of deliberation was critical for transforming power and fostering families' collective agency. Such systems leadership practices demonstrate how co-design works to *both* surface "old" normative dynamics (in this case, about white space and what counts as "rigorous" or "professional") *and* facilitate families and staff in working to disrupt them and chart "new" paths for moving forward.

Theories of Systemic Change: Scaling Up or Only Local Activity?

Because all the administrators in this effort were district actors, the question of *systemic* co-design continually arose in our discussions. Kelly's effort to enlist principals in co-designing a "welcoming environment" as part of implementing the district's new racial equity policy became an opportunity to reflect on how co-design might move beyond local contexts to reshape broader overlapping activity systems across the entire district. All three district leaders worried that co-design was "very time-consuming" and wondered how to "go to scale" with trust and relationship building, interventions in complex, powered interactions, and iterative process, particularly when there was such urgency to address racial inequities in the system. They initially approached the question as one of *either* scaling up *or* doing co-design as locally specific family engagement on the margins of schools. In this either/or paradigm, the district leaders also worried about all the variation that existed in a system with different school contexts; different cultural, racial, ethnic, and identity-defined communities; and a wide array of leaders with their own positionalities and learning trajectories for enacting new forms of leadership and collaboration. Picking up on the improvement-science notion that "variation in performance is the core problem to address" (Bryk et al., 2015), Kelly, Justin, and Keisha saw this variability as a key barrier and constraint on the "efficacy" of co-design across a system.

However, after discussing scripted data from the principal co-design professional development session, the district leaders began to question their either/or framing of change as *either* replication-focused scaling *or* context-specific, local family engagement activity. Kelly related that he had given principals an assignment to try out co-design, and they mostly took it up as "one more thing" to add to their already full plates. We discussed a transcript excerpt of a debrief meeting about this dynamic, in which an individual prompted the team to think differently about how they positioned the openings for co-design to principals:

> Alita (at the end of the debrief meeting): Wait a minute. Maybe we should be thinking about, where are the opportunities already, not how do we add this onto something else that I'm not doing yet?

That is, Alita suggested that principals currently saw co-design as another task to add to their lists in part because the district focused on what they were *not* doing, rather than identifying opportunities to use a co-design approach to address existing decision points. In reporting out our ensuing discussion to the larger group, Kelly explained:

> [Before, we] were like, "Where are we doing family engagement that you might want to do this [co-design]?" But it's not so much about family engagement, this is about shifting power and how we make

> decisions. And so the question might be, the question that's a tackle for how to get started might be, "Where are you making the decision that will impact the whole school?" And then look at that. So we talked about planning for the Black Lives Matter Week. Could you have done, if we had time, could you have done a co-design with families and kids about Black Lives Matter Week? Or if you're going to change your homework policy, you *could* just make the decision. The teachers *could* just make the decision, but that's an opportunity for co-design, so where are we making the decisions that are impacting the community?

After this session, Kelly worked to "scale down" his efforts a bit (his words, riffing on Erickson's article, as discussed below, which I had assigned as a class reading in anticipation of the topic arising in this site visit). His theory of systemic change began to focus more on building capacity and leading others in co-design by collaborating around important decisions in the life of schools, with the ambition that collaborators would, in turn, go on to other contexts and bring valuable experiences and learned capacity with them.

Kelly recognized shortly afterward that the need to hire a new principal at one of his schools represented a perfect opportunity to take a co-design approach to *his* core existing work. After he brought in a partner to co-lead the process, he held multiple parent meetings, with parents inviting other parents to fully reflect the diversity in the school. The group identified student, family, and staff priorities and redesigned the hiring process. Two parents of color from those sessions collaborated with staff to create interview questions, and separate panels of 10 parents, 10 students, and 10 staff interviewed the top candidates and made their own recommendations to the superintendent. The outcome was a unanimous choice, and Kelly suspected that he would probably have made the same decision on his own. But more importantly, Kelly's leadership practice ensured that students, families, and staff—not just the "usual suspects" but also families who are pushed to the margins—had real influence, which began to repair the damaged trust between the community and the district. One student told Kelly, "Why don't we do this when we hire teachers and our vice principals? We're the ones who have to sit and listen to them. We should have a say!" Likewise, two parents of color were so grateful that they reached out to school board members to tell them about how the process had rebuilt their trust in the district.

In the case of this dilemma, then, Kelly and the other leaders did *not* both undertake replication at scale and focus on local activity alone. Rather, their deliberations challenged the underlying logics of scaling premised on a factory model of schooling. They began to center people, relationships, and collective capacities in their approaches to co-design, recognizing that people have to *participate* experientially in co-design in order to be able to facilitate it. In this notion of systemic change, then, young people, families, and communities of color cannot be confined to a set of events slotted periodically through the academic calendar. As Kelly reflects in the closing exercise, systemic change toward justice requires the expertise of families of color in the core work of schools:

> I used to think that co-design was about . . . engaging, teaching and equipping families. Now I think that families of color . . . have expertise and cultural strengths that our education system does not have that are critical to reinventing schools and making decisions about schooling that serves all students.

Likewise, at the close of the discussion that prompted Kelly to "scale down," Keisha also reflected on her understanding of systemic change as related to capacity, exploring questions about how we build others' capacity to do this kind of work across multiple spaces and places. In this way, I might reframe their leadership practice as evolving more toward an orientation of *both* systems change *and* local activity as a means of building collective capacity and enacting new practices.

CO-DESIGN AS "SOLIDARITY-DREAMING"

Scholars of participatory design argue that the expansion of co-design activity and the proleptic ("future in the present moment") commitments interwoven into it offer a way forward for systemic change that imagines transformative possibilities beyond our current education system. Leigh Patel (2017) argues:

> We pay dearly for having incremental approaches to single issues. We become challenged to imagine into existence a reality in which all living beings, human and nonhuman, are afforded well-being, care, and dignity. When we can't imagine it, it has no chance of emerging or being remembered into being. Neither does it have the chance to struggle through the rough patches, the failures, the revisions we need to radically face in making a society into existence that is not based on incremental acceptance or domination.

Thus, co-design offers the opportunity to imagine beyond incremental changes. Patel's reference to "incremental acceptance" constitutes a kind of window dressing over the existing paradigm, such as *more* parent nights (done the same ways we've always done them) or flyers translated into several languages instead of only English (but still put in a child's backpack as the sole form of communication about a school activity). This might also take the form of structural shifts, like family liaison positions—that still come with the expectation that doing the job well means assimilating families into white normative school expectations and behaviors.

Given the urgency of the problems facing our young people, their families, and schools, educators and families alike may well feel we don't have time to do this kind of "big" imagining. Or perhaps that we are not allowed to do it. As another Leadership for Learning graduate, Dr. Sandra Powell, once reminded me, the system has conditioned some families of color to think they cannot ask for anything greater than incremental acceptance. To this, Dr. Patel raises a compelling challenge for all of us: If we cannot imagine educational justice and community well-being—or the dignity of all beings—how do we think we will test it out and realize it?

A design discussion primarily between Keisha, Justin, and a third person in our last formal session together provides a glimpse into the potential space that systems leaders might open and help hold for this kind of "solidarity-dreaming." The exchange offers a vivid example of these leaders' growing co-design expertise and their collaborative efforts to support their colleague in helping to reshape education in community-defined and -centered ways. Due to confidentiality concerns, I am not able to share the full transcript data of the dialogue itself, as it too easily places a particular community, but I do hope to narrate the broad strokes enough to help you to see the co-design "moves" they were making. Most of the local community members had left by this time, so as part of a small group of primarily systems leaders from other contexts, Justin and Keisha had been asked to generate potential questions to launch an intergenerational co-design session in this particular nondominant cultural community. While others (including myself) participated in this conversation and helped evolve the concepts, Keisha and Justin played pivotal leadership roles, so I have homed in on them in this exchange.

> We are in a beautiful space filled with light, air and cultural art in the heart of a community we have been graciously invited into as guests and learners. We pause to consider what questions could shape their upcoming co-design session, and Keisha references a story shared with us by a community member and educator who opened our day together. Keisha suggests that a concept from that story about intergenerational relationships might be a good prompt to open a broader community session. In this move, she *begins with families and communities* by centering a community member and her hopes and dreams for her grandchildren.
>
> The group discusses and refines this idea a bit, then one administrator suggests instead using the goal of 100% graduation rates and how to achieve it as the opening question for the session. Justin intervenes at this point in a move that *transforms power* from the dominant white cultural norms of schools toward

community-centered understandings of education: "That's going to focus them on the . . . school house. You're not allowing them to think outside the box with that question." To this, the administrator responds quickly, "That's their goal."

Keisha acknowledges the goal but then draws on histories embodied in the community space we are meeting in to explain, "I think those are goals . . . but this is like, something a lot bigger than that. This sounds like healing that they want to have happen with this community. And so we're talking about the certain narrow kind of focus on graduating—to what?" Justin wonders, "Just to be colonized?" Keisha references a recent tragic incident with a local youth that had been mentioned earlier and says, "So this is so much bigger, it seems, than high school graduation."

At this point, Keisha turns to the poster of values and identifies two that relate to creating a "healthy" community and moving through the world in "good" ways. She wonders aloud if that's what education should be about. Others jump in to tie Keisha's musing to the task of crafting questions for an opening design session: What does it mean to this community in their cultural context to move through the world in "healthy" and "good" ways? The move again grounds the questions in community and opens the potential to *foster reciprocity and agency* across generations.

Justin agrees, adding, "And it doesn't have to happen in a particular space." Keisha concurs, "It doesn't have to happen in the spaces they [others] have constructed."

This exchange demonstrates how these two district leaders considered how to facilitate nondominant community members in "social dreaming" about transformative educational possibilities (Espinoza, 2008). They drew on community histories (both long past and recent incidents), historicized notions of "schoolhouse" space, cultural practices, and community values as resources for helping the community to reimagine education in that space. Although neither of them was part of that community and neither had much direct experience teaching young people of those backgrounds, they were able to recognize and leverage the differences and variation they were learning about as resources in reimagining the possible. When their colleague suggested they focus instead on graduation rates, they intervened skillfully to expand the focus from "the schoolhouse" to broader family and community histories, concerns, dreams, and values. Keisha and Justin were not saying that these conventional measures of academic success—test scores, grades, graduation—were unimportant. Rather, they were suggesting that community well-being and education justice reach for far more—and require both remembering and imagination. Through this short exchange, Keisha and Justin provide us with a glimpse of how to cultivate solidarities across disparate communities, geographies, histories, and spaces.

ON SOLIDARITIES

When I introduce the idea of fostering solidarities with systems-based leaders, the discussion often feels elusive. I suspect this is because in our dominant culture society and educational institutions, we have so few examples and models of how we might move from a stance of solidarity, rather than from self-interest. In fact, I've gotten into arguments with dear friends who cannot imagine any other way to conceptualize what makes people act either individually or collectively. When I start talking about our families, though, people begin to open the door to consider motivators other than self-interest. As a parent, I am often up at unhappy hours of the night with one of my young children. Perhaps they are sick, wet the bed, or have some kind of pain that makes it difficult for them to sleep. Whatever it is, I do not stay up with them and comfort them out of self-interest. Yes, perhaps I will be able to go back to sleep if I deal with whatever issue is bothering them, but at the end of the day, we do these things out of something other than self-interest. In this case, we do it out of love.

Scholars and leaders from bell hooks and Paulo Freire to Martin Luther King, Jr., and Gloria Anzaldúa have argued for love as an organizing principle, the search for which many claim constitutes a search for our humanity. Most recently, Mónica Byrne-Jiménez and Irene Yoon (2019) have proposed that we undertake educational leadership as a practice of love. They argue for leaders to reclaim "courageous love" and "tap into the deep well of their love for children, for their work, and a deep belief in the power of education."

Although this kind of "strong love" calls me, it is also hard for me to imagine operating out of love toward whole educational systems and communities of educators, children, youth, and families whom I know, at best, from a distance. But my argument here is not that any one way of conceptualizing a different ethic or stance is better or right, but that we have possibilities *other* than the conquest of land, colonization, and dispossession rooted in self-interest.

Thus, I often wonder what it might be like to foster solidarities centered around difference and interdependence, rather than surface notions of sameness or around temporary interest convergences. Ruben Gaztambide-Fernández (2012) discusses how necessary this shift in understanding solidarity is if it is to be useful in the work of decolonizing education:

> Understanding solidarity in relationship to social cohesion or as a source of collective action for groups in competition with each other has the effect of reissuing the colonizing logics of European social sciences, both classic and contemporary. A decolonizing pedagogy of solidarity must shift the focus away from either explaining or enhancing existing social arrangements, seeking instead to challenge such arrangements and their implied colonial logic. . . . It is about imagining human relations that are premised on the relationship

between difference and interdependency, rather than similarity and a rational calculation of self-interests. (p. 49)

As Tuck and Yang (2018) argue, justice projects of different sorts entail multiple theories of change; our work suggests that solidarities as one possible "hinge" in a theory of educational systems change. The evolving understandings and practices of the district leaders in this chapter offer insights for "bending" systems leadership toward educational justice.

CONCLUSIONS (AND NEW OPENINGS)

> I used to think co-design was a strategy for family engagement . . . now I think co-design is . . . for engaging others in decision making as well as further attuning my lens on how shifting/rebalancing power toward those most impacted may be one of our best strategies to engaging in authentic equity work. (Keisha, closing reflection)

Equitable collaborations are not something we undertake for the benefit of families so they can feel included in an inequitable and colonizing system. Rather, at their core, the theories and practices in this chapter are about leading change and realizing more just schools. Keisha's closing comments above reflect a shift that I hope has been conveyed through the research, concepts, and examples in this book. Beginning with families and communities, transforming power, building reciprocity and transformative agency, and undertaking change as collective inquiry are each and all only starting places, strands of DNA for growing our practices and expanding our collective capacity. Equitable collaborations constitute a call to approach our work, relationships, and everyday interactions in and out of schools in fundamentally different ways. My aim in this parting section is not to narrate the end of the journey and the (check box) accomplishment of equitable collaborations as a predetermined destination but to raise provocative questions and "tee up" the next phase of the voyage, a phase that looks to cultivating solidarities and enacting transformative multilevel systemic change.

Keisha, Justin, and Kelly are not alone in struggling with questions of scale across a system. However, Megan Bang and Shirin Vossoughi (2016) argue, "In an era in which scalability has become a routine question and desire but has largely failed to bring about espoused outcomes, it seems warranted that as a field we carefully re-examine the assumptions that drive such efforts" (p. 187). They turn to Erickson (2014) to suggest that a paradigm of (Taylorian) efficiency and control undergirds efforts at "scaling up," "best practices," and "high fidelity implementation." The notion of "scaling" privileges an object or process as a relatively technical matter that can be replicated "with fidelity" in larger and larger arenas. Although scholars of policy implementation often foreground notions of "adaptation" across contexts rather than "fidelity" these days, the core aim of taking something small and replicating it reliably and predictably on a larger scale remains. Because these efforts rely on the same underlying hierarchically powered, ahistorical and apolitical assumptions that enable racial inequities to regenerate at multiple levels of the system, scaling often tends to sustain or merely enhance the status quo ways of doing business.

Solidarity-driven co-design rests on a different logic. Bang and Vossoughi (2016) describe participatory design (of which solidarity-driven co-design is one "flavor") theoretically as "driven by proleptic commitments and sensibilities predicated on always evolving and reconstructed subject-subject relations" (p. 187). In other words, what if, instead of a factory model of educational systems organized to routinely and efficiently produce a particular standardized outcome (e.g., uniform achievement rates or graduation), we instead imagined systems as organic ecosystems. In this model, we might instead center people, relationships, and interactions—along with the co-constructed objects of their activity (i.e., *both* solidarities *and* the outcomes they engender). What if we then recognized these relationships and solidarities as constantly in motion, shaped by histories, power and politics, and local contexts? Such a system might entail adapting structures, evolving routines, and ongoing collective work to shift and grow the future in the present moment. In such a living systems model, variation might be a *resource* we can leverage toward these aims, rather than a *problem* we need to surmount—or eliminate.

It doesn't take much in this model to imagine that the "variation" represented by nondominant families and communities might—through collaboration with them—help us to together construct new ways of going about the core work of teaching and learning in and beyond schools. What has historically been constructed as "the problem"—the behaviors, knowledge, perceptions, languages, practices, and agency of young people of color, their families and communities—might become not merely assets but the expertise and solidarities we have needed all along to envision and begin to realize transformative possibilities beyond our outmoded factory-model educational systems.

Working from a model of a living ecosystem helps us to escape the "rut" of thinking in singular, linear ways about systemic change and forcing us into a false binary of *either* top-down *or* bottom-up. Rather, as some learning scientists have begun to help us theorize, we might conceptualize individuals and their relationships as "carriers" of particular practices across different spaces and places (Zavala, 2016); we might see how individuals in a particular co-design process might cultivate "sister spaces" elsewhere in or beyond a given system (Vossoughi in Melendez et al., 2018); and we might envision how change might instead "ripple" or expand outward from local co-design projects as a form of sustained *and* constantly evolving activity (Bang & Vossoughi, 2016).

These concepts may sound a little radical for a book you thought was going to help you communicate better with parents or foster family advocacy for more responsive schools or policies. These ideas are not new, however. Such understandings certainly represent a different kind of animal in the realm of education reform, policy, and normative school-centric leadership, but Indigenous communities have long understood the dynamism and systemic interdependence of human and nonhuman relations (Cajete, 2016; Smith, 2012; Vizenor, 2008). Community leaders (including a subset of educational leaders), organizers, and social movements, likewise, recognize human relationships, power, and leadership as central organizing units for change, not initiatives, data, outcomes, or policies (Warren, 2014; Zavala, 2016). A growing body of work both within and outside of the field of education offers theory and research about complex systems and change (Barton et al., 2004; Sullivan et al., 2015). And scholars, families, communities, and educators have begun to take up the challenging work of "creating the future in the present" as we imagine and work to realize transformative change in education (Ishimaru, Bang, et al., 2019). Paulo Freire encapsulated the power of collaboration at the crux of such efforts to envision and enact transformative possibilities and practices:

> Teachers and students (leadership and people), co-intent on reality, are both Subjects, not only in the task of unveiling that reality, and thereby coming to know it critically, but in the task of re-creating that knowledge. As they attain this knowledge of reality through common reflection and action, they discover themselves as its permanent re-creators. (Freire, 1970, p. 69)

In other words, educators, leaders, students, families, and communities can not only rehumanize each other through the process of unveiling history and power in education, they can also create knowledge and practices to reshape education as vehicle of liberation.

Thus, I end with a call for evolving our research-practice, our processes and theories of change, and the measures we rely on to signal what matters and what counts. We can aim our sights beyond narrowly defined academic achievement for a few individuals to "escape" from their communities. We can move beyond research that describes problems and showcases unique exceptions to the rule. We must discard the "incremental inclusion" practices that persist under the banner of "equity and justice." Community well-being and educational justice call us to the "strenuous" work of collaborating *with* families and communities to build solidarities across difference and enact transformative change that reimagines what education might become. *Kodomo no tame ni.* For our shared children and future.

Initial Partnership Assessment Tool

The distinctions between conventional partnerships and equitable collaborations elaborated in Table 2.1 (p. 50) can be used as a tool with a group of school, family, and community leaders to catalyze initial assessments and conversations. In practice, the contrast between conventional partnerships and equitable collaborations represents more of a continuum than a dichotomy, so the activity below suggests a starting place for collecting data from the group.

Keep in mind that systems-based actors almost always perceive greater equity and inclusion than nondominant families and communities themselves. Examining perceptions from multiple actors—formal leaders, educators at different levels and varied racial and cultural backgrounds, as well as nondominant families and community leaders—will give you the most robust view of the dynamics in your system.

Start by choosing one dimension (roles, goals, strategies, context/change process) and asking each person to place a colored dot or note on the line to indicate where they perceive your school, district, or organization to be on the continuum between conventional partnerships and equitable collaborations. Emphasize that there are no right or wrong answers, but that this is a first step in coming to a common understanding about where to begin. You might want to color-code the dots by role (e.g., blue for families, green for teachers, orange for administrators, etc.). After each person has placed his or her dot or note, initiate a conversation about the experiences or understandings that led them to that placement—start with family and community members to center their voices and perceptions! As a group, note key themes and differences, particularly if there are differences by role.

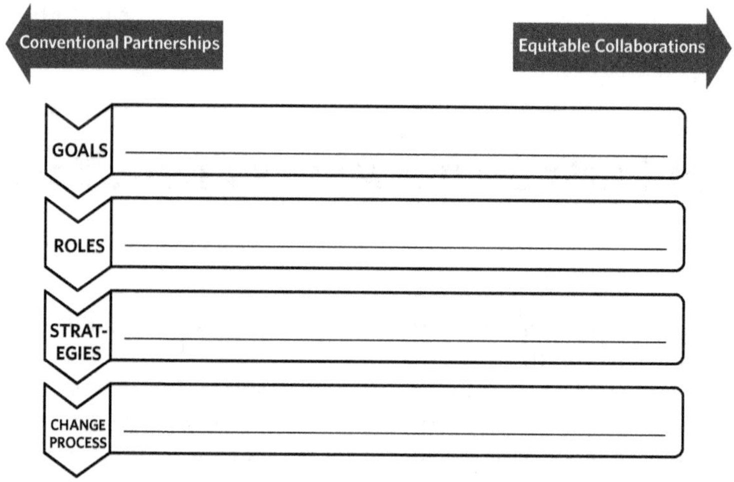

Most systems and organizations find that their approaches to nondominant families and communities lie somewhere between the conventional deficit-based paradigm and sustained and equitable collaborations. For instance, perhaps your school or district has taken up home visits or has an increased emphasis on building proactive, positive parent–teacher relationships. Perhaps there's a parent/family leadership council or designated parent slots in building leadership teams or district taskforces. These are important assets from which to begin, and the group might discuss the extent to which these are more than token representations. You can use the principles that undergird the book to further assess the quality of those activities and opportunities (for example, to what extent do those opportunities transform power and build reciprocity and transformative agency?)

Your group or team might also want to consider a more detailed *organizational* leadership assessment of your organization's equity practices, such as rubric from the LEAD Tool (see Ishimaru & Galloway, 2014; Galloway & Ishimaru, 2015).

Final Lesson Topics and Design Principles

Co-Designed Parent Curriculum Lesson Topics

Lesson 1: Communication Part 1
Lesson 2: Communication Part 2
Lesson 3: Ensuring Academic Success
Lesson 4: Addressing Bullying
Lesson 5: Fostering Positive Racial and Cultural Identities, Part 1
Lesson 6: Fostering Positive Racial and Cultural Identities, Part 2
Lesson 7: Parent Advocacy and Leadership

Lesson Design Principles

The five principles emerged through an iterative process with the Design Team to shape the learning process designed into the curriculum. Learning should enable families to:

1. **Build relationships with other parents/family members.** Activities should provide meaningful opportunities for family members to meet and make connections with one another, sharing their hopes and dreams for their children, families, and community, and sharing their common concerns or struggles. These relationships and trust are foundational for the other principles.
2. **Share their experiences, ideas, resources, concerns, and priorities with each other.** Lessons should provide opportunities for parents and family members to share personal experiences with issues in their children's education in order to learn from each other and to tap into their own collective knowledge and expertise. Through the sharing of these experiences, parents can exchange ideas, solutions, and resources with each other, create an ongoing network, and begin to work toward identifying and prioritizing common problems that should be addressed.
3. **Interact, collaborate, and reflect with one another to develop new or alternative understandings.** Through interactive activities such as skits,

games, dialogue, and opportunities for collective reflection, parents/family members can develop new shared understandings of issues that affect their children's school life.

4. **Foster student success beyond academic achievement.** Parents and families want their children to succeed academically, yet academic achievement is but one part of a more holistic approach to their children's learning, development, and education. Lessons should enable parents and family members to engage with topics that they feel are relevant to the success of their children in the broadest sense.
5. **Develop capacity to take action to support their children and work with other parents to improve the school.** Beyond simply providing information, learning should enable parents and family members to develop and practice skills and strategies they can use to create change. Although equitable transformation requires educators and schools to change as well, ultimately parents and families should feel they have the knowledge and capacity not only to support their children but to influence decisions at their school.

Downloadable at: education.uw.edu/sites/default/files/programs/epsc/ParentCurriculum-FINAL-Print.pdf

Notes

Introduction

1. The term "nondominant" here refers to historically marginalized communities, including Indigenous, Black, Latinx, Asian, Pacific Islander, immigrant, refugee, and other intersecting communities systematically excluded or oppressed by formal systems. While recognizing that these groups have distinct histories, experiences, and dynamics in education and society, the term highlights the power asymmetries inherent in the relationship of these groups to the dominant culture (Gutiérrez, 2006).

2. Scholars have suggested this term as an expansion to the ableist language of "colorblindness" that uses dis/ability as a metaphor for that which is undesired. This term also acknowledges that avoiding talking about race is a form of power that ignores the experiences of people of color (Annamma et al., 2017).

Chapter 1

1. My children's preschool teachers shared this with my children, likely based on Claude Steiner's *The Original Warm Fuzzy Tale.*

2. For a thorough treatment of this history, see Ta-Nehisi Coates's (2015) in-depth essay about the historical contexts and enduring influence of the Moynihan Report on "The Black Family in the Age of Mass Incarceration" in *The Atlantic.*

3. Scholars also highlight how this myth has been used to maintain anti-Black racism. The model minority myth has been used to advance colorevasive agendas and ideologies of cultural racism (Poon et al., 2016).

4. The Parent–Teacher Association (PTA) refers to a formal organization, whereas PTO is a more generic term for school-based parent organizations that may or may not be affiliated with the National PTA. However, "PTA" is the more commonly recognized acronym for any such organization in schools, so I use that here.

5. Research I conducted at Rainier Beach High School highlights an example of parent leaders who used their PTA as a lever of community-based, equity-focused change (Ishimaru, 2018). Teaching for Change has also developed a series of tools and resources to support parent groups in fostering inclusivity and equity in gentrifying school communities (www.teachingforchange.org/parent-organizing/equityinparentorgs, Syeed, 2018).

Chapter 2

1. John Gast, *American Progress*, 1872. Chromolithograph published by George A. Cofutt. Source: Prints and Photographs Division, Library of Congress.

Chapter 3

1. Standard 8: "Effective educational leaders engage families and the community in meaningful, reciprocal, and mutually beneficial ways to promote *each* student's academic success and well-being" (National Policy Board for Educational Administration, 2015, p. 16).

Chapter 4

1. This is actually the name of the Washington State Indigenous education curriculum.

2. See, for instance, Stanford Social Innovation Racial Equity blog, the 2015 Collective Impact Forum focus on equity, and a significant number of sessions at the StriveTogether network convening with the words "equity" or "justice" in the title.

3. Sociologist Pierre Bourdieu (Bourdieu & Passeron, 1977) argued that the knowledge, skills, and social networks of the middle and upper classes constitute valuable forms of "capital" in a hierarchical society that enable the reproduction of social inequality. Yosso (2005) turns Bourdieu's notion on its head using Critical Race Theory to identify the forms of capital—the community cultural wealth—possessed and used by students and families of color, including aspirational, navigational, social, linguistic, familial, and resistant capital.

4. The Parent Teacher Home Visits Project grew out of a community organizing practice developed in Sacramento. See www.pthvp.org for more information.

Chapter 5

1. See Ibram X. Kendi's October 2016 blogpost for an extensive history of standardized testing in "Why the Achievement Gap is a Racist Idea" (Kendi, 2016).

2. I use "joint work" here to highlight the importance of building capacity and agency through consequential shared effort, not merely through conversations or relationship building situated off to the margins of daily work. Joint work comes out of sociocultural learning theories related to the notion that learning happens through participation within "communities of practice" (Lave & Wenger, 1991; Rogoff, 1994).

3. Many in the field have begun to refer to this as the school-to-prison "nexus" because a "pipeline" does not account for all the ways that ideologies, policies, and practices interlock to move particular young people from schools to prisons (Meiners, 2011).

4. A term and concept developed by the Family Leadership Design Collaborative.

5. This chapter draws from multiple phases of research in each setting: (1) In 2013–2014, the Equitable Parent-School Collaboration (EPSC) research team (including Co-Principal Investigator Dr. Joe Lott, Dawn Cameron Williams [chapter coauthor], and other doctoral students) conducted a qualitative study of the data carousel planning and event at Community Place, which led to a research-practice partnership the next year, and has now continued to evolve on its own; (2) In Riverview, we engaged in a research-practice partnership with Dr. Melanie Quaempts (formerly Strey) and other district and community partners to collect data and support implementation; and (3) We engaged Southeast Seattle Education Coalition (SESEC) in a research-community partnership with Dr. Jondou Chen taking lead with Aditi Rajendran (chapter coauthor) as part of the EPSC research team. That

work laid the foundation for our subsequent co-design partnership as part of the Family Leadership Design Collaborative. Please see the EPSC website for more information, tools, and resources: www.education.uw.edu/epsc/

6. Community Place and Riverview are pseudonyms, whereas SESEC and CISC are the actual names of the organizations. All individual's names are pseudonyms, with the exception of Erin Okuno, the executive director of SESEC.

7. The survey had been collaboratively developed in another context, iteratively piloted and refined, and was available in English, Spanish, Vietnamese, Russian, and Somali.

8. Specifically, the school with the 45% overall response rate included 60% of primarily English-speaking families, 35% Spanish-speaking families, and 46% of the Vietnamese-speaking families in the school. For context only, school-based response rates in a neighboring district tended to range between 10% and 20%, within which 84% of respondents mostly or always spoke English at home.

9. Amharic, Chinese, Oromo, Russian, Somali, Spanish, Tagalog, Tigrinya, Vietnamese, and English

10. See SESEC blogpost for more information: www.sesecwa.org/2016/03/01/sesec-summit-2/

Chapter 7

1. Special thanks to Valorie Jones for her "nudge" out of the proverbial nest into the broader field.

2. You can find many resources, publications, and more information about the FLDC on our website: familydesigncollab.org

3. FLDC core design principles toward community well-being and educational justice: Beginning with family and community ecologies; refusing and disrupting normative power dynamics; enacting solidarities in collective changemaking; creating ongoing transformative possibilities.

4. We owe a debt of gratitude to current superintendent of Flint Community Schools Dr. Derrick Lamar Jones Lopez for paving the way for our systems-based leaders and for his generosity and transparency in sharing his own systems leadership practice and co-design work.

References

Achinstein, B., & Ogawa, R. T. (2011). *Change(d) Agents: New Teachers of Color in Urban Schools*. New York, NY: Teachers College Press.

Anderson, G. (1998). Toward authentic participation: Deconstructing the discourses of participatory reforms in education. *American Educational Research Journal*, *35*(4), 571–603.

Annamma, S. A., Jackson, D. D., & Morrison, D. (2017). Conceptualizing color-evasiveness: Using dis/ability critical race theory to expand a color-blind racial ideology in education and society. *Race Ethnicity and Education*, *20*(2), 147–162. doi.org/10.1080/13613324.2016.1248837

Anyon, J. (2009). Progressive social movements and educational equity. *Educational Policy*, *23*(1), 194–215.

Anzaldúa, G. E. (Ed.). (1990). *Making face, making soul/Haciendo caras: Creative and critical perspectives by feminists of color* (1st ed). San Francisco, CA: Aunt Lute Books.

Au, W. (2009). *Unequal by design: High-stakes testing and the standardization of inequality*. New York, NY: Routledge.

Au, W. (2017). When multicultural education is not enough. *Multicultural Perspectives*, *19*(3), 147–150. doi.org/10.1080/15210960.2017.1331741

Auerbach, S. (2007). Visioning parent engagement in urban schools. *Journal of School Leadership*, *17*(6), 699–734.

Auerbach, S. (2009). Walking the walk: Portraits in leadership for family engagement in urban schools. *School Community Journal*, *19*(1), 9–32.

Auerbach, S. (2011). Beyond coffee with the principal: Toward leadership for authentic school–family partnerships. *Journal of School Leadership*, *20*(6), 728.

Bang, M., Curley, L., Kessel, A., Marin, A., Suzukovich, E. S., III, & Strack, G. (2014). Muskrat theories, tobacco in the streets, and living Chicago as Indigenous land. *Environmental Education Research*, *20*(1), 37–55. doi.org/10.1080/13504622.2013.865113

Bang, M., Faber, L., Gurneau, J., Marin, A., & Soto, C. (2015). Community-based design research: Learning across generations and strategic transformations of institutional relations toward axiological innovations. *Mind, Culture, and Activity*, *26*(1), 1–14. doi.org/10.1080/10749039.2015.1087572

Bang, M., Marin, A., Faber, L., & Suzukovich, E. S. (2013). Repatriating Indigenous technologies in an urban Indian community. *Urban Education*, *48*(5), 705–733. doi.org/10.1177/0042085913490555

Bang, M., Medin, D., Washinawatok, K., & Chapman, S. (2010). Innovations in culturally based science education through partnerships and community. In M. S. Khine & I. M. Saleh (Eds.), *New Science of Learning: Cognition, Computers and Collaboration in Education* (pp. 569–592). doi.org/10.1007/978-1-4419-5716-0_28

Bang, M., & Vossoughi, S. (2016). Participatory design research and educational justice: Studying learning and relations within social change making. *Cognition and Instruction*, *34*(3), 173–193. doi.org/10.1080/07370008.2016.1181879

Bang, M., Montaño Nolan, C., McDaid-Morgan, N. (2018). Strong families, strong nations: Indigenous family engagement. In E. McKinley & L. Smith (Eds), *Handbook of Indigenous education* (pp. 1–22). Singapore: Springer.

Baquedano-López, P., Alexander, R. A., & Hernandez, S. J. (2013). Equity issues in parental and community involvement in schools: What teacher educators need to know. *Review of Research in Education, 37*, 149–182.

Barajas-López, F., & Ishimaru, A. M. (2016). "Darles el lugar" A place for nondominant family knowing in educational equity. *Urban Education, 55*(1), 38–65. doi.org/10.1177/0042085916652179.

Barton, A. C., Drake, C., Perez, J. G., Louis, K. S., & George, M. (2004). Ecologies of parental engagement in urban education. *Educational Researcher, 33*(4), 3–12.

Bell, D. A. (1995). Who's afraid of critical race theory. *University of Illinois Law Review, 1995*, 893.

Bell, P. (2004). On the theoretical breadth of design-based research in education. *Educational Psychologist, 39*(4), 243–253.

Bensimon, E. M. (2005). Closing the achievement gap in higher education: An organizational learning perspective. *New Directions for Higher Education, 2005*(131), 99–111. doi.org/10.1002/he.190

Bernal, D. D. (2002). Critical race theory, Latino critical theory, and critical raced-gendered epistemologies: Recognizing students of color as holders and creators of knowledge. *Qualitative Inquiry, 8*(1), 105–126. doi.org/10.1177/107780040200800107

Bertrand, M., & Marsh, J. A. (2015). Teachers' sensemaking of data and implications for equity. *American Educational Research Journal, 52*(5), 861–893. doi.org/10.3102/0002831215599251

Bertrand, M., & Rodela, K. C. (2018). A framework for rethinking educational leadership in the margins: Implications for social justice leadership preparation. *Journal of Research on Leadership Education, 13*(1), 10–37. doi.org/10.1177/1942775117739414

Bonilla-Silva, E. (2010). *Racism without racists: Color-blind racism and the persistence of racial inequality in the United States* (3rd ed). Lanham, MD: Rowman & Littlefield Publishers.

Booher-Jennings, J. (2005). Below the bubble: "Educational triage" and the Texas accountability system. *American Educational Research Journal*, 42(2), 231–268.

Booker, A., & Goldman, S. (2016). Participatory design research as a practice for systemic repair: Doing hand-in-hand math research with families. *Cognition and Instruction, 34*(3), 222–235. doi.org/10.1080/07370008.2016.1179535

Bourdieu, P., & Passeron, J.C. (1977). *Reproduction in education, culture and society.* London, England: Sage.

Brayboy, B. M. J. (2006). Toward a tribal critical race theory in education. *The Urban Review, 37*(5), 425–446. doi.org/10.1007/s11256-005-0018-y

Brown, S., Souto-Manning, M., & Tropp Laman, T. (2010). Seeing the strange in the familiar: Unpacking racialized practices in early childhood settings. *Race Ethnicity and Education, 13*(4), 513–532.

Bryk, A. S., Gomez, L. M., Grunow, A., & LeMahieu, P. G. (2015). *Learning to improve: How America's schools can get better at getting better.* Cambridge, MA: Harvard Education Press.

Bryk, A. S., & Schneider, B. L. (2004). *Trust in schools: A core resource for improvement.* New York, NY: Russell Sage Foundation.

Bryk, A. S., Sebring, P. B., Allensworth, E., Easton, J. Q., & Luppescu, S. (2010). *Organizing Schools for Improvement: Lessons from Chicago.* Chicago, IL: University of Chicago Press.

Burch, P. (2007). Educational policy and practice from the perspective of institutional theory: Crafting a wider lens. *Educational Researcher, 36*(2), 84–95.

Byrne-Jiménez, M. C., & Yoon, I. H. (2019). Leadership as an act of love: Leading in dangerous times. *Frontiers in Education, 3*(117), 1-9. doi.org/10.3389/feduc.2018.00117

CADRE. (2017). *How can you love the kids but hate the parents? A shadow report on the unfulfilled promises of LAUSD school discipline reforms in South LA.* Los Angeles, CA: CADRE. Retrieved from cadre-la.org/newhome/wp-content/uploads/2018/02/Final-SR-Report.CADRE_.Oct-2017.ENG_.pdf

Cajete, G. A. (2016). Indigenous education and the development of indigenous community leaders. *Leadership, 12*(3), 364–376. doi.org/10.1177/1742715015610412

Cammarota, J., & Fine, M. (2008). *Revolutionizing Education: Youth Participatory Action Research in Motion*. New York, NY: Routledge.

Carreón, G. P., Drake, C., & Barton, A. C. (2005). The importance of presence: Immigrant parents' school engagement experiences. *American Educational Research Journal, 42*(3), 465–498. doi.org/10.3102/00028312042003465

Carter, D. (2008). Achievement as resistance: The development of a critical race achievement ideology among Black achievers. *Harvard Educational Review, 78*(3), 466–497. doi.org/10.17763/haer.78.3.83138829847hw844

Carter, P. L. (2005). *Keepin' it real: School success beyond black and white*. Oxford, England: Oxford University Press.

Carter, P. L., Skiba, R., Arredondo, M. I., & Pollock, M. (2017). You can't fix what you don't look at: Acknowledging race in addressing racial discipline disparities. *Urban education, 52*(2), 207–235.

Chase-Lansdale, P. L., & Brooks-Gunn, J. (2014). Two-generation programs in the twenty-first century. *The Future of Children, 24*(1), 13–39.

Coates, T. (2015, October). The black family in the age of mass incarceration. *The Atlantic*. Retrieved from www.theatlantic.com/magazine/archive/2015/10/the-black-family-in-the-age-of-mass-incarceration/403246/

Coburn, C. E. (2003). Rethinking scale: Moving beyond numbers to deep and lasting change. *Educational Researcher, 32*(6), 3–12. doi.org/10.3102/0013189X032006003

Coburn, C. E., & Turner, E. O. (2011). Research on data use: A framework and analysis. *Measurement: Interdisciplinary Research & Perspective*, 9(4), 173–206. doi.org/10.1080/15366367.2011.626729

Cole, M. (1998). *Cultural psychology: A once and future discipline*. Cambridge, MA: Harvard University Press.

Coleman, J. S., Campbell, E., & Hobson, C. (1966). *Equality of educational opportunity*. Washington, DC: U.S. Government Printing Office.

Collins, P. H. (1998). *Fighting words: Black women and the search for justice*. Minneapolis: University of Minnesota Press.

Cooper, C. W. (2009a). Parent involvement, African American mothers, and the politics of educational care. *Equity & Excellence in Education, 42*(4), 379–394.

Cooper, C. W. (2009b). Performing cultural work in demographically changing schools: Implications for expanding transformative leadership frameworks. *Educational Administration Quarterly, 45*(5), 694–724.

Crenshaw, K. (1990). Mapping the margins: Intersectionality, identity politics, and violence against women of color. *Stanford Law Review, 43*, 1241.

Crow, G. M. (1998). Implications for leadership in collaborative schools. In D. Pounder (Ed.), *Restructuring Schools for Collaboration: Promises and Pitfalls* (pp. 135–153). Albany, NY: SUNY Press.

Crowson, R. L., & Boyd, W. L. (2001). The new role of community development in educational reform. *Peabody Journal of Education, 76*(2), 9–29.

Darling-Hammond, L. (2015). *Flat world and education how America's commitment to equity will determine our future*. New York, NY: Teachers College Press.

de Brey, C., Musu, L., McFarland, J., Wilkinson-Flicker, S., Diliberti, M., Zhang, A., Branstetter, C., & Wang, X. (2019). *Status and trends in the education of racial and ethnic groups 2018* (NCES 2019-038). Washington, DC: National Center for Education Statistics. Retrieved from nces.ed.gov/ pubsearch/

Dee, T. S. (2004). Teachers, race, and student achievement in a randomized experiment. *The Review of Economics and Statistics, 86*(1), 195–210. doi.org/10.1162/003465304323023750

Delgado-Gaitan, C. (1994). Consejos: The power of cultural narratives. *Anthropology & Education Quarterly, 25*(3), 298–316.

Delgado-Gaitan, C. (2001). *The power of community: Mobilizing for family and schooling.* Lanham, MD: Rowman & Littlefield Publishers.

Delpit, L. D. (1988). The silenced dialogue: Power and pedagogy in educating other people's children. *Harvard Educational Review, 58*, 280–299.

Derrick-Mills, T. (2015). *Understanding data use for continuous quality improvement in Head Start preliminary findings* (OPRE Report #2015–33). Washington, DC: Urban Institute.

Design-Based Research Collective. (2003). Design-based research: An emerging paradigm for educational inquiry. *Educational Researcher, 32*(1), 5–8.

Diamond, J. B. (2012). Accountability policy, school organization, and classroom practice: Partial recoupling and educational opportunity. *Education and Urban Society, 44*(2), 151–182.

Diamond, J. B., & Cooper, K. S. (2007). The uses of testing data in urban elementary schools: Lessons from Chicago. *In* Moss, P. (Ed.) *Evidence and Decision Making, National Society for the Study of Education Yearbook*, (pp. 241–263). Malden, MA: Blackwell Publications.

Diamond, J. B., & Gomez, K. (2004). African American parents' educational orientations: The importance of social class and parents' perceptions of schools. *Education and Urban Society, 36*(4), 383–427.

Diamond, J. B., Randolph, A., & Spillane, J. P. (2004). Teachers' expectations and sense of responsibility for student learning: The importance of race, class, and organizational habitus. *Anthropology & Education Quarterly, 35*(1), 75–98.

Doucet, F. (2011). (Re) Constructing home and school: Immigrant parents, agency, and the (un) desirability of bridging multiple worlds. *Teachers College Record, 113*(12), 2705–2738.

Dunbar-Ortiz, R. (2014). *An indigenous peoples' history of the United States.* Boston, MA: Beacon Press.

Duncan, G. J., & Murnane, R. J. (Eds.). (2011). *Whither opportunity? Rising inequality, schools, and children's life chances.* New York, NY, Chicago, IL: Russell Sage Foundation, Spencer Foundation.

Dyrness, A. (2009). Cultural exclusion and critique in the era of good intentions: Using participatory research to transform parent roles in urban school reform. *Social Justice, 36*(4) (118), 36–53.

Engeström, Y. (2001). Expansive learning at work: Toward an activity theoretical reconceptualization. *Journal of Education and Work, 14*(1), 133–156.

Engeström, Y. (2007). Enriching the theory of expansive learning: Lessons from journeys toward co configuration. *Mind, Culture, and Activity, 14*(1–2), 23–39.

Engeström, Y., & Sannino, A. (2010). Studies of expansive learning: Foundations, findings and future challenges. *Educational Research Review, 5*(1), 1–24.

Epstein, J. L. (1995). School/family/community partnerships: Caring for the children we share. *Phi Delta Kappan, 76*, 701.

Erickson, F. (2001). Co-membership and wiggle room: Some implications of the study of talk for the development of social theory. In *Sociolinguistics and social theory* (pp. 152–181). New York: Pearson Education Limited.

Erickson, F. (1994). Where the action is: On collaborative action research in education. *Bulletin of the Council for Research in Music Education, 123*, 10–25.

Erickson, F. (2014). Scaling down: A modest proposal for practice-based policy research in teaching. *Education Policy Analysis Archives, 22*(9), Retrieved from epaa.asu.edu/ojs/article/view/1473/1198

Espinoza, M. L. (2008). *Humanization and social dreaming: A case study of changing social relations in a summer migrant educational program.* (Unpublished doctoral dissertation). Los Angeles, CA: University of California, Los Angeles.

Fabricant, M. (2010). *Organizing for educational justice: The campaign for public school reform in the South Bronx.* Minneapolis, MN: University of Minnesota Press.

Faircloth, S. C., & Tippeconnic, J. W. (2013). Leadership in Indigenous education: Challenges and opportunities for change. *American Journal of Education, 119*(4), 481–486.

Fan, X., & Chen, M. (2001). Parental involvement and students' academic achievement: A meta-analysis. *Educational Psychology Review*, *13*(1), 1–22.

Fielding, M. (2001). Students as radical agents of change. *Journal of Educational Change*, *2*(2), 123–141.

Fine, M. (1993). [Ap] parent involvement: Reflections on parents, power, and urban public schools. & responses. *The Teachers College Record*, *94*(4), 682–729.

Fine, M. (2008). An epilogue, of sorts. In *Revolutionizing education: Youth participatory action research in motion*. New York, NY: Routledge.

Fordham, S., & Ogbu, J. U. (1986). Black students' school success: Coping with the "burden of 'acting white.'" *The Urban Review*, *18*(3), 176–206.

Fox, M., Mediratta, K., Ruglis, J., Stoudt, B., Shah, S., & Fine, M. (2010). Critical youth engagement: Participatory action research and organizing. In L. R. Sherrod, J. Torney-Purta, & C. A. Flanagan (Eds.), *Handbook of Research on Civic Engagement in Youth* (pp. 621–649). Medford, MA: John Wiley and Sons.

Freelon, R. (2018). Transformational resistance and parent leadership: Black parents in a school district decision-making process. *Urban Education*, 10.1177/0042085918801886.

Freidus, A. (2016). "A great school benefits us all": Advantaged parents and the gentrification of an urban public school. *Urban Education*, *54*(8), 1121–1148.

Freire, P. (1970). *Pedagogy of the oppressed*. New York, NY: Herder and Herder.

Fryberg, S. M. (2010). When the world is colorblind, American Indians are invisible: A diversity science approach. *Psychological Inquiry*, *21*(2), 115–119.

Galloway, M. K., & Ishimaru, A. M. (2015). Radical recentering: Equity in educational leadership standards. *Educational Administration Quarterly*, *51*(3), 372–408.

Garces, L. M., & Gordon da Cruz, C. (2017). A strategic racial equity framework. *Peabody Journal of Education*, *92*(3), 322–342.

Garcia, J. (2019). Critical and culturally sustaining Indigenous family and community engagement in education. In S. Sheldon & T. Turner-Vorbeck (Eds.), *The Wiley handbook of family, school, and community relationships in education* (pp. 71–90). Medford, MA: John Wiley and Sons.

Garner, B., & Horn, I. S. (2016). *Epistemic foundations of educators' data use*. Paper presented at the annual meeting of the National Council of Teachers of Mathematics Research Conference, San Francisco, CA.

Garner, B., Thorne, J. K., & Horn, I. S. (2017). Teachers interpreting data for instructional decisions: Where does equity come in? *Journal of Educational Administration*, *55*(4), 407-426. doi.org/10.1108/JEA-09-2016-0106

Gaztambide-Fernández, R. A. (2012). Decolonization and the pedagogy of solidarity. *Decolonization: Indigeneity, Education & Society*, *1*(1), 41–67.

Geller, J. D. (2016). Ensuring that family engagement initiatives are successful, sustainable, and scalable. *Voices in Urban Education*, *44*, 2–5.

Geller, J. D., Alcantara, V., Boucher, D., Catone, K., Lopez, R. M., & Tung, R. (2015). What does it take to form meaningful connections among cultural brokers, parents, and teachers? Lessons from a federal grant. *Journal of Family Diversity in Education*, *1*(4), 22–44.

Geller, J. D., Doykos, B., Craven, K., Bess, K. D., & Nation, M. (2014). Engaging residents in community change: The critical role of trust in the development of a Promise Neighborhood. *Teachers College Record*, *116*(4), 1–42.

Gershenson, S., Hart, C. M. D., Hyman, J., Lindsay, C., & Papageorge, N. W. (2018). *The long-run impacts of same-race teachers* (Working Paper No. 25254). Cambridge, MA: National Bureau of Economic Research. doi.org/10.3386/w25254

Gorski, P. C. (2008). Peddling poverty for profit: Elements of oppression in Ruby Payne's framework. *Equity & Excellence in Education*, *41*(1), 130–148.

Green, T. L. (2017). Community-Based Equity Audits: A Practical Approach for Educational Leaders to Support Equitable Community-School Improvements. *Educational Administration Quarterly*, *53*(1), 3–39. doi.org/10.1177/0013161X16672513

Gregory, A., Skiba, R. J., & Noguera, P. A. (2010). The achievement gap and the discipline gap: Two sides of the same coin? *Educational Researcher, 39*(1), 59–68. doi.org/10.3102/0013189X09357621

Gullo, D. (2013). Improving instructional practices, policies, and student outcomes for early childhood language and literacy through data-driven decision making. *Early Childhood Education Journal, 41*(6), 413–421. doi.org/10.1007/s10643-013-0581-x

Gutiérrez, K. (2006). White innocence: A framework and methodology for rethinking educational discourse and inquiry. *International Journal of Learning, 12*(10), 223–230.

Gutiérrez, K. D., & Jaramillo, N. E. (2006). Looking for educational equity: The consequences of relying on Brown. *Yearbook of the National Society for the Study of Education, 105*, 173–189.

Gutiérrez, K. D., & Jurow, A. S. (2016). Social design experiments: Toward equity by design. *Journal of the Learning Sciences, 25*(4), 565–598. doi.org/10.1080/10508406.2016.1204548

Gutiérrez, K. D., & Rogoff, B. (2003). Cultural ways of learning: Individual traits or repertoires of practice. *Educational Researcher, 32*(5), 19–25.

Gutiérrez, K. D., & Vossoughi, S. (2010). Lifting off the ground to return anew: Mediated praxis, transformative learning, and social design experiments. *Journal of Teacher Education, 61*(1–2), 100–117. doi.org/10.1177/0022487109347877

Haapasaari, A., Engeström, Y., & Kerosuo, H. (2016). The emergence of learners' transformative agency in a Change Laboratory intervention. *Journal of Education and Work, 29*(2), 232–262. doi.org/10.1080/13639080.2014.900168

Hagerman, M. A. (2018). *White kids: Growing up with privilege in a racially divided America.* New York: NYU Press.

Hands, C. (2014). Somewhere between a possibility and a pipe dream: District-level leadership that promotes family inclusion and engagement in education. *Journal of Family Diversity in Education, 1*(2), 88–111.

Hands, C. M., & Hubbard, L. (Eds.). (2011). *Including families and communities in urban education.* Charlotte, NC: Information Age Publications.

Hargreaves, A., & Fullan, M. (2012). *Professional capital: Transforming teaching in every school.* New York, NY: Teachers College Press.

Harris, C. I. (1993). Whiteness as property. *Harvard Law Review, 106*(8), 1707–1791. doi.org/10.2307/1341787

Heath, S. B. (1983). *Ways with words: Language, life, and work in communities and classrooms.* Cambridge, England: Cambridge University Press.

Heifetz, R. A., & Linsky, M. (2002). *Leadership on the line.* Boston, MA: Harvard Business School Press.

Henderson, A. T., & Mapp, K. L. (2002). *A new wave of evidence: The impact of school, family, and community connections on student achievement.* Austin, TX: National Center for Family & Community Connections with Schools, Southwest Educational Development Lab.

Henderson, A. T., Mapp, K. L., Johnson, V. R., & Davies, D. (Eds.). (2007). *Beyond the bake sale: The essential guide to family-school partnerships.* New York, NY: The New Press.

Henig, J. R., Riehl, C. J., Rebell, M. A., & Wolff, J. R. (2015). *Putting collective impact in context: A review of the literature on local cross-sector collaboration to improve education.* New York, NY: Teachers College, Department of Education Policy & Social Analysis.

Henrich, J., Heine, S. J., & Norenzayan, A. (2010). Most people are not WEIRD. *Nature, 466*(7302), 29. doi.org/10.1038/466029a

Hill, L. A. (2003). *Becoming a manager: How new managers master the challenges of leadership* (2nd ed). Boston, MA: Harvard Business School Press.

Hill, N. E., & Tyson, D. F. (2009). Parental involvement in middle school: A meta-analytic assessment of the strategies that promote achievement. *Developmental Psychology, 45*(3), 740–763. doi.org/10.1037/a0015362

Holcomb, E. L. (2004). *Getting excited about data: Combining people, passion, and proof to maximize student achievement* (2nd ed.). Thousand Oaks, CA: Corwin Press.

Hong, S. (2011). *A cord of three strands: A new approach to parent engagement in schools.* Cambridge, MA: Harvard Education Press.

Honig, M. I. (2004). District central office-community partnerships: From contracts to collaboration to control. In W. Hoy & C. Miskel (Eds.), *Educational administration, policy, and reform: Research and measurement* (pp. 59–90). Greenwich, CT: Information Age Publishing.

hooks, b. (1994). *Teaching to transgress: Education as the practice of freedom.* New York, NY: Routledge.

hooks, b. (2003). *Teaching community: A pedagogy of hope.* New York, NY: Routledge.

Horsford, S. D., & Sampson, C. (2014). Promise neighborhoods: The promise and politics of community capacity building as urban school reform. *Urban Education, 49*(8), 955–991. doi.org/10.1177/0042085914557645

Horsford, S. D., & Vasquez Heilig, J. (2014). Community-based education reform in urban contexts: Implications for leadership, policy, and accountability. *Urban Education, 49*(8), 867–870. doi.org/10.1177/0042085914557647

Horvat, E. M., Weininger, E. B., & Lareau, A. (2003). From social ties to social capital: Class differences in the relations between schools and parent networks. *American Educational Research Journal, 40*(2), 319–351. doi.org/10.3102/00028312040002319

Howard, T. C., & Navarro, O. (2016). Critical race theory 20 years later where do we go from here? *Urban Education*, 0042085915622541.

Howland, A., Anderson, J. A., Smiley, A. D., & Abbott, D. J. (2006). School liaisons: Bridging the gap between home and school. *School Community Journal, 16*(2), 47.

Ikemoto, G. S., & Marsh, J. A. (2007). Cutting through the "data-driven" mantra: Different conceptions of data-driven decision making. *Yearbook of the National Society for the Study of Education, 106*(1), 105–131. doi.org/10.1111/j.1744-7984.2007.00099.x

Ippolito, J. (2015). Reading interventionist research in two urban elementary schools through a discursive lens. *Urban Education, 53*(10), 1265–1290.

Irby, D. J. (2018). Mo' data, mo' problems: Making sense of racial discipline disparities in a large diversifying suburban high school. *Educational Administration Quarterly, 54*(5), 693–722. doi.org/10.1177/0013161X18769051

Ishimaru, A. M. (2013). From heroes to organizers: Principals and education organizing in urban school reform. *Educational Administration Quarterly, 49*(1), 3–51. doi .org/10.1177/0013161X12448250

Ishimaru, A. M. (2014a). Rewriting the rules of engagement: Elaborating a model of district-community collaboration. *Harvard Educational Review, 84*(2), 188–216.

Ishimaru, A. M. (2014b). When new relationships meet old narratives: The journey towards improving parent-school relations in a district-community organizing collaboration. *Teachers College Record, 116*(2), 1–49.

Ishimaru, A. M. (2018). Re-imagining turnaround: Families and communities leading educational justice. *Journal of Educational Administration, 56*(5), 546–561. doi.org/10.1108 /JEA-01-2018-0013

Ishimaru, A. M., & Bang, M. (2016). *Toward a transformative research and practice agenda for racial equity in family engagement.* Seattle, WA: A Family Leadership Design Collaborative, University of Washington.

Ishimaru, A.M., & Bang, M. (2017). *Solidarity-driven decision-making: Enacting equity in partnering & decision-making, Phase 2 Process Brief.* Seattle, WA: Family Leadership Design Collaborative, University of Washington. Retrieved from familydesigncollab.org/wp-content /uploads/2018/07/Solidarity-Driven-Decision-Making_FLDC-Phase-2-Process.pdf

Ishimaru, A.M., Bang, M., Valladares, M. R., Nolan, C. M., Tavares, H., Rajendran, A., & Chang, K. (2019). *Recasting families and communities as co-designers of education in tumultuous times.* Boulder, CO: National Education Policy Center. Retrieved from nepc .colorado.edu/publication/family-leadership.

Ishimaru, A. M., Barajas-López, F., & Bang, M. (2015). Centering family knowledge to develop children's empowered mathematics identities. *Journal of Family Diversity in Education, 1*(4), 1–21.

Ishimaru, A. M., & Galloway, M. K. (2014). Beyond individual effectiveness: Conceptualizing organizational leadership for equity. *Leadership and Policy in Schools*, *13*(1), 93–146. doi.org/10.1080/15700763.2014.890733

Ishimaru, A. M., Lott, J., Fajardo, I., & Salvador, J. (2014). *Towards equitable parent-school collaboration: Developing common parent engagement indicators for the Road Map Project*. Seattle, WA: College of Education, University of Washington.

Ishimaru, A. M., Lott, J., Torres, K. E., & O'Reilly-Diaz, K. (2019). Families in the driver's seat: Catalyzing familial transformative agency for equitable collaboration. *Teachers College Record*, *121*(11). Retrieved from www.tcrecord.org/Content.asp?ContentId=22819

Ishimaru, A. M., Lott, J., & the Equitable Parent-School Collaboration Research Project. (2014). *Charting a course to equitable collaboration: Learning from parent engagement initiatives in the Road Map Project*. Seattle, WA: College of Education, University of Washington.

Ishimaru, A. M., Rajendran, A., Nolan, C. M., & Bang, M. (2018). Community design circles: Co-designing justice and wellbeing in family-community-research partnerships. *Journal of Family Diversity in Education*, *3*(2), 38–63.

Ishimaru, A. M., & Takahashi, S. (2017). Disrupting racialized institutional scripts: Toward parent–teacher transformative agency for educational justice. *Peabody Journal of Education*, *92*(3), 343–362. doi.org/10.1080/0161956X.2017.1324660

Ishimaru, A. M., Torres, K. E., Salvador, J. E., Lott, J., Williams, D. M. C., & Tran, C. (2016). Reinforcing deficit, journeying toward equity: Cultural brokering in family engagement initiatives. *American Educational Research Journal*, *53*(4), 850–882. doi.org/10.3102/0002831216657178

Jepperson, R. L. (1991). Institutions, institutional effects, and institutionalism. *The New Institutionalism in Organizational Analysis*, *6*, 143–163.

Jeynes, W. (2012). A meta-analysis of the efficacy of different types of parental involvement programs for urban students. *Urban Education*, *47*(4), 706–742.

Jeynes, W. H. (2007). The relationship between parental involvement and urban secondary school student academic achievement: A meta-analysis. *Urban Education*, *42*(1), 82–110. doi.org/10.1177/0042085906293818

Jeynes, W. H. (2005). A meta-analysis of the relation of parental involvement to urban elementary school student academic achievement. *Urban Education*, *40*(3), 237–269. doi.org/10.1177/0042085905274540

Jeynes, W, H. (2015). A meta-analysis on the factors that best reduce the achievement gap. *Education and Urban Society*, *47*(5), 523–554. doi.org/10.1177/0013124514529155

Jezewski, M. A. (1990). Culture brokering in migrant farmworker health care. *Western Journal of Nursing Research*, *12*(4), 497–513.

Jimenez-Castellanos, O., & Gonzalez, G. (2012). Understanding the impact of micro-aggressions on the engagement of undocumented Latino immigrant fathers: Debunking deficit thinking. *Journal of Latinos and Education*, *11*(4), 204–217. doi.org/10.1080/15348431.2012.715492

Johnson, R. S., & La Salle, R. A. (2010). *Data strategies to uncover and eliminate hidden inequities: The wallpaper effect*. Thousand Oaks, CA: Corwin.

Jordan, W. J. (2010). Defining equity: Multiple perspectives to analyzing the performance of diverse learners. *Review of Research in Education*, *34*, 142–178.

Kania, J., & Kramer, M. (2013). Embracing emergence: How collective impact addresses complexity. *Stanford Social Innovation Review*, pp. 1–7.

Kao, G. (1995). Asian Americans as model minorities? A look at their academic performance. *American Journal of Education*, *103*(2), 121–159.

Kao, G. (2004). Parental influences on the educational outcomes of immigrant youth. *International Migration Review*, *38*(2), 427–449. doi.org/10.1111/j.1747-7379.2004.tb00204.x

Kendi, I. X. (2016, October 20). Why the academic achievement gap is a racist idea. [Blog post]. Retrieved from www.aaihs.org/why-the-academic-achievement-gap-is-a-racist-idea/

Khalifa, M. (2017). *Centering ancestral knowledges: Leadership in learning environments*. Seattle, WA: Family Leadership Design Collaborative. Retrieved from familydesigncollab.org/wp-content/uploads/2018/07/Ancestral-Knoweldges_FLDC-Research-Brief_07.25.18.pdf

Khalifa, M. (2018). *Culturally responsive school leadership*. Cambridge, MA: Harvard Education Press.

Khalifa, M. A., Jennings, M. E., Briscoe, F., Oleszweski, A. M., & Abdi, N. (2014). Racism? administrative and community perspectives in data-driven decision making: Systemic perspectives versus technical-rational perspectives. *Urban Education*, *49*(2), 147–181. doi.org/10.1177/0042085913475635

Khalifa, M. A., Khalil, D., Marsh, T. E. J., & Halloran, C. (2018). Toward an Indigenous, decolonizing school leadership: A literature review. *Educational Administration Quarterly*, *55*(4), 571–614. doi.org/10.1177/0013161X18809348

Khalifa, M., Dunbar, C., & Douglasb, T.-R. (2013). Derrick Bell, CRT, and educational leadership 1995–present. *Race Ethnicity and Education*, *16*(4), 489–513. doi.org/10.1080/13613324.2013.817770

Kirshner, B., & Jefferson, A. (2015). Participatory democracy and struggling schools: Making space for youth in school turnarounds. *Teachers College Record*, *117*(6), 1–26.

Knapp, M. S., Copland, M. A.,& Swinnerton, J. A. (2007). Data-informed leadership: Insights from current research, theory, and practice. In P. Moss (Ed.), *Evidence and decision making: the 106th Yearbook of the National Society for the Study of Education* (pp. 74–104). Chicago, IL: University of Chicago Press.

Kohli, R. (2018). Behind school doors: The impact of hostile racial climates on urban teachers of color. *Urban Education*, *53*(3), 307–333. doi.org/10.1177/0042085916636653

Koretz, D. M. (2008). *Measuring up: What educational testing really tells us*. Cambridge, MA: Harvard University Press.

Kovach, M. (2019). Conversational method in Indigenous research. *First Peoples Child & Family Review*, *14*(1), 123–136.

Kulago, H. A. (2016). Activating Indigenous knowledge to create supportive educational environments by rethinking family, community, and school partnerships. *Journal of Family Diversity in Education*, *2*(1), 1–20.

Lac, V. T., & Mansfield, K. C. (2018). What do students have to do with educational leadership? Making a case for centering student voice. *Journal of Research on Leadership Education*, *13*(1), 38–58. doi.org/10.1177/1942775117743748

Ladson-Billings, G. (1998). Just what is critical race theory and what's it doing in a nice field like education? *International Journal of Qualitative Studies in Education*, *11*(1), 7–24. doi.org/10.1080/095183998236863

Ladson-Billings, G. (2006). From the achievement gap to the education debt: Understanding achievement in U.S. schools. *Educational Researcher*, *35*(7), 3–12. doi.org/10.3102/0013189X035007003

Ladson-Billings, G., & Tate, W. F. (1995). Toward a critical race theory of education. *Teachers College Record*, *97*(1), 47–68.

Lareau, A. (2003). *Unequal childhoods: Class, race, and family life*. Berkeley: University of California Press.

Lareau, A., & Horvat, E. M. (1999). Moments of social inclusion and exclusion race, class, and cultural capital in family-school relationships. *Sociology of Education*, *72*(1), 37. doi.org/10.2307/2673185

Lave, J., & Wenger, E. (1991). *Situated learning: Legitimate peripheral participation*. Cambridge, United Kingdom: Cambridge University Press.

Lawrence-Lightfoot, S. (2004). *The essential conversation: What parents and teachers can learn from each other*. New York, NY: Ballantine Books.

Lawson, H. A. (2013). Third-generation partnerships for P-16 pipelines and cradle-through-career education systems. *Peabody Journal of Education*, *88*(5), 637–656.

LeChasseur, K. (2016). Re-examining power and privilege in collective impact. *Community Development*, *47*(2), 225–240. doi.org/10.1080/15575330.2016.1140664

Lee, C. D. (2001). Is October Brown Chinese? A cultural modeling activity system for underachieving students. *American Educational Research Journal*, *38*(1), 97–141. doi.org/10.3102/00028312038001097

Lee, S. J. (2006). Additional complexities: Social class, ethnicity, generation, and gender in Asian American student experiences. *Race Ethnicity and Education*, *9*(1), 17–28. doi.org/10.1080/13613320500490630

Leithwood, K., Louis, K. S., Anderson, S., & Wahlstrom, K. (2004). *How leadership influences student learning. Review of research*. New York, NY: The Wallace Foundation.

Leithwood, K. A., & Riehl, C. (2003). *What we know about successful school leadership*. American Educational Research Association Division A. Retrieved from olms.cte.jhu.edu/olms2/data/ck/file/What_we_know_about_SchoolLeadership.pdf

Lewis, A. E., & Diamond, J. B. (2015). *Despite the best intentions: How racial inequality thrives in good schools*. New York, NY: Oxford University Press.

Lewis-McCoy, R. L. (2014). *Inequality in the promised land: Race, resources, and suburban schooling*. Stanford, CA: Stanford University Press.

Lightfoot, D. (2004). "Some parents just don't care": Decoding the meanings of parental involvement in urban schools. *Urban Education*, *39*(1), 91–107. doi.org/10.1177/0042085903259290

López, G. R. (2001). *On whose terms? Understanding involvement through the eyes of migrant parents*. Paper presented at the annual meeting of the American Educational Research Association, Seattle, WA.

López, G. R., Scribner, J. D., & Mahitivanichcha, K. (2001). Redefining parental involvement: Lessons from high-performing migrant-impacted schools. *American Educational Research Journal*, *38*(2), 253–288.

Lopez, M. L., & Stack, C. (2001). Social capital and the culture of power: Lessons from the field. *Social Capital and Poor Communities*, 31–59.

Mackey, H. J. (2015). Educational administration in Indian country: The peculiar position of Indigenous languages, tribal self-determination, and federal policy. In A. Normore, P. Ehrensal, P. First, & M. Torres (Eds.), *Legal frontiers in education: Complex law issues for leaders, policymakers and policy implementers* (pp. 165–180). Bingley, England: Emerald Publishing.

Mandinach, E. (2012). A perfect time for data use: Using data-driven decision making to inform practice. *Educational Psychologist*, *47*, 71–85. doi.org/10.1080/00461520.2012.667064

Mansfield, K. C., Welton, A. D., & Halx, M. D. (2012). Listening to student voice: Toward a more inclusive theory for research and practice. In C. Boske & S. Diem (Eds.), *Global leadership for social justice: Taking it from field to practice* (pp. 21–41). Bingley, England: Emerald Publishing.

Mapp, K., & Hong, S. (2010). Debunking the myth of the hard to reach parent. In S. L. Christenson & A. L. Reschly (Eds.), *Handbook of school-family partnerships* (pp. 345–361). New York, NY: Routledge.

Mapp, K. L., & Kuttner, P. J. (2013). *Partners in education: A dual capacity-building framework for family–school partnerships*. Austin, TX: SEDL. Retrieved from www.sedl.org/pubs/framework/FE-Cap-Building. pdf.

Marsh, J. A., & Farrell, C. C. (2015). How leaders can support teachers with data-driven decision making: A framework for understanding capacity building. *Educational Management Administration & Leadership*, *43*(2), 269–289. doi.org/10.1177/1741143214537229

Marsh, J. A., Strunk, K. O., Bush-Mecenas, S. C., & Huguet, A. (2015). Democratic engagement in district reform: The evolving role of parents in the Los Angeles Public School Choice Initiative. *Educational Policy*, *29*(1), 51–84.

Martin, D. B. (2011). What does quality mean in the context of White institutional space? In B. Atweh, M. Graven, W. Secada, & P. Valero (Eds.), *Mapping Equity and Quality in Mathematics Education* (pp. 437–450). Netherlands: Springer. doi.org/10.1007/978-90-481-9803-0_31

Martinez, M. A., Chang, A., & Welton, A. D. (2017). Assistant professors of color confront the inequitable terrain of academia: A community cultural wealth perspective. *Race Ethnicity and Education, 20*(5), 696–710. doi.org/10.1080/13613324.2016.1150826

Martinez-Cosio, M., & Iannacone, R. M. (2007). The tenuous role of institutional agents: Parent liaisons as cultural brokers. *Education and Urban Society, 39*(3), 349–369. doi.org/10.1177/0013124506298165

Mawhinney, H. B., & Smrekar, C. (1996). Institutional constraints to advocacy in collaborative services. *Educational Policy, 10*(4), 480–501.

McWayne, C. M., Melzi, G., Schick, A. R., Kennedy, J. L., & Mundt, K. (2013). Defining family engagement among Latino Head Start parents: A mixed-methods measurement development study. *Early Childhood Research Quarterly, 28*(3), 593–607. doi.org/10.1016/j.ecresq.2013.03.008

Mediratta, K., Shah, S., & McAlister, S. (2009). *Community organizing for stronger schools: Strategies and successes*. Cambridge, MA: Harvard Education Press.

Meiners, E. R. (2011). Ending the school-to-prison pipeline/building abolition futures. *The Urban Review, 43*(4), 547. doi.org/10.1007/s11256-011-0187-9

Melendez, J. W., Radinsky, J., Vossoughi, S., Marin, A., Bang, M., Nolan, C. M., . . . Hall, R. (2018). Community-based design partnerships: Examples from a new generation of CHAT/DBR. In Kay, J. and Luckin, R. (Eds.) *Rethinking Learning in the Digital Age: Making the Learning Sciences Count, 13th International Conference of the Learning Sciences (ICLS) 2018, Volume 2*. London, UK: International Society of the Learning Sciences.

Meyer, H.D., & Rowan, B. (2006). *The new institutionalism in education*. Albany, NY: SUNY Press.

Milner, H. R. (2013). Rethinking achievement gap talk in urban education. *Urban Education, 48*(1), 3–8. doi.org/10.1177/0042085912470417

Mirra, N., Filipiak, D., & Garcia, A. (2015). Revolutionizing inquiry in urban English classrooms: Pursuing voice and justice through youth participatory action research. *English Journal, 105*(2), 49–57.

Mitra, D. (2006). Increasing student voice and moving toward youth leadership. *The Prevention Researcher, 13*(1), 7–10.

Moll, L. C., Amanti, C., Neff, D., & Gonzalez, N. (1992). Funds of knowledge for teaching: Using a qualitative approach to connect homes and classrooms. *Theory into Practice, 31*(2), 132–141.

Motha, S., & Varghese, M. M. (2018). Rewriting dominant narratives of the academy: Women faculty of color and identity management. *Race Ethnicity and Education, 21*(4), 503–517. doi.org/10.1080/13613324.2016.1248826

Moynihan, P. (1965). *The Negro family: The case for national action*. Washington DC: Office of Policy Planning and Research United States Department of Labor.

Nakagawa, K. (2000). Unthreading the ties that bind: Questioning the discourse of parent involvement. *Educational Policy, 14*(4), 443–472. doi.org/10.1177/0895904800144001

Nasir, N. S. (2011). *Racialized identities: Race and achievement among African American youth*. Stanford, CA: Stanford University Press.

Nasir, N. S., & Hand, V. M. (2006). Exploring sociocultural perspectives on race, culture, and learning. *Review of Educational Research, 76*(4), 449–475. doi.org/10.3102/00346543076004449

Nasir, N. S., McLaughlin, M. W., & Jones, A. (2009). What does it mean to be African American? Constructions of race and academic identity in an urban public high school. *American Educational Research Journal, 46*(1), 73–114. doi.org/10.3102/0002831208323279

Nasir, N. S, Snyder, C. R., Shah, N., & Ross, K. M. (2012). Racial storylines and implications for learning. *Human Development, 55*(5–6), 285–301. doi.org/10.1159/000345318

National Policy Board for Educational Administration (2015). *Professional Standards for Educational Leaders 2015*. Reston, VA: Author.

Nisbet, E. (2018). Local-level philanthropic partnerships in public education: Dilemmas for equity and public responsibility. *Journal of Urban Affairs, 0*(0), 1–19. doi.org/10.1080/07352166.2017.1421432

Noguera, P. (2003). *City schools and the American dream: Reclaiming the promise of public education*. New York, NY: Teachers College Press.

Oakes, J. (1985). *Keeping track: How schools structure inequality*. New Haven, CT: Yale University Press.

Oakes, J., & Rogers, J. (2006). *Learning power: Organizing for education and justice*. New York, NY: Teachers College Press.

Okuno, E., & Chen, J. (2016). *SESEC Equitable family engagement report*. Seattle, WA: SESEC.

Olivos, E. M. (2006). *The power of parents: A critical perspective of bicultural parent involvement in public schools*. New York, NY: Peter Lang.

Olivos, E., & Mendoza, M. (2009). Immigration and educational inequity: An examination of Latino immigrant parents' inclusion in the public school context. *Journal of Latino/Latin American Studies, 3*(3), 38–53. doi.org/10.18085/llas.3.3.k12913266121047h

Orfield, G., & Frankenberg, E. (2014). Increasingly segregated and unequal schools as courts reverse policy. *Educational Administration Quarterly, 50*(5), 718–734. doi.org/10.1177/0013161X14548942

Pang, V. O., Han, P. P., & Pang, J. M. (2011). Asian American and Pacific Islander students: Equity and the achievement gap. *Educational Researcher, 40*(8), 378–389. doi.org/10.3102/0013189X11424222

Paredes, M. (2011). Parent involvement as an instructional strategy: Academic parent-teacher teams. (Doctoral dissertation). Arizona State University, Tempe, AZ. Retrieved from cdn.ymaws.com/www.cpedinitiative.org/resource/resmgr/docs/DiPs/Paredes.pdf

Park, S., Hironaka, S., Carver, P., & Nordstrum, L. (2013). *Continuous improvement in education*. Stanford, CA: Carnegie Foundation.

Park, V., & Datnow, A. (2009). Co-constructing distributed leadership: District and school connections in data-driven decision-making. *School Leadership & Management, 29*(5), 477–494. doi.org/10.1080/13632430903162541

Patel, L. (2016). *Decolonizing educational research: From ownership to answerability*. New York, NY: Routledge.

Patel, L. (2017, July 27). Rejecting a politics of inclusion. [Blog post]. Retrieved from decolonizing.wordpress.com/2017/07/27/rejecting-a-politics-of-inclusion/

Payne, C. M. (2008). *So much reform, so little change: The persistence of failure in urban schools*. Cambridge, MA: Harvard Education Press.

Pekel, K., Roehlkepartain, E. C., Syvertsen, A. K., & Scales, P. C. (2015). *Don't forget the families: The missing piece in America's effort to help all children succeed*. Minneapolis: MN: Search Institute. Retrieved from www.search-institute.org/downloadable/SearchInstitute-DontForgetFamilies-Report-10-13-2015.pdf

Pérez, M. S., & Saavedra, C. M. (2017). A call for onto-epistemological diversity in early childhood education and care: Centering global South conceptualizations of childhood/s. *Review of Research in Education, 41*(1), 1–29. doi.org/10.3102/0091732X16688621

Pollock, M. (2009). *Colormute: Race talk dilemmas in an American school*. Princeton, NJ: Princeton University Press.

Poon, O., Squire, D., Kodama, C., Byrd, A., Chan, J., Manzano, L., Furr, S. & Bishundat, D. (2016). A critical review of the model minority myth in selected literature on Asian Americans and Pacific Islanders in higher education. *Review of Educational Research, 86*(2), 469–502.

Posey-Maddox, L. (2014). *When middle-class parents choose urban schools: Class, race, and the challenge of equity in public education*. Chicago, IL: The University of Chicago Press.

Powell, W. W., & DiMaggio, P. (Eds.). (1991). *The new institutionalism in organizational analysis*. Chicago, IL: University of Chicago Press.

Quezada, M. S. (2016). Strengthening relationships with families in the school community: Do school leaders make a difference? *Voices in Urban Education*, *44*, 23–32.

Raftery, I. (2018, October 29). Here's why rich Seattle schools can afford extra teachers and fancy gadgets. *KUOW*. Retrieved from www.kuow.org/stories/some-seattle-school-ptas-can-afford-extra-teachers-should-they-spread-the-wealth

Ray, V. (2019). A theory of racialized organizations. *American Sociological Review, 84*(1), 26–53. doi.org/10.1177/0003122418822335

Rogers, J., Freelon, R., & Terriquez, V. (2012). Enlisting collective help: Urban principals' encouragement of parent participation in school decision-making. In S. Auerbach (Ed.) *School leadership for authentic family and community partnerships: Research perspectives for transforming practice* (pp. 55–77). New York, NY: Routledge.

Rogoff, B. (1994). Developing understanding of the idea of communities of learners. *Mind, Culture, and Activity*, *1*(4), 209–229. doi.org/10.1080/10749039409524673

Rogoff, B. (2003). *The cultural nature of human development*. Oxford, England: Oxford University Press.

Rosen, S. M. (2019). "So much of my very soul": How youth organizers' identity projects pave agentive pathways for civic engagement. *American Educational Research Journal*, *56*(3), 1033–1063. doi.org/10.3102/0002831218812028

Rubel, L. H. (2017). Equity-directed instructional practices: Beyond the dominant perspective. *Journal of Urban Mathematics Education*, *10*(2), 66–105.

Ryan, J. (2006). Inclusive leadership and social justice for schools. *Leadership and Policy in Schools*, *5*(1), 3–17. doi.org/10.1080/15700760500483995

San Pedro, T., Carlos, E., & Mburu, J. (2017). Critical listening and storying: Fostering respect for difference and action within and beyond a Native American literature classroom. *Urban Education*, *52*(5), 667–693. doi.org/10.1177/0042085915623346

Sandall, S. R., Schwartz, I. S., & Lacroix, B. (2004). Interventionists' perspectives about data collection in integrated early childhood classrooms. *Journal of Early Intervention*, *26*(3), 161–174. doi.org/10.1177/105381510402600301

Sannino, A., & Nocon, H. (2008). Special issue editors' introduction: Activity theory and school innovation. *Journal of Educational Change*, *9*(4), 325–328. doi.org/10.1007/s10833-008-9079-5

Schutz, A. (2006). Home is a prison in the global city: The tragic failure of school-based community engagement strategies. *Review of Educational Research*, *76*(4), 691–743.

Scott, J. (2013). School choice and the empowerment imperative. *Peabody Journal of Education*, *88*(1), 60–73.

Scott, W. R. (2013). *Institutions and organizations: Ideas, interests, and identities*. Thousand Oaks, CA: Sage Publications.

Sensoy, Ö., & DiAngelo, R. J. (2017). *Is everyone really equal? An introduction to key concepts in social justice education* (2nd ed.). New York, NY: Teachers College Press.

Sheldon, S. B., & Jung, S. B. (2015). *The Family engagement partnership: Student outcome evaluation*. Baltimore, MD: Center on School, Family and Community Partnerships, Johns Hopkins University.

Shirley, D. (1997). *Community organizing for urban school reform* (1st University of Texas Press ed.). Austin, TX: University of Texas Press.

Siddle Walker, V. (1996). *Their highest potential: An African American school community in the segregated South*. Chapel Hill, NC: University of North Carolina Press.

Skiba, R. J., Michael, R. S., Nardo, A. C., & Peterson, R. L. (2002). The color of discipline: Sources of racial and gender disproportionality in school punishment. *The Urban Review*, *34*(4), 317–342.

Small, M. L. (2006). Neighborhood institutions as resource brokers: Childcare centers, interorganizational ties, and resource access among the poor. *Social Problems*, *53*(2), 274–292. doi.org/10.1525/sp.2006.53.2.274

Smith, L. T. (2012). *Decolonizing methodologies: Research and indigenous peoples* (2nd ed.). London, England: Zed Books.

Solórzano, D. G., & Bernal, D. D. (2001). Examining transformational resistance through a critical race and latcrit theory framework: Chicana and Chicano students in an urban context. *Urban Education*, *36*(3), 308–342. doi.org/10.1177/0042085901363002

Souto-Manning, M., & Rabadi-Raol, A. (2018). (Re)centering quality in early childhood education: Toward intersectional justice for minoritized children. *Review of Research in Education*, *42*(1), 203–225. doi.org/10.3102/0091732X18759550

Stanton-Salazar, R. D. (2010). A social capital framework for the study of institutional agents and their role in the empowerment of low-status students and youth. *Youth & Society*, *43*(3), 1066–1109. doi.org/10.1177/0044118X10382877

Starkie, B. (2012). *Data sharing through parent portals: An exploration of parental motivation, data use, and the promise of prolonged parent involvement.* (Unpublished doctoral dissertation). Retrieved from search.proquest.com/docview/1039154195/?pq-origsite =primo

Stone, C. N., Henig, J. R., Jones, B., & Pierannunzi, C. (2001). *Building civic capacity: The politics of reforming urban schools*. Lawrence: University Press of Kansas.

Suárez-Orozco, C., & Suárez-Orozco, M. M. (2001). *Children of immigration*. Cambridge, MA: Harvard University Press.

Sullivan, A. L., & Artiles, A. J. (2011). Theorizing racial inequity in special education: Applying structural inequity theory to disproportionality. *Urban Education*, *46*(6), 1526–1552. doi.org/10.1177/0042085911416014

Sullivan, A. L., Artiles, A. J., & Hernandez-Saca, D. I. (2015). Addressing special education inequity through systemic change: Contributions of ecologically based organizational consultation. *Journal of Educational and Psychological Consultation*, *25*(2–3), 129–147. doi.org/10.1080/10474412.2014.929969

Superville, D. (2019, June 18). A district knew it was failing some students. How it's using parents to help. *Education Week*, pp. 1–11.

Syeed, E. (2018). There goes the PTA: Building parent identity, relationships, and power in gentrifying schools. *Equity & Excellence in Education*, *51*(3–4), 284–300.

Takahashi, S. (2011). Co-constructing efficacy: A "communities of practice" perspective on teachers' efficacy beliefs. *Teaching and Teacher Education*, 27(4), 732–741. doi .org/10.1016/j.tate.2010.12.002

Takaki, R. (1989). *Strangers from a different shore: A history of Asian Americans*. New York, NY: Little, Brown and Company.

Terriquez, V. (2011). Schools for democracy: Labor union participation and Latino immigrant parents' school-based civic engagement. *American Sociological Review*, *76*, 581–601. doi.org/10.1177/0003122411414815

Tilly, C. (1998). *Durable inequality*. Berkeley, CA: University of California Press.

Trujillo, T. (2014). The modern cult of efficiency: Intermediary organizations and the new scientific management. *Educational Policy*, *28*(2), 207–232. doi.org/10.1177 /0895904813513148

Tuck, E. (2009). Suspending damage: A letter to communities. *Harvard Educational Review*, *79*(3), 409–428. doi.org/10.17763/haer.79.3.n0016675661t3n15

Tuck, E., & Gaztambide-Fernández, R. A. (2013). Curriculum, replacement, and settler futurity. *Journal of Curriculum Theorizing*, *29*(1), 72–89.

Tuck, E., & Gorlewski, J. (2016). Racist ordering, settler colonialism, and edTPA: A participatory policy analysis. *Educational Policy*, *30*(1), 197–217.

Tuck, E., & Yang, K. W. (2012). Decolonization is not a metaphor. *Decolonization: Indigeneity, Education & Society*, *1*(1), 1–40.

Tuck, E., & Yang, K. W. (Eds.). (2018). *Toward what justice? Describing diverse dreams of justice in education.* New York, NY: Routledge, Taylor & Francis Group.

Turner, C. S. V. (2002). Women of color in academe: Living with multiple marginality. *The Journal of Higher Education, 73*(1), 74–93. doi.org/10.1353/jhe.2002.0013

Turner, E. O. (2015). Districts' responses to demographic change: Making sense of race, class, and immigration in political and organizational context. *American Educational Research Journal, 52*(1), 4–39.

Turney, K., & Kao, G. (2009). Barriers to school Involvement: Are immigrant parents disadvantaged? *The Journal of Educational Research, 102*(4), 257–271. doi.org/10.3200/JOER.102.4.257-271

Tyack, D. B. (2000). *The one best system: A history of American urban education* (15. print). Cambridge, MA: Harvard University Press.

U.S. Department of Education (2016). *The state of racial diversity in the educator workforce.* Washington, DC: Office of Planning, Evaluation and Policy Development, Policy and Program Studies Service. Retrieved from www2.ed.gov/rschstat/eval/highered/racial-diversity/state-racial-diversity- workforce.pdf.

Vakil, S., McKinney de Royston, M., Suad Nasir, N., & Kirshner, B. (2016). Rethinking race and power in design-based research: Reflections from the field. *Cognition and Instruction, 34*(3), 194–209.

Valdés, G. (1996). *Con respeto: Bridging the distances between culturally diverse families and schools: an ethnographic portrait.* New York, NY: Teachers College Press.

Valencia, R. R., & Black, M. S. (2002). "Mexican Americans don't value education!"—On the basis of the myth, mythmaking, and debunking. *Journal of Latinos & Education, 1*(2), 81–103.

Valenzuela, A. (1999). *Subtractive schooling: U.S.-Mexican youth and the politics of caring.* Albany, NY: State University of New York Press.

Villanueva, E. (2018). *Decolonizing wealth: Indigenous wisdom to heal divides and restore balance.* Oakland, CA: Berrett-Koehler Publishers, Inc.

Virkkunen, J. (2006). Dilemmas in building shared transformative agency. *Activités, 03*(3–1). doi.org/10.4000/activites.1850

Vizenor, G. R. (2008). *Survivance: Narratives of Native presence.* Lincoln: University of Nebraska Press.

Vygotsky, L. S., & Cole, M. (1981). *Mind in society: The development of higher psychological processes.* Cambridge, MA: Harvard University Press.

Wallace, T. L., Kelcey, B., & Ruzek, E. (2016). What can student perception surveys tell us about teaching? Empirically testing the underlying structure of the Tripod Student Perception Survey. *American Educational Research Journal, 53*(6), 1834–1868. doi.org/10.3102/0002831216671864

Wang, M. T., & Huguley, J. P. (2012). Parental racial socialization as a moderator of the effects of racial discrimination on educational success among African American adolescents. *Child Development, 83*, 1716–1731.

Warikoo, N., & Carter, P. (2009). Cultural explanations for racial and ethnic stratification in academic achievement: A call for a new and improved theory. *Review of Educational Research, 79*(1), 366–394. doi.org/10.3102/0034654308326162

Warren, M. R. (2014). Transforming public education: The need for an educational justice movement. *New England Journal of Public Policy, 26*(1), Article 11. Retrieved from scholarworks.umb.edu/nejpp/vol26/iss1/11

Warren, M. R., Hong, S., Rubin, C., & Uy, P. (2009). Beyond the bake sale: A community-based relational approach to parent engagement in schools. *Teachers College Record, 111*(9), 2209–2254.

Warren, M. R., Mapp, K., & Community Organizing and School Reform Project. (2011). *A match on dry grass: Community organizing as a catalyst for school reform.* New York, NY: Oxford University Press.

Warren, M. R. (2005). Communities and schools: A new view of urban education reform. *Harvard Educational Review*, *75*(2), 133–173.

Warren, M. R., Mira, M., & Nikundiwe, T. (2008). Youth organizing: From youth development to school reform. *New Directions for Youth Development*, *2008*(117), 27–42. doi.org/10.1002/yd.245

Wayman, J. C., & Stringfield, S. (2006). Technology-supported involvement of entire faculties in examination of student data for instructional improvement. *American Journal of Education*, *112*(4), 549–571. doi.org/10.1086/505059

Weiss, H., & Lopez, M. E. (2011). Making data matter in family engagement. In S. Redding, M. Murphy, & P. Sheley (Eds.), *Handbook on family and community engagement* (pp. 21–28). Lincoln, IL: Academic Development Institute. Retrieved from www.schoolcommunitynetwork.org/downloads/FACEHandbook.pdf

Wilson, C. M. (2019). Critical approaches to educational partnerships with African American families: The relevancy of race in ideology and practice. In S. Sheldon & T. Turner-Vorbeck (Eds.), *The Wiley handbook of family, school, and community relationships in education* (pp. 51–69). Medford, MA: John Wiley and Sons.

Wolfe, P. (2006). Settler colonialism and the elimination of the Native. *Journal of Genocide Research*, *8*(4), 387–409.

York, B. N., Loeb, S., & Doss, C. (2019). One step at a time the effects of an early literacy text-messaging program for parents of preschoolers. *Journal of Human Resources*, *54*(3), 537–566. doi.org/10.3368/jhr.54.3.0517-8756R

Yosso, T. J. (2005). Whose culture has capital? A critical race theory discussion of community cultural wealth. *Race Ethnicity and Education*, *8*(1), 69–91. doi.org/10.1080/1361332052000341006

Yull, D., Blitz, L. V., Thompson, T., & Murray, C. (2014). Can we talk? Using community–based participatory action research to build family and school partnerships with families of color. *School Community Journal*, *24*(2), 9.

Zavala, M. (2016). Design, participation, and social change: What design in grassroots spaces can teach learning scientists. *Cognition and Instruction*, *34*(3), 236–249. doi.org/10.1080/07370008.2016.1169818

Zhou, M., & Bankston, C. L. (1999). *Growing up American: How Vietnamese children adapt to life in the United States*. New York, NY: Russell Sage Foundation.

Index

The letter *f* after a page number indicates a figure; the letter *n* after a page number indicates a note.

About the Author

Dr. Ann M. Ishimaru is an associate professor of educational policy, organizations, and leadership at the University of Washington College of Education. Her scholarship focuses on the intersection of leadership, school–community relations, and educational justice in P–12 education. Her community-based research seeks to leverage the expertise and leadership of nondominant students, families, and communities to realize equity in education. She is a principal investigator of the Family Leadership Design Collaborative (with Dr. Megan Bang), a national transdisciplinary research project aimed at co-designing research and practice with nondominant families and communities, practitioners, and scholars to transform educational systems. Dr. Ishimaru also co-leads a national study of district-level equity leadership and a research-practice partnership examining racial equity teams as a catalyst for equitable instructional and organizational practices. She is the recipient of the 2017 AERA Exemplary Contributions to Practice-Engaged Research Award and the 2016 UCEA Jack A. Culbertson Early Career Award in Educational Administration. Prior to becoming a faculty member, Dr. Ishimaru earned her doctorate at Harvard Graduate School of Education and her master's at Stanford University School of Education. She has worked as an environmental educator, middle and high school science teacher, and director of a community-based cultural arts organization. She lives with her husband, three children, and two cats in Seattle, Washington.

MW00659107

THERE OUGHT TO BE SHADOWS

To –
Stephanie
Keep reading!

[illegible]

THERE OUGHT TO BE SHADOWS

KRISSIE K. WILLIAMS

Quill & Crow

There Ought to Be Shadows
By Krissie K. Williams
Published by Quill & Crow Publishing House

This book is a work of fiction. All incidents, dialogue, and characters, except for some well-known historical and public figures, are either products of the author's imagination or used in a fictitious manner. Any resemblance to actual persons, living or dead, or actual events is purely coincidental. Although real-life historical or public figures do appear throughout the story, these situations, incidents, and dialogues concerning them are fictional and are not intended to depict actual events nor change the fictional nature of the work.

Copyright © 2024 Krissie K. Williams

All rights reserved. Published in the United States by Quill & Crow Publishing House, Ohio. No portion of this book may be reproduced in any form without permission from the publisher, except as permitted by U.S. copyright law.

Edited by Cassandra L. Thompson and Tiffany Putenis

Cover Design by Fay Lane

Printed in the United States of America

ISBN (ebook): 978-1-958228-32-6

ISBN (print): 978-1-958228-33-3

Publisher's Website: quillandcrowpublishinghouse.com

Content Warning: Please be advised that this book includes themes that may prove triggering for some including death, domestic violence, and historical accounts of slavery and racism.

The thief does not steal in an unfamiliar place.

- African Proverb

Et tu, Brute?

- William Shakespeare, *Julius Caesar*

Chapter One

MARILYN

For a moment, I thought about surrendering to death.

It could work… It would be easier.

Instead, the natural urge we as living creatures all have filled my veins: the determination to claim my destiny. To live. *To live…* I read the letters imprinted on the inside of my brain as I allowed myself to fight for breath and unwillingly swallowed another gulp of bath water.

His strength was more focused now, pressing on the top of my head where I often parted my hair. I had only pushed myself up a little. Great Grandmother stood in my peripheral vision while the monster hovered over me, bent on extinguishing me from this Earth. I could see her outline in the mirror above the sink. She always appeared to me in a crisis. Lately, it seemed like she had been appearing a lot more frequently.

Bubbles formed around me from my splashing and writhing. I managed to get one arm out of the water. He was so intent on holding me under that he didn't notice.

The razor I'd grabbed sliced the flesh of his right arm. Bright red blood ran down and dripped into the bathwater. *To live…to live*...I repeated it over and over in my mind. Unfazed by my movements, he kept pushing my head down. I cut him again, this one deeper into the sensitive skin of his inner arm. He released his grip on my head and slumped back against the toilet with wide eyes.

He seemed more surprised than angered by my actions. I caught him off guard. Silence fell. The light above the sink flickered a little. It had been doing that since the power outage the week before.

In a few short breaths, my destiny changed. The blood from his arm flowed more heavily now, scattering droplets on the tile floor. He grabbed a mint green hand towel I had purchased on sale and used it to apply pressure to the wounds. His eyes rolled back in his head.

Then he stood up, towel still in hand, and left. The wooden floorboards creaked beneath his heavy boots.

And so it was. The end of our marriage.

Chapter Two

MARILYN

I stood in the old mirror fastened to the bureau in my bedroom. Still wrapped in my towel, my skin was wet and flushed from the ordeal. Hands shaking, I struggled to comb the knots out of my hair. One knot refused to budge. Frustrated, I stuck my right hand into one of the drawers, searching for the scissors I kept underneath my socks. I grabbed them, and with a decisive snip, the knot of hair was no longer a part of me. *There,* I thought.

"Is he coming back?" I said out loud, half hoping that Great Grandmother would answer. Shortly after he left the bathroom, as I collected myself enough to climb from the old clawfoot tub, I heard the front door open and shut. Normally, there would be a tug and heave whenever we left to make sure the door was in place so it could be locked. Over the years, we'd meant to get it repaired. We never did.

Just like children. We talked about it but never got around to having them. There was always too much to do. It wasn't regret I felt at the thought, but relief. There was always something more important. Another job. Another promotion. Another house.

Another goal. Another success. I didn't think I could have lived with myself if I had brought a child into this madness.

My mind drifted off to a memory of eight years ago.

"So what do you think?" I'd asked him on the sidewalk in the drizzling rain by the Spanish moss-covered palmetto tree.

Colby glanced at the property. The yard was unkempt. There was a beautiful, weathered wrap-around porch that lay in front of them. It was obvious there was wood rot on the trim work. It had always been a dream of mine to refurbish an antebellum home. The windows were single pane: there would be drafts on cooler days. He was turning it over in his head; I could see it in his face. He raised his eyes and kept studying the house. The storm drains needed to be replaced. It was going to be one massive migraine. One massive migraine and a series of hapless errors and unexpected expenses. We knew it.

"Let's do it."

I could tell by his tone that he wasn't convinced it was worth it. But he was in. Hell, I won.

Two and a half months later, we found ourselves walking on battered floors over a series of weekends spent covered in various shades of gray and eggshell white paint. There were always handymen coming and going. In the summer, it seemed like the grass grew a foot overnight. There was always something that needed to be taken care of. And if we could focus on the house, we didn't have to focus on our marriage.

But I loved that I could open the windows in the spring and inhale the sultry air. I wasn't a garden expert, but I loved to go to the local nursery and buy big potted plants to set on the porch every year. I put fresh linens on the bed every week and sprayed the room with lavender. Occasionally, we would have another couple over for dinner and drinks. The dining room table could seat eight, but I never felt comfortable feeding more than four people at a time. I didn't have good entertaining skills; I could do enough to get by. Salmon was always my favorite. It was simple to cook; I could toss it on pasta or serve it with rice and a vegetable medley. Colby never complained.

In the sixth year I lived in the gilded cage, Great Grandmother began to show up. It was around the time our fights started. My pair of beloved pearl earrings went missing. They were from a former boyfriend, Jax. He gave them as a gift to me for my thirty-fifth birthday. I only wore them on special occasions. It was the only gift from any of my exes that Colby allowed me to keep.

"I don't like that you still have them. It's like I'm competing with a ghost," he said as he helped me put on my coat. We were on our way to one of his work functions. He shrugged his shoulders and grabbed his keys from their spot on the foyer table. "Let's go." A ripple of nerves went through my stomach. I could tell this would not be the end of the conversation.

I quieted myself in the car for fear of having another showdown this week. I'd barely survived the first two days, and it was only Wednesday. I didn't know why I'd worn the earrings. *Am I being passive-aggressive?* I wondered as we drove down the darkened streets. Or was I simply longing for a time when life had been kind to me? Both were possible. Nonetheless, a month later, they weren't in the gold tin box where I normally kept them.

Great Grandmother had moved my pearl earrings. I knew it, didn't like it, and there was nothing I could do about it. It was her way of letting me know from her celestial space that trouble would soon be afoot. I shoved the idea out of my mind. I wanted to stay on autopilot, enjoying life and denying that the fabric of my marriage was tearing into strips, little by little, every day.

But there she was, always hovering in odd places at odd times, reminding me that something was about to go awry. I can remember it so clearly. Two days after my earrings went missing, Colby hit me for the first time. In the span of one and a half seconds, I became a battered housewife.

I was shoved into my new existence as a result of his disapproval that I accepted a new job offer. It was just that quick. Suddenly, I was like the young women I counseled at the community center's general pseudo-therapy group as a part of their outreach effort. I could no longer afford to look down on them. Now, when they told their stories, I hung my head. Sometimes, I wished I could pursue a side conversation with one of them and ask them how they got out. Or beg them to tell me any tricks to try at home to deafen the violence. But instead, I held it all in, wearing various sympathetic facial expressions and telling them I would keep them in my thoughts.

Shaking off the past, I looked up. Great Grandmother sat in my bedroom chair, smoking a cigarette. Her long baby-blue nightgown fluttered up and down with the tap of her foot as she moved it back and forth. Her shock of gray hair gleamed. I wondered if that meant it was going to be a long night. I didn't know if Colby was going to come back or what my next move should be. Should I gather some things and run while I have the chance? I had very few friends in this town, even fewer who would understand what I was going through. I needed to move quickly. I grabbed a bag from the closet and began stuffing it with anything I might need.

Great Grandmother stood up from the chair and raised her hand. "You're safe, child. He won't be back. Go to bed."

Chapter Three

MARILYN

I sat in my silver Lexus SUV, sobbing. An intense panic attack seized me as soon as I pulled off the highway. There I was in my black pantsuit with a fastener firmly planted in my hair while streaks of MAC foundation slid down my cheeks. My hands shook. I gripped the steering wheel to make them stop and closed my eyes. *I am surrounded by love and light,* I repeated to myself in the rearview mirror as I breathed deeply. *I am surrounded by love and light…*

There weren't too many cars in the parking lot. I noticed Cousin George's blue pickup truck as soon as I pulled in. I expected to see him here; he was always kind to me. I could hear organ music playing inside the church. I was late for the service, but I wanted to be. If I had shown up at the house on time to ride with the rest of the family, I would have been forced to make small talk with Cousin Janet, and nobody wanted to talk to Cousin Janet. I found tissues in my purse and dabbed under my eyes, doing my best to fix the damage caused by my crying. It was now or never.

Christ Rock Church didn't loom over me today as it had

when I was a child. Its location at the edge of a field made it look even smaller. Unlike other places of worship, it hadn't grown exponentially as time passed. They still had one service on Sundays and a weekly Bible study on Wednesdays. Bingo took place every other Tuesday evening. Aside from the outreach to the sick and shut-in, that was about it. Pretty boring, run-of-the-mill religious service stuff. The congregation was primarily composed of ordinary people, many of whom had never even crossed the county line.

It felt strange to be back home. I didn't miss it. I'd hightailed it out of there as fast as I could the minute I got the chance. Even now, after I made the hard decision to come back, my guard was up. I could have started over in a different city after my marriage blew up, but that took so much effort. I would have to find a new job, make new friends, and get a new place to live. Too much effort. I didn't need effort, I needed safety.

Great Grandmother told me to come back home. Her message was confirmed by a phone call from my mother. Uncle Niles had passed peacefully the night before. She told me not to worry about attending the funeral. "I know you have quite a bit going on. They, umm…they all know about you and Colby," she said.

"Mom, I'd appreciate it if you stopped telling people my business. The divorce isn't final yet. If someone asks me about it… well, it's a real trigger for me."

She paused. "I'm sorry. I only told them you two were separating, not the reasons why. I figured it would be easier for you, so you wouldn't have to field as many questions. It's just that everyone is always asking about you and how you're doing."

I knew they didn't care about how I was doing; they were just nosy. It was part of the reason why I struggled with going to Uncle Niles's funeral. Not to mention the ghosts of the past I was sure to encounter. I secretly hoped that I would not have to revive the amount of dead carcasses I left in the wake of my exit from this wretched place. Regardless, I decided to pay my respects to one of the few family members I trusted. I missed him. I felt guilty about losing contact with him over the past year, even though it was a difficult one. I barely resembled my former self now. Sustained trauma made me feel like I lost all of my soul. Sometimes, it comes back.

Mine will never come back.

If you blinked twice, you would most likely miss Moonstone, South Carolina. But it was a place of beauty, full of Spanish moss trees and old plantations dotting the map of the town. People still dressed for dinner and went to church on Sunday. They drank bourbon on the back deck and played chess. But it was also the kind of a place a person didn't need to go to unless they had a reason to. Folks here were pretty tight-knit; they didn't like too many outsiders. To fit in and make a life here isn't easy. Better to try your luck and go to Atlanta instead.

Nonetheless, year after year, season after season, someone doesn't get the memo. They show up. Some are running from the ghosts of their past. Some come because they are excited for the next chapter of their future. Some come because they long for the stillness. Some come because a horrendous set of circumstances forced them to be in exile from their true home. And some come because they are just plain dumb.

Beware of Moonstone. It reflects what you want to see.

The sound of the organ startled me, reminding me why I was there. I closed my car door and walked into the church. I slunk into a pew at the back of the church, hoping not to be noticed just yet. But it was too late. Several people saw me and started waving. *Ugh...* The pit in my stomach grew.

Standing before me in the nave, Uncle Niles's casket was a beautiful shade of polished mahogany. I peered over someone's shoulder to get a closer look. I could see they dressed him in a gray suit with a black tie. I heard another person make a remark as they took a seat next to me. "I saw him at the wake yesterday. I don't know why they colored his hair so black."

I wonder whose idea that was, I thought.

I tried to amuse myself by counting the different shades of color in the stained glass windows while Pastor Judge continued with the eulogy. It reminded me of when I was forced to listen to him drone on when I was a child. Sometimes, I wanted to rip the ribbons out of the two pigtails on each side of my hair while I was sitting in the pew and yell. I felt my inner child bubbling to the surface as I sat there, feeling trapped and helpless, surrounded by the past. My mother turned around in her seat and beckoned me to come up front and sit with the family. I shook my head no. I didn't want to cause a commotion; I wanted to stay in the back and be left alone with my thoughts.

I hated Pastor Judge. He was a self-serving, narcissistic prick. He had committed too many sins over the years at Christ Rock Church. Embezzlement, sexual harassment, assault, thievery, and an assortment of others. He answered for none of his crimes. The congregation readily accepted any explanation he manufactured to exonerate himself.

It was the preying—not praying—on women that bothered me the most. He would call the single women up to a special altar call every service telling them he would ask Jesus to send them a special "God-fearing" mate. He reminded them that as long as they stayed "pure" and "had faith," he would come. When God did send them a "mate," they needed to cherish their blessing.

"If you don't take care of your man, someone else will, and God will take him away from you. Make sure he is the head of the household and be diligent in all of your wifely duties," he would say in a booming voice. Huge drops of sweat would roll down his punchable face.

I remember when I became a teenager, I began to understand the hypocrisy. Why were the women called to the altar but not the men? What about the men? He looked at the single women as if they were lepers, and he was Jesus himself, anointing them with his thick, overloaded gospel. There were always one or two, overwrought with emotion, that decided it was time for their debut—that this was it, Broadway or bust. After days of rehearsing in the mirror, they went for it, heaving and falling out onto the floor while he screamed his false prophecy, pretending they were overcome with the Holy Spirit.

When I was young, my best friend Jamie and I used to bet on who would give the best performance.

"Fifty cents on Sister Carol. She's been divorced for ten years. She's desperate. I think she'll go down first," Jamie said confidently in between sucking on her jumbo lollipop. It was a Saturday, and we were hanging out in the church parking lot after a youth choir rehearsal.

"My money's on Aunt Bessie," I replied. "She's always hollering about how she's so sad and lonely since her man left her for that young girl. You know, the one whose family just started coming? That girl's only nineteen, and she run off with him. He's forty-seven. Ew."

"Nineteen is OLD. That girl's not young." Jamie always had to fight me on everything. She kept licking her lollipop, which had become sticky in the hot South Carolina heat.

"Well, I guess she is old to us. But to Aunt Bessie and them, she is young. Too young to be with him."

I could tell by Jamie's face that she was turning over what I said in her head.

I remember one particularly hot day around noon, Jamie and I were playing jacks on the front porch while her mother was in the kitchen baking a chocolate cake for the church's anniversary dinner. She had asked us to keep an eye on Joey, Jamie's younger brother, while we played. Unfortunately, he ran off into the woods behind the house, which was never a good sign. No good ever came from him running off on his own. Whenever he returned, there were sure to be scrapes and cuts somewhere on his body. Afterward, there would always be a lecture or scolding by Jamie's mother about him not being somewhere where his sister could keep an eye on him. Joey was the poster child for the word daredevil.

I was about to pick up five jacks when a rush of wind knocked the ball out of my hand.

"Whoa. Did you see that? Where did that come from?" Jamie asked excitedly. "There's like no trucks or cars on the street to cause it! That was crazy."

"I dunno," I replied. I looked up at the sky, but there wasn't a cloud in sight.

"You two, stop playing right now and come help me find your brother. I told you all to watch him. We'll split up. God only knows what that boy's got himself into." Jamie's mama shook her head in frustration. "Jamie, you go left down by the ditch. Marilyn, walk down the cut-through to the old golf course. He goes there to meet his friends and play kickball."

I hated that path. Huge, overgrown trees formed a covered bridge in the sky, blocking out the sunlight. I could barely see where I was going, but I could see the shadows. And the shadows could see me. I hurried as quickly as I could to get to the old golf course, tripping on a branch. Blood ran down my skinned knee as I wiped away the dirt. Grasping at a branch from a tree, I closed my eyes and took a moment to breathe. I hoped that this escapade with Joey would end soon.

All of a sudden, Great Grandmother was standing there. I yelped. I rubbed and readjusted my eyes to make sure that the sun wasn't playing tricks on me. It wasn't. A horrendous scream escaped from Jamie's mother, echoing in the distance. By the time it reached my ears, I knew it was too late.

I blinked back the memory. Funerals make you remember other funerals. Uncle Niles's service made me remember Joey's.

Two days later, I was still thinking about his death. How Jamie's mother found him crushed under the large branch of a tree, his young body succumbed to its weight. How he was gone before we got there.

Jamie held my hand so tightly throughout the entire funeral that the corner of three of my fingernails started to bleed. She even followed me to the bathroom when I had to go in the middle of Pastor Judge's eulogy.

There was the shrieking of the masses in the house after the service. The prayer team gathered outside on the porch. Jamie's mother was inconsolable. Her father was numb and rarely responded to anyone. They would fix him a heaping plate of food and set it down in front of him. He would push it aside. He had been doing that since the day Joey died. I can still see the oil from the macaroni and cheese dripping onto the paper tablecloth. I can still smell the fried pork chops. I still felt the humidity in the kitchen.

My mind drifted back to the funeral. The congregation was standing and aligning into a procession to view Uncle Niles one last time. A few minutes later, I stood outside with the rest of the family talking.

"I knew you were gonna be late," my mom gently chided.

"You know I can't deal with Cousin Janet," I replied.

"Nobody can deal with Cousin Janet. That's why it's a family effort."

"Agreed. I'll do better next time," I said, knowing I wouldn't.

My mother was in full funeral regalia, draped in a black skirt suit with a wide-brimmed black straw hat and her oversized Jackie O sunglasses. If there were a fashion magazine called *Church Monthly*, she would surely make the cover. Julia Maxwell wore church like a second skin.

"Are you coming with us to the cemetery and the repass?" she asked me.

"Yeah, I'm coming." I swallowed hard; I knew this was a losing battle as soon as I walked into the church. No way was I getting out of family commitments for the rest of the day. If I was going to live in this town for a while, I was going to have to deal with them.

After the burial, we all clustered into the tiny church basement for the repass. Four ushers piled rice, yams, collard greens, and turkey onto our flimsy paper plates. The heat from outside mixed with the smell of the food drippings and sweet cakes, merging with the ever-present odor of cheap perfume and cologne worn by some of the congregants. The scent was overwhelming. People gathered around tables in tight circles, making small talk while they waited in line.

All eyes were on me. I felt their gazes drifting over me as I chatted with some of my relatives. I forced myself to make small talk with my distant cousins, Chelsea and Patricia. They were twins I had never been able to tell apart when I was young. Now, it appeared they had both gained a tremendous amount of weight over the years. I tried to hide my surprise at their new physical appearance. When we were in high school, they ran with the pretty girls, or rather, the Mean Girl Squad.

At times, they would ask me to attend their sleepovers. I knew it was a forced invitation and that their mom put them up to it. I didn't want to go, but my mother said that they were family and sometimes, with family, we have to do things that make us uncomfortable. Angela, Chelsea and Patricia's mother, always liked to be in my mother's good graces. She knew the family name meant prestige in Moonstone.

When I arrived, there were two new girls, usually someone they met at the latest Jack and Jill Foundation event. I felt bad for them because I knew what was to come. For the next six hours, they would be subjected to a night of bullying and teasing by

Chelsea, Patricia, and their merry band of idiots. It would always end with the intended victims cowering in a corner, making fun of the girls, telling them they were fat, had no money, or were not pretty enough to be with them. The girls looked like they were wingless birds trying to escape from a halfway-open cage.

I would sit silently and not intervene. I felt like people needed to fight their own battles, and this was one of them. I had no voice: even if I spoke up, they wouldn't listen. Sometimes, I would ask Aunt Angela if it was okay to watch TV upstairs rather than be in the basement with them. I would feign that I didn't feel well. She would ask me if I wanted to go home. I told her no. I wanted to stay for the make-your-own sundae bar they always had. She would acquiesce and not call my mom to pick me up.

In the morning, the two girls would emerge looking a bit haggard with puffy eyes from sobbing the night before. Aunt Angela would be in soccer mom mode, flipping slightly dark brown around the edges pancakes for us to eat. Their father would be sleeping off the previous night's liquor. He was a terrible alcoholic. She would ask us if we had fun as we inhaled orange juice and water, dehydrated from our sugar coma the night before. The victims would lie through their teeth that they had a great time. The Mean Girl Squad would eye them threateningly from across the table, forbidding them to speak about the incident.

Sometimes, I wondered if their mother was in on it. Aunt Angela never interjected, and I know she could hear the faint cries of helplessness from the basement. From what my mother told me, she wasn't well-liked in high school and was often a target of bullying herself. Vowing for her kids to never be like she was, she trained them in tactics of dominance.

Although it seemed The Fates had something else in mind for them. After years of tormenting people they deemed less than them, they had become the old "high school hero, life zero" cliche. After declaring they were going to college and medical school after graduation, my mother told me they were back home within a year or two. It turned out that Chelsea and Patricia weren't as bright and smart as everyone thought. When they went to college, and the rubber met the road, they couldn't cut it academically. I guess all of those years of cheating on tests and bullying other students into completing their homework and research papers for them didn't pay off. They came home and found that they no longer had an audience for the Mean Girl Squad to harass. People had moved on with their lives: attending college, going into the military, getting married, and so forth. Since there were no people to persecute, they were left to themselves. So they worked regular nine-to-five jobs and went to fish fries, cookouts, and church. They didn't marry and never traveled further than the county line.

Now here they were, across the table from me, smiling with broken teeth, their arms squeezed too tightly in short sleeve blouses while large teardrops of sweat dripped down their necks in the heat. I smiled back through clenched, pearly white teeth, my lips painted with red MAC Ruby Woo lipstick I bought from Sephora. I pride myself on being a good person, but I must be honest.

I relished this small victory.

Oh, I knew they would go home and talk about me, how I looked prim and proper, but they could tell I was a mess inside. They would remark about my car and how wealthy I was because they would surely walk outside with me after the repass to observe it. And there would be a flutter of conversation about who is getting what in the divorce and how nasty it was. Then, they would get on their cell phones and chirp to the three friends they had between them. I would be the hot topic of conversation for the next month or so, and then they would move on. They were vultures, after all; once they picked my bones clean, they would find someone or some other situation to serve as a feast. Until I became a hot topic again.

But I relished this victory. The horror that I had just encountered with my soon-to-be ex-husband degraded my soul. However, this was a small needle to grasp in a field of weeds.

An eye for an eye. For once, and probably the only time I could remember, The Fates got it right.

Chapter Four

RAWLING

I have a penchant for always getting into things I'm not supposed to. I can't help it. I try to be good every day. In the morning, when Mama tells me to say my prayers, I clasp my hands so tightly together. Sometimes, there's an angel I look at that she hung on my bedroom wall. I ask the angel to please guide me through the day. *I don't want to do any bad things today,* I think as I get dressed to go to school.

This school, St. Benedict's. Mama said I have to go here because the public schools wouldn't understand me. When I asked her why, she told me they wouldn't understand me and my penchant for trouble. But St. Benedict's would. I asked her why they would understand me. She told me they would because she gave a lot of money to the school every year. I nodded my head yes, though I felt that it was a pretty crappy reason for anyone to be able to get away with anything.

Right now, I'm bored, so I decide to draw on my desk. The teacher is going over a spelling lesson with us. I'm actually pretty good at spelling. Matter of fact, I'm good at everything when it comes to school. I don't have to try very hard. That's why the nuns hate me. I'm too smart. I am the first one to finish every test. The first one to figure out the math problem, the first one to finish the science experiment. But I can do very bad things, and therein lies the paradox.

I look out the horizontal window near my desk. There are streaks on it and I can tell it had been cleaned the night before. Cleaned, but not thoroughly wiped dry. If it were one of our housekeepers, Mama would have made her redo all of the windows in our house before she paid her, and she would have taken some money from her salary to compensate her for the stress she caused her by not having the house sparkling clean. Sometimes, I questioned why Mama was so mean to the help. I asked her once. She said they needed to be thankful they had jobs in this economy.

"Oh," I remarked.

"Besides, it's just the pecking order of the universe," she continued. "If I don't treat them like they are nothing, then someone else will. They will simply have to learn to pull themselves up by their bootstraps or get used to eating the scraps that fall off the dining room table. Don't worry; you'll get the hang of this world."

We often had these conversations on our way home.

Mama tried to pick me up every day. I'd loosen my private school plaid tie and run down the front steps of the school, filled with excitement that St. Benedict's was over for the next fifteen or so hours. She would be sitting outside in the parking lot with the convertible top down on her late-model, icy blue Mercedes sedan, flicking the ash off a cigarette. She would yell at me to hurry up and get in the car. I would slam the door behind me and throw my bookbag in the backseat. Whenever I saw her smoking, she would tell me that she was still trying to quit, but it wasn't going so well. I knew it wasn't going well whenever I went into the kitchen cabinet above the marble counter and noticed two rows of Oreos missing from the package. She told me, at times, she would rather be dead and a size six in a Chanel suit in the coffin than fat. *Another of those lessons from Mama…* I thought to myself.

We live in a cookie-cutter mansion in a gated community. I have an entire wing to myself in our house. It's on the second floor. I see my mother disappear down the long hallway toward the other side of the house. I don't see her until she picks me up from school again tomorrow.

At night, I am left to my thoughts. I do not like them.

There is another side of me that wants to take over. The side of me that does very bad things. This is why I pray so hard. I want to be a good kid.

Sometimes, when I brush my teeth in my bathroom at night, I blink. I think there is something behind me. A shadow of some sort. I check the entire bathroom and pull back the shower curtain to see if anything is there. There is nothing, but the curtain billows slightly as if something was there.

The students at St. Benedict's are attracted to me and afraid of me at the same time. They feel bad because I have very few friends. Nobody chooses me for games at recess because they are afraid I will do something to hurt them or their friends. I can't blame them. Because I will. Just like I did to that bird. I saw her struggling on the dirt road. Something or someone must have hit her. If I was a decent kid, I would have scooped her up and taken her home. I'm sure one of our housekeepers or gardeners would have tried to save her. But I didn't. I picked up a rock and smashed it into her. I stood back and watched her struggle. She wiggled a little. Then she gave in to death.

I cannot help myself. I am noticing that if I see something that is down on its luck, I have to take advantage of it. It's like there's a fire in me that spurs me on. A voice in my head that tells me to do these things. If I don't do what it wants me to, the voice gets louder. Especially at night.

Sometimes, I wish Mama wouldn't disappear down the long

hallway, leaving me alone for the night. I would like it if she would stay with me, at least until I fell asleep. But she is never there.

At night, the shadow takes over.

Sometimes I am scared of the shadow, like when it visits me in the mirror in my bathroom when I am brushing my teeth. At other times, I like the shadow. It gives me a strange power that I never had before. I am beginning to understand what Mama said about the pecking order in this universe. I am at the top.

One night, I did see Mama. She had on a long red dress with a split on the side. She wore sparkly silver shoes with it. She never leaves the door open to her bedroom. That is why I normally don't see her. But this time, it was; I cautiously tiptoed down the long hallway to peek inside. She saw me as she gazed in her mirror, fastening her diamond earrings. I stopped. I thought she would be mad at me for disturbing her. There was a pause between us.

"Mama, where are you going?" I asked her curiously.

She looked at me in the mirror, picking up her glass to take a sip of her wine.

"Mama's going hunting," she replied.

Chapter Five

MARILYN

My mother never talked about Great Grandmother when I was a child. We never visited her, even though she only lived about five miles away from us before she passed on. One time, when I was a child, about six years old, I saw her at the Pick-N-Pay grocery store. My mother was in aisle three, perusing over her choice of canned stewed tomatoes. I was holding onto my mother's hand for dear life. I hated to go out in public; I was afraid of the world. Whenever I was scared, I sheepishly hid behind her, sucking on my thumb. It was only when I peeked out from behind my mother that I saw Great Grandmother's shock of gray hair. There she was—live and in color. I had never seen her before or been introduced to her. But I knew it was her there at the end of the aisle.

"Ma, that's Great Grandmother. Isn't that her?" I asked with dinner plate-sized eyes and crooked pigtails.

My mother barely raised her gaze to look where I was pointing. "Almost done, Marilyn. Give me another sec."

My mother locked eyes with Great Grandmother. She stood there for a minute, so still, it was almost as though she had stopped breathing. Not intimidated, just stoic. She dropped the can of stewed tomatoes in the shopping cart and steered us in another direction. She stayed quiet through the checkout line and during the walk to the car in the parking lot.

"Marilyn, how did you know that was your Great Grandmother?" she finally asked.

"I dunno." I shrugged my shoulders. "I just had a feeling."

"Did she say anything to you or motion for you to come near her?"

"No."

My mother bent down to about the same height as me and grabbed my arms.

"Listen. If you ever see her again, I want you to run. Run as fast as you can and find me. Do not speak to her."

I was bewildered. Why didn't my mother want me to be with her? She was my great-grandmother, after all.

Great Grandmother did not begin appearing to me as an apparition until I was ten years old. At first, I was terrified. I thought I had done something wrong. At times, I would be in a brightly lit room when she would appear, lingering in a corner with her shock of gray hair flowing down her lithe frame. I never told anyone. I buried the secret deep in my soul's ocean. A soul now stolen away and hiding in a hinterland because of my soon-to-be ex-husband's hateful words and even more hateful hands.

I remember being confused by her behavior. But I nodded my head yes as if I understood, though the conversation left me with more questions than answers.

The day Great Grandmother died, I sat straight up in bed at the exact time she was transitioning. I didn't know why, but I heard a swarm of bees burrowing inside my head. It was tumultuous. I knew she was gone.

It wasn't so much grieving for Great Grandmother—my mother would not allow me to mourn her. The only interaction I had with her was that day at the Pick-N-Pay. What I felt was more of a longing. An unrequited love. A locked attic to which there was no key.

A few years passed. In that time, I grew from an awkward, skinny Black girl to an awkward, skinny Black teenager. In hindsight, I felt like the steps to young adulthood for awkward, skinny Black girls were jagged and compressed. Emotional skids and races to glory with epic ski slope letdowns. From time to time, I would pinch myself to make sure I was still me. Sometimes, I would check the birthmark behind my left ear to make sure it was there. I would hop on the sink's counter in my bathroom and pull my left ear down, craning my neck to look in the mirror to see if it moved. When I saw it, my anxiety would release for a moment. My birthmark was my North Star.

I often wondered why Great Grandmother didn't come to visit me sooner after her death, before my awkward, skinny black girl years. Why didn't she make herself known? Perhaps it was because she felt I wasn't ready. Truth is, I don't think I was ever ready. The sight, or The Hanging as I called it, was thrust upon me at the most inopportune time.

Enough of this…

I shook myself out of my reverie and pulled into the circular cobblestone driveway of my new home. It was one of the features I loved most about it. I had recently acquired the property, thanks to the generous trust fund my father provided for me upon his death. After taking off my shoes and changing clothes, I made myself a steaming cup of lavender tea and got to it. Large boxes surrounded me, filled with items that needed to be unpacked. The best thing for me to do with my grief was to keep busy. Just like my old house, this one needed work, too. I didn't know how long I was going to stay or how much money I wanted to put into it, but it needed to feel like home while I was there. After a few hours of work, I sank into a chair and promptly fell asleep among the dust bunnies. I didn't wake up until the next morning. My phone vibrated next to me on the arm of the chair.

"Hey, it's Denise. How are things going down there? I read your email. I'm so sorry to hear about your uncle."

"Hey. I'm okay. I'm trying to settle in."

"Can you settle in a little faster? You're on a deadline. We need something by the end of the year."

I swallowed hard. "What does something mean? The whole book, half of it, or chapters?"

"The first few chapters I read are a great start. But you need to get moving. We need the entire manuscript done by next spring. I'll firm up the date and email you. We have to do line edits after that. I'd like to send it to some interested editors soon."

"No problem. I'll get on it." Anxiety swelled in my chest.

"That's what I wanted to hear. I would like to have it placed with a publisher by the summer—fall at the very latest. Gotta go. I'll touch base with you in a couple of weeks to see how you're progressing."

"Talk to you then," I replied.

I hung up and sighed. There was so much work to be done. Why was there always so much work to be done?

I had been surprised by my good fortune when I met Denise Halstead at a friend's holiday party the year before. We chatted it up and became fast friends before I learned she was a literary agent. At the time, I wasn't sure if I was ready to reveal the dark parts of my life to strangers, but I summoned up the courage to tell her about an idea I had for a nonfiction book about African American women surviving domestic abuse. She seemed interested, and I ended up signing with her by the end of the week. I liked Denise and didn't want her to think I was just using her for her connections. But she wasn't fazed by it. She never asked if that was all I wanted out of our friendship. She just let it ride.

Leaving the unpacked boxes and chair behind, I moved to my computer. I'd managed to set that up, at least. The cursor blinked on the computer screen incessantly while my eyes ping-ponged from my book proposal to the notes jotted on my steno pad.

Spending time in the mire of the worst part of my life wasn't going to be a pleasant experience. After several deleted lines, I was absorbed in my writing. I barely realized that sundown was dripping through my windows. A long night was ahead.

I didn't like the night. My worst experiences had happened at night. Letting out a deep sigh, I turned off my desk light and hauled myself up the stairs, falling into bed without even taking my sleeping pill.

A few hours later, I awoke to the faint sound of running water from the bathroom. I sat up confused. I'd fallen asleep without even washing my face. *It's an old house,* I thought.

I crawled out of bed, squinting in the dark. As I edged closer to the door of the bathroom, the flow of the water sounded heavier. Much too heavy to be coming from the sink faucet. I flipped on the light and saw a stream of water pouring from the bathtub spout. Even more curious, the tub was filling up with water, although the drain was open. I rushed to turn it off and dipped my fingers into the tub to feel the temperature of the water, trying to determine if it had been running for a while.

A skeletal hand reached out of the water, grabbing mine. A second hand emerged and grabbed my other arm. A gray face with white hair floated just under the surface; I heard the sound of wind roaring through the figure's gaping maw. I fought, struggling to push back against the force trying to pull me below.

As quickly as the assault started, it abruptly ceased. All was quiet. I was bewildered about what just happened. I fell back onto the floor, shaking from fright. This was the second attack on my life this year. It felt like there was a dark entity that had recruited members from here and beyond to assist in my death. I did not know what I did to deserve this fate.

WHERE THE FUCK IS GREAT GRANDMOTHER?

I screamed it over and over in my mind. Why wasn't she here?

After the bathtub incident, I sat in my living room shivering, eyes big as full moons, propped in an armchair with all of the lights on. Even the slightest sound terrified me. I sat there all night, waiting until it was time to get dressed to go to Mom's house for breakfast.

WHERE THE FUCK IS GREAT GRANDMOTHER?

She did not show up and warn me about this. She did not teach me how to prepare for something like this. She did not warn me that my life was in danger.

I got dressed mechanically and drove to my mother's house for breakfast.

The Hanging is what I call it. My clairvoyance. Pictures that appear to me before suddenly cutting off, leaving me desperate to hang on, to see the next picture. I tried to keep it at bay, but it wasn't easy...it never worked out. The Hanging always won. I shivered, trying not to think about the face in the water.

My family was already outside when I arrived, eating on tables in the backyard while bees swarmed, trying to pick at the assortment of sweet breads and bagels. The smell of bacon and eggs drifted through the air as I crossed the threshold.

Every year, Mom held a memorial breakfast in honor of my father, who passed on several years before from pancreatic cancer. As divine timing, Uncle Niles's funeral date coincided with this. I was happy that I was able to attend after missing it the last few years. Colby did not allow me to attend the last couple of years we were together.

My mother and father had been a power couple in Moonstone. A successful man, he was beloved by the town for his philanthropy, rare for a man of his wealth. When I thought about him, my heart swelled with sadness. Oh, how I missed him. The hot biscuits he made from scratch for me before church on Sundays. The bedtime stories—my favorite was *Charlotte's Web*. I would be completely asleep and he would still finish the book. We must've read it a hundred times, but it never got old. He was patient, kind, and slow to anger. They didn't make men like him anymore.

They didn't make couples like Julia and Matthew Maxwell anymore, either. Mom fell in love with him when she was in high school, but she didn't tell him. He was the popular guy, coming from a well-to-do family. His family owned a small chain of hardware stores throughout the South and had built considerable wealth within a short period of time. Their status elevated them to the level that white folks felt comfortable enough to have a conversation with them and even call them friends, while the other Blacks in their lives were treated like the help.

In a town as small as Moonstone, Blacks treated the Maxwells like demigods. I had grown accustomed to a life of finer things—little satin ribbons in my hair, white patent leather shoes to wear every Easter, and fresh, clean linen on my canopy bed to pave the way for candy dreams. My mother held her head high whenever she walked into their bank; she married up, and she knew it. She was very conscious of her social status and did not hesitate to introduce herself to anyone who didn't automatically recognize her.

Every Christmas Eve, we rented the town hall and provided dinner for the less fortunate. We were given a list of needy families from the local churches and schools. If you were invited to participate in serving dinner, you were deemed "in" by Julia and her friends. The invitation always arrived the Saturday after Thanksgiving. The phone rang incessantly from that Saturday night through the next Sunday afternoon. The answering machine tape would be full. *Of course, I would LOVE to serve dinner. I've been looking for a way to give back...blah blah blah.* The answering machine tape became worn from the amount of fakeness coming through its speaker. I would roll my eyes as I heard the messages.

It was as if all the wannabes in town got their chance to be initiated into a secret society.

While I knew that giving back was important, all I really wanted to do was eat sweets and watch reruns of *Rudolph*, *Jack Frost*, and *A Christmas Story*. Thanks to the Maxwells's holiday tradition, I couldn't get to my TV until about 10:00 in the evening. By midnight, I was asleep from the sheer physical exhaustion and excitement for the day ahead. I always got everything I wanted on Christmas. All I had to do was keep good grades and stay out of any major trouble. That was the beauty of being an only child—the parents could solely focus on you. Unfortunately, this set me up for some painful life lessons in the future. Sometimes, no matter how good you are, you don't get everything you wrote on your list.

The strong coffee and smell of pancakes snapped me back to the bristling heat of the present. My memories had given me a brief respite from it. And while I wished I could wrap myself in the happier moments like a cool towel, they weren't going to help me with my dilemma. Great Grandmother still had not appeared, and in a matter of hours, I would be back in my house alone. I resolved myself to the fact that I would not sleep tonight, whether my tormentor came back to finish me off or not.

"I saw you at the funeral, but I didn't get a chance to say hello."

Fuck... It was Cousin Janet. I was trapped with no one to rescue me. Janet's wig looked exceptionally cheap today, its fat curls stuck to her forehead. Sweat formed a puddle on her upper lip from the steam coming from her plate.

"Hey, Cousin Janet. How've you been?" I feigned a smile.

"I've been hanging in, you know. My Daddy's death is tough."

"Yeah, I know. I'm so sorry. I miss him too."

"Thank you for coming back in time for the service. We appreciate it." Janet sat her fat ass down in the adjacent chair.

I sighed internally. This was going to be a marathon session. I knew Cousin Janet only wanted to hear all the sordid details about the downfall of my marriage to Colby. Her sitting next to me was nothing more than a fishing expedition.

"There was no problem. I just adjusted my timeline. He meant a lot to me." I stabbed my fork into my pancakes rhythmically, cutting them into neat squares. My eyebrows were wet and my sunglasses fogged up from the humidity.

"How's the house? Do you need any help fixing it up? 'Cause you know I'm retired now…"

"No, I'm good. I like the work. It's cathartic for me."

Cousin Janet looked disappointed she couldn't inspect my new digs. I didn't want to let her into any part of my life—I had enough to deal with.

"Are you sure, baby? 'Cause you know I'm really good at painting. I painted the church basement last year—"

"No. I got this. I got this." I had kept repeating this to myself since the end of my marriage. It was my new mantra, even if I felt like I was one cold cup of coffee away from losing my shit.

"Well, baby," Cousin Janet said as she leaned in close and grabbed my hand. "I want to be there for you. I know you've been having a hard time. You can tell me what really happened. I promise I won't tell anyone."

So much for subtlety. "No, thank you. I'm fine. And if you ask me again, I will choose to end this conversation. You know how you got drunk at the family Christmas party five years ago and took a crap next to the potted plant in the den? And my mom had to rip the carpet out and replace it? Remember how you cringe whenever you hear someone whisper about it when you are in the room? It's kind of like that for me. Except I didn't take a shit in my sister's den, and I'm not embarrassed. Things just didn't work out. Stay the fuck out of my business."

Stunned into silence, Cousin Janet sat back in her chair. As if on cue, my mother stepped onto the back porch.

"Everything okay?" she asked.

"Um yes, everything is fine. Everything is fine. I was just catching up with Marilyn. She was telling me all about her adventures when she lived in Raleigh." Cousin Janet put on another fake smile, revealing the pink lipstick on her front teeth. If there was one thing Cousin Janet feared most, it was the wrath of Julia Maxwell. She stood up and smoothed out her skirt.

"I think I'll go visit with Betty. I haven't seen her in a while. So many people reached out to me and I need to make my rounds. Nice talking to you, Marilyn." She sauntered away, heading toward her next victim.

Mom rubbed my back to comfort me. "What happened, baby?"

"What happened? What happened is that I'm just *done* with people."

Chapter Six

MARILYN

Being Black. Being Black in America. Being a Black woman in America. Being a divorced, formerly abused Black woman in America living in a small town.

I jotted all of the labels I currently wore down in my notebook. I felt like a cardboard box being mailed somewhere with the packaging tape that read *Fragile* on it. I was going to have to wear these labels for the rest of my life. Oh—add one more to the list: being a divorced, formerly abused Black woman in America living in a small town who had The Hanging.

My ghastly visitor had not come to me since the first night. I was three weeks in and no repeat visit. *Maybe they got mixed up,* I thought. *That happens sometimes with the spirit world.* Perhaps they meant to attack someone else. Thankfully, the second attempt on my life so far this year was done, I felt confident I could finally focus on my writing. I sauntered to the kitchen to make myself another cup of coffee before I got to work.

And there it was—the vintage pen my father gave me as a gift when I first told him I was entertaining the thought of writing a book when I was in my early twenties. It seemed like a lifetime ago that we had that conversation. Great Grandmother was back.

I hadn't seen the pen since before I moved. It was one of those items you knew was there somewhere, but it wasn't needed, so you didn't break your back trying to find it. I figured it would turn up at some point when I wasn't looking for it. Great Grandmother was up to her old tricks again.

Anger fell on me like rain. I knew the day was coming when Great Grandmother would show up. Now that she was nearby, she had some explaining to do.

"When you're ready, we need to talk."

I waited a few seconds. No stirring. No worries—it was only a matter of time before her spirit appeared. I decided to carry on with today's writing. I continued outlining the major plot points I wanted to address in my book.

The wind chimes that I hung up a few days before on the tree near my window began to clang. I looked up from my computer. Great Grandmother was standing in my makeshift home office in a black nightgown. It contrasted with the shock of her gray hair like a blood moon in the night sky. She seemed frenzied. I could tell that something was off.

"Where have you been?" I asked. "I've been down here alone. A few weeks ago, I had to fight for my life."

Great Grandmother put her hand over my lips.

My anger quelled.

"Chile, I've been around. You know damn well I don't have to announce myself every time I come to this space."

I lowered my eyes sheepishly.

Great Grandmother pulled me in for a hug. I felt her embrace. "I'm glad you safe, girl." She pulled away from our embrace and began floating around the room. "I been tryin' to git some information. Who came to you and why."

I stared into the pools of my ancestor's eyes. I believed her.

"More importantly, how do we stop it from happening

again?" I asked. "I don't have any enemies down here. Do you have any?"

Great Grandmother laughed. "Chile, we all gots enemies. Seen and unseen. Yes, including me. Especially in this line of work. I got an inklin' it might be a wraith. She comin' after you for something I mighta did to her family a long time ago."

"What did you do?"

Great Grandmother glanced around as if she were looking for someone or something that might interrupt our conversation. She shrugged her shoulders. "It ain't time for the story now. I got to go."

Her body began disappearing in translucent chunks from my vision. "In the meantime, she shows up, I got ya some pieces of jade to keep on ya till we figure out what to do to kill her. It's got *juju,* so it'll do the trick. At least temporarily."

I looked on the windowsill to see the green stone necklace she left behind.

The next day, the wraith showed herself while I was cooking dinner. I was filling my pot with water from the kitchen sink when the familiar skeletal hand reached through the drain. My heart jumped a little, but not as much as the first time. I grabbed the jade I'd hung around my neck and threw it down the drain. There was a loud howl as the hand shrunk back from me. Great Grandmother was right—it worked. At least temporarily.

Great Grandmother came back the next day. The encounters between me and her were always different in the daylight. She was a bit less terrifying in the sun.

She stood at the edge of one of the kitchen counters, smoking a cigarette. "When your Great Grandaddy and me were young, we were sharecroppers. We made do. Didn't really git much of anything after the harvest every year. Never did. But what we got, we took a little each time and saved it up. Said to ourselves, we's gonna git some of our own land someday. Somethin' to pass to our children." She inhaled deeply and blew out swirls of smoke that dissipated into her diaphanous presence.

"Mr. Cochrane, our landowner, told us to go see Mr. Fuller, as he had heard somethin' 'bout his family owing a bunch of money to some other family. They lost a big lawsuit. I remember somethin' about their boy gettin' mixed up in sum trouble. He stole some cattle from his neighbor. I think he broke sum tools, too.

"So he says go to see Mr. Fuller. He owned about five hundred acres and was lookin' to sell about fifty or a hundred of 'em. Git himself out of sum debt. That lawsuit wasn't the only debt they owed. From what we heard, there was a line that began at the center of town and ran all de way to their place. So we's went and had a little talk with Mr. Fuller. We looked at de land and says we like to buy it."

"Oh, okay," I interjected. "That's how we got the land by the Industrial Park. If you can even call it an Industrial Park."

Great Grandmother nodded. "So Mr. Fuller talks to his lawyer and says he'll make us a contract. We agreed to pay him one-fifty a month. That was a lot back then, but we figured it was worth it to be landowners. We was just gonna use it for farming anyway. So de contract say we pay him that amount of money for thirty years. After we signed it, we took it to a white lawyer that was nice and fair to Black people. His name was Mr. Ernie." She took another puff of her cigarette and let out a deep sigh.

"Mr. Ernie says there was some problems. De contract interest rate was way too high. We would never pay it off. De contract also said if we don't pay it off before we die, then Mr. Fuller and his family can take it back! And all de money we paid, we lose! It's not even like our family can keep payin' on it so dat we can keep it in our family."

I shook my head in disbelief. It was not uncommon to swindle Black people out of land, work, and money in the South, even though many years had passed since slavery was abolished. Many rural people of color still did not know how to read and write and had very little access to good legal advice.

"I was pissed. Your great-granddaddy was upset, but he said we would put our heads together an' figure it out. Well, I figured it out alright. I went down by the creek across from de old golf course—which wasn't even built yet. I went to see Wind. She was half-Native American an' half-Black. She had De Hanging, too, like you. I told her what was going on. She was a good conjurer. She could make *juju* like you wouldn't believe. Many people been blessed wit her results. She specialized in justice. I was gone git my justice." She floated around the kitchen and peeked her head out of the window, rendering her almost invisible in the light. The sun shifted and the tree shadows cut shards into her face so she looked splintered.

"I miss de weather. Sometimes it git real cold when I have to go out now." Although it was winter, the temperature was a mild sixty degrees outside. Great Grandmother's voice was full of longing. I wondered if she sometimes wished to be back among the living.

"So Wind put some *juju* on 'em. It worked. About ten days later, one of Mr. Fuller's children died. My heart stopped when I heard. De *juju* worked so quickly! Mr. Fuller was devastated. So devastated he died himself. A year later, his wife had to sell the rest of de land to pay off more debts. She was real bitter. She went to go see another conjurer who was white, I think her name was Melda. She wasn't dat good at *juju*, either, but she was cheap. She made a lot of mistakes. Mr. Fuller's wife went to her to try to fix me and Great Grandaddy after she found out I fixed her. So Melda tried to make a spirit that would attach to me. Follow me 'round and make me crazy."

The room began to rumble slowly. Sometimes this happened when other spirits followed Great Grandmother into the physical world. They liked to hitch a ride.

"You come out now! I told you 'bout coming along to places

you ain't been invited to. You gone git yerself in some trouble you can't git yerself out of."

I could hear muffled voices under the floor. Sparks that looked like little firecrackers singed the floorboards. Finally, after a few seconds, all was quiet.

"Good. They decided to leave. Troublemakers."

"So why is a wraith after me instead of you?"

"I reckon when the conjurer did magic, somethin' went wrong. That can happen you know, when people don't know what they doin'."

I nodded.

"Somehow, de wraith got out. She been hidin' herself all these years, but now she shows her face. It probably was directed by some relative of theirs who's still mad at me and Great Grandaddy even though we been dead for so long. Somebody knows I been travelin' here and back. They know about you. They know you and me are kin and close. De best way to hurt me is to git to you. We got to kill dis wraith. Don't leave her alive. She may come back and do the same thing again. I may need to contract dis one out. Part of the killing is that you need to git at it when it is in a weak state. Lemme find someone dat is willing to do that—weaken it. They may even be able to kill it and we don't have to worry about it. De wraith probably got sum enemies. If she attached to dat family, Lord knows she got sum enemies."

If there was anything that defined Great Grandmother's character the most, it was revenge. She did not suffer fools gladly in her life or the afterlife. Her manner in fixing Mr. Fuller's family after being hoodwinked in a land deal did not surprise me. She stood here in front of me in all her enormity: abounding of wisdom, conjure, sorrow, acrimony, hindsight, foresight, and unadulterated love. And yet, though all of those words were adequate enough to describe my ancestor, the word 'revenge' still stood out above them. When someone wronged someone else,

Great Grandmother's efforts always lay there first. She did not care if there would be retaliation later.

She took the trouble as it came.

Great Grandmother

"I ain't got no time for your foolishness. I'm here to see Bune," Great Grandmother said authoritatively to a lesser demon outside his office. She noticed they had changed the decor. Everything looked gaudy like it was straight out of the Gilded Age. There was a large gold chandelier that hung in the middle of the ceiling. Its lights were brightly colored, almost casting various shades in every direction. The carpet was now orange, covering the old concrete floor that was there before. In the far right corner, a large Greek statue of the Trojan horse of Troy stood. An old tune by Elvis played through the speakers of a radio. She felt like she had walked into a disco in the 1970s.

The demon sized her up. "He's a little backed up today. Then he's on vacation for the next two weeks." He turned his head and continued to watch the Celtics play on a small flat screen hanging on the wall. He clenched his hand and banged on the table as one of the players missed a shot. "That's gonna cost me big!"

Great Grandmother rolled her eyes. "You tell him I'm here, or I'll tell him you been taking side contracts from other gods. I'm sure he won't like dat too much. There ain't enough enchantment spells in the world to help ya when he finds out you been freelancing."

The demon reluctantly set down his coffee and pressed the buzzer to let her in.

Bune sat at the table studying a book on Greek mythology. He snapped it shut when Great Grandmother came in and stood to give her a hug.

"One of my favorite spirits to see." Bune smiled, baring his jagged-edged teeth. "How you been?"

"I been okay, I reckon. Can't get any worse—I'm already dead," she replied.

"How do you like what we've done with the reception room?" he asked.

"I ain't too keen on it," she said. "It's very loud."

He winced. "Yeah, some people have said that. But I want those who visit for business to have an experience. Something they can never forget. I want them to feel energetic and excited. I want them to know I'm the MAN."

"Well, I reckon it definitely screamin' dat," she replied.

He motioned for her to take a seat beside him.

"I prefer to stand. I ain't got much time. Can't get too comfortable."

"I guess you're not having a drink, then." Bune stepped over to the credenza and poured himself a glass of Bordeaux. "This was one of Napoleon Bonaparte's favorite drinks. He didn't drink much, but when he did, it was Bordeaux. I miss him. He's not around so much these days." Bune looked wistfully into the dead air.

"What happened to him?"

"I dunno. It was a falling out of sorts. Never mind me, I'm rambling. What do you need?"

"I got a wraith after my great-granddaughter."

"Oh, wraiths—they are nasty business. I had to kill one last year that was after a family member. It took me four tries. What's this one after your great-granddaughter for? I know she has The Hanging, but doesn't conjure."

"De wraith is after her to get back at me."

"Oh, I see," Bune said. "You must have really pissed someone off. I guess it comes with the territory."

"I need you to send somethin' to de wraith to weaken it. What you got?"

Bune shrugged his shoulders. "Depends on how powerful she is. On a scale of one to ten, ten being the highest, what do you say?"

"I reckon she might be 'bout an eight or nine. I only seen one more powerful than her since I been doin' this."

"Well, technically, you need something very holy to knock that out. The old rules used to say that the person it was after needed to be the one that killed it, but that's changed."

"Dat's good. Takes her out of de whole process. Most of de ones I deal wit got sins. They ain't too holy."

Bune took another sip of his Bordeaux. "Oh my. I tell you, this is some good wine. Let me go through my contacts. I'm sure there's someone that can help you."

"It has to be done quickly."

"Of course. Time is of the essence," Bune replied. "There is the discussion of payment. How would you like to do that? In years of service, an eye for an eye, or souls? I need to know before I can negotiate this deal."

Great Grandmother thought long and hard for a moment. Determining how she would pay was difficult because she didn't know the mercenary who would be doing the deed. "An eye for an eye works best for me."

"Splendid, I'll be sure to pass it on. When I get confirmation, I'll let you know."

Great Grandmother shook his hand. "It always be a pleasure doin' business wit you."

"Same here. Same here."

He walked her to the door.

For a second, she thought she heard her husband wailing below. The bars that trapped souls beneath Bune's office often shook from the screaming. She wanted to turn back to see if it actually was him but decided against it.

When someone stops for a visit in demon territory, their mind can play tricks on them.

Chapter Seven

RAWLING

Junior High School. I'm an eighth grader. I finally convinced Mama to let me give public school a try after going to St. Benedict's for all of elementary school. She was worried they wouldn't understand me as St. Benedict's did, but she reluctantly agreed in the end. Most of my fellow classmates like me. There are kids who invite me to their parties and on holiday trips. Sometimes I go, sometimes I don't. It's a little game I like to play with them. *When will the Prince of Moonstone arrive?* I think to myself and smile.

I'm pretty handsome, and I handle this early teenager thing okay. I play basketball on the school team; the coach says I am very talented. I was also elected class president. All the people in my orbit think I'm a great kid.

But they shouldn't. Because the shadow still takes over.

Their stupidity fascinates me. I now know what Mama was talking about when she said there was a pecking order in the universe. Most people are of low intelligence. They want to believe the best in people. They want to believe that everyone has morals. This is why they are easily misled, like sheep. But I am the wolf.

I wanted to be captain of the school basketball team. I wanted us to win the middle school state championship. And I wanted to date Carrie. There was only one problem: him. His name was George Alves.

At first, I was intimidated. I saw how the seventh and eighth-grade girls swarmed around him during lunch. I had my friends, Tom and others, that I sat with. It's not as if I was a social outcast. But it irked me. Every now and then, I would glance in his direction. He and his minions would bellow laughter from something they watched on TikTok or Snapchat. A surge of anger sent ripples up in my chest inside me.

I told Mama one day when she picked me up from practice.

"If that's what you want, then get it. By any means necessary," she replied. "When I was young like you, my mother used to always say, 'Be nice, Savannah. You have to be nice in this world. Because this world has enough mean people.'" She snorted as if the thought was ridiculous. "Well, Rawling, that's bullshit. Because nice girls finish *last.*"

She slowed down and stopped at the red light. She took out her makeup case and smudged her lips with a bright, shocking pink.

I double-blinked because the sun was blinding my eyes with the lipstick color. The traffic light changed to green. She pressed the gas pedal like she was driving in the Indy 500.

"Do you know why we have such a good life? It's because your mama takes what she wants. I'm on husband number four. When I'm done with this one, I'll walk away with a fat check and a big smile on my face. That's why I tell you not to get too close to them when I marry them. They're only temporary. It's not about their feelings, it's about climbing up and staying at the top. Figure out a way to take him down."

Sometimes, I wondered if Mama knew about the shadow. The shadow has become a part of me; I am no longer afraid of it like I used to be. At times, I think she did know.

The shadow allows me to breathe. I feel bottled up and trapped most of the time. Like the bird I killed when I was younger. Half wingless, hanging on for dear life. But when the shadow takes over, I soar. Nothing hurts me because I hurt it first.

The shadow talks to me. As a matter of fact, I speak to the shadow more than I talk to Mama or my friends. My nightly routine of brushing my teeth in my bathroom was where we had our best discussions.

The shadow gave me the idea to get rid of George.

"I'll make it an accident. I can do it for you. You won't have to struggle for much in this world as long as I am a part of you. But if you set this event in motion, you can never go back," the shadow explained one Thursday afternoon. It was after basketball practice, and I was pissed. Coach had just announced that George Alves was going to be Captain this year, and I would be Assistant Captain. It wasn't fair. I had been there longer; he just moved to Moonstone with his family. He had no ties here. There was no family legacy. The only reason he got to be Captain is because our coach was best friends with his father.

He did not deserve to date Carrie. She was too pretty for him. She would look better with me.

A few days later, they announced at school that George and his father were killed in a car accident. Apparently, a truck blew a stop sign; it was a head-on collision. Tragic. I feigned empathy at the funeral, even though I really didn't care. He was gone. Carrie was soon to be mine, and I am now Captain of the basketball team.

All thanks to the shadow.

Chapter Eight

MARILYN

Icy rain pummeled Moonstone. I pulled up the collar of my raincoat so that it covered my neck and hurried inside the house. I was terrified.

For the past three nights, I had been having Hangings about a baby. Every time the mother went to look at the baby's face, there wasn't one. When I woke up from the nightmare, my skin was covered in gooseflesh.

Naturally, I told Great Grandmother about it. As she stood there, with her shock of gray hair flying in the air, she raised her eyebrows. "De dreams about babies is the worst. That foretell somethin' very bad gonna happen. And you didn't see de baby's face? Something very bad gonna happen indeed."

"Behind it, there was a dark figure looming, whispering in its ear," I told her. "The baby was flailing its arms and screaming at first, but then it calmed down. The figure began to cuddle it like it was rocking a baby to sleep."

"You might need to talk to De Secret Keeper about dis."

I looked at her in disbelief.

No one knew too much about The Secret Keeper. Any information shared was on a need-to-know basis—the universe wanted it that way. There were more rumors than facts that surrounded their existence. Where did they live? Was it in the woods, as cliché as that sounds, or did they live a double life? Maybe they were your child's teacher at elementary school. Maybe it was the choir member you made fun of that sang off-key at rehearsal two weeks ago. Maybe it was the lady who cleaned offices at the Industrial Park on Sizemore Road. It could literally be anyone.

I'd only heard of their existence mentioned twice in conversation in my lifetime. The Secret Keeper was an undercurrent of our community; people knew the being was there, but they didn't dwell on it. It could cause massive anxiety, like a spider dangling mid-air from its web over your head when you wake up in the morning. Your first instinct is to jump out of the way. Then you swat at it and usually end the poor spider's life. And you're done with it.

Except with The Secret Keeper, a person can never really get away. They can never escape their deeds. And what did The Secret Keeper know? Did they possess eternal or earthly knowledge or both? What was the secret about? Was it good or bad? Was the secret harmful or helpful? Or is the secret no longer important due to the passage of time? What span of a person's life did the secret or secrets cover? Could a person afford to part with the secret if it got out?

The biggest concern people had surrounded how The Secret Keeper collected information. They did not beg, nor borrow, nor steal. As if by magic, when someone wished to visit them, the thought was released into the air, and The Secret Keeper knew. If The Secret Keeper wanted to make a deal with them, cryptic instructions were sent for a meeting.

The Secret Keeper existed simply to be there when the weight of the world suppressed someone so much that they needed to confess. A sin eater of sorts. People who left their classified information with The Secret Keeper knew they must never tell that they visited and purged their souls. Punishment for loose lips could mean death for them or someone dear to them.

So why risk it all? Why deal with The Secret Keeper in the first place? Because with The Secret Keeper, all knowledge was safe after being revealed. It was as though it never happened. But the gamble lay in the fact that, at any time, The Secret Keeper could dispense justice or revenge. That was The Secret Keeper's power. Making a deal with them had the potential to be more dangerous than a deal with the devil.

In eternal pursuits, things were quite different. The spiritual realm divulged gems of wisdom about what was to come. It was up to The Secret Keeper to decide whether to share them with the person or persons who would be affected. Sometimes The Secret Keeper worked through intermediaries—saints, ghosts, gods, goddesses, angels, demons, whoever could disseminate the knowledge. But it wasn't their responsibility to check and see if the information reached its intended party. That's why The Secret Keeper had to be careful who they did business with. There was almost always a transaction involved, a favor for a favor tucked away for future use. Sometimes, it involved a soul being bound for a certain time to them. The cost could be anything. After all, nothing comes for free.

"I didn't ask for this," I told Great Grandmother. "This life of misery. This life of solving dilemmas that don't have anything to do with me. Like the wraith."

"I told you I took care of dat," she interjected.

"But how long until the next monster shows up? Monsters under the bed. Monsters in the closet. Monsters in the basement. Monsters in the attic. Monsters in my teacup. Monsters in the trees. Monsters everywhere." Hysteria rose with each thought I spoke aloud.

"I know dis hard for you. I'm sorry 'bout dat. But there's nothin' I can do about it beyond what I'm doin'."

I was quiet. The question I desperately needed the answer to was pushing to the surface. "Great Grandmother that night—the night Colby tried to kill me. All the other times before when he hit me. Why didn't you help me?"

Great Grandmother lit up another cigarette to smoke with her Bic. "I can't. Least not right now," she continued. "I ain't got the right to. I can't do no work when it come to love. Not love between two people on dis earth." She exhaled deeply. A large swirl of smoke interweaved with her gray hair. "Love between two people on dis earth got to be figured out by them."

"Wow. I never knew that." I stared blankly into the vapor.

"You got to go see De Secret Keeper. Lemme let them know you'll be seeing them. I'll see what I can find out from my contacts. The problem be dat De Fates be changing the rules and the game all de time. Sometimes we know, sometimes we don't."

"The sooner we know, the better."

"Agreed." Great Grandmother replied. She hesitated for a moment. "I wonder if dis got somethin' to do with De Awful Evil. What do you think?" she asked as she continued to smoke, appearing unbothered by her comment.

"Great Grandmother! Nobody mentions that." My eyes grew wide. "We do not talk about The Awful Evil. Talking about it could give it life again. The Awful Evil is over. At least that's what I heard a few years ago."

"I heard dat, too. I just trying to make some sense out of things that been happening on de other side. And now you tell me 'bout the nightmares you been having. I'm just trying to put it together. Not trying to make you more frightened than you are. You got enough on your plate." She placed her bony fingers on my shoulder. "I best be leavin'. I got work to do and so do you. By de way, there are some unexpected visitors coming your way, and they ain't of the spirit kind either."

Then she disappeared, whistling her favorite song by Etta

James, *"At last, my love has come along…"* as she melted into the floor like chocolate candy left outside on a hot day.

The boy was back.

I hadn't seen him since a few days after he died. Quite a bit of time had passed between us--with me growing from a girl with pigtails to curly long hair and Chanel jewelry, him from flesh to apparition. Even now, when I saw him, his eyes still betrayed a whimsy about him mixed with mischievousness. Lurking behind him was sadness, like someone who was forced to relive an unfulfilled dream over and over. I knew that feeling all too well.

He and I didn't speak. We never did. When I was young, he showed up to me six nights in a row after his death. Every night at exactly 3 am, I would wake up to him hovering at the edge of my bed. I peed in my bed those nights. My mother wondered what was wrong with me. She chided me for drinking too much juice so close to bedtime.

He always wore the same overalls with red sneakers and beat-up shoestrings with the plastic tips hanging off of them. There was a bit of dirt on his cheek from being outside playing. It was like he was just bothering me because he was bored and wanted to clown around.

Meanwhile, I didn't know how to process this as a child. First, Great Grandmother's spirit, and then seeing Joey shortly thereafter. I was half a person for the rest of that school year. I withdrew into myself. I read copiously. *Sweet Valley High* books were my favorite. I thought to myself: if I could be one of these white girls, then my life would be okay. The only thing they worried about was if the boy they were crushing on felt the same way about them. They didn't have the Olympic-size problems that I did at an early age. Seeing dead people ain't for the weak.

Still, I did not for the life of me know what he wanted with me now. I had enough going on. Did he come to warn me about something? I already had Great Grandmother for that. And although she dropped the ball with the wraith initially, she showed up just in time. I wondered if he was lost. Perhaps he wasn't where he was mandated to be–-just floating in a netherworld until he got some direction. Nonetheless, my wits would have to adjust to seeing him again. Whenever he showed up now, there was an angst about me; a restlessness settled in my limbs and chest. I was hoping that I could wish him away.

Sensing that supernatural pursuits would take up quite a bit of my time in the future, I focused most of my day on putting my thoughts down on paper. It was a difficult process. No one wants to relive the most hellish part of their life. After writing about the first time Colby hit me, I stopped for the whole day. It was as if my soul stopped breathing at the moment I typed the period at the end of the last sentence. There was just nothing left. The moment he decided to unleash his wrath on me was the moment quiet sadness walked into the room, sat down, and decided to make itself at home. I sat back in my desk chair and closed my eyes.

What would have become of me if it never happened? I wondered.

Would I have been the powerhouse professor with a doctorate in history, sociology, or political science? A professor who guest lectured around the country and had written several bestseller books? Would Colby and I have decided to adopt a child after we had both attained our career goals? After all, it would have most likely been too late for me to conceive on my own. Would we have been able to afford that quiet little getaway on the Cape that we both longed for?

The quiet sadness didn't announce itself like a broadcaster at a buzzer beater win in a basketball game. It just came in, found a chair, and stretched out its legs. It read novels with me, helped me strip old paint from the walls when we were renovating the house.

It ate meals and drank with me. There were always three people in my bed when I was married; the quiet sadness slept beside me.

After my marriage ended, the quiet sadness decided to invite its friends, resentment, and apathy, to visit. They took shifts regulating my life. There would be times when they gave me the day off. I might laugh at a joke or receive a beautiful gift from someone. But I never deluded myself—I knew all three of them would be back. My happiness was temporary.

Sitting in my kitchen, I kept turning Great Grandmother's statement about The Awful Evil over in my head. I had a sense that whatever was coming to Moonstone was beyond sinister, and I did not want to be a part of it, no matter what it was. It simply wasn't fair that The Fates kept choosing me for their intrigues.

Chapter Nine

MARILYN

I found myself on the living room sofa in my mother's house, determined to ask the questions that had lingered in my mind for the better portion of my adult life.

"Mom, why don't we talk about Great Grandmother? We talk about everyone else except her."

Mom lowered her eyes, deep in thought. I was surprised at her body language, sure I was going to get a tongue-lashing. Whenever controversial family topics came up, I could never be sure what to expect.

"Why are you asking about Great Grandmother? She's dead and gone. It's not like you looking to build a relationship with her. She was a very toxic person. So toxic that your grandmother left at an early age. If you want to focus your energies on getting to know your ancestors, then focus on the rest of the family."

"Did your mother ever speak about what happened between them?"

"No. I was very young when she left me, and I probably wouldn't have understood anyway. All I know is that she left early and died unexpectedly in an accident." Mom shut her laptop and got up. "I want some tea, do you want some, too?" She didn't wait for an answer. "I'll get it. Miss Eliza is off today."

I felt defeated, but I wasn't done asking questions. "Mom, what about The Awful Evil?"

My mother spun around, staring at me as if I was an alien.

"We don't talk about that, Marilyn," she snapped. "You know better."

"But if we don't talk about it, why did we hear all these stories when we were little? For example, why couldn't we swim in the pond after midnight? What would happen? And what about The Crooked Woods? My friend Jamie used to tell me she heard that there were people living in the water around here—The Sea People. She even heard from a neighbor's daughter that she was related to them."

"You heard those things from the church and school. We told you all that to keep you safe. No child should be swimming that late anyway. The water's muddy. And you can get lost in The Crooked Woods. There's no cell service. The people that go down the paths—if they are smart, they turn around after the first mile or two. The dumb ones keep walking, thinking they'll discover some magic treasure or a leprechaun or something. Then they disappear. They go missing. Search teams are sent out, and they can't find anything or anyone."

She leaned against a column next to a wall. "They did find one, though. I remember Lucy's son, Sam. He got it in his dumb head to go into The Crooked Woods. His college buddies dared him to when he was home on Christmas break. You were little then."

"I remember that vaguely," I said as I followed my mother into the kitchen.

"So anyway, you know he was super smart. But not bright at all when it came to common sense. Common sense ain't common. Like the kind of kid that will walk in the pouring rain with an umbrella in their hand and never use it. He was a follower." My mother opened the pantry door and went to her tea box. She pulled out two tea bags that were labeled Black Currant.

She placed the kettle under the faucet and began to run water. Then she set it on the stove for the water to boil. "We can have these peanut butter cookies with our tea. Miss Eliza baked them yesterday."

"Yum," I said as I sat at the oversized farmhouse table.

My mother's cell phone rang. I could tell it was someone from the church.

She rolled her eyes as she picked up the phone. "No, you need to get those funds approved before you buy that with your own money. I've told you that several times. We have a budget," she said. After a little while longer, she ended the conversation. "Whew, that girl can talk." My mother threw the phone on the island in the middle of the kitchen. "And she doesn't know how to do anything by herself. It's always 'How do I do this?' and 'How do I do that?'"

"What is it, another fundraiser for the church?" I asked as she poured the hot water into our mugs. "If it is, count me out. I may have come back to Moonstone, but I'm not coming back to that church. I don't know how you still go there after all these years, with Pastor Judge's shenanigans."

"I go because I worship the Lord, not because of Pastor Judge. I can separate the two. You never could."

"You're right, I can't. I can't support someone that pretends they are repping for the Lord, and what they're really repping for is their own delusions of grandeur."

"Well, he's old now. He won't be there much longer," my mother said as she stirred honey into her tea.

"I'm sure one of his minions will take over. He's taught them all the tricks of the trade." I pursed my lips together.

I could tell my mother noticed I'd become more cynical since my marriage ended. I was also more on edge and depressed. I had always been quirky, but I was missing my spunk. That get-up-and-go I always had. When I left Moonstone for good, I was excited. I had decided to try out a career as a professor after finishing my Master's degree in Sociology. I jumped at the opportunity to live in Philadelphia for a while. I could tell she wanted that version of Marilyn back.

However, my mother didn't know the new me. She kept remarking that I was too thin, almost gaunt, with circles under my eyes and unruly hair. Well, to be fair, my hair had always been unruly, but now it was downright disorderly. My wild, loose curls swung every which way when I walked. Underneath the eye circles and skin bruised by the sun's heat was a layer of tiredness that had never been there before.

You know the kind of tired I'm talking about. That *just let me go to bed* tired. That *ain't nobody cooking tonight* tired. That *I ain't answering the phone because it's another crisis I have to deal with* tired.

And now I wanted to talk about The Awful Evil. I knew it was taboo territory. For as much as Julia Maxwell was taught to fear The Secret Keeper, she was taught to fear The Awful Evil much more.

She stopped analyzing me with her eyes and turned the topic back toward The Crooked Woods. "So what were we talking about before the phone rang—oh yes, Sam. So one afternoon in the winter, he decides he's gonna take a little walk in The Crooked Woods. Two days later, his mother filed a missing person report. Search dogs went out and scoured as much as they could. When the sun was setting, they knew it was time to call it a day. The search team went out for five more days. No Sam. Lucy kept begging them to go deeper down the paths. But the search teams were smart. They would turn around and only search within a three-mile radius. When they saw a teardrop of the sun going down for the day, they always ended it.

"Anyway, twenty-seven days later, Sam is found wandering around the old golf course. Some kids found him when they were messing around out there. He was disheveled, and his clothes were torn. He was walking in circles, mumbling to himself. No one could really make out what he was saying. It was some weird language. But his mother was just happy he had returned." She sighed, swirling her spoon around in the mug.

"But he hadn't returned—only his physical body. Lucy took him to the hospital. They gave him some special tests and therapy. The doctors could never figure out what actually had happened to him while he was missing. They prescribed him meds because he kept cutting himself. In the end, he was more of a zombie than a human because of the drugs.

"After a while, things started going better. He transferred to one of the local colleges and got his BA and then a job. He married a pretty girl from Savannah. They bought a starter house, settled down, and had two kids here. Two girls, I think."

"That sounds a little too neat and tidy," I said.

Her mother nodded in agreement. "So a few years pass, and one day, your father is reading the newspaper while eating breakfast. And he screams, 'Julia! Come here quick!' I was nervous. I thought something had happened to him or you. Maybe an accident." She took another bite of a cookie and then took a deep breath. "Well, chile, your daddy points and shows me a story in the newspaper on the front page. It says: *Father Kills Entire Family in Fire.* There was a picture of Sam next to the article. He set the entire house on fire and locked all the doors so no one could get out, including himself."

"Wow. These days, they call that family annihilation," I said.

"Call it what you want, I call it crazy. Maybe he ate too many of those orange berries that grow in The Crooked Woods while he was missing. I'm sure he was hungry at some point, and those berries are poisonous. I don't know what it all got to do with The Crooked Woods, but there definitely is something unnatural brewing in there."

Great Grandmother

Great Grandmother fluttered around The Secret Keeper's cottage. She was filled with apprehension from the conversation.

"This honey is rather thick," The Secret Keeper remarked as they poured some into their tea. "The bees been working overtime."

"I'm worried. Very worried about dis. What we askin' Marilyn to do might be too much," Great Grandmother said.

"Well, if we prepare her well, she will emerge—but not unscathed. And the goal is for her to get out. The Renegades leave a stain on your soul. Always."

"What she got to do?"

"Same as you did in the past. Stay focused and adhere to the task. I don't know what hell they will set her up with."

"Don't I know it," Great Grandmother said as she remembered her excursions there. She never wanted to go back.

"Marie Laveau is there right now. The Fates sent her."

"Why did they do dat?" Great Grandmother asked, circling The Secret Keeper's table.

"They send her there from time to time for work purposes," The Secret Keeper explained. "But there is more I must tell you. For sixteen consecutive nights, I have been tirelessly researching the meaning of the silver ring around the last secret I threw into the fire. I tried to make sense of it. A silver ring hasn't been seen in the fire since 1925–-the year Idi Amin was born. His connection to Moonstone is a mystery in itself. There are rumors that some of his ancestors migrated here after the Emancipation Proclamation, but this data cannot be verified. He became a brutal dictator in Uganda in the 1970s, committing atrocities and violating human rights for power and money. By the end of his reign, he was forced to live in exile, which he did until he died. He left a dire legacy of terror and death. The Fates sometimes allow darkness to do as it pleases."

"Dat's somethin' terrible," Great Grandmother remarked.

There was a whirring in the kitchen.

"Ahh, Father Kelly must be here," she said. The weathered apparition of an older white man with a nose red from a bit too much drinking emerged from the air. He was dressed in a priest's clothing.

"Hello, all. Sorry, I'm a little late. It was a bit of a crazy trip."

The Secret Keeper ushered him in to take a seat by the fire casting shadows on the walls in the room.

Father Kelly stared warily at The Secret Keeper, like a schoolboy who was in trouble in the principal's office. "I know I've got some nerve coming here to see you after I pissed you off the last time. Sorry about that."

The Secret Keeper eyed Father Kelly suspiciously as if unsure of whether he was being authentic or not. "Don't do that shit again. Pay your debts," they finally replied.

"What's dis about?" Great Grandmother asked, surprised there was bad blood between the two.

"Some business we did a long time ago," The Secret Keeper told her.

"Duly noted," Father Kelly said, relaxing. "Let's get to it. There was a child born. The child should be about seventeen or so now."

"Getting ready to come into his own power," Great Grandmother added.

"Yes. Do we know who this child is?" Father Kelly asked. "Although he's not a child anymore…"

"More importantly, why didn't the secret burn up in the fire? Usually, that means that a person is gonna do somethin' that the course of action can't be changed. De Fates won't have any of it. I done talked to them. They are clueless."

"You got in to talk to The Fates? Wow, how did you pull that off?" asked Father Kelly. He was rather stunned by the accomplishment.

"Well, they owed me a favor. Somethin' they needed long ago."

"That must've been some favor you helped them with. I know people who have waited hundreds or thousands of years and never gotten in to see them." Father Kelly sat back, still in disbelief.

"I reckon De Fates got to figure out who or what is messin' with them. Wonder if they know but ain't letting nobody know. Nah," Great Grandmother continued, "on second thought, I don't think they know."

The Secret Keeper shrugged their shoulders. "This is some kind of mess. Usually, we know what's happening in Moonstone. But there's been no clue this time."

"Well, who is the child? I know you know the father."

"I can't open The Book unless two or more from the other worlds are present."

"That's why I'm here," Father Kelly said. "I heard through the grapevine you needed some assistance. I contacted Great Grandmother and told her I would accompany her to your house. After all, it's the least I can do to make up for my last time dealing with you. I know this is important to Moonstone."

The Secret Keeper nodded. They kept all of the secrets in their mind, but they still kept everything in The Book. It held most of the secrets in Moonstone. It was a backup copy, insurance. It made a giant thud when placed on the table. A face appeared in the hardbound cover.

"What's the password?" The Book asked.

"Secret Keepers are trap keepers," The Secret Keeper answered.

There was a loud click, and a thousand papers flew out into the air.

"What decade? What's the date?" asked The Book.

"This one is it." They plucked the paper with their thumb and forefinger.

All the papers fell into one complete and accurate pile by date and The Book closed shut. The face on the cover disappeared.

All three of them gathered together.

Father Kelly began reading out loud.

> *"January 21, 2007. A child born to Giselle Tucker and Ezman Reynolds. Birthplace: Moonstone, South Carolina. Name of Child: Rawling Tucker. This child was born to a parent who wishes its identity be unknown. So mote it be."*

Each of them stepped back from the paper. The Secret Keeper reopened The Book. The secret paper fluttered in the air and slid into its correct place in the papers. The Book clicked shut again. The Secret Keeper placed it back into the cabinet and locked it.

"We have the mother's name. That's a start," said Father Kelly.

"I didn't know that before," The Secret Keeper said. "If there are names of other parties involved, I can't see them sometimes. It's like a glitch in the program. I can only see who asked for the secret to be burned."

"Didn't know nothin' 'bout that," Great Grandmother scoffed. "I thought you knew everything."

"Nobody knows everything. Sometimes, people know just enough to make themselves dangerous. That's me."

"I reckon you right if De Fates don't know who's out to change a plan," she said. She lit up a cigarette.

"So, how do we find out more?" The Secret Keeper sighed.

"You got to talk to my great-granddaughter 'bout this. I already told her. What you need her to do?"

"She has to go to The Renegades," the Secret Keeper replied. They knew that wasn't what Great Grandmother wanted to hear.

"That ain't no place for her. That ain't no place for nobody.

Friend or enemy," Great Grandmother said with trepidation in her voice.

"I have heard stories about that place. Not everybody makes it out," Father Kelly said as he adjusted his hearing aid.

"Why she got to go there? Why not you? Why not anybody else?" She flicked ashes into the air.

"Because she has The Hanging. Plain and simple. The Fates told you one day, they might need her. Today is that day."

"Dis ain't fair." Great Grandmother sulked.

"Since when is dealing with The Fates fair?" Father Kelly took out a flask and started drinking.

"She needs to come see me first. She can't go there without knowing what she's up against," The Secret Keeper replied.

Chapter Ten

MARILYN

I hear my alarm go off on my cell phone. It pierces the tranquil silence that I was experiencing while I was sleeping. I don't want to get up. I don't want to encounter the world. I just want to lay here and think about *him*.

Him is Jax.

Two days ago, when I was cleaning out one of the storerooms, I found an old picture in a dusty antique silver frame of an African American couple. The picture was dated and in black and white. The dark-skinned woman was dressed in early 1920s glamor, with a white cloche hat and pearls fastened around her neck. Her dress was modest. It looked to have a long ribbon sash tied around her lower hips. She sat adoringly in front of her husband (at least, I am assuming it was her husband). A rather tall, copper-skinned man stood behind her with his hand on her shoulder. He had a scar on his left cheek. His hair was parted in the middle and slicked down on each side. She had a slight smile. He remained poised. He looked almost afraid to show any emotion toward her. *I wonder if it was a marriage of convenience,* I thought to myself, *like Colby and I.*

They did not resemble Mr. and Mrs. Marshe. I concluded they must have been members of an extended family or close friends. I knew very little about the Marshes, the family that lived here previously, except that they did business with my father from time to time. Mr. and Mrs. Marshe had both passed on to the afterlife a few years before. Their children let the house deteriorate into a dire set of circumstances, forcing them to sell as is because they couldn't afford the renovations. I wanted to do the right thing, seeing as it could be a memento that the family that used to live here might want. Perhaps they were in a rush to pack up the house, and it was overlooked. When I contacted their realtor, she relayed that the photo was of no interest to them and I could throw it away. Still, I could not let it go, so I found a place for it on the wall next to the fireplace among faded wallpaper in the living room.

Two mornings later, I woke to the people in the picture frame staring at me from my bedroom dresser. The husband appeared much happier. He was affectionately kissing his wife on her hand. Although their poses had changed. I was a bit surprised, but I know that most houses come with their own sect of spirits. Some are trapped; some merely hang around because this was the time they were happiest. Some are wailing from the pain that never left them once they departed from this Earth. Though I still did not know if they were related to the Marshes, they had woven a tapestry in this house and hence, now my life too. I needed to ask Great Grandmother about them. She didn't know about all matters associated with Moonstone but perhaps she could provide me some clues.

Nonetheless, staring at the couple in the frame made me miss him. Even with all the supernatural things happening around me, Jax was all I could think about.

It felt like a lifetime ago. He came into my life like a wild stallion.

I was teaching at a local college in Philadelphia before I met

Colby. I was in between classes one day and decided to take a walk to Starbucks for a latte. It was sunny, but there was a hint of a chill in the air—a perfect fall day. The baristas at Starbucks knew me well, as I frequented it at least three times a week. They were exceptionally busy that day, and I found myself waiting in a long line. Finally, I was able to give my order.

"Grande latte, please. And I'll take a slice of pumpkin loaf bread." The barista grabbed my treat and shouted my order to the person working the coffee bar. Then she rang me up.

"No charge. You're good."

"Huh?" I looked at her quizzically.

"No charge, ma'am. Someone already paid for you. They took care of your order."

I had heard about this paying-it-forward thing, I just never expected it to happen to me. I scanned the shop, looking for who it might be.

"Is the person still here? I'd like to thank them."

"No. They're not here anymore."

Not wanting to hold up the line any longer, I accepted the kind act and moved toward the area where customers picked up their orders.

Two days later, I had a craving for another latte and pumpkin bread. I once again found myself in Starbucks.

"I'll have a grande latte and a slice of pumpkin bread."

"Sure." The same barista rang up my order.

"All set. Someone already paid for you."

I was more than surprised. "Again?"

Chelsea, the barista, chuckled. "Yes, ma'am. Again."

"Is it the same person that paid for me before?"

"Yes ma'am, it is."

"Well then, okay. This is weird. I guess I have a latte angel." I wanted to know more, but once again, the line was getting long and I didn't want to hold it up any longer.

"Thanks," I said, beginning to feel a bit paranoid.

Three days later, I placed the same order at Starbucks. There was a different barista behind the counter.

"No charge, ma'am. You're all set."

"Let me guess, someone already paid for it," I said sarcastically.

"Yep. Someone paid it forward." The barista smiled.

"Listen, while I appreciate it, can you please tell the person who is paying for me that I don't want them to anymore? It's kind of creeping me out. Do you know who is it? Can you at least describe them to me?" I was beginning to feel like I had a stalker.

"No, I can't. They gave me a hundred dollars to keep it anonymous."

"A hundred dollars? What the fuck is going on here?" I asked.

The barista looked nervously at me. "I'm sorry. Do you want anything else or are you all set?"

I walked away with a mix of frustration and anger. Then I decided to have a seat. I was going to get to the bottom of this mystery once and for all. When things settled down a bit, I walked up to the counter to resume the conversation.

"Can I talk to you for a minute? I'm sorry about my outburst. I didn't mean to scare you. It's just a little unnerving, that's all. I appreciate the gesture, but part of me feels like I'm being stalked. Is it a guy or a girl? Help a sista out."

"Can't do it," she said in a sober voice.

Who was this master of puppets? I thought to myself.

I decided to turn the tables. I scribbled a note on the notepad I kept in my school bag: *Thanks for my free lattes. But I'm a little weirded out by your generosity. What's your name?*

I handed the note to the barista. "Can you give this to whoever keeps paying for me? I don't have a hundred dollars, but I promise I'll leave you and Chelsea alone about it. Does this person come here a lot? Maybe I'll hang out one day and try to catch them."

"Yeah. They're here enough. That's on you, though. I wouldn't waste my day waiting for him—"

"Him! It's a him! I had a feeling," I shouted as I pointed a finger at her.

The barista had a look of disappointment on her face. She had messed up big time.

"You slipped up. Don't worry, I'll keep the secret." I winked and handed her a five-dollar bill. Excited that I was closing in on my latte stalker, I ran out of the door to teach my next class.

Later that afternoon, I decided to forget about the mystery latte man and concentrate on the weekend. The Hanging wasn't helping me out with who it might be. Even if it was creepy, it still was a bit endearing that someone gave a shit about making my day. Maybe if I had time on Sunday, I would try to stake him out.

"Girl, that's some crazy shit. Cute, but some crazy shit." my friend Starr said while we were shopping that Saturday. "And you couldn't pick that up with your spidey sense?"

"No. It doesn't work that way. It only appears when it feels it needs to appear."

"Well, that's super annoying," she replied, sipping on her soda. "Girl, you betta get yourself a plan to see him. Who knows? He might be single and cute."

"Let's not get too ahead of ourselves. With my luck, he'll look like a werewolf on a full moon."

"If I were you, I would just ride it out. Fuck it. I know you sent him a note. You should have let it go. You could probably get free Starbucks for the rest of the semester. Don't ask any more questions, and rock the boat. That's like seven bucks you're saving each time. I'm just saying, it's a question of economics."

After the weekend, my curiosity became even more piqued. On Monday, I found myself in my favorite haunt.

"He replied to your note!" Chelsea said jubilantly. She handed it to me with my latte.

"Thanks." I was excited but decided to read it when I got

outside. I took a deep breath and unfolded the napkin, struggling to read the hastily scribbled words.

My name is The Smartest Man In The Room.

"Oh, you're arrogant. Very arrogant indeed." I arched an eyebrow but smiled to myself.

Game on. GAME ON.

A few days later, I was in stealth mode in my car, going on a fact-finding mission.

I put on my Ray-Ban sunglasses and hung out in a parking spot a few doors down from my favorite Starbucks. It was game time. Well, not quite game time—but amateur investigative journalist time.

After further five-dollar bill incentives to Chelsea, the barista provided more tidbits of information regarding my mystery latte sponsor. She still didn't tell me his name, but she did provide several possible time slots in which he might appear.

I didn't want to ambush him and show up at the same time he was there. If I was dealing with some kind of nutcase, who knows what would happen? I just wanted to see who he was and try to find out where he worked or lived. After all, he still was paying for my lattes; I figured that, at this point, it was way over the fifty-dollar mark. I did know that he usually wore a black jacket, was about 6 feet or so, and Black.

It was 7:37 am. I was losing hope. I figured I wasn't going to see him. Just then, the Starbucks door swung open. A well-dressed Black man with a light black jacket stepped outside with a grande coffee.

Fuuuuck. He's cute… I had been secretly hoping he was ugly so I could dismiss the whole event. No such luck. I couldn't follow him on foot because what if he turned around? I wanted to take my chances and drive in his direction…*nah…too obvious.* I talked myself out of it quickly. My best bet was just to turn my head and stretch over the backseat as far as I could to see what direction he was walking toward.

He took a right turn.

I still remember the rush I felt at that moment. My body was mixed with jitters and excitement. I didn't have a solid plan; it was more just a hunch that I could pinpoint a geographic location. City blocks are longer than average size blocks to walk. I would have to be quick.

I turned right around the same corner as he did. I slowed down a bit, perusing restaurant windows and boutiques for any signs of life. Outside tables were set up for fresh-air dining and obstructed some of my views. I was about to call it a day after the second block. *Damn, why'd I wear these sandals today?* My shoes weren't built for fast walking.

A bright red door flung open. A waiter in jeans carried piles of pasta on a large tray on their way to an outdoor table. Through the window, I saw my mystery latte sponsor. He was talking to one of the staff who looked like a hostess. I could see him but he couldn't see me because of the angle.

"Excuse me, who's that? He looks familiar," I said to the waiter.

"Oh, that's Jax. He's the owner."

"Thanks," I said and left.

The next day, I stopped a waitress outside during her shift. "Could you do me a favor? I'm in a hurry. Can you give this to the owner?"

"Umm. Sure, no problem." The waitress looked a little perplexed but stuffed the envelope in the pocket of her apron.

I hustled myself back to work. I pictured him smiling to himself after he read the notecard with a monogrammed M that simply read:

To The Smartest Man In The Room,

Gotcha.

And thus, the greatest love of my life started with a simple gesture of kindness. With every passing day inside these house walls, as the people in the photo changed positions, my sentiments swallowed me whole like a whale. Yet in the middle of the whale's stomach, there was nothing: only grief and misery. I was mourning the life that could have been for both of us if only The Fates had allowed us the chance.

"De Secret Keeper said you need to go see them 'bout dis. It ain't pretty," Great Grandmother said to me as she stood by my pillow the next morning. She had literally woken me up from a dead sleep. I knew this was going to be a hellish conversation.

"So what's the plan?" I asked as she straightened her covers around her.

Great Grandmother stood up and floated back and forth for a minute. "You got to go to De Renegades. I ain't too sure about dat for you. Every heartbreak or broken dream you done had will be there, live and in color. You will feel all of it. Every bit. You don't wear heartbreak well. I can dress mine up with red lace and some pearls. You wear it and you be looking like a peasant."

Fear was stuck in my throat. "I've never heard you talk about this before. Have you been there?"

"I been three times. Barely survived de second time. So many paths to keep you from going to get what you went there for."

"Why do I need to go? Did The Secret Keeper tell you that?"

Great Grandmother shifted from one leg to the other. She lit up a new cigarette with shaking hands. I could tell she was nervous; I had never seen her act this way before. There was an undercurrent of anxiety in her voice that I rarely heard.

"How did you survive?" I asked.

"Well, de trick is you got to focus. You can't let nothin' sidetrack you. You gone see people and situations that hurt you and others you love. You be wanting to go back and fix it."

My mind flashed to Jax.

"But don't go back. It's a trick. 'Cause when you stop to fix it, there be another problem right next to it. Then you spend all your time tryin' to change the past and not looking for what you need. All de while De Renegades are draining your life." She inhaled her cigarette. "De Secret Keeper gone help you. They said you two need to meet."

"Why would they help me, Great Grandmother?" I asked. "I heard they only help people that they can get something out of."

"We's all in this together. We's all got a stake in it. Whatever comin', it's gonna affect all of us."

"What did they show you? What did you try to go back and fix when you were there?" I was curious. I wondered if she had tried to fix her relationship with her daughter.

"Never you mind 'bout dat. Dat's not important. De important thing is I made it out alive. De Secret Keeper gone tell you who you need to see and what you need to get. Go there, get what you need, and get out."

A few days later, I received instructions from The Secret Keeper to meet them that night.

I stumbled up the steps to The Secret Keeper's house. They opened the door for me to enter and I stood there, wringing my hands with pools of sweat in my palms.

"You don't have to be afraid of me. Do right by me, and I will do right by you."

"Fair enough," I replied.

"The Renegades are a strange place. It doesn't matter who goes, human or spirit, you will be affected by your journey for the rest of your life." The Secret Keeper lit a candle and sat down next to it. "You must go because you are the one The Hanging came to. It doesn't just go to anyone. That vision of the baby turning into smoke marked you."

I studied The Secret Keeper for a moment. *So, this is what so many people fear*, I thought. I decided to keep my questions to myself, as I was still filled with trepidation.

"Great Grandmother told me what to expect."

"Good. I cannot stress this enough—DO NOT STOP until you reach the party you need to talk to. Time has a way of getting away from you when you're there. I can't help you when you're there, and Great Grandmother can't help you. Nobody outside of the realm can. I have to limit my interaction there due to my business. Great Grandmother can't take another chance. However, you are allowed to bring along one other traveler."

"Oh. That's interesting. Although I don't know who would be crazy enough to go there with me. I don't have any close connections here."

"If you do find someone, be sure to pick a person who has some powers. The more supernatural help you have, the better."

"Okay," I replied.

"When you get there, go see an old friend of mine. Ever heard of Marie Laveau?"

"Who hasn't? You know her?" I was surprised.

"Of course I do."

"Wow. I'm humbled I get to meet her."

"If you can reach her."

"Why does Marie Laveau live in The Renegades?"

The Secret Keeper pondered my answer before they spoke. "Because she figures if someone can withstand all that fear and regret enough to get to her, then they must be someone substantially worth her time. But she doesn't live there. She just does business there occasionally."

The Secret Keeper gave me a moment to process.

"One last thing," they added. "I had to make an appointment for you to go. Your ticket will be on your kitchen table on the day of your trip. Once you pick up your ticket, that's it. You're on your way. Get some rest. You're going to need all your energy."

I stood up and crossed to the fireplace to warm my hands. I felt a bit more at ease with The Secret Keeper. "I'm assuming we'll talk once this is over?"

"I'll know when you're back. You'll get instructions to see me again. In the meantime, be safe. And remember, at some point, you'll need something from me. I'll take care of it."

I looked at them quizzically. I didn't have any secrets they needed to get rid of. Was The Secret Keeper seeing something in my future that I wasn't aware of yet? I pushed the thought aside and bid them goodbye.

Later that evening, I awoke to a loud pounding on my front door and a fierce rainstorm. It scared me to death. *Was Colby coming to finish the deed?*

I flew down the steps and ducked into the kitchen, grabbing the largest knife I could find. The person was still pounding on my door. I went to the living room and peeked out the window. A hovering figure in a dark coat stood on my stoop. *Perhaps it's someone in distress,* I thought. I took a deep breath and unlocked the deadbolt.

The door flung open violently due to the wind from the storm. A scared woman in drenched clothes stood before me.

"Hi, Jamie," I said with a sigh of relief.

"Hi," she replied, trembling from the freezing rain. Her hair was matted around her wet face. "Are the monsters back?"

"Come in. Let's get you warmed up." I grabbed Jamie's hand and pulled her inside. A crack of thunder startled us as I closed the door.

I took off her coat and hung it up on a hook.

Jamie smoothed out her wrinkled t-shirt and jeans as if to dry herself but to no avail. She was soaked.

"I'm going to go get you a towel. Have a seat." I glided into the guest bathroom and pulled a fluffy gray one out of the linen closet.

Jamie, shivering, looked around the room. "This is Mr. Marsh's old place?"

"Yes. I bought it from his daughter."

"Why you wanna live here? Why not live at home with your mama?"

I went into the kitchen and put on the tea kettle. "I need to get you warmed up. What a nasty storm. I didn't even know it was going to rain. Look at you! You walked all the way over here in this?"

Jamie kept staring at me, undeterred. "Why you wanna live here? Why not live at home with your mama?" she repeated.

I went over to her, bent down, and grasped her hands gently. "We talked about this a long time ago. Remember? I wanted some independence from my family and when I live at home, I miss my father a lot."

Jamie's eyes grew big. "Oh yeah. Now I remember."

A silence fell between us that only old friends could understand. A flash of lightning burned in the pitch-black sky outside.

Jamie leaned in a few inches. "Are the monsters back?" she asked again.

I took a deep breath. Jamie always knew when something sinister was happening that involved me. "Yes, the monsters are back," I solemnly replied.

"I had a feeling you needed me. Someone told me to come see you."

"Who was it? Was it a spirit or human? Was it Great Grandmother?"

"No, not Great Grandmother. Somebody new. A spirit."

"Be careful. Not everybody who visits us is there to help. There's lots of shenanigans when we are dealing with the other side; Great Grandmother told me so." The tea kettle began to whistle.

I rushed to the kitchen to turn the kettle off and poured the hot water into two mugs. When I returned, Jamie had sunken into a trance like she did when we were younger. She sat with her mouth half open and dead eyes. Drool trickled down her chin. I set the tea down and ran over to her.

"Jamie!" I shouted.

She snapped back to attention. "I was doing it again, wasn't I?" She began to chide herself. "I can't help it. I'm sorry. I'm sorry, Mama. I should have watched Joey more carefully. I should've played with him. Then he wouldn't have run off. He's dead, Mama. He's dead and it's all my fault!" She began sobbing uncontrollably.

"Jamie! This is Marilyn. It's not your fault. Your mama's not mad at you. It was an accident. Do you remember she told you it was an accident? Right before you went into the hospital the first time? She died a long time ago." I hugged her.

Jamie wiped away some of her tears. "Yes, I remember now. Okay. It's all done."

I went back to get the tea and handed Jamie a mug. "It's lavender," I told her. "For your nerves."

She sipped it gratefully.

"Are you still taking your meds?" I asked.

"Yes," she said. "But they don't always work. I don't want to ask them for a higher dosage. Sometimes they make me too sleepy."

"Well, you should still tell the doctors they aren't consistently working. I'll make an appointment for you and take you there myself."

"Marilyn, I have to go with you to The Renegades. That's what the spirit told me."

I was shocked at what she said. "What do you know about that, Jamie? That's not exactly public knowledge." I didn't like that the visiting spirit told her what she was needed for.

"I dunno. He just said I needed to see you, and we have to go to The Renegades."

I sighed heavily. "I don't know if you could handle it, Jamie.

You're already in a fragile state. I'd hate to make it worse." I wasn't sure I was going to make it out of there alive, let alone my fragile childhood best friend.

"Please let me go. It's a chance for me to make things right. I know something bad is going to happen in Moonstone. We have a chance to stop it. You know I have the powers."

I had thought about who would be brave enough to come with me in my circle of friends; there weren't many. I had considered Jamie as a choice ever since my conversation with The Secret Keeper, but I could never be sure what Jamie's state of mind was.

I hadn't visited her since she returned to Moonstone. Jamie was like the sun. I know it's out there; even though we don't have much interaction with it, I know I need its warmth.

Jamie hadn't been the same since the accident. Joey's death propelled her into a catatonic state. She didn't function during her teenage years. There were no sleepovers or sweet sixteen parties for her, no curfews to break. No jubilant graduation party to congratulate her on acceptance to a prestigious university.

Her mother died of a broken heart. She grieved for both her son and daughter. She never got the opportunity to shop for prom dresses with her or comfort her when her first boyfriend broke her heart. All that was left was emptiness. Her mother filled her days with needless errands and threw herself into the church. She did anything she could to survive.

There was a glimmer of hope when Jamie was transferred to the last hospital. They had made strides with her. She began to speak again and tried to reconnect with people. Unfortunately, most of Moonstone had turned their back on her, moving on to the next tragedy. I even overheard someone in a line at the deli laughing not more than a few days ago, referring to her as 'the crazy lady who lives by the creek.'

That crazy lady that lives by the creek has the ability to save people from death, I wanted to say to them.

It was almost as if The Fates gave her power in exchange for her grief over the loss of her brother. Did The Fates feel guilty for allowing such an abhorrent event to occur? No one would ever know the answer to that, at least not on this Earth.

The first time it happened, we were teenagers. Jamie was functioning well that day, which was unusual. A little girl ran into the middle of Forte Street and was hit by a car. Her tiny body flew into the air and landed six feet away. Jamie ran to the girl's side; she lay there, convulsing and coughing up blood onto the black tar while onlookers watched in panic. Jamie crouched down to her level. She stared at her and covered her eyes with her hands.

"Breathe, girl," she whispered into her ear. "You got a lot of life left in you. Even if you do live in Moonstone."

All at once, the girl stopped shaking and began heaving. Blood poured out of her nostrils. She sat up, brushing the dirt away from the wounds on her knees and arms. Then she stood up unsteadily. People were amazed, but they also were afraid. That's why they called her 'the crazy lady who lives by the creek.' Or by her nickname, The Evader. People either loved, loathed, or feared her.

Although her powers worked in this realm, I wasn't so sure they would in The Renegades. Her power only intervened when it chose to. There was no rhyme or reason, no pattern of specific people to save from death. I was afraid to further damage Jamie's psyche by subjecting her to the burdensome experience of The Renegades without a guarantee that her powers would work there. However, with so much at stake and so many unknown factors, I felt I didn't have a choice.

I sighed. "Okay. You're in."

Chapter Eleven

RAWLING

I remember when Mama took me to The Crooked Woods one time when I was little. I think I was seven years old.

She woke me early one Sunday morning and told me to get dressed. She told me we weren't going to church. Instead, we were going on a little field trip. I was bewildered by what she said. She and her latest conquest traveled every so often, but the only time I got to travel to other places was on school trips. Miss Josie, my nanny, would be in charge of me when she left.

When I was young, I loved spending time with Miss Josie. She didn't have any children, so she liked to spoil me. She would bake chocolate cakes for me, and we would decorate them together. One time, she even put my name on it. She wrote *Rawling* in big cursive letters in blue frosting. That cake ended up being different than the rest. The day after we made it, I went to eat another piece, but it tasted awful. I can't describe it. It was still moist, but it tasted like sour milk.

Miss Josie scowled with her first bite. She took two more. "They taste the same," she said, wincing as she put her fork down.

"Mine too," I replied.

Miss Josie mentioned all of the ingredients she used. "None of these would have done this to the cake. I don't know what happened. I know you love your chocolate cake. I'm sorry, Rawling," she said.

I was upset, but I didn't let her know I was really looking forward to another piece of cake.

I remember being so terrified of The Crooked Woods at that age that I thought to myself, I'd rather make another sour chocolate cake with Miss Josie than go there with Mama.

I can still feel the heavy mist in the air as me and Mama drove with the top down in her convertible. We pulled off the main highway and made a right turn. We traveled down several winding roads, which made me nervous. It seemed The Crooked Woods was almost another planet away. I remembered the stories about what happened there—none of them good. I heard about them one day from a classmate. There were thick trees, heavy rocks, and endless spider webs the size of small bushes. Thorns from plants could cut you at any moment. It was very easy to get tangled up in the overgrown brush. It was eerily quiet: you could never hear any birds chirping or other animals scurrying around. There were many mazes inside of it. Pools of quicksand sought to devour your legs. There was a rumor that at its center, something malevolent existed, although no one knew what it was.

The Crooked Woods reminded me of *Grimm's Fairy Tales*. Everyone met trouble in the woods. *Little Red Riding Hood. Hansel and Gretel. The Hut in the Forest.* I had a big book of all of these stories when I was little. It was given to me by one of Mama's ex-boyfriends as a Christmas gift.

Mama parked and slammed the door open and shut, then put her keys in her purse. She took one last drag of the remainder of her cigarette and stamped it out. She adjusted the top of her blue denim shorts and pulled her red and white checkered crop top down to cover her belly a little more. She took my hand and tugged it tighter.

"Why are we here?" I asked.

"Your mama needs a couple of things. Hold this bag for me," she replied.

I gripped the small canvas bag she handed me. Then she bent down to be at eye level with me.

"Listen," she said. "Don't you go and run off. Stay right next to me. I mean it. I know what people say about The Crooked Woods. No one should wander in there because they might not come out. Truth is, that is only for certain people. If you know what you're doing, then they'll let you pass and leave you alone. After we get what I need and leave, don't you go scurrying back here with anyone. They know me, but they won't know you without me."

I was so scared I couldn't speak, so I just nodded.

We walked down what seemed like endless tiny dirt paths. I thought Mama didn't have to warn me about not coming back; it was too confusing anyway. Finally, we stopped at a brook near a small moss-covered hill. I watched the water gurgling up and bobbing down over the rocks.

"We're here," said Mama.

She took her canvas bag from me and laid it on a nearby rock. She bent down and plunged her hand into the brook. After several tugs, she pulled up a handful of bright red flowers. I marveled at how they were in full bloom when they came up from the water. She grabbed another handful, put them into her bag, and we left.

She paused and bent down so she could take me by the arms. "You must never speak of this experience. No one is to know that we were here. No one." Her fingers dug into my skin.

We drove home in silence. Mama knew I was still scared, but she said nothing to soothe my fears. When we arrived, I ran up the steps and straight into Miss Josie's arms.

"What's wrong with you, child?" she asked as she ran her fingers through my thick blonde curls.

Tears flowed down my face. I didn't say anything. I just hugged her tighter to my tiny body. I was so weak then and such a loser.

Mama walked gracefully past me. "He's fine, Josie. Just a little tired. We took a long walk today. Make him lunch. Then, put him down for a nap. When he wakes up, give him some sweet tea and oatmeal raisin cookies as a snack."

"Yes, Mrs. Giselle," she replied.

A few days later, Mama was engaged to a new man. His name is George. So far, they are still together. I wonder if she loves this one. She might. Who cares? He has a lot of money. We live well. Maybe that's why she needed the bright red flowers that day from The Crooked Woods. He's husband number five.

Now that I am older, I am no longer afraid of The Crooked Woods.

Last August, on one hot summer night, the evil shadow told me to go there.

It was as if I was possessed. It stirred me so badly, I had to get out of bed. I was afraid when I arrived, something terrible would happen. But the evil shadow assured me I would be okay. I didn't need to sneak out of a window. Now that I am older, I pretty much come and go as I please. Besides, Mama just had cosmetic surgery and was fast asleep on pain meds. Not that I saw her at night anyway. I threw on some faded jeans and an old Led Zepplin t-shirt and drove there. It was remarkable I remembered the way to navigate to the same place.

I walked easily in between the trees by moonlight. Every few feet, the trees would adjust themselves to different positions. Paths would open and close. What was once a path became covered and invisible.

"Stop here," the evil shadow said to me. "Pick up some of the dirt and eat it. You need to absorb some of its contents. It will strengthen you."

I was repulsed, but I obeyed. The dirt tasted sweet as I gulped it down. I wiped my face with my hands.

"How did it taste?" the evil shadow asked.

"Sweet," I replied.

"Good. That means you are the Chosen One. You and I will do great things together."

I didn't know then what it meant by that statement but I knew it was nefarious. I didn't care. I was ready to be king of the world.

Chapter Twelve

MARILYN

Jamie and I woke up to the smell of fresh garbage. At first, I scoured the house looking for something I may have forgotten to throw away: a half-eaten sandwich, salad, or sour milk. When I reached the kitchen and saw the ticket glowing bright orange, I knew it was time.

How should I dress for The Renegades? I wondered. *How do I dress for entrance into a realm that fully intends to devour me by the end of my excursion?*

I opted for jeans and a tee. It was the best I could do under the circumstances. Jamie stood behind me in the kitchen as I picked up the ticket. I grabbed her hand as the world spun, rendering us both unconscious.

When we awoke, we found ourselves sitting in a waiting room.

"Where are we?" Jamie asked me in a half-dreamlike state.

"Your guess is as good as mine," I said as my eyes adjusted to the smoke. The smell of musky perfume permeated the air, burning my throat. "Ugh. That smell is going to make me nauseous." I winced.

"Me too," Jamie replied.

I nervously scanned the room. It was covered in 1980s wallpaper with hot pink shag carpet on the floor. There were several rows of desks with women and men working on old desktop computers and handheld calculators. They were all speaking loudly to their clients in the chair next to them. Several other people sat in chairs around Jamie and me, waiting for someone or something.

"Is that Barry Manilow?" Jamie asked. There was elevator music playing in the background.

"Indeed, I think it is."

A butterball squat woman with her hair neatly pinned in a bun stood in the front of the room, yelling numbers and names. "1006? 1006? Richardson, you're next."

"That's me." An older white man stood up and smoothed out his trousers. He walked over to her.

"Come with me," she said, turning her back to the rest of the people in the waiting room.

"This is so weird. Like I thought we were gonna be there as soon as we picked up the ticket," Jamie said. "I wonder if I'll see Joey or Mama."

I bristled at the sound of her words. *Jax.* Great Grandmother said that every sorrow or fear you ever had would manifest itself here. My confidence faltered, and I wondered if we would get out alive.

"1007? 1007? Maxwell, you're next."

I jumped at the call of my last name. We were up.

"That's me." We stood up and followed the woman to one of the desks. She ushered for me to have a seat. Jamie stood next to me.

A light-skinned Black woman with long stiletto white nails began typing.

"Marilyn Maxwell," she said as she continued reading, "is this your first visit to The Renegades?"

"Yes."

"And is this your traveler? What's her name?"

"Jamie. Jamie Travers."

The woman eyed her up and down. Then she pushed her glasses back up the bridge of her nose.

"What are the computers and calculators for?" Jamie asked.

"That is on a need-to-know basis. And you don't need to know." She picked up her extra large Big Gulp soda and sucked on the straw so hard that her cheeks fell inward on her face, and she looked like a deformed alien.

"What are the computers and calculators for?" Jamie asked again. She was becoming fixated again.

The woman looked at me and raised her eyebrows.

"Jamie." I grabbed her hand. "That's enough. The lady said you don't need to know."

"What is the purpose of your visit?"

"To visit Marie Laveau."

The lady's eyes widened a bit. "Oh, I see. An audience with the queen." She continued, "All set. Good luck."

A rush of wind surrounded us, transporting us to a wasteland. An explosion rocked our eardrums.

"What the hell is that?" I asked. I saw a flash of orange light with smoke and debris flying.

"Attack!" Soldiers in what appeared to be old army uniforms were knee-deep in mud.

"I'm going over!" another yelled as he climbed up out of the trench. Heavy shelling surrounded them.

"We're in the middle of some kind of war!" I yelled as we ducked behind sandbags in a trench.

It appeared as though everyone around us could see us but didn't interact with us. Another soldier fell back into the trench. He was bloody and missing his left arm. Burnt clothing stuck to his wounds. His fellow soldiers pulled him out of No Man's Land back into the trench. There was a stench of dead burned bodies around them. Planes sputtered above them, continuing to drop bombs.

"I think we're in World War I," Jamie pointed to a soldier handing out gas masks. He handed one to both of us.

"This is just in case." He grabbed his bayonet and charged into the deadly atmosphere.

The soldier who was missing an arm groaned in pain.

"How do you know?" I replied.

"I did a lot of reading at the hospitals. I love history. This fighting is trench warfare." Jamie pointed to the higher ground. The soldier who lost an arm was placed on a gurney.

"Excuse me," he said to me. "Can you please deliver this letter to my family? Just in case I don't make it?" He held a letter in his trembling hand.

I started to take the letter.

"No." Jamie intervened. "Marilyn, we don't have time for that. He's tugging at your heartstrings. If you take the letter, I think others will do the same. There'll be a thousand soldiers asking you to take letters to their families. We'll lose time."

I turned away from the American soldier.

He grabbed my hand. "Please," he said. "I want them to know how much I loved them."

I fell into a trance when I looked into his eyes. I held my other hand out to take the letter.

"We gotta get to this door." Jamie said. A few feet away stood a bright red door. "I think if we get to this door, we get to the next level or something. Kinda like a video game." A thick yellow cloud of mustard gas moved through the air.

"Put on your gas mask," Jamie ordered.

I did as I was told. We crouched down in the trench and made our way to the door. At first, it wouldn't open. Flashes dotted the sky like lightning rods. Jamie turned the knob again. With a creak and a click, it opened. We hurried through the door.

The scent of magnolia trees surrounded us, our faces warmed by the sun. Jamie and I stood on a dirt road next to a wooden fence. Dust flew in our faces from a hot breeze.

"It's peaceful. I'm sure it won't last." I said to Jamie. "I don't know what's going to happen to us next," I continued. "It could be anything."

The sound of a wagon and hooves trotting in the distance echoed around us. As the wagon approached, two white men slowed the horses.

"Y'all best be going now. The scramble for slaves is gonna be happening soon. You got to git there to get the best ones. I need me two strong men and a woman for breeding. What y'all need?"

Jamie and I looked at each other incredulously. We could tell from the men's clothing and the horses that this time period was definitely before World War I.

"I best be going. See y'all there." The man tipped his hat and pulled on the horses to signal he was ready to go.

"I got a bad feeling about this one. I think we're in the South during slavery," I said.

"Did you see how he asked us what we needed? I think to him we look like slave owners, not Black girls."

"We have to get out of here," I told her.

We walked down the dirt road. At the end, there was all sorts of commotion. Throngs of white men stood hovering and shouting at the opening of a large fence. Several men dressed in black suits were accepting payments.

As Jamie and I edged closer to the scene, we were horrified. Black bodies, some half-naked, were inside a pen. Babies screamed in the arms of their mothers. Men yelled in various languages as they were poked with sticks, their hands were tied with rope. An elderly man was struck on the side of his head. Blood fell down his ear.

A white man shot his gun in the air. Chaos and confusion ensued. A stream of people waiting outside rushed inside the pen. They began lassoing Black bodies. People shoved each other, wrestling to acquire the slaves they wanted. A whip crackled several times, adding to the insanity.

"Oh my God. This is a slave auction," I said in a panic. "This is a slave auction!"

Slave owners chained them together and escorted them out of the pen when they were satisfied with their purchase. Blacks were crying: some were trying to loosen the chains.

"No!" a mother yelled as a slave owner pulled her away. "Please let me have my baby. Please, sir," she sobbed.

"I only paid for you. Nobody else. I need you to breed."

One of the auctioneers grabbed her baby girl and handed her off. "Someone else wants your child. They paid a lot for her."

"Please! Can you buy me and my Willa?" She turned to me. "She's just a baby. She'll never know who her mother is. I promise I can work good. Just let me keep my baby." She fell to her knees.

"I-I'm sorry. I can't do that…" My voice faltered. I could still hear the baby crying in the distance.

"How cruel can you be? My baby needs me."

"We can't do anything about this, Marilyn," Jamie said. "Remember, if you help her, then you have to help all of them."

Just as we began to leave, an elderly slave began shrieking as she was being whipped. I stopped dead in my tracks. "This isn't right. Maybe I can buy her freedom."

Jamie tugged on me again as the woman wailed. Her dress began to fall off of her, revealing scars on her back from previous whippings, blood cascading over them.

"Close your eyes and don't look back. Follow me." Jamie guided us to the next red door, which was unexpectedly ajar, and we pushed the rest of the way open. Night stars gleamed in the sky. A full moon hung low between the branches of a tree.

Marie Laveau sat in a luxurious leather chair, sipping tea.

"Hello," she said. "You made it."

Jamie and I were stunned. The journey was shorter than we expected. Yet here sat Marie Laveau in front of us, in all her regalia and beauty. The books, portraits, and photos didn't do her justice.

"Please, have a seat," she said. "The Secret Keeper tells me you have a matter of great importance to discuss. Have some tea."

We settled ourselves on the couch and sat to face her. We were surrounded by tufts of brightly colored hibiscus flowers, while our feet were covered in dark moss. There was a lightness to our mood, which was unusual as to what we had encountered just before. She appeared very comfortable in her power, the Voodoo Queen of New Orleans. During her time she was alive, many sought her expertise on matters of the heart, legal issues, and money. She rose through the ranks to become one the most revered women in the city, as many important people trusted her with their deepest dreams and secrets. I wished I could be like her: secure in my existence. I feel those virtues still escape me. I was a shrinking spirit, afraid to look at myself in the mirror sometimes. Especially after Colby.

"I know navigating The Renegades is tricky. You must be very careful when leaving. The journey to the exit will be harder. That is why so many people don't make it out. The Renegades—how you say—*saves the best for last.* Enjoy this brief respite now."

"We need to know why the baby was born," I said. A star flickered in the midnight sky.

"The stars are flickering. Danger is near. I will get to it then." She sipped her tea. "I'm not going to tell you when and how The Awful Evil was born in Moonstone. That's forbidden knowledge.

But I will tell you that it has been a part of your community for centuries, feeding off the fears and misery of the people it touches. There is no rhyme or reason to who is affected by it. It merely rests and, when it is hungry, it strikes."

Marie Laveau shifted her gaze toward the sky. "Everything in our life is in a state of flux. One minute you feel one way, and the next, you feel different. It is our myriad of emotions that keep us literally alive. You cannot feel happy without also feeling sadness. You cannot feel love without feeling hate. How would you know how to cherish something if you had never lost something important to you?"

"So, there is a balance we must keep. That's how the universe operates," Jamie said.

"Yes—but what if there is a disruptor? What if there is someone who stays angry or in love too long? What if all someone experiences is winning, but never losing? They would not know how to build resilience and come back stronger."

"Does The Awful Evil seek to disrupt the balance?" I asked.

"Yes," she said. "The Awful Evil can only take hold of someone for a specific moment in time. You have seen unexpected murders and suicides in Moonstone. However, if it is used in conjunction with a human specifically born for this purpose, it has way more power. The person has the ability to manipulate time, so to speak. For if someone is in an enraged state of mind, they can stay in that state for however long it wants them to. The longer you are there, the more damage a person might do—violence, murder, or hurt themselves. And what if The Awful Evil was able to control other humans through its host? Moonstone, and eventually other towns like it, would be completely destroyed."

"You mean there are more towns like Moonstone?" Jamie asked.

"Wow. I didn't know that." My eyes became large pools.

Marie Laveau laughed. "Surely you didn't think you were the

only ones on the planet that experienced The Awful Evil, along with other anomalies. Rest assured, you are not alone."

I felt a little relieved and scared at the same time. It was nice to know others were dealing with the same madness across the world. On the other hand, to know there were more Awful Evils, or something similar to it, spread out across the planet was a sobering thought.

"The child was born to usher in greater power. Tucker. His name is Rawling Tucker. He started off with easy tricks, like telling the sixth-grade bully to take someone's lunch. Or having someone trip a kid at recess. But lately, he's experimenting more. Testing to see how far he can go. He's already killed. Did you know that?"

Great Grandmother's theory was confirmed. The child and The Awful Evil were intertwined.

"No, we didn't," I told Marie. "I haven't heard about any strange deaths in Moonstone lately."

"He killed a middle school boy he was having trouble with. He and his father died in an awful accident."

"Oh my," I replied. "How does The Awful Evil choose someone to manipulate?"

Marie Laveau lowered her eyes and became pensive for a moment. "That is arranged by The Fates, from what I understand. They provide The Awful Evil with a child before they are born. It is kept a tight secret. Even The Secret Keeper doesn't know how the host is chosen. They only have the means with which to find out. The Secret Keeper has asked The Fates, but they have not replied with an answer. I am not sure why they don't want The Secret Keeper to find out. However, from what I understand, with this particular person, The Fates were unaware. This one was chosen by someone, or something, else. The Fates are a little nervous about this. It was a curveball. They are unsure as to how to respond."

"Ah, I see," I replied.

"When people talk to him, they go into a trance. He can manipulate them to do anything."

"What's the endgame? Is he going to plan something grand? Like a mass murder or something?" I asked.

Marie Laveau sat quietly and thought for a minute. "Not too sure. But you need to stop him before he does. The Awful Evil speaks to him and guides him through his thoughts. They decide who will be the next one harmed."

"So he is aware that he is evil and what he is doing is wrong? Or is he a victim?" asked Jamie.

"He is very much aware. Very much indeed. He is not captive to its power. On the contrary—he is learning to master it."

Marie Laveau looked upward to the black sky.

"So how do we kill it?" Jamie said, leaning forward in her chair. I was surprised by her frankness.

"You can't kill him," Marie said. "You can only try to sever the connection he has to The Awful Evil. Hopefully, that will be enough. Now that you know its purpose, Great Grandmother, The Secret Keeper, and others can help you with that. But it is your journey, not to be influenced by me."

The direness of the situation overwhelmed me.

"Well, I'm afraid our time is up." Marie Laveau stood and smoothed out her long, bright red skirt. "I have many appointments tonight. Remember, The Awful Evil and Moonstone have respected each other uneasily throughout time. But now they are unbalanced. And that can cause great calamities."

Jamie and I stood up and began to prepare for the hellish journey out of The Renegades.

"Remember, climbing out is harder than climbing in." Marie Laveau smiled and pointed to a pink door that had magically appeared. "Farewell."

With a wave of her shawl, she disappeared. The pink door grew larger by the second. Soon it loomed over us.

"Buckle up. Let's do this." I took Jamie's hand and we walked through.

Instantly, we were somewhere else. I remembered that day. I remembered the heat. I remembered the smell. I saw the ladybugs on the concrete in front of the house. I saw our younger selves sitting on the ground playing jacks.

"Oh no," I said, filled with dread.

Jamie ran to Joey's apparition and hugged him. "Joey. Joey, don't run off and play. Stay here."

He looked at her, puzzled. Then he pushed back from her embrace and dashed off.

"Joey, don't go! Don't go!" Jamie began to run after him.

"Jamie! Jamie!" I took off after her.

Joey turned down the path in the woods where he would be killed. I could hear the branch of the tree snap. By the time Jamie and I had caught up with him, it was too late. He yelled out in pain.

"Get up, Joey. Get up, Joey," Jamie repeated frantically, trying to pull the large tree branch off him. He was pinned down and shaking. Sobbing, Jamie bent down and took his hand. I watched her will every emotion in her body to help him escape death, closing her eyes tightly. "Joey, hold on. Hold on."

Blood filled his mouth, staining his face. His eyes grew still.

"Joey! No. No. I'm going to change this. Get up. Get up." Jamie helplessly seized more twigs and brushed the dirt off his face.

"Jamie. We've got to go. We'll die here. I can feel myself fading."

"No! Don't tell me that. I can save him. I wasn't there the first time, but I'm here now. I need to concentrate. If I can concentrate harder, I can save him. Dammit. Why isn't my power working?" She was hysterical.

To the far right corner, I could see the next door. "We have to go, Jamie. This was meant to be. If it weren't for him, you wouldn't have your power."

"No. I don't need my power. I need my brother." She cuddled his head to her chest.

I looked up and winced at the sun. My legs buckled, and I was beginning to feel weak. My life force was draining out of me.

"We gotta get outta here."

As if on cue, Jamie fell into a stupor. I dragged her to the door.

In the next breath, we were in a church full of impeccably dressed people. The crowd was smiling, chatting, and taking pictures. I looked around to see if I could recognize anyone. I didn't.

But I recognized one of the faces at the altar.

Jax.

Climbing out is harder than climbing in.

The entire sanctuary smelled of dahlias. His bride was beautiful, standing in a silk gown with a cascading trumpet train.

"Jax, Jax," I dropped Jamie to the ground and continued calling his name as I ran up the aisle. "Jax, don't do this. You don't have to do this. You don't have to ruin us." Tears tumbled down my cheeks. I felt as if my lungs would explode from emotion. All the old wounds I'd tried to suppress came bubbling to the surface.

"Jax!" I tried to take his hand. "Listen to me. You're the love of my life. I'm sorry I didn't tell you sooner. We can do this. You don't need her. Please don't marry her."

He looked at me as if I was a stranger, then turned his back to me as the minister began reciting the wedding vows.

I fell to my knees. "This can't happen. Please don't do this. I love you. I love you more than life itself." All the knots of pain I had experienced over the years wound themselves into one gargantuan weight and sat squarely on my chest.

I had never felt so alone in my life. Jamie was still there but hadn't woken from her stupor. I had to fight this battle alone.

"This is it. I can't go on," I said out loud. "I can't go on." All I could do was sit with my knees pressed to my chest and rock back and forth.

"I can't go on."

I closed my eyes and surrendered to the swell of emotions enveloping me.

Climbing out is harder than climbing in.

Chapter Thirteen

RAWLING

I sit in the back of English class, twirling my pencil around my fingers. If I hear one more comment about the rubric for the reflective essay due in a couple of days, my head is going to explode. There should be an exemption for students who get all As. We shouldn't have to be forced to listen over and over to teachers who must repeat themselves for idiot kids. It was a time waster. I had more important things to do with my life. The bell for lunch rings and I'm relieved. I'm starving.

"Move outta my way, loser," I say jokingly as I bump into my best friend Tom on purpose. At first glance, you would think that Tom was an athlete with his muscular physique. No such luck; he couldn't dribble a basketball or throw a football if his life depended on it.

"What delectable delights do we have today?" Tom says to me as we continue down the hall. "Lemme guess—mystery meat."

I make a gagging gesture. "I'll stick to the day-old pizza. Last time I had mystery meat, I was in the bathroom for two days."

"Gross," Tom laughs.

Kids call us the dynamic duo.

We breeze our way through the line in the cafeteria and sit at our usual table. No one dares sit with us unless invited. Another boy, full of anticipation, sits nervously at the edge of a table adjacent to us. Other kids in the cafe barely glance over at the potential interaction between us.

"What do you think? You wanna make his day?"

"Sure," I reply. I was ready to get into some shenanigans. I point my finger at him and beckon him over.

He smiles and picks up his lunch tray.

"Hey, you're new. What's your name?" I ask the boy, sizing him up. I can tell he isn't rich, but he isn't poor either. *That Polo shirt is undeniably from two seasons ago,* I think.

"Yeah. I'm Mike."

"Hi, I'm Rawling; this is my partner in crime, Tom."

"What's up?" Tom adds, nodding his head. He jams some fries into ketchup and stuffs them in his mouth.

"Have you made any friends yet?" I ask.

"Um, a few. I know Jack on the track team. He's in my precalc class." The new kid sucks down some soda through one of the paper straws they gave out in the line.

"Oh yeah. We know him. He's cool. But a bit of a lightweight when it comes to drinking games." Tom looks at me and we both laugh.

"One time, we got him so drunk off beer pong, he ended up in the hospital for alcohol poisoning. That was a fun night."

"It was epic," Tom agrees.

I see Mike smile anxiously. I know he's already heard about my reputation. I'm sure that, from what kids at school have told him, he was scared of me. He would be swimming with sharks if we allowed him in our circle. I'm sure all his life, this kid has been bait. I know he wants to be a shark instead.

"I see you did a dance with the mystery meat today. You'll pay for that later. Mystery meat has its consequences."

Mike pushes the meat aside from his mashed potatoes on the plate. "I didn't know that. God, I hope I don't get sick."

"You probably will." Tom turns sideways, swinging his legs so they stretch out across the empty bench. "So where do you live? What part of town? Why the hell did you move to Moonstone?"

Mike shuffles his fingers through his hair. "Umm…my dad. He inherited a diner from my aunt who died a few months ago."

"Sorry about that," I say. "Which one is it?"

"The Speakeasy Diner, across from the movie theater," Mike replied.

"Oh yeah, I know that place. Good milkshakes," Tom said.

"Thanks. My dad was sad about it. He had just lost his job in Savannah, so he decided we should have a new start."

"So, is it just you and Dad? Or Dad and Mom? Any sisters and brothers?" Tom plays with his jello with a plastic spoon.

"Umm…just me and Dad. Mom left us a few years ago. We live in the West Bank development. You know, that little housing development they just built?"

"Yep. I know it." I turn over in my head how and what use I could put Mike to. I love to play games with ordinary people or STUPIDS, as both me and Tom call them.

"Hey Mike, watch this." I take an open bottle of red Gatorade and chuck it in the air. It hits the wall and explodes on a couple of students. Streaks of red run down the wall. All the kids crack up in the café except the ones that got hit. Tom bellows with laughter.

"What the fuck, Rawling? I hate you guys." James, a sophomore, stands up, shaking his hair to get rid of the droplets of liquid that landed on his head.

"Tucker, come with me." Mr. Sands, the Assistant Principal, and my arch nemesis, tells me as he marches over to my table. "Grab your stuff; you're going to in-school suspension for the rest of the day."

"Adios, suckers," I tell Tom and Mike as I throw up the peace sign with my right hand. I smirk as I follow Mr. Sands out of the cafeteria.

I'm sure Mike was a little shocked at what I did. It totally came out of the blue. He probably even secretly felt bad for the students who got sprayed with the blood-red liquid. But I could tell he didn't feel bad enough to abandon me and Tom and ask the others if they were okay.

My plan to land an in-school for the rest of the day had worked. I checked earlier in the day when I walked past the room. There was only one kid in there; rumor had it he was given an in-school because he was caught stealing an answer key to a math test. *What a light consequence for stealing. This fucking place has no rules. We get away with murder around here,* I think. I sign in and take a seat in the back. It was perfect. I could use the first half of my time there to write a monster history paper. The second half? A conversation with my shadow, The Awful Evil.

But The Awful Evil is impatient today, demanding to speak immediately after a few minutes of working on my paper.

"Way to go, hitting James with that soda. Fucking awesome."

"Thanks," I say in my head.

"You hate that kid, right? Something about him sleeping with your ex-girlfriend?"

I nod. I have my AirPods in so to the teacher, I look like I'm just jamming to a good song. "So, what do I do with Mike? Is he acceptable? I know you were losing faith after the last one I chose."

The Awful Evil is quiet for a moment. "Yeah, we can use him. He's got some mommy issues. Let's turn them into more anger. He's stronger than the other one. Start to train him now. That way when it's time, it will be second nature to him."

"Cool. We need to make sure this can't be traced back to me. I still haven't heard from Yale. And why did it take so long for you to decide we should do this?"

"It took so long because I felt you weren't ready yet. And it won't get back to you. I have that under control. When Mike's done, he won't remember a thing." The Awful Evil cackles. "Have I ever failed you? And yes, you'll get into Yale. You got a future. I have many plans for you. For us."

I smile.

"What's so funny?" Mrs. Price, the teacher on duty, asks me.

I smirk at her and shook my head.

"You've got a bad attitude." She rolls eyes lined with fake eyelashes and heavy mascara and continues correcting papers.

"Add her to the list." The Awful Evil chuckles.

"Will do."

"Stick with me, kid. Stick with me. Let's shake the world."

Chapter Fourteen

MARILYN

I stared at the thick yellow envelope on the kitchen table. Dixon & Gerard, Counselors at Law—my divorce papers had finally arrived. I was relieved that Colby signed them. I was afraid he was planning to drag this whole messy affair out for controlling purposes. It would have been his last attempt at subterfuge.

Instead, he chose to cut his losses. The night he walked out after trying to kill me, he never came back. At first, I expected him to burst through the door at any moment with rage-filled fists to pummel me into submission. I had nightmares where he would come to pick up his things and decide to hold me hostage. I had seen a story on the news about a wife held captive by her husband. She was reported missing on a Friday. By the end of the weekend, they found her in the house, dead. He had lied to her family and friends the entire time, telling them she took a short trip somewhere. I thought what I would do if that was also my fate; I would beg him to release me, trying to manipulate the situation to my advantage. I doubted he would go for it because I would be negotiating with a psychopath. Luckily, that didn't play out in reality. Instead, he had asked his friends to collect his things from me. Everything else was handled through the lawyers.

In lieu of anger, there was silence. A peace took root in my mind that had been missing for quite some time. I never longed for the love I lost with him. I merely rolled the stone back in place to seal the cave of desolation shut.

I hadn't written anything since my journey to The Renegades. My unfinished manuscript sat on the laptop screen, staring back at me, mocking my attempt to be a writer. The Secret Keeper had said that once you survived The Renegades, you wouldn't be the same. I wondered if this is what they meant.

Jamie was in the hospital again. The brunt of our excursion had destroyed what little sanity she had left. She lay there, a feeble, half-broken numbness in her lifeless eyes, curled up on the bed. She didn't speak much, only asking for her needs and giving one-word responses. I had been to visit her twice after I initially dropped her off. Destroyed by regret and guilt, I couldn't muster enough strength to visit her again. At least not for the time being.

My mother tried to contact me for a couple of days after I returned. When I finally did pick up the phone, I lied and told her I had been under the weather for a few days. In full 'mother hen' mode, she stopped by with a care package cultivated by Miss Eliza, her maid. Reluctantly, I forced myself to have a conversation with her, though I barely heard what she was saying. About fifteen minutes in, I collapsed on the couch and fell asleep. I had no energy left to do anything, let alone be forced to combine words into specific sentences.

Yet there was still so much to do. There was always so much to do.

I needed to meet with The Secret Keeper again. I needed to talk to Great Grandmother. I needed to know what I was up against. And I needed warriors to help me. The Secret Keeper knew I had returned. I suspected they were giving me a few days to recuperate. When they were ready to meet, they'd make sure I knew.

And in the midst of all of this holy mess, The Fates decided to throw in another curveball.

My email sat open in one of my many browser windows; an unopened email waiting. The browser icon blinked in the taskbar, a constant reminder. It had been sitting there for three days. Three days too long. But I couldn't muster the courage to open it. I just couldn't.

I sighed heavily and clicked on the icon to retrieve the message.

Hey. I don't know if you still use this old email address or not, but I thought I would try. I'm sorry we never got to touch base over the last few years. We definitely have some unfinished business. I'd be grateful if we could talk.

Take care,

Jax

The sight of his name took me back.

A thousand thoughts raced through my head as I stood there, wringing my hands on top of the shopping cart, wondering if that was really her. Alexandra Dempsey. I did not want my mind to play tricks on me. Not here. I did not want to walk up to her only to notice when I turned around that it wasn't his mother. And if it was her, should I take the lead and begin the conversation? What if it is her and she recognizes me first?

I spiraled as I was caught in this predicament. What do we discuss? Do I casually bring up the point that I haven't heard from Jax in a while? Did Alexandra know that already? Or was she just as in the dark as me?

It was too late. The lady lifted her head in my direction; she appeared surprised and waved.

Sheepishly, I waved back. Maybe that's enough, I thought. But it wasn't. Now Alexandra Dempsey was making a full-on beeline to me.

"Hi! How are you?" Alexandra hugged me.

"Hi, Alexandra," I replied. "I never see you in here."

"I don't come here very often. I was just in the area and had to pick up some snacks for the girls' night I'm on my way to."

"Oh, that sounds fun." I was barely holding my own, trying not to break down sobbing. I didn't want to be forever remembered as that crazy Black girl who had a crying fit in Whole Foods.

"So, have you spoken to my son?"

My stomach dropped. "No, I haven't talked to him in quite a while," I said, my voice wavering.

Alexandra rolled her eyes in disdain. "I tell you, I don't know what's going on with Jax. I haven't heard from him in days. We used to talk two to three times a day. Ever since the wedding…" Her voice trailed off at the sight of my face. She realized I had no idea what she meant.

"What wedding?" I asked, my voice cracking. I was petrified of the answer.

Alexandra's face fell. "Oh, Marilyn, I'm so sorry. He told me that things between you two were over and you were still friends. He told me he told you everything and that you had met someone, too. He said it was amicable."

At this point, I was convinced that my heart was pounding outside my chest. I couldn't breathe.

"Are you okay?" his mother asked me. "You look like you're going to faint. Oh my God, I'm so sorry. I'm gonna kill him. Why did he tell me you knew everything when clearly you didn't?" She gripped my arm tighter to help me steady my feet.

"I-I don't know. I haven't talked to him in a while. When was the wedding?"

"About two weeks ago," she replied. "I raised my son better than this. I always told him to finish something before he began something else."

My hands were visibly shaking from the news.

"I don't like her. If it's any consolation. I always thought you were the one for him." Alexandra grasped my hands, an anchor in the storm of emotion she must have seen on my face.

"Apparently, he didn't think the same." I released Alexandra and gripped

the shopping cart. "He didn't think anything at all. He didn't even think enough of me to tell me the truth."

Her face became overwhelmed with empathy for me. "Well, I've said too much. Much too much. I should leave. They'll be calling my number in the line soon."

Relief flooded me as I realized that she was ending the conversation.

"Nice to see you, Marilyn. Take care of yourself." She gave me another light hug and walked away.

I drifted back to the present from the memory of Jax's betrayal, staring at the email on the screen. *What fresh hell is this?* I thought after I read the message again. I wondered if my trip to The Renegades had ushered in this communication. My old, dysregulated emotions filled me again, like a swarm of hornets beneath my skin. I didn't want to deal with him. I wasn't going to respond to the email. It wasn't his right to ask me to have a conversation with him.

Of course, I wondered what he had been up to all these past years. I had ventured to clear the karma between us a few years before. I was in a particularly bad space with Colby and felt myself being pulled back into the past. I remembered the good days we had. I wanted to make contact with him, grasp anyone that was real and genuine because the Colby I knew when we married wasn't the same man he became. But there was no response, so I washed my hands of it.

At times, my mind would wander, even though I struggled not to think about him. I had imagined that he would be still married, with two or three kids, living a fairytale life. The life I got robbed of. Nice girls finish last. It wasn't fair.

"About time you looked at dat email. It's been hovering for three days."

I jumped in my chair. "Great Grandmother, you startled me."

"Sorry bout dat. I didn't mean for you to jump outta your skin. I'm glad you made it through De Renegades."

"Thing is, I don't remember how me and Jamie got back. Got back to here, that is," I replied.

"I reckon someone might have asked Marie Laveau to take care of you. You was there on important work, after all."

"Who would do that?" I asked.

"I reckon someone who might be on our side of things. Remember, *the enemy of my enemy is my friend.*" Great Grandmother flicked her Bic lighter a few times before she lit her cigarette. She wore a silk purple nightgown with matching bedroom slippers. "But be careful. They may be on our side now, but not later. Tell me what you found out."

"We're dealing with someone who talks to The Awful Evil. They were born to help it accomplish its goals."

"Oh my. Dat's some nasty stuff. What we got to do 'bout it?"

"We have to sever the tie that it has to him. Of course, it's a damn near mammoth task."

"How we gonna do dat?" she continued. "I ain't even know dat was possible."

"Apparently, it is. Although I suspect it would just be to bide our time. We need to save lives. Lives that have a purpose for The Fates. I don't think The Awful Evil will ever be gone from Moonstone for good, though."

"You got dat right. Separating De Awful Evil from Moonstone would be harder than separating a mama from its child."

Swirls of hot red smoke surrounded us. There was a roar under the floor.

"Here we go." Great Grandmother's shock of gray hair grew whiter as she stomped her foot down in her house slipper. "Git outta here. If you come bother me again, you'll have hell to pay."

"More spirits trying to hitch a ride?" I asked.

"Yep. They been getting bolder. I wonder what be going on dat making them want to be here in Moonstone." She stomped her foot down again. The fervor quelled into silence.

"They gone now." She inhaled the smoke from yet another

cigarette. "We can't look into dat now. We got to deal with this boy and De Awful Evil. How you think we gone finish this?"

"That's the six million dollar question. I'm hoping The Secret Keeper will know."

"You don't have to visit them. I'll fill 'em in and let you know the next step. I get de sense they want you to rest before your next task." Great Grandmother studied me for a second, sitting there with her unkempt hair and her disdain for life. "You look wild, child. Like a billion storms done did you in. It's De Renegades. It'll do dat to you."

I sat awestruck by Great Grandmother. It was amazing the way she spoke in half-English, half-slang with a speech impediment and wound it tightly around melancholy phrases that spoke to your soul. *Like a billion storms done did you in…* I repeated the words to myself. *Like a billion storms done did you in… Like a billion storms done did you in…*

The house rattled from the wind. I was unfocused, still feeling the effects of my trip to The Renegades. Since the weather wasn't beckoning me to venture outdoors, I decided to stay in and work on polishing up a few rooms in the house I hadn't gotten a chance to fix up yet. One room I particularly liked. It had some cracked paint on the trim and was painted a dusty pink. The carpet was ratty; I'd need to replace it. There was an old satin pink and white pinstripe lounge chair in there, left behind by the previous residents. It wasn't the primary bedroom, but its square footage was just a little less. So, I settled myself into creating a dressing room with it. The extra closet space was needed for my clothes, and I had purchased an old Gilded Age-era standing mirror from an estate sale when I was married to Colby. It meant a lot to me. When the movers took it, I had prayed it wouldn't shatter on the trip. It was perfect for this room.

I put the room together methodically, casting jewelry onto an old table with cabriole legs. Like the trim, I knew that it would need another coat or two of paint. But it would have to do for now. There was a shaggy eggshell-colored rug I'd purchased online that I threw in the middle of the floor, covering the worst section of carpet.

Deciding to move some of my fancier clothes into the room, I took an armful of summer cocktail dresses and opened the French doors of the oversized closet to put them in. I knew it was expected often that you dress for dinner in the South and they would come in handy. There was dust and what smelled like a hint of lavender in the air. The light was still working, to my amazement. I hung the dresses up and continued to unpack. Shortly after, the light flickered and I tripped over an old hat box left by Mrs. Marshe. I picked it up, expecting it to be lightweight, but there was a heaviness to it. I wondered if perhaps there were old documents or cash inside. Lots of elderly people hide money in their houses.

I pulled the white ribbons loose and opened the teal-colored box. Sneezing from the cloud of dust that escaped, I pulled out a brown leather book. There was no name or title on the cover. Some of the tattered papers were loose, falling out of the binding. I quickly grabbed a few of them before they landed on the floor. Curious, I perused the contents.

It read as a who's who of Moonstone and their histories. The book discussed some of Moonstone's origins. There were family trees on some pages, tracing back generations. I pondered if the Marshes were a part of the lineage of the town's founding families and I looked for connections. I became lost in the paragraphs and photos tucked in between the pages. Histories always fascinated me. Especially on a weary, windy, and rainy day in Moonstone.

Halfway through the book, there were only blank pages left. I assumed that this was because of the expectation that someone else would continue recording the history. Disappointed that I didn't discover any new information about The Awful Evil, I tried to shut the book.

But it would not close.

The harder I tried, the more it seemed determined to remain open. Exasperated from frustration with my arms aching, I put the book aside on the settee and attempted to get up. A force seized my legs; I tried to move several times to no avail.

Images and thick black ink appeared on the empty pages of the book. Heavy cursive script wrote words one by one in a matter of seconds.

I was meant to be here. I was meant to read this book. I gripped the pages, pulled them closer, and began reading:

> “ *In 1801, The Abbotts purchased one hundred slaves from an auction at a nearby town. Originally from West Africa, they arrived during the summer months after a period of seasoning in the Caribbean. Secretly wishing to die, they knew it was a curse that they survived the atrocious ordeal. It was thought that, if they could withstand the brutal conditions of the horrendous experience, they would be more docile to bear the full weight of slavery in the United States.*
>
> *The Abbotts owned one plantation at that time, but they were ambitious. After much discussion about what crop to produce, they settled on growing King Cotton. With the invention of the cotton gin by Eli Whitney a few years earlier, securing contracts with factories in New England made it a profitable venture. There would be more than enough money for their family for generations.*
>
> *The overseers at the Abbott plantation were particularly mean. One of them, Mr. Greenley, liked to punish the slaves for the slightest insults. If a person was late to the field, they were whipped three lashes. If someone was found working too slowly the result would be missing supper. Any slave could expect to be hung over an open fire with flames dancing at their legs and feet for the slightest infraction.*
>
> *Mr. Abbott took pleasure in raping young slave girls, some*

as young as seven years old. This resulted in several illegitimate children, who grew up to become slaves to their own father. Mrs. Abbott did not take too kindly to her husband's pursuits. She was known to scold and discipline the female slaves who were his victims. Those who worked in the house with her received the worst treatment. She was known to beat a poor slave with a wooden spoon till blood spurted from her scalp if she did not like how she arranged the curls in her hair for a party.

Eventually, the Abbott's slaves began to plot ways to hold their owners accountable for their abhorrent deeds.

On Sunday, church attendance was mandatory and they were on their best behavior. During the service they feigned smiling and sang the deceitful spirituals, appearing grateful to be given to such graceful masters who took care of them. If there was one thing slaves knew how to do, it was to behave dubiously to accomplish bigger intentions.

They wondered how they and other white-skinned people like them could call themselves to be part of this religion called Christianity. How did they sleep at night knowing that they separated families, murdered someone, or sexually assaulted women and children? This Christianity was not their religion. It did not speak of justice, ancestor worship, and caring for the land that you eat from and live.

No, this Christianity was not their religion.

The Abbotts did not know that their slaves were among some of the best conjurers south of the Mason-Dixon line. Elders taught their craft to their descendants, sharpening their skills generation after generation. They resisted.

On Monday evenings, they braided each other's hair in cornrows with intricate patterns indicating various maps with ways of how to escape from the plantation. They broke tools to slow down the cultivation of crops. Old man Jim, one of the elder slaves, carefully concocted libations that were laden with herbs and roots for Mr. Abbott. Whenever one was given to him, he always fell asleep and didn't remember what happened the day before.

They arranged ceremonies a few miles into the woods at night and on holy days. They called on their god Ogun to administer justice to the Abbotts. They asked their god Anyi to afflict them with disease and ill health. There was a reason why John Abbott drank too much. There was a reason why his wife couldn't conceive children.

The slaves at the Abbott plantation knew how to sow seeds of discord. They knew the old ways. And when those ways were not to their satisfaction, they cultivated a more malignant path.

It may have been the first or second generation. No one knows. But for thirteen nights in a row one summer, the Abbott slaves made a pact with the land they toiled every day. They took roots, herbs, and honey, and prayed and worshiped the Earth. Over time, the curse morphed into an entity of its own: not only devouring the descendants of the Abbott family but also others who were innocent in the wake.

The Awful Evil was born from the wicked belief that white-skinned folk were superior to dark-skinned folk. The Fates allow for The Awful Evil to exist because they don't have a choice. Moonstone merely serves as a void between realms, including the afterlife. And generations after generations, regardless of color, would become a casualty of its hunger…

There was a reason why The Crooked Woods were dangerous, I thought. *There was a reason why Elias Abbott became a murderer.*

A sharp knock at the door interrupted me.

The book fell to the floor and shut itself.

Chapter Fifteen

MARILYN

"Jax, why are you here?" I asked.

Anxiety washed over me like water.

"I went to your mother's house and introduced myself. She gave me your new address. Cute little town you live in." He stood on the porch, shifting nervously from foot to foot.

I shot him with a stare cold enough to freeze ice in a polar vortex. "It's rather assuming for you to drive all this way and think I would agree to see you," I said. "I'm on a deadline. I have to write."

I could barely look at him because I was still so attracted to him. The way his eyes locked on me when he was serious about what he was saying had always made me melt.

"Oh, you're writing. That's great. I remember you said you wanted to write a book someday."

I stopped for a moment. "No. You don't get to do this. You don't get to walk back into my life after all this time and act like you didn't implode our relationship. You have no right to be here. I'm closing the door now." Fire flashed in my eyes. "Standing here on my doorstep like I owe you something. This is bullshit. After what you did to me all those years ago? How dare you?"

I slammed the door in his face.

Are you fucking kidding me? I thought.

I did not want him here. He had hurt me too deeply; I did not want him to get close to me or this town. Moonstone has a way of sticking to people like a piece of chewing gum sticks to the sidewalk on a hot day. I did not need any more guilt on my hands after Jamie's breakdown from The Renegades.

I wondered if my trip there had ripped open this chasm in my life. I remembered the anguish I felt when I saw him standing beside his bride. The feeling of the knife twisting in my chest. It felt as if all the stars were sucked out of the galaxy. I thought about the past years, the false hopes that maybe if I reached out to him one more time, he might communicate with me. I had navigated life as best I could, all the while feeling that something—or rather, someone—was missing. The other half of me.

After my fourth attempt to contact him was met with rejection, I convinced myself that it was for the best. We simply weren't meant to be. I sealed my regrets from the past away. Everything changed when I met Colby. He wasn't necessarily exciting, but he was safe. If I only knew then…

"I see The Universe got lots of shits and giggles today." Great Grandmother's apparition unfolded beside the kitchen window. Her gray hair billowed in the soft breeze from the ceiling fan.

"Great Grandmother." I breathed a sigh of relief. "I'm glad to see you."

"Hey, chile. I got to tell you something bout how we defeat De Awful Evil."

"I have to tell you something too," I replied.

"You out wit it first."

I hesitated for a moment, then told her about everything I'd just read.

She took a deep breath, so deep that my curtains ballooned

out from the window. "So dat's De Awful Evil. Dat's the whole story."

She crossed her thin arms across her chest. "Dat's what we been chasin' for de last few hundred years. It make sense though. There's a lot of hate in dis world. And de hate affect everyone, not just us Black people. De Awful Evil take root whenever it can and there be a lot of people dat die from it. I ain't surprised De Fates know. They can't do anything about it. I'm sure they tried but de *juju* never been strong enough."

I nodded.

"We got to go raise someone from de dead."

"Say what now? Are you kidding? What—"

"Hush now and listen," Great Grandmother interrupted. "I got it taken care of. My friend gonna get us some help."

"What's raising the dead have to do with anything?" I said.

"It's a dead person named Calem. He been dead one hundred years. He is known to be the only one dat could defeat De Awful Evil's purpose and put it to sleep for some time. Dat sleep is de only time dat Moonstone git to breathe from De Awful Evil. We got to dig him up and cut off one of his hands."

"Did you know about this Calem?" I asked.

Great Grandmother chuckled. "No. I been dealin' with De Awful Evil for a while, but I didn't know bout dis Calem 'til now. So the story is De Awful Evil chose Calem to help him, just like Rawling. Only somethin' went wrong, don't know what. Turns out, he marked to do something else. It started bonding with him, then something stopped it."

"I see. Interesting and terrifying story." I sat in my chair, already depleted by the morning's events. "Great Grandmother, how do you propose we dig up a body and cut the hand off of it? In the middle of the night? Why do we need his hand?"

Great Grandmother inhaled her cigarette. "Well, dat is part two. After we git it, we got to go visit someone. De *Loa* Legba. He be in charge of De Crossroads. We got to present to him the hand for identification and make our request. Then he will make a decision after we present all de facts to him."

"I need a drink," I said. I headed over to the bottom cabinet and got out a bottle of Chardonnay. I quickly poured a glass and gulped it down before I slammed the glass back down on the counter.

"That's better," I said. "When we gotta do this little deed?"

"I gonna get de hand tonight. I'll come see you tomorrow."

"I had a feeling you were going to say that." I brushed some of my unkempt hair out of my face. "Well, if we're doing this soon, I need to get my head together for what's to come. And there goes finishing my chapter this week. Thanks, Universe, for screwing up another potentially productive day."

"You don't get to dictate how to help Moonstone when it's convenient for you, chile," Great Grandmother quipped. She never approved of whining. I could tell she was annoyed with me.

"I'm sorry, Great Grandmother."

"Okay, chile. I'll see you tomorrow. Like I said, my friend gonna help me get de hand tonight. His family has a long history here. He's got some unusual powers, just like you. His mom owes me a few favors."

"Oh, I see. Is this person reputable? I'm just concerned. You know I have anxiety."

"Chile, you got to trust me on dis. Some folks I deal with ain't pretty or have morals, myself included. But he's a good one."

I didn't respond.

She narrowed her eyes, studying me. "You saw him. I can tell. I sensed he was de one comin' to see you."

I lowered my eyes. I knew she was talking about Jax.

"I know it's hard. I know you miss him. Even after all this time. Dis, for you, ain't just another heartbreak." She caressed my face and long, disorderly curls. Then she kissed me gently on the cheek.

"It's been a long time, and I still feel like a piece of me is missing. And when I saw him, it all came back to me," I replied.

"Listen chile, life is hard. Sometimes there are things you just got to accept." She kissed me again on the cheek. "You got to forgive or accept it. My problem is I don't forgive. But I do accept. Bye, chile. I got business to take care of."

Great Grandmother dissipated into the antique white wall.

Great Grandmother

Great Grandmother looked at the massive, hulking figure in front of her in the moonlight. "Nice to meet ya. I been hearing about you a lot. Tell your mama thank you for helping me out. Though I know she didn't have much choice in the matter."

Henry looked at her reluctantly. "No problem. It's not like I had anything else going on."

"I been watching you over de years. Watching your body grow big and long as the oak trees in de Carolina heat." Great Grandmother knew Henry's mother Selma when she was young. As Selma grew older, she unofficially kept an eye on her. She often made poor decisions and was easily influenced by her friends. She gave birth to Henry at a young age, the result of a drug-fueled weekend in Las Vegas. She spent three days partying with unholy spirits while throwing away what little self-esteem she had left. It was as if each chip she placed on the table contained a piece of her soul incarnation. She winced at the outcomes of each game, secretly knowing that her heart would be bound to some supernatural being for an undisclosed amount of time. And yet, something kept compelling her to play again and again… Now Henry was left to pick up the pieces.

He looked at her surprisingly. "I didn't know that. I never saw you around when I was a kid."

"Dat's because I didn't want to scare you. I figured you had enough going on with your mama. She be a handful. I got her outta trouble more than a few times."

Henry's birth was quite a stupendous event. She was in labor with him for over twenty-four hours. At hour twenty-seven, The Fates decided it was time for his arrival. Selma had shrieked like she was being murdered—her epidural hadn't worked. When Henry appeared, he was enormous—eleven pounds and eight ounces. The doctor and nurses were amazed at his size. Selma passed out as soon as she was done pushing.

Henry relaxed and Great Grandmother could tell he felt more at ease. She knew she had a reputation in Moonstone and was sure it frightened him.

"So what's this business about? Why are we at the oldest cemetery in Moonstone in the middle of the night?" he asked.

"We got to git a hand. An important one. We looking for Calem. Calem Bishop." She pointed to a piece of paper on which the name was written.

They both looked around the cemetery. Battered headstones with half-etched names surrounded them. Great Grandmother floated around, searching for his name. Then she zoomed into the sky. "He be there," she said as she pointed toward the right. "He be right there."

Henry's large legs stepped over the larger headstones with ease. Great Grandmother met him at the grave. He took his shovel and began digging furiously.

Flecks of dirt scattered in chunks. In a matter of minutes, he was done.

"Wow. I knew your strength would come in handy for this," she said.

He dug the shovel into the opening of the coffin. The wood was deteriorated, so it was fairly easy to crack open. A loud hissing sound escaped from it.

"Oh, dis be important in de universe. I ain't never heard no sound like dat coming outta a coffin," Great Grandmother continued.

Henry reached into the coffin and snapped the right hand off of the dead body, putting it in a black sackcloth bag. He brushed some dirt aside and closed the coffin. "Do we need to cover it back up?" he asked.

"Yes, we don't want people knowing dat it was us who disturbed the grave. Even if it is for the greater good."

He heaped piles of soil back onto the coffin. When he was done, he rubbed the dirt from his hands on his t-shirt. "Are we finished here?" he asked.

Great Grandmother inhaled her cigarette. "Here, yes. But there's one more thing we got to do..."

Chapter Sixteen

MARILYN

It's amazing how two people can weave in and out of each other's lives. But the threads are never tied at the end to make it permanent. And thus, we unravel. We travel to the land of should-of-could-of-would-of. We toss and turn at two in the morning. We are wide awake but never present. An explosion could happen within earshot and jolt us. But a few seconds later, our mind wanders back to the land of should-of-could-of-would-of. There's a wanting in a person's soul that makes them feel like something's not right. Everything and everyone could be perfect, but it still isn't quite right.

Jax felt like this.

And here he was outside of my front door again two mornings later.

I stood inside, my body trembling. I didn't know what to do. Should I let him in, have this uncomfortable conversation, and wash my hands of it all? Or should I block him out of my life? Pretend that I never met him? Much easier said than done. In the end, the desire to finish this with him won out. I didn't want him hanging around Moonstone right now with all the danger. After all, what if The Awful Evil decided to hurt him to get to me? As much as I hated him, I didn't want to see him dead.

Jax rang the doorbell a few more times.

"Marilyn, can you just talk to me? Please?"

I opened the door slowly. I stood there, barefoot in a sundress, like I was a billboard for summer. My hair was disheveled, my brown skin dewy, with a hint of cherry lip gloss on my lips. I knew he saw beauty, but underneath it all, I knew he could tell misery lurked, too.

"You look beautiful," he said. "Still beautiful, just sad."

"A long time of melancholy will do that to you," I replied.

"I'm sorry that you're having a hard time right now," he continued. "Whatever's going on, you don't deserve it. I'm sorry for being such an asshole to you. I should have been truthful. I should have told you I met someone else. Even if that someone else was all wrong for me; I married her, and it was a disaster six months in."

"Am I supposed to feel bad for you?" I asked.

"No, no, I didn't mean for you to take it that way. I was totally selfish. I didn't take your feelings into account."

"Why did you run from us? From me? Was it something I did? I thought I wasn't good enough for you—"

"No," he interrupted me. "That wasn't it at all. It was the opposite. I didn't think I was good enough for you. I didn't think we could make it work. You living in Philly, me living there. So I sabotaged our relationship." He shrugged his shoulders.

"I tried to reach out to you over the years," I continued. "You still rejected me. I said to myself, even if he is still married, he could have at least responded to my attempts. Told me the truth instead of leaving me in limbo. And when you never did, it just sent me further into a downward spiral." I lowered my eyes, looking away.

Jax asked hesitantly. "Did you ever wish we ended up

together—even after it was all over? Do you think we would have worked out in the end?"

I looked at him angrily. "Do you want to know what I wished for? I wished that every day I could wake up to a good morning text from you. And every night before I go to sleep you would send me one telling me to have sweet dreams. I wished that when you looked at me, Venus, the Moon, and the whole damn galaxy ended with me. That there was no one else you could possibly want. That twilight melted and covered us. And when you thought about me, you said to yourself, 'There she is, my woman. The one made especially for me.' But I learned the hard way that dog won't hunt."

I began to close the door, but he stopped me.

I turned to face him again. "Right before you went silent, I felt like I had to compete for your attention. It was exhausting. Like I was another box to check on your to-do list. Like whenever I contacted you, you were cordial, but secretly, you wanted to say, '*What do you want? I'm busy.*' I started to feel like someone or something would always be more important than me. I felt like I was fighting for scraps of your attention. It shouldn't have to be that way. Because if you truly want to be with someone, it should be an easy decision. That person is always at the top of the pile. Always a priority. Sure, odds and ends will come and go: problems, issues, people; all of it will make your head fuzzy. But in the end, the rest of the world is just noisy chatter. And when the mist clears in your mind, you know who you belong with. And who belongs with you." A massive weight lifted from my shoulders. All of my thoughts from the past sixteen years were finally free.

"I loved you, Marilyn. Still do."

A surge of anger came roaring back. "Perhaps you did love me. But you didn't love me enough to blow up your life for me. Not when I needed you to. And there were many, many times when I felt like I needed you, but you weren't there for me." I thought about all of the hard times I had encountered when I felt that I needed support. I had felt abandoned by him, here to slay these demons—on earth and beyond—without any help. "Well, that's enough for today. I think you should leave."

"Would it be okay if I contacted you every now and then in the future? I'd like for us to be friends."

I eyed him suspiciously. "I have enough friends. I'm not too sure how I feel about that. There are a lot of scars and bruises between us."

"Fair enough. But you know me. I don't give up too easily. I need you in my life. Even if I have to start buying you more lattes." He flashed a quick smile. I could tell he was crestfallen by my answer.

"Oh yeah. I forgot about that," I replied, secretly knowing that I never did forget. "Bye, Jax." I closed the door and pressed my head against the it, heavily weighing the words he said during their conversation.

I had always wanted that permanent kind of big love. The one that makes you feel terrified and safe. But sometimes love like that is too volatile, a mystical experiment that could rupture at any moment. It seemed he wanted that big love, too.

Great Grandmother unwrapped the dirty cloth and threw it on the kitchen table.

"Oh my God! It's a hand!" I jumped back.

"It's *de* hand," she continued. "Calem's hand. De one we need to go see Papa Legba about. We need to travel to De Crossroads."

I edged closer to the table and studied the bones. "I'm afraid I'll break it if I hold it."

"Never you mind, chile. It still holds de energy we need. We need de energy, not the bones."

"Oh, I see," I replied. "Did you have any trouble getting it?"

"Naw, no problem at all. My friend Henry got it. He's got super strength. That's his gift."

"How did you meet him?" I asked.

"Me and his mama did some business together," she said. "When de business was over, we decided to be friends. He's gonna come wit us to see Papa Legba. I ain't never been to see him personally, and I don't know what's in store."

"Gotcha."

"Dis journey similar to de last. You gonna see the ticket on the table and grab it. I'll be waiting on the other side for ya. Henry gonna get a ticket at his house too."

"Okay." I felt the jitters in my body growing. It was one thing to fight supernatural battles on Earth. Then, we had the home-court advantage. But it was quite another when I traveled to someone else's realm, let alone a *loa*. I'd heard many stories about Legba, mainly from Great Grandmother, who overheard them from spiritual gossips. They ranged from him being a docile and nice *loa* to a narcissist who insisted on total loyalty. It depended on whether he liked you or not. Others said he could be quite vengeful if he felt wronged. I felt like we were walking into a spiritual minefield.

The next morning, Great Grandmother and I found ourselves in front of a large iron gate. Storm clouds gathered overhead. I was startled by a crack of thunder as lightning danced in the clouds above us.

Henry stood across the field. He waved and ran to greet us. As he got closer, I could see he was a large, hulking man with biceps the size of Christmas hams. His hair was chestnut, which was unusual. I hadn't seen too many Black men with chestnut hair in my lifetime.

"Great Grandmother, how are you on this fine day?"

By the smile on his face and the soft tone of his voice, I thought he resembled more of a gentle giant than a mercenary. I couldn't help but wonder just how much help he would be if we got ourselves into some trouble. The rain began to pick up, falling like coins on us.

"I reckon I be okay. Dis here is my great-granddaughter, Marilyn."

"Hi, Marilyn. Nice to meet you." He stuck out his huge hand to shake mine.

"Likewise." I flinched at the grip of the handshake.

"I'm sorry. Sometimes I don't know my own strength," he said.

We stared at the looming gate at the intersection while a streak of lightning flashed behind it, and I scanned our surroundings for any signs of life. It was eerily quiet except for the rain. I had imagined bustling activity from other spirits and the dead crossing into the afterlife. We continued standing for about five minutes, unsure of what to do.

"I guess we got to read de words." Great Grandmother took out a small piece of paper from the pocket of her housecoat. She unfolded it and read:

Papa Legba, open the door
Your children await
Open the door, Papa Legba
So that I may pass
When I return, I will thank the loa

Within a breath, a small man appeared, sitting on a stoop outside of the gate. He was bald and had kind eyes. "What you need? Why you here?" He spoke in a sharp voice.

"Henry, give me de hand." Great Grandmother took the wrapped cloth out of his outstretched arms.

"Who you be? Who you all be?" Legba's voice grew louder by the second.

"I'm Great Grandmother. Dis here is my great-granddaughter. She got De Hanging. And dis here my friend, Henry. He got

De Strength," she continued. "We here on some serious business."

"Get to it."

"We need this man. Calem Suthers. Born 1922." She unwrapped the cloth and gave Legba the bony fragments of the hand.

Papa Legba grasped them firmly. "Mmm. I know this Calem. He was special. He stopped bad stuff from happening in your town. Moonstone."

"Yes," she continued. "We need to borrow him again. Just for a while. We havin' some real big problems right now. A boy need to get De Awful Evil off his back. Calem is de only one who can do it."

"I see. I'll allow it. But before you take him, know you have to do something for me in the future."

Great Grandmother eyed him cautiously. "What do you need?"

"Sometimes we have to send someone back. They not ready yet to crossover. Next time I have someone that I think has some promise, I'm sending them to you two, Marilyn and Henry."

Henry and I looked at each other apprehensively. It was a deal we had no choice but to accept.

"I'm new to this game. What do we have to do with them?" Henry asked.

"Never you mind. I will determine that when the time comes."

Henry began shifting from side to side. I could tell he was confused and nervous.

Papa Legba motioned for one of his assistants to come over. "Find this man," he said authoritatively to him.

The man took the skeletal hand and scurried behind the gate. Eventually, he dissipated.

"It may be a little bit of time before he returns," Papa Legba said as he stood to walk away from us. "I have a couple of things to take care of. I'll be back shortly."

After he disappeared, Henry looked at us. "What are we going to do with Calem?"

"I reckon we ask him to do the same thing he did to De Awful Evil some time ago," Great Grandmother said. "And if dat don't work, we go back to De Renegades to try to get more information."

"I'm not going back to The Renegades," I said. "No way in hell."

"That will be our last resort," Great Grandmother replied.

A few minutes later, a white man appeared next to us. He was dressed in a white shirt with black pants and suspenders.

"Hello. I'm Calem."

Great Grandmother's face brightened. "Calem. We need you."

"What's this about?" he asked as he snapped his suspenders. "Nobody really comes around to see me so it must be important. What do you need? Papa Legba wouldn't have granted permission for me to see you unless it was big."

"It is big," Great Grandmother told him. "It's De Awful Evil big."

Calem rolled his eyes into the back of his head. "I almost died fighting that thing. It really had me going for a while. I thought I was invincible. Then it asked me to kill the girl I was sweet on. I was all set to do it. I worked it all out. It was going to be grisly." He looked visibly embarrassed by his former thoughts and shook his head.

"So what happened? Why couldn't you go through with it?" I asked.

"Because of my grandmother. Soon after The Awful Evil began talking to me, my personality changed. It was my grandmother who noticed first. She was a healer. I was becoming meaner to my friends. I resisted listening to my mother. Fear seized her heart. She had heard stories about The Awful Evil. This time, she decided to investigate herself. After speaking with another healer who only dealt with extreme spiritual matters, she told me to drink from a stream on the other side of The Crooked Woods. It's not there anymore. I drank from the stream for three days straight. I was nauseous and in great pain. But on the third day, I noticed that my soul wasn't so heavy. It just quietly passed away, like a cold or a fever."

Calem looked thoughtful. "Somehow, I was able to break it. I had something supernatural inside of me, although I don't know if it came from angels or demons or what. But it was enough."

"Too bad that stream is gone," Henry said.

Calem sighed. "Yes, it is. I don't know if it dried out naturally or if The Awful Evil got rid of it. Sometimes the misery overflows on the good."

I thought about what he said; I could not have agreed more.

"So what is The Awful Evil doing now?" Calem asked.

"It attached itself to a boy," Great Grandmother told him. "He already making trouble. You de only one been able to put De Awful Evil in its place."

"I don't know how to do it," Calem said as he scratched his beard. "Unless I breathe into him. Whatever this elixir is I had, it's still a part of me. Of my being. If I can get close enough to him and breathe it into him, it may do the job."

Henry looked visibly nervous. I felt the same.

"I ain't too sure dat's gonna do it. Seems too simple," Great Grandmother said.

"Agreed," Henry and I said at the same time.

"Well, we have to try. I'm willing to do that for you. I may not make it out. And I promise you, it won't be dead. But I will make it sleep for a few years. That's all you really need—time. Time to figure out what you need to do in the future to end it. If you ever can."

"Dat will have to do," Great Grandmother said.

Calem nodded. "I need to get close enough to ambush the boy. Once I'm done, he will be free—and the others he is controlling for The Awful Evil will be free, too. I'm afraid we don't have much time. It could happen at any second. Now that we have spoken about him, I can feel The Awful Evil's energy."

"Let's get you over to Earth now," Great Grandmother said. "De sun is setting here and dat means it's rising in Moonstone."

Legba had returned. He pointed a bony finger to beckon us over to him. A long scroll appeared before a table with a dimly lit candle. We bent over to read:

> *We the undersigned hereby agree to acquire Calem Suthers in the mission to save Moonstone, South Carolina from The Awful Evil. Calem Suthers will remain in our care until his return to Papa Legba. Great Grandmother, Marilyn Maxwell, and Henry Upton agree to return Calem Suthers to the Crossroads within a reasonable timeframe after the deed is complete. If not delivered at the designated time, then Great Grandmother, Marilyn Maxwell, and Henry Upton's relatives' lives will be shortened by five years. In exchange, Papa Legba will have permission to send someone (deity, demon, angel, or human) to Great Grandmother, Marilyn Maxwell, and Henry Upton. They will train and care for this person in the manner in which Legba wishes, for an unspecified amount of time.*

Henry raised his eyebrows. "This contract gives him too much power to interfere in our lives."

Great Grandmother shrugged her shoulders. "It'll be okay. No need to worry bout dat. It will get figured out when it needs to."

We wrote initials next to our names in the air.

"Farewell," Legba said, tipping his hat in our direction. "As in all things, hurry. Time is not on your side. The only moment when it is on your side is in death."

Chapter Seventeen

RAWLING

The Awful Evil was gracious enough to show me the events unfolding with Mike on the morning of our big day.

I watched as Mike looked at himself in the mirror and played with his cowlick. He dabbed some more gel on his hair to smooth it down and get it to behave. His hair seemed different, not quite as light a brown as it used to be.

"See how his hair is getting darker? It's because I'm taking over," The Awful Evil said to me. I could tell he was excited.

"He feels like he can show his mom that he's not a loser anymore," The Awful Evil told me.

"I see," I said. *He'd probably never been a part of anything meaningful before in his life,* I thought.

"In order to do this important work, you have to be able to master others' emotions to manipulate them," The Awful Evil explained.

I saw Mrs. Price walk hurriedly out of her house, keys in hand. It was still slightly dark outside. She was mumbling about something under her breath.

"Hi, Mrs. Price." Mike waved to her at the driver's side window.

She jumped and rolled it down. "Oh Mike, hi. How are you? You're up early. You're usually late to school." She put her travel mug full of hot coffee in the cup holder.

"Yeah, I am."

Mrs. Price eyed him suspiciously. "Do you need a ride or something? I'm going to be late, so I've got to go. I'll see you at school."

"Actually, yeah. I do need something."

"What?"

Mike reached inside his track jacket. He pulled out a knife and swiftly slit her throat. I watched him as he struggled to comprehend what he had just done. It must have been more difficult than he thought. I smirked. At least he'd followed the plan I laid out for him and Tom the night before.

She gasped for air until her facial muscles gave a final flinch and then she slumped over. Her car horn blew for a few brief seconds. Mike reached back inside the vehicle and pushed her over a bit so it would stop.

His black Nikes hit the ground and he started running.

It had begun.

An hour later, I stood in the attendance office, waiting to be checked in.

"Rawling, late as usual," Ms. Reynolds, the attendance secretary said. "What's your excuse today?"

I gave her one of my big smiles. "I dunno, Ms. Reynolds. Maybe it's just because I like saying hello to you. It brightens my day."

Ms. Reynolds blushed, smiling. "You are such a lady killer. I don't know why other teachers don't like you. I've always said, well, he's nice to me so I don't know what you're talking about."

I grabbed my pass and continued on to class. I always knew when to turn on the charm to get what I needed. Of course, she didn't mark me as an unexcused late. She marked me late with an official excuse, which meant I didn't have to make up the tardy in detention.

Today was the big day.

Mrs. Price had already been killed, Mike had others on his kill list—the kill list he helped build. We had decided that shooting would be too messy. It was too common for us to do. But if several random people were stabbed in the building, we might be able to pull it off. The Awful Evil's job was to interfere with time. It would freeze it for a few minutes so Mike could move on to the next person.

The bell rang and students emptied into the hallway.

A couple of minutes later, Tom stood in between the doors to the auditorium on the first floor, watching my ex-girlfriend walk toward him. I hid in the doorway and peered around the corner; I didn't want to be seen.

"Rawling, look at you. Who are you peeping at? You are such a weirdo. Get to class." James, another senior, said to me as he was bounding down the stairway.

I shot him a fiery glare. "Shut the fuck up."

There must have been something in my eyes and voice that scared him a little. He shrugged his shoulders and continued on his journey. I decided to go to class.

"No worries. I'll show you what's going on," The Awful Evil whispered to me. "Just look at your phone in class. Tell your teacher you need to look at yesterday's notes to study for the quiz."

I nodded and settled in a seat in the last row. I hid my phone behind my bookbag on my desk and continued watching. I saw Tom and Lacy walk into the auditorium. Old props from previous shows dotted the stage.

Hey guys, I'll catch up with you later, she texted her friends. She sucked her breath in.

"What do you want?" she said to Tom.

"Can we just talk for a few seconds in here?"

"This place reeks," she said. "Make it quick."

Tom shifted nervously from one foot to the other. "Listen, Rawling really misses you."

"Oh please, Tom. I am so over him. He knows this. Did he put you up to this? I'm already late to English." She ran her fingers through her blonde curls and began to walk off.

"Wait!" He stepped in front of her. His expression became darker.

Her face melted into a look of fear. "Tom, what's wrong? What's going on?" she asked shakily.

Tom thrust the knife into her stomach. She fell back on the floor and moaned low in her throat. A pillow of dust surrounded her limp body. I smiled.

I could tell Tom was shocked at what he did; it looked like he grew numb for a little while. Trembling, he hastily pulled off his t-shirt and changed into the new one he had stashed in his bag. He wiped the knife off with a washcloth he took from home and tucked it into his backpack. Lacy was still moaning, although her voice became softer and softer each time. *Get your shit together, Tom…* I thought. I was sure no one saw him because the cameras outside of the auditorium were broken. The school couldn't afford to get new ones until summer when next year's budget took effect.

"Well done," The Awful Evil told me.

A small gathering of teachers around the main office began to swell. They were speaking in hushed voices, but I could decipher some of what they were saying—something about Mrs. Price being assaulted. Word had gotten out about what happened. Many immediately pulled out their phones and began texting people. I stayed in the circle of chaos. Everything was unfolding like a movie playing out in front of me. My legs were cemented to the ground.

Mr. Morse, our principal, spoke to everyone on the intercom.

He told all teachers and staff to clear the hallways and that our school was going into lockdown.

Panicked, people scattered everywhere. Several teachers and administrators went to guard the entrances to the auditorium.

"You need to move. NOW!" The Awful Evil snapped me back to reality. I shifted gears and hurried in the opposite direction from the commotion. It was difficult due to the amount of students rushing to their classes.

Abruptly, I was pulled into an oversized custodian closet. The door shut and a large body held me from behind, his mammoth hands wrapping around my chest.

"What the fuck?" I screamed. At that very same moment, I could hear a couple of students yelling in shock further down the hallway.

"Oh my God, it's Lacy!" a girl yelled. "She was stabbed!"

Once inside the closet, the energy changed. I no longer felt like The Awful Evil was in charge. Instead, I felt like there was a tug of war ensuing inside my chest. I soon realized who these people were.

They were here to stop the plan.

"I know why you're here," I snarled. "You're here to stop me. Me and The Awful Evil. But it's too late. It's already begun." I wrestled inside of the huge arms of whoever had me in restraint.

"We have to hurry," a woman said to the other two people inside the closet.

"Well, if it isn't the magnificent Marilyn Maxwell. I've heard about you. You and your Great Grandmother." The Awful Evil spoke through me to her. I did not know about this woman and who she was. What connection did she and these other people have to The Awful Evil?

She stumbled backward in surprise when I said her name.

Two apparitions then amassed around both me and the guy who was holding me. I began to choke. One was a man dressed in clothes that appeared to be from the roaring 20s, the other was an old woman in a nightgown with long gray hair.

An unknown surge separated me from the man and my strength returned.

"Calem, is that you?" The Awful Evil laughed. "You'll never stop me. I'll merely go to sleep and wake up hungrier than before."

"Calem, you got to do it now!" The older apparition in the nightgown said as she lunged toward me.

I put my hands up in defense and knocked her away. A large hand from the massive man grabbed me and pulled me down to the ground. It held onto me as the person The Awful Evil called Marilyn took out a tiny piece of paper from her jeans pocket.

She began to recite strange-sounding words as swirls of red and gray smoke surrounded me. I realized it was Latin.

"Expelle malum. Expelle malum!"

Then she began reciting some words in what sounded like some sort of tribal language.

"Ondoa uovu. Ondoa uovu!"

A flash of light flew from the elder's hand. My chest rose. Calem pinched my nostrils and began to pour a heavy mist and smoke into my mouth. I found myself and The Awful Evil struggling to resist.

Objects began flying around the closet. Old canisters jumped off the shelves and hit them. Somehow Calem kept pinching my nose and pouring swirls of breath into me. I broke free from the man holding me, flew up in the air again, and dropped down to the floor. I groaned, my head spinning. I could no longer feel The Awful Evil near me.

A fury of clamor swelled outside of the closet.

"We gotta get out of here," I heard the large man say. He ran and opened a back door to the closet that was used for freight deliveries.

Calem followed after him.

I lay on the floor helpless, and too weak to move. I could feel a presence still hovering over me. I opened one eye. It was Marilyn. She took the small paper with the words and she recited it and pinned them to my chest. She then climbed out of the window in the closet and ran away as I felt myself lose consciousness.

Chapter Eighteen

MARILYN

All four of us gathered at The Secret Keeper's house.

"Tell me everything," The Secret Keeper demanded as they poured us tea.

"We caught all three of them," I told him. "Henry and Calem did their part with Rawling. Mike never showed up for school; Tom stayed in school to avoid suspicion. But he was the last person to be seen with the girl before she went missing. Although they won't remember how they were involved, they will take the fall for it. The Awful Evil and Rawling put a lot of planning into it all."

"Rawling will move on, but in a more average state of affairs than The Awful Evil promised him. As a matter of fact, he'll be catatonic for a while," The Secret Keeper said.

"Whatever de case, I'm glad dis business is over with," Great Grandmother said as she smoked her cigarette. Her hair bobbed up and down in the breeze coming through the open window. "There are some things I need to keep an eye on. Some potential trouble."

"Does it involve any of us or Moonstone?" I asked nervously.

"Not too sure bout dat. I'm just tryin' to gather information right now," she replied. "But just know de work in Moonstone ain't never done."

I nodded, then stood up. "I have to go."

"I can go with you in case you need help," Henry offered.

"No, I've got this," I said.

The Secret Keeper walked me to the door. "I know what you want to do, Marilyn," they whispered in my ear. "Don't do it. Some books should never be read."

I looked at them quietly. "Like I said. I got this."

The Secret Keeper nodded in uneasy agreement and bid me and Calem farewell.

A few minutes later, we stood in my kitchen, waiting to be summoned by Papa Legba for Calem's return. Apprehension swallowed my voice. I knew that what I was about to do could change my reality as I knew it. The brevity of my request for him began to affect my body. My hands were shaking.

"Everything okay, Marilyn?" Calem asked.

"Fine, I'm just tired. I'm glad we got back in time." I smiled gently at him.

There was a whirring sound and we were transported back to The Crossroads. Legba appeared beside me.

"Thanks for honoring your end of the deal," he said. "I trust everything worked out for the greater good?" He puffed on a thick cigar.

"Yes—at least for the time being," I replied. "Calem, thank you so much."

Calem smiled.

"You best be going. I got some other business to finish up with Marilyn," Papa Legba said.

Calem nodded.

One of Papa Legba's assistants motioned for him to come to him.

"I bid you farewell, Ms. Marilyn." Calem walked gently down the road.

Papa Legba met me eye to eye. "I know why you here, Marilyn. It's not just because you had to return Calem. You want information. Information on your family." He let out a big sigh. "She not here. Your grandmother, Celia Belas. She not here. She not at the Crossroads."

I looked at him in disbelief. "How did you know I was going to ask you about her?"

He grinned. "Intuition. I don't know why she's not here. That is a question with a million answers in a million realms. I don't know where she at, but I can tell you how it happened." He blew a puff of smoke from his cigar into the air.

"What do you mean?" I asked. I was dizzy with eagerness for any scrap of information I could grasp. The question that had haunted my entire life enveloped me.

Papa Legba took a seat on his milk crate.

"I can tell you who and how it happened. I'm taking a big risk here. But I believe everyone should know their family secrets, especially if the future is at stake." Papa Legba removed his hat. He rubbed his brow with his elbow. The midnight sky turned purple around them.

"Please," I asked him helplessly. My patience had run out.

"Great Grandmother killed your grandmother. She killed her daughter."

My mind split in two.

"Are you serious? Why?"

Papa Legba's chest heaved up and down. He put his hat on his lap.

"Celia, your grandmother, never had a good relationship with Great Grandmother when they were alive. They fought like two cats trapped in a box. Celia was rebellious, to say the least. She knew about Great Grandmother's ties to The Fates and others. She didn't like it, even at her young age. She sensed not all of

The Fates were not on the same page—that perhaps there were some with nefarious plans, and they were manipulating events to serve their own purposes."

"Did this disturb Great Grandmother?" I asked.

"Great Grandmother never knew. She never told her. She decided to keep it to herself. Celia thought it might benefit her in the future. Your grandmother was smart—too smart."

"Oh. I see."

"Before your grandmother met your grandfather, she fell in love with a demon," he continued. "Great Grandmother was beside herself. She knew the problems if the romance was to continue, so she killed him. Celia never forgave her for that. For the rest of the time she was on Earth, she made it her mission to wreak havoc on all of Great Grandmother's missions. Then, the order came in from The Fates that she had to die."

My mouth dropped open. My heart was racing.

"So The Fates had her killed?" I asked.

"Yes. There is a rumor about some of them being involved in shifty business but that was never confirmed. No one knows the real reason why she had to die."

I fell onto the road and seized my chest. The greatest revelation I had been seeking had finally been revealed to me. I felt free and tied to a chain at the same time.

"I think you must go back now. What you do with our discussion doesn't faze me. But I figured you at least deserved to know."

"Yes. Thank you for helping me." I turned and walked to the edge of the road.

I was afraid. But I knew I had to confront Great Grandmother.

Chapter Nineteen

MARILYN

I sat at home nervously tapping my fingernails on my kitchen table. I hadn't seen Great Grandmother in a few days. To say my mind was uneasy from the conversation I had with Papa Legba would be an understatement. What was going to happen when I asked Great Grandmother if she killed her daughter? Would she lie, or would she tell the truth? Deep down inside, I hoped that she would lie. The truth was more devastating.

Now that I knew Great Grandmother betrayed my mother, I didn't know how to feel about her. How could I trust her? But as Great Grandmother herself says, some things you have to forgive or accept.

I was also wrestling with Jax in my mind and heart. I did not know whether to trust or leave him where he was. Since he came to visit me, I could not get him out of my head. Even with everything that happened. It was as if the end of me was the beginning of him. I had felt that way since the day we met in person. If we truly were meant to be together, then this time would be different.

I never asked Great Grandmother about the couple in the frame.

Yesterday, I looked at them and they had changed positions again. Now, they were embracing each other and kissing. There were words etched at the bottom of the picture. I picked it up and was surprised to read the names, Marilyn and Jax. Perhaps we were together in a past life. Taking this as a sign, I asked The Fates for once to allow love to be cast in my favor.

When and if the timing became right, I might tell him about my other life: the childhood trauma, The Hanging, and Great Grandmother. He always had an eternal way of making me feel that no matter what, everything would be alright.

It was one in the morning. I knew he was catching a red eye at 3:30 am back to Philadelphia. He had told me this when he stopped by. I had held off trying to contact him. I wasn't ready to have a conversation with him yet, but I wrote him a note. If it reached him before he left, then I knew we had a chance to start over. If not, perhaps the stars would align sometime in the future. No matter, I had met my true love, and if we were meant to be then eventually we would reach our destiny.

I hastily stuffed myself in a pair of faded-out Lee jeans and a t-shirt, grabbed my keys, and rushed to his hotel.

A light rain was beginning to fall. I walked into the lobby. There were two people at the hotel bar soaking their heartache away in martinis. The lights were dimmed because it was after hours. I went to the front desk.

"Can I help you?" a younger woman asked me. She looked at me nervously, unsure why someone would check in so late.

"Jax-Jax Dempsey. I believe he has a room here."

"I'm sorry. We're not allowed to give out that information," she said.

"I know he's here. I was wondering if you could give him this note." I pulled out a card-sized envelope with my initials monogrammed on the back.

She sighed but nodded.

"Thank you," I said. I handed it to the woman behind the desk.

The note read:

Jax,

Give me time and space to figure out some things.
When I am done, I promise I will find my way back to you.

- The Smartest Woman In the Room

The next evening, I woke up around 3 am to the sound of the crystals I kept on my dresser in a small bowl clattering. I felt a force inside of me, stirring me to get up. She was here.

"I'm just checking on you, chile," she said. "I'm glad you decided to give Jax another chance. You two had somethin' good. I reckon it'll work out this time. Your great-grandfather and I had trouble, too. It took a while, but we worked it out."

"I hope so," I said hesitantly.

Great Grandmother sat on my dresser smoking. She flew over to my bed.

"So, aside from Jax, how you been?' she asked me.

"I'm okay, I suppose. I've been exhausted. I'm trying to mentally wrap my head around a few things. Like what we do if The Awful Evil comes back. I wonder if we'll be strong enough next time."

"You don't need to worry bout dat right now. Finish writing your book. I'll take care of anything else dat comes up."

It was obvious that I was dancing around the topic that needed to be discussed.

"Out wit it, child. What you wanna know? Somethin' on your mind dat you're not saying."

I took a deep breath. I had been nervously wringing the fringe on the edge of my pajamas.

I sensed she wouldn't have asked this question unless she knew the answer.

"I spoke to Legba last time I was at The Crossroads. He told me some troublesome information. Information about you."

"Hmm. What did he say?"

It was now or never.

"He told me that you killed my grandmother Celia. He said you had your reasons." There was an uncanny silence between us.

"Yes. Yes, I killed my daughter."

My heart broke.

"Sometimes I think there ought to be shadows to hide us from de terrible truth 'bout things in this world. Sometimes, I think there still wouldn't be enough of them." Her shock of gray hair dimmed a bit, turning black and purple in some places.

"I didn't tell you because I didn't want you to feel de pain I got to feel. It's my burden to bear; I knew it when I did it. De Fates and I had to do what had to be done. Your great-grandaddy complied because he loved me and knew I had to do it. Ain't nobody gonna understand it. They don't need to."

Tears crowded in my eyes, spilling between my lashes. To hear the words from Great Grandmother's mouth washed my soul in anguish. I loved this woman. Protected her. I couldn't understand why there wasn't another way. Even when my mother said she was a spiteful, unpleasant person, I told myself I knew differently.

Julia Maxwell said that Great Grandmother and my grandmother, Celia, had a rocky relationship. But in my heart, I knew there was more to the story. However, my assumptions were never as heinous as the truth Great Grandmother just confirmed.

"Does my mother know you killed her?"

"Yes," she answered softly. "She never told you because she, like me, thought it best to keep it to ourselves. Now you know de source of her hate for me. This why your mama wanted to keep me away from you. She was afraid dat I would do the same to you dat I did to her if it came to it."

The tears running down my face began to soak the collar of my t-shirt.

"Your mama has always known you had De Hanging. Your father, too. He was afraid right up till his deathbed dat somethin' would happen to you. We never discussed it." She continued, "When you was little, they tried to make believe it didn't exist. But that day at the Pick N Pay, when you saw me, she knew you had it. Why else would I be following you to make sure you were okay? The way you immediately looked at me and knew who I was and you had never seen me before. She knew alright. She knew."

I began to sob uncontrollably.

"Marilyn, ain't nothin' you can do 'bout de past. It's done," Great Grandmother said in a rather somber tone. She refrained from touching and consoling me, knowing it would make things worse.

I struggled to understand how she could be so callous after confirming that it was true.

"How do you expect me to go on? Knowing what I know now? What happens to us?"

"Well, I don't know dat. It's up to you." She flicked ash away from her cigarette. "I'm going away for a little while. I'm going to leave you for a thousand suns. Give you some time to figure out and adjust. You won't be hearing from me." She threw away her final cigarette in the air. When it landed, she stamped it out with her bedroom slipper. "Before I go, I got to tell you some more truth about your ancestors and de relatives you are kin to in Moonstone."

"I thought I knew everyone that I was kin to."

Great Grandmother snapped her right hand fingers. A long

scroll appeared beside her. "I was plannin' on giving you this today. Even though our talk turned about me. Hopefully, this might help you learn 'bout your heritage in Moonstone. Your destiny will always be tied to this town." She placed the scroll in my hands.

"Take care of yourself, chile," she said softly. "And remember, I love you. Even if you don't feel it, I do."

Great Grandmother fluttered from my window into the open evening sky. A minute later, I saw a star brighten in the dark. I figured it was her in the constellations, glowing brighter as she reached her intended place.

I wiped away my tears with the sleeve of my shirt. I was not sure what was to come and if my soul could endure another shock at this moment. Truth spurned me on. Hands shaking, I unfurled the old document and began to read what it said: T*he Sea People.*

> *The Sea People lived on the outskirts of Moonstone. They took careful steps to hide from earthlings. They skulked along the edges of the coastline, crouching and cowering under the shadows of the cliffs that evolved from the water above and around them. They huddled in the thick of the coral reefs. If there was any disturbance from The Land People they retreated to their underwater caves out of fear they would be discovered.*
>
> *At night, they searched for shiny objects that The Land People had tossed overboard or lost that they could use for exchange and trade for favors. A ring here, some coins there, a metal hook from a fishline could land them enough payment for a bit of clothing to wear: perhaps a warm shawl to use for the cooler months when they were hunting. Sometimes, they would fetch something rather large, such as a silver cup or gold watch. These items were worth much more. They often coveted*

them and kept them stored away for a time when they would be needed the most.

Amari and his wife lived in an underwater cave not too far from The Crooked Woods. It was a hard life but a quiet life. He immersed himself in his community. Every Saturday, he brought some of his wares to market. He liked to go to the local pub and make mischief with his comrades. On clearer days when the water wasn't so choppy, they would play a round of sea games, leveraging items they scavenged as bets on the winners.

His wife, Saphima, did not interact too much with the other Sea People. She contained herself in the tiny space they called home. It was modest. A rusty side table was used to dine. They had fashioned their eating utensils and a few plates out of whalebone. There was a small mattress made out of dried seaweed and various rocks that they smoothed out to lay upon. While he hunted at night, she would amuse herself by knitting or sewing. Sometimes she would be lucky, and he would find a bauble of sorts to bring her: a scarlet hair ribbon or bracelet. Saphima was magical at repurposing any trinkets she received. She could spin beauty into anything ordinary.

Whenever Amari returned from hunting in the early morning, she would have fresh coffee and some salty dried fish waiting for him. For some reason, today, he was especially excited to eat his breakfast. Coffee was a luxury he could never live without. The first sip he took daily reminded him of the old world.

In the old world, every morning, he would drink coffee while the sun would be snooping over the lines of trees. He would meet with his tribe to discuss possible places where they might pursue larger prey, perhaps enough to sustain the entire village. Saphima and her friends would ask for blessings from their loas *on their hunt. She would give him cowrie shells.*

They served a dual purpose. First, as amulets to protect him from danger from animals and tribes with whom they were not allies. Second, they could be used for trade should he need to unravel himself from any unwanted situation.

Saphima would wait with the other wives anxiously for them to return. If they were successful, she would throw her arms around him and kiss him on the cheek. They would spend the rest of the afternoon cleaning and preparing their kill for dinner. After the evening meal, there would be drum dancing to thank the loa Ogun for their fortune. At night they would retire to their beds for slumber, satisfied with their accomplishment.

That was their life before the ship.

One morning, their village was ambushed by angry, dark-skinned men. They carried elder sticks they had borrowed from older people in their tribe with them. They carried spears with them.

They carried greed with them.

They carried malevolence with them.

They carried spite with them.

Amari, Saphima, their kin, and others were rounded up like the wild boars they captured for meals. Amari did not recognize these angry men although they had dark skin like him. These dark-skinned men spoke to other men that did not look like them. The men they spoke to were white-skinned. Amari, Saphima, their kin, and others had never seen white-skinned men before.

Within a matter of hours, they were given to these white-skinned men. In return, the white-skinned men gave the angry dark-skinned men shiny objects, spices, new weapons, and barrels of something dark-colored to drink.

They were taken to the Ivory Coast where they stayed in confusion. They spoke amongst themselves about how strange the men with white skin looked. Amari, his kin, and others wondered if they were being punished by the loas *because they did not give them enough offerings of thanks. On the Ivory Coast, they waited for days, frightened and flustered. They did not know why the white-skinned men were shouting at them all the time and why they would get mad when they did not comply with their orders. They only knew that if they did not respond, then the white-skinned men would beat them. What Amari, his kin, and others did not understand in language the white-skinned men made sure they understood with violence.*

Amari did not see Saphima while they were on the Ivory Coast. He merely caught a glimpse of the back of her head as they walked onto the ship. He saw her frazzled braids and purple bruises on her skin. He screamed out her name, but she could not hear him. He felt helpless as a man. As her husband, he was supposed to protect her from peril. Now here she was, in their darkest hour and he could not fight for her. He could not comfort her. He could not save her.

On the ship, Amari was chained to other men as they were led below. Again he looked for his beloved Saphima but could not find her. There were women shrieking. One was going into labor. She was taken by one of the white-skinned men to a room with two other women from his tribe. From there, he heard more cries of misery.

While he was lying next to other tribesmen in the bow of the ship, they tried to discuss a possible mutiny in their language. Every night they plotted their revenge. However, soon Amari felt that no one was brave enough to execute the mission. Eventually, the talk fell on closed ears. And then the talk became a whisper and a few broken words that dissipated in the air when they left his lips. He concluded that most people among him felt perhaps it was better if they accepted their fate.

The ocean became an enemy of Amari, Saphima, their kin, and others. They did not understand why. They had always worshiped it and the loa Mami Wata. For some reason, the ocean became angry and punished them. When some did not do what the white-skinned men wanted they were thrown overboard to be swallowed by it as an example for others as to what might happen if they did the same. Amari also watched others jump to their deaths. The ocean filled them with so much trepidation and despondency they felt they had no choice. They did not know what awaited them when they reached the new land. They did the only thing they could to stop it from arriving. The water predators took notice of the ship and followed it. The smell of decay attracted them. They devoured the dead bodies.

Some of Amari's friends began to learn some of the white-skinned men's words. They could tell by the tones in their voices what their emotions were. Soon there was talk on the ship that there might not be enough food to sustain them for the rest of the voyage. It was decided that they would not follow their intended course. They were going to try a different navigation to arrive at the new land quicker.

The different navigation sealed the ship's fate.

A crackle of thunder, unlike any other they ever heard, startled them one night out of their sleep. The ship was not stable. It began to rock hard from side to side. Sheets of rain pummeled it. Wind punched holes in the wood. There was scattered commotion and arguing between the white-skinned men. Chaos fell. A large snap happened. Wave after wave deluged the ship and the ocean inhaled it. Amari and others tried to free themselves from the shackles so they could swim. They could not. He wondered if Saphima had freed herself in time. Secretly he knew she didn't.

He knew it was over.

Or so he thought.

Amari and others were suffocating in the water. He closed his eyes and held his fellow friend's hand as death enveloped them. He prayed to Mami Wata that his demise would be swift.

But he did not die.

Time passed and Amari, his kin, and others floated in a dreamlike state in the water. They were not disturbed by the water predators. As they swam by them from time to time, they saw them not as a meal, but in reverence to them. All of them were being pulled by an invisible magnet to the waters that lay aside Moonstone. It was here that they made their home in the New World. It was here that Amari found his beloved Saphima again. He was grateful they were reunited.

Amari, Saphima, his kin, and the others realized they were now half-human and half-water spirits. They weaved in and out of the water like stitches in a garment. They never ventured or spoke to The Land People. They did not trust them. It was The Land People who betrayed them, kidnapped them, and cast them into their watery future.

At times, they would dive far and wide to see the shipwreck. They would remember the horror. Some of the passengers on the ship did not become half-human and half-water spirits. For those who did not pass on to their new life as a deity, they paid their respect to them. They mourned them. They cursed the white-skinned men's remains that were still there. If they needed something, sometimes they would go back to pick up the remnants of objects that still lay in the ship at the bottom of the sea like vultures. Then they would return to their underwater sea cave homes.

On their last journey to the shipwreck, there was talk that there could be some trouble coming. No one knew why or from whom. Some of the half-human/half-water spirits heard it from people in the other worlds. Everyone was frightened. The Fates still had not spoken about it, so they did not know how large the trouble was. They did not know if they should prepare. Many wondered if now would be a good time to select a leader of The Sea People to address such matters. Many said that Amari should be the leader. He was not so sure.

The Sea People wanted an audience with The Fates. This was a most difficult task. That is why they collected and saved their shiny objects. They would serve as payment for the visit if they were selected to talk with them.

Amari rubbed his beard and rested his hand on Saphima's as he continued sipping his coffee. He did not want to scare her by verbally acknowledging his concerns. However, they almost always knew what each other was thinking. They held this conversation in silence.

I sat down and let my heart absorb the information about the lineage of my ancestors. An immense sadness captured me about their lives. I felt compelled to find my people. We all needed to discover the mystery behind the rumor that something wicked, inherently more than The Awful Evil, was going to arrive. If there was trouble, we had to stop it.

The enigma of Moonstone took root in my soul, even when I ran away and tried to deny it. It was a deep well full of conjure, secrecy, mysticism, and malevolence. No matter how hard you try, you will fall into it.

As Marie Laveau warned us in The Renegades:

Climbing out is harder than climbing in.

Acknowledgments

It wasn't until I became older that I realized what a profound effect both of my grandmothers had on me. Although they were vastly different in terms of personality, their traits are interwoven in my soul. Callie Spann, mother of my mother, was prim and proper and always poised. A preacher's wife, you would never catch her without her hair dyed jet black or her white gloves on for Sunday service. She looked and acted like she stepped out of an etiquette magazine. It was from her that I learned at times to be reserved and disciplined. I always thought of her as strict. However, I can see why in hindsight. After all, she raised four children in the deep South during segregation and the wrath of the Ku Klux Klan. How she and her husband, my grandfather survived physically and emotionally is beyond explanation. I thank her for inspiration.

Rosalyn Williams, mother of my father, was the salt of the earth. Her sense of humor was unmatched. My father was an only child and he was the center of her universe. In between her incessant cigarette smoking, she talked tough and didn't take any crap from anyone. I fondly remember my summer vacations in the south as a child playing on her farm, feeding chickens and stray animals, and looking like Pig Pen from playing in the dirt all day as the sun went down from all of the day's shenanigans. I remember swimming at the community pool with my cousins. I can't forget cousin Carrie always braiding my hair on the porch to give my mom a break from fixing my pigtails. These fond summer memories in South Carolina with both sides of my family shaped this novel.

I wouldn't be who I am today if it weren't for Sue and Charles Williams. They raised me and my sister to be strong, kind, and have perseverance—and do it all with a laugh. I have the kind of parents that made sure education came first. When the Scholastic Book Fair came to my school, they always let my sister and I buy whatever we wanted because they knew reading was important. Mom, I don't think I could have been prouder than the day you graduated and received your Ph.D. It is now wonderful to see you two as my friends at this stage of life. Thank you both for allowing me to smile, cry on your shoulders, and giving me a pep talk when things weren't going right. I was a very creative child and kind of quirky. I'm sure you didn't quite understand me at times—but you and Dad threw your hands up in the air and went along with it. It is your love of education and your encouragement of reading at home for me that inspired me to write.

Earron, you rock. I am so proud of you. Thanks for being such a wonderful baby sister.

Thank you to the extended Spann and Williams clan for your support in my endeavors, as well as my friends and family from my hometown of New Haven, CT.

To Veronica, Erika, Darlene, and Sharon, I will always look at you as my big sisters. You got me through some dark days when I was a child. I want you to know I will always remember that.

I want to thank Wilbur Cross High School Class of '92 and all my teachers, especially Ms. C., my art teacher, and Mrs. Stephenson who taught me how to drive. You were brave. My high school experience taught me to embrace all cultures and learn from people who didn't look like me.

To Providence College, I want to thank you for the free education (via scholarship). There were the lessons in Western

Civ class and there were the life lessons. You taught me how to navigate as a Black woman in a predominantly white environment. I remember falling in love with Charles Dickens while taking an English class about his books. My favorite novel we read that semester was *Bleak House.* I appreciate the former Balfour Center for Multicultural Affairs as it was our home away from home on campus. Oh, and thank you Providence for fostering my current obsession with NCAA Division I and NBA basketball. I am a Friar for life.

I also want to thank my PC crew for friendships that still carry on to this day. You know who you are. What a wild ride and I couldn't have had better people to share it with. Gina, Taniedra, Tayna, Erika, Kima, Cre, the guys, and everyone else in between gave me friendship and emotional stability. Gina, I thank your family, your mom—as I affectionately call her Aunt Cheryl—and your late father, Uncle Al for fostering me. I knew I always had a seat at your table for Sunday dinner and the holiday cookouts. Allison, you were the best roommate ever.

To Michelle Bonner Zagorski, I am so happy we recently rekindled our friendship. Thank you for allowing space in your life for us to continue laughing and making mischief. To the city of Philadelphia, I never realized how much I missed you until I left.

I'd like to thank all my colleagues and friends at Barnstable High School. What is wrong with us? Public education is crazy and we keep showing up everyday to teach. You all are rockstars. My neighbors in the 2600 hallway, I thank you! To the Social Studies and Business teachers, I could not work in a better department. Thanks for the support and humor during the breakdowns. Hope and Alik, thank you for providing me mentorship, friendship, solace when I needed it, and a good meal. BHS GALS—you know who you are. My gratitude cannot go deep enough. I love you deep.

Michelle, Sara, and Amy at The Spa At Sea Street, I thank

you for keeping me sane, as well as looking and feeling good, and yelling at me when you knew I wasn't taking care of myself.

I want to thank the lovely ladies of the Theta Epsilon Omega chapter and all of Alpha Kappa Alpha Sorority, Inc. Each one of you inspires me to accomplish what our ancestors only dreamed. I am honored to be a part of such a legacy of phenomenal Black women.

To Mike and Kate, we knew something had to be done about racism after the murder of George Floyd. When you both contacted me out of concern, I told you I had an idea and asked for your help. You two agreed without any hesitation. Thank you for creating the Barnstable Ally Group with me. To the Barnstable Ally Group leadership team, thank you for graciously giving up your time and hearts to a worthy cause. This past year has been busy and I appreciate you all shouldering responsibilities to keep our ship running. To all of our members, thank you for restoring faith in humanity and attempting to leave our earth in a better way than we found it.

Amy, Kevin, Mike and Jess thank you for always supporting me. Can't wait for our next crazy adventure.

To my dear friend Neil, I thank you for many years of friendship.

To Bella, the Williams's family dog and Luna, my cat, you are wild creatures that continue to teach me the concept of unconditional love.

I would like to also thank my lovely new little family at Quill & Crow Publishing House. To my editing team, thank you for pushing me to be a better writer. It was a hard process and I can be stubborn. To Cassandra, I believe that the universe aligns with divine time and that's why we fell into place. You are a dynamic Editor in Chief. Thanks for picking *There Ought to Be Shadows* up out of the slush pile and believing in my story.

Wholeheartedly, I want to take time to acknowledge everyone that encouraged me, congratulated me, or wrote or sent me kind words when I announced that I signed with Quill & Crow Publishing House for *There Ought To Be Shadows.* I thank you for the check ins on how I was doing, and my mom calling me and asking me if I wanted her to drop me off dinner because she knew I was writing.

Lastly, to all my readers, I thank you for agreeing to go on this wild journey with Marilyn and Great Grandmother.

About the Author

Krissie K. Williams is the author of several novellas. She earned her B.A. in History/Secondary Education from Providence College and M.A. in Learning and Thinking from The Graduate Institute. She is a high school history teacher and also is founder of Barnstable Ally Group, a local civil rights and social justice organization. She is also a member of Alpha Kappa Alpha, Sorority, Inc..

When she is not teaching or writing you can find her doing retail therapy, soaking up a historical tour (in which ghosts may or may not be involved), and traveling. She also spends as much time as she can with her merry band of misfit friends and laughing with her mom, dad, and sister. She lives on Cape Cod, MA with her mischievous black cat Luna.